Most Humble Servants

Most Humble Servants

The Advisory Role of Early Judges

Stewart Jay

Yale University Press

New Haven and London

Copyright © 1997 by Yale University.

Printed in the United States of America.

Library of Congress Cataloging-in-Publication Data

Jay, Stewart.
  Most humble servants : the advisory role of early judges / Stewart Jay.
    p. cm.
  Includes bibliographical references and index.
  ISBN 0-300-07018- 7 (cloth : alk. paper)
  1. Advisory opinions—United States—History. 2. Judicial opinions—United States—History. 3. Advisory opinions—Great Britain—History. 4. Judicial opinions—Great Britain—History. I. Title.
  KF8775.J39   1997
  347.73.14—dc21   97-8983
                                                   CIP

A catalogue record for this book is available from the British Library.

The paper in this book meets the guidelines for permanence and durability of the Committee on Production Guidelines for Book Longevity of the Council on Library Resources.

10 9 8 7 6 5 4 3 2 1

For my dear wife, Lisa Kennedy

Contents

Acknowledgments

I owe my wife, Lisa Kennedy, special thanks for editing the entire manuscript. More especially, she and our children sustained me through the years required to write this book.

I wish to thank the readers of this manuscript for their helpful comments: William Casto, Richard Fallon, Daniel Farber, William Fletcher, Robert Frankel, Jr., Thomas Green, Wythe Holt, Maeva Marcus, Arval Morris, James Oldham, John Orth, Hugh Spitzer, and Louis Wolcher. William Casto and Wythe Holt were particularly generous in giving my work a thorough reading; their corrections and suggestions were invariably valuable. I am grateful to James Oldham, whose expert advice on the sections dealing with Chief Justice Mansfield greatly improved my understanding. Several research assistants contributed to producing this book. Richard Marens deserves thanks for his diligence and sound advice on the British chapter. Erin Williams checked hundreds of citations. Claudia Caruthers proofread the manuscript and gave me especially valuable editorial assistance. My manuscript editor, Julie Carlson, and production editor, Margaret Otzel of Yale University Press, offered excellent editorial advice.

I have the great fortune of being associated with an institution that has a superb library. Without the library staff at the University of Washington School of Law, completing this project would have been far too difficult for me. In some way or another, I could thank every member of the library for contributing to this work. Two research librarians, Mary Whisner and Martin Cerjan (now at the University of Maine), aided this book in more ways than I could possibly list, but most of all by quickly and accurately answering often obscure questions. Three staff members of the same library, Laurie Blakley, Patricia Roberts, and Michael Madin, promptly located and retrieved the hundreds of books and materials that made this work possible.

Another indispensable research source was the Documentary History of the Supreme Court 1789–1800, a project compiling and reprinting documents related to the early Supreme Court. Citations to the project's published volumes appear throughout the notes. In addition, the director of this project, Maeva Marcus, kindly gave me access to copies of scores of unpublished documents, and she patiently showed me the way to learning this subject (to the extent that I have). Robert Frankel, Jr., an associate editor, carefully read a late version of the manuscript, corrected several errors, and provided important documents.

The research and writing of this work could not have been accomplished without the summer grants and other support that I received from the University of Washington Law School Foundation over the past few years.

Chapter 1 is based on my 1995 article, "Servants of Monarchs and Lords: The Advisory Role of Early British Judges," in volume 38 of the *American Journal of Legal History*.

When primary sources are quoted, spelling and grammar have been left in their original form.

Introduction

In the summer of 1793, Secretary of State Thomas Jefferson requested on behalf of the Washington administration that the Justices of the Supreme Court advise the executive on certain questions concerning American obligations and rights as a neutral party in the ongoing war among European powers. Jefferson explained that these "abstract questions" were "often presented under circumstances which do not give a cognisance of them to the tribunals of the country." Five of the six members of the Court signed a letter in response, refusing to provide answers on the ground that there were "strong arguments against the Propriety of our extrajudicially deciding the questions."[1]

Chief Justice John Jay's biographer, Richard Morris, commented that the "memorable argument" presented by the letter was "unanswerable, and that ended the matter." And so it did as a matter of constitutional principle. Thomas Sergeant wrote in his 1822 treatise on the U.S. Constitution that the Justices had declined because the Court's work was confined to "the decision of controversies brought before them in legal form," and the questions did not grow "out of a case legally brought before them." Likewise, Justice Story's

Commentaries on the Constitution stated that the judicial "branch of the government can be called upon only to decide controversies, brought before them in a legal form; and therefore are bound to abstain from any extra-judicial opinions upon points of law, even though solemnly requested by the executive." From the formative period of the United States to the present, this view has persisted as the standard interpretation of the Supreme Court's unwillingness to assist the executive some two centuries ago.[2]

Historians of early America, whether legally trained or not, have with few exceptions read the Justices' letter at face value. Julius Goebel typifies this understanding by reciting in his history of the early Supreme Court that the refusal "was grounded on the separation of powers and on the impropriety of extrajudicial decision of the questions proffered." Even accounts of the Washington administration's political struggles that otherwise provide minute details of the period tend to treat the incident of the letter as having been resolved on purely constitutional grounds. Forrest McDonald, for example, in his biography of Alexander Hamilton, indicates merely that "[t]he Court . . . refused on constitutional grounds to give an advisory opinion." A classic account by Charles Thomas of the Washington administration's foreign policy in 1793 concludes that "[t]he Justices explained the refusal solely on constitutional grounds. There is no reason for attributing any other motive to them."[3]

One of the initial issues left unaddressed by these explanations is that Supreme Court Justices in the 1790s did counsel the executive on a number of occasions after having been expressly asked to do so by the administration. Chief Justice Jay provides the most notable example of this, as he not only rendered advice on numerous occasions but actually served as Secretary of State while retaining his membership on the Court. In other instances, the Justices attempted to influence legislation through formal and informal contacts with Congress. Both members of the Supreme Court and lower federal judges also performed statutorily assigned duties that seem contrary to Charles Warren's assertion that the federal judiciary under Jay "established itself as a purely judicial body."[4]

Mindful of these facts, several historians have contended that the Justices in 1793 were making a deliberate effort to distinguish between their role as individuals in service to the nation and their obligation as members of the Court, an institution they wished to separate strictly from the two other branches of the federal government. Referring to the Justices' letter to the Washington administration, Maeva Marcus and Emily Van Tassel argue that the Justices "did not want the executive branch to think that it was a part of their official duty to advise the president when asked, for in the justices' minds that could be an interference with their primary constitutional duty to be impartial judges in the last resort." Similarly, Russell Wheeler has asserted that the Justices "realized they would be setting a precedent for public advice-giving on legal questions which could arise before them in litigable form." Wheeler contends that this might have made "the Court appear an executive appendage." Worse yet, "[i]f the Court's advice were not followed the Court would appear weak, and if a case arose based on such an action there would be a tendency for the public to interpret a decision opposed to the President as vindictiveness and to regard a decision upholding him as obsequiousness."[5]

The views of these scholars and others have advanced our understanding of the early Supreme Court's attitude about extrajudicial service by judges, and many of the details they offer in support of their theses will be considered in this book. It is difficult to quarrel with the contention that the Justices were attempting to distinguish between the tasks a judge might perform in an individual, albeit "official," capacity, and the tasks the Court itself could carry out as a branch of the federal government. Further, the contention that they were endeavoring to protect the institutional autonomy of the Court in its formative years is persuasive.

Beyond these general conclusions, however, a great deal more remains to be said. Why did the Justices wish to establish this formal separation between their individual and institutional capacities? If anything, the prior history of judicial advisory opinions in both England and the American states would have countenanced at least some advice by the Court to the executive outside a formal adjudication. As it happens, the letter to the Justices was not an isolated occurrence; rather, it transpired in the midst of a grave political crisis. This book presents the thesis that the surrounding political climate and the ideological orientations of key political players, some of whom were on the Court, directly influenced the Justices' decision to decline answering. Moreover, the Justices had an interest in fostering the independence of the Court and the federal judicial system as a whole, an interest that was not hypothetical but rather driven by a number of political threats to the national judiciary. How the federal judiciary would evolve in both structure and influence was an open question in 1793, and the Justices were aware that their actions could have a direct bearing on the future of the system.

More than a decade after these events involving Washington's letter, on the other side of the Atlantic, the opposition in the British Parliament strongly protested the appointment of Chief Justice Lord Ellenborough to the cabinet. The effort to prevent Ellenborough from serving in the cabinet was based on the supposedly "recognized feature of the English constitution, to keep separate and distinct the legislative, executive, and judiciary powers of state." But the parliamentary attack failed decisively. To refute the opposition's argument, the government's ministers cited numerous examples to demonstrate "that from the earliest periods of our history, the judges have been employed and consulted by the crown, in the executive department of the state." As to separation of powers, the ministers replied: "It is idle to talk of the separation of the legislative, executive, and judiciary powers in England, where one of the branches of the legislature was the supreme court of law, and had usually for its speaker the first law-officer of the kingdom; where the servants of the crown sat in both houses of parliament, and where the chief justices were privy counsellors and sworn advisers of the crown, in all matters relating to the honour of the king and to the good of the people."[6]

The government was not misrepresenting the facts. For centuries British judges had been called upon to advise the Crown and its ministries, often by providing formal advisory opinions on legal questions. These were extra-judicial decisions rendered by the judges apart from any ongoing case. Whether the consultation was with all the twelve principal judges of England or with some lesser number, the advice always was given as part of the official duties of the judiciary. In the Ellenborough controversy, the government might have added that English judges had been formally involved with the House of Lords as advisers on legislative and adjudicative matters since the inception of that body.

British courts would take a considerably longer time to reach a conclusion similar to that of the U.S. Supreme Court in 1793. As the House of Lords declared in a 1957 decision, "it has by many been thought an unwise practice to try to anticipate judicial decisions extra-judicially by obtaining the opinion or advice of the judges, the reason being that it is regarded as tending to sap their independence and impartiality."[7]

The rejection of advisory opinions by the Supreme Court, and ultimately British authorities, typically is justified as an aspect of separation of powers, and accordingly reflects a basic outlook about the judicial function. In the 1910 decision of *Muskrat v. United States*, for example, the Supreme Court used the Justices' rejection of the Washington administration's inquiries to illustrate the meaning of the constitutional term "cases and controversies," saying that federal courts were limited to hearing "claims of litigants brought before the courts for determination by such regular proceedings as are established by law or custom for the protection or enforcement of rights, or the prevention, redress, or punishment of wrongs." Likewise, Lord Diplock remarked in a 1977 House of Lords case that "the jurisdiction of the court is not to declare the law generally or to give advisory opinions; it is confined to declaring contested legal rights, subsisting or future, of the parties represented in the litigation before it and not those of anyone else." Commentators have elaborated on this theme by identifying functional justifications for the ban on advisory opinions, emphasizing the importance of resolving legal issues against a concrete set of facts, refined by an adversary presentation, which in turn "limit[s] the scope and broad policy implications of the legal determination, and . . . aid[s] . . . its accurate interpretation."[8]

Given this depiction of courts as passive adjudicators of contested cases, it is unremarkable that in recent years the proscription against advisory opinions so often has been linked to the issues of standing, mootness, ripeness, and political questions. In explaining the connection, the Supreme Court said in a 1984 case that this family of doctrines sprang from "the idea of separation of powers on which the Federal Government is founded. . . . 'All of the doctrines that cluster about Article III—not only standing but mootness, ripeness, political question, and the like—relate in part, and in different though overlapping ways, to an idea, which is more than an intuition but less than a rigorous and explicit theory, about the constitutional and prudential limits to the powers of an unelected, unrepresentative judiciary in our kind of government.'" Invoking similar themes, students of this aspect of constitutional law have suggested that prohibiting advisory opinions serves "[t]he value of having courts function as organs of the sober second thought of the community appraising action already taken, rather than as advisers at the front line of governmental action at the stage of initial decision."[9]

The purpose of this book is not to explain, much less to question or even justify, the present vision of the judicial office. Rather, this book is a historical inquiry into the respective roles of early British and American judges as advisers to executive and legislative bodies. A comparison of judicial practices in the two countries during overlapping chronological periods spanning several centuries and ending in the eighteenth century reveals a contrasting picture of the role of courts in society. For the greater portion of England's existence, judges were not confined to deciding contested cases. Instead, their official responsibilities included diverse tasks of a legislative and executive nature that today would be considered entirely inappropriate for the judiciary.[10] A major focus of this book (see chapter 1) will be the history of the service by British judges as advisers to the Crown and its ministers (referred to interchangeably as the executive),[11] as well as to the House of Lords. At the same time, we will find that these practices were consistent with the prevailing constitutional theories in that nation.

One possible explanation for the contrasting attitude of American and

British authorities about extrajudicial advisory activities in the late eighteenth century is that the respective cultures had built their judicial institutions on fundamentally different constitutional foundations. In addition to the starkly dissimilar conceptions of separation of powers, other principles of democratic government that inform the present insistence on confining the unelected judiciary to deciding concrete, adversarial disputes had not taken root in England. Indeed, to the eighteenth-century and earlier worlds in which government scarcely was representative of the people's will, the point of keeping appointed, life-tenured judges from advising the government may not have seemed especially relevant.

Although an interpretation along these lines seems plausible, one should be careful not to indulge too quickly in the assumption that differing views of separation of powers generated divergent judicial institutions. A better approach is to start by tracing the origins of the advisory role played by English judges. One outstanding feature of the English tradition was the ancient lineage of the practice, which began long before separation of powers became a controlling feature of constitutional government. In the earliest formulation of English courts, judges were the King's surrogates—his servants—for dispensing justice. Similarly, the relationship between the judges and the House of Lords grew out of the historical link between the King and the Lords, who themselves were considered advisers to the monarch. Because the judges formally ranked as servants of the royalty, the Lords were able to call upon their services for legal advice. Over time, even though the Lords and the Crown evolved into independent institutions, the judges continued to have ties with both the executive and the upper house of Parliament.

Calling on the judges for counsel was thus by long tradition a prerogative of monarchs and Lords. And in the England of this period, traditions of the sort that allocated political privileges were not discarded easily. The British constitution itself was not contained in a document outlining the structure of government but rather consisted of largely unwritten understandings about the legal rights and responsibilities of British society's members. As the chiding of the opposition by the ministers in the Ellenborough affair demonstrated, any attempt to advance a novel constitutional theory would have been met with a chorus of denunciations based on a defense of traditional practices. Consequently, if the customary role of judges as advisers underwent change, the likely source of explanation would not be an abstract constitutional theory along the lines of separation of powers. Instead, the more probable explanation would lie in the events that shaped the political and social history of the times.

It might be said that this history proves that the decisive force in the development and decline of the judiciary's advisory role was the larger theories behind separation of powers—even if the immediate actors in the political process appeared to be unaware of them. As constitutional theories evolved to insist on defining distinct branches of government, the judiciary accordingly became cabined into a distinct role of adjudicating contested cases. This would explain nicely why the Americans were ahead of the British in rejecting advisory opinions, as the United States from the beginning insisted on separated branches. Consistent with such an understanding, it could be claimed that the Supreme Court Justices appropriately refused to give extrajudicial advice because doing so would have contradicted their roles as impartial judges of conflicts. To explore this perspective, the later chapters of the book detail the American experience in rejecting advisory opinions. After this study is complete, it will be evident that such constitutional doctrines as separation of powers afford at best a partial explanation of both the British and the American developments.

Judges served as advisers during times of strong royal rule as well as during the period in the eighteenth century when Britain began its transition to cabinet government. Curiously, however, the British judges apparently issued no advisory opinions to the executive after 1760. In that year, the principal judges in England gave their last recorded advisory opinion to the King, accompanied by a fairly heavy suggestion from Chief Justice Lord Mansfield that such advice should be sought only in unusual circumstances. No dramatic change in British constitutional theory lay behind this development. Chief Justice Ellenborough's subsequent appointment to the cabinet shows that there was scarcely any support for the view that judges should eschew a formal connection with the executive. A further complication to explicating a theory for the decline of advisory opinions in Britain is that the judges continued to perform their historic role as assistants to the House of Lords for more than a century after they stopped counseling the executive.[12]

There is always a danger in trying to rationalize historical events with theoretical explanations that the people of the relevant period did not recognize. Ideology has its place as a motive of human conduct, yet we should keep in mind that people operate not only from a backdrop of ingrained expectations and ideological inclinations but also in response to immediate needs and personal idiosyncrasies. In the main, both British and American attitudes toward advisory opinions are the product of historical circumstances and not the result of an overriding vision of the respective constitutions. To be sure, the use of judges as advisers to both executive and legislative branches fits harmoniously with the then-current theory of the

British constitution, and in fact the practice was never successfully questioned. This is unremarkable considering the nature of the British constitution—the theory would be obliged to justify the advisory role. On the American side, the freshly minted Constitution did not offer an express answer to the question whether federal judges could serve as advisers to the other branches of government. A thorough review of the evidence shows that constitutional principles of separation of powers alone do not explain why the Justices in 1793 balked at assisting the Washington administration. This does not deny that the Justices' letter elevated the issue to constitutional status by invoking the concept of separation of powers. Rather, the point is that the choice made was neither inevitable nor necessary under the contemporary understanding of the constitutional role of judges.

A reasonable explanation exists for the decline of advisory opinions to the British executive, but much like the American experience, it lies buried in the intricacies of national politics. At the heart of these affairs during the reign of George III we find Lord Mansfield, Chief Justice of the Court of King's Bench from 1756 to 1788. Not only was Mansfield the principal jurist in the land and a preeminent member of the House of Lords, but he also carried on an extensive relationship with a series of administrations. An exploration of his public life suggests that the decline of advisory opinions to the executive may be a product of Mansfield's own predilection for exercising influence while avoiding political exposure. As to the continuing relation between the judges and the House of Lords, the probable answer is that there were no serious political obstacles preventing the arrangement, yet the necessity for the practice was considerable.

At the end of chapter 1 it will be possible to relate the British side of the history of extrajudicial advising to larger themes of constitutional development. It seems likely, for example, that the judges' ability to decline giving advice to the executive was made possible by the guarantee of lifetime judicial tenure that became effective in the eighteenth century. This judicial independence was itself the product of a reaction against the notorious abuses of the courts by the Stuart monarchs in the previous century. Nonetheless, several generations of such independent judges continued giving advice to the executive, and many more thereafter would serve the Lords. The essential point is that judicial independence created the possibility for courts to insist on a formal separation from the partisan political branches. For an explanation of why particular arrangements evolved thereafter, we must consider the political circumstances of the times.

After examining the treatment of judicial advisory opinions in British practice, we will turn our attention to the American colonies and states, and to the debates at the federal Constitutional Convention of 1787. An important part of this discussion will relate to American attitudes regarding separation of powers. With this foundation laid, our inquiry can turn to the sequence of events leading to the Supreme Court's refusal to answer the questions in Jefferson's letter. To explain this incident fully, three lines of development must be analyzed. One of these involves the variety of official and semi-official functions performed by federal judges outside the course of ordinary adjudications. The second factor is the political history of the Washington administration up to 1793—especially the tensions that emerged between Hamilton and Jefferson—and, more generally, the ideological struggles that led to the creation of America's first political parties. Finally, we take into account the special concerns of federal judges for the inchoate national judicial system.

Apart from telling the specific history of the advisory role played by British and American judges prior to the nineteenth century, the larger purpose of this book is to describe in detail how a fundamental principle of governmental structure evolved. In effect, this account provides an insight into the evolution of political ideologies over a period spanning hundreds of years. By examining American developments alongside the British system, we add the complexity of a parent society producing a breakaway offshoot that eventually acquired its own distinctive political and social characteristics, while retaining many of the older relative's attributes. This in turn allows us to isolate the key factors responsible for the constitutional progression.

Lawrence Stone remarked a few years ago that constitutional histories tend to be "sterile and meaningless." It is true that more than a few constitutional histories deserve this label, if for no other reason than their common assumption that theories of government arise out of reasoned deductions from established principles. In particular, judges who venture into legal history in their opinions often succumb to this tendency. Certainly logic and abstract theory play a part in constitutional change. Of far greater significance, however, are the actual political circumstances behind the issue, including the personal outlooks and interests of those figures who are in a position to influence the developments. These elements blend together, much as paint on an artist's canvas, to produce a picture whose distinctive appearance nonetheless bears the traces of the disparate elements. In a manner of speaking, there *always* must be an explanation deeper than the official version that appears in legal opinions or in the public statements of political figures. And the tales to be told about this deeper aspect of constitutional change are rich in force and meaning.[13]

1

The Advisory Role of Judges in Great Britain Through the Eighteenth Century

Sir William Blackstone wrote "that all jurisdictions of courts are either mediately or immediately derived from the Crown, their proceedings run generally in the king's name, they pass under his seal, and are executed by his
officers." Accordingly, the King, "in the eye of the law, is always present in
all courts, though he cannot personally distribute justice. His judges are the
mirror by which the king's image is reflected." Despite the considerable
fiction in this statement, the "[j]udges were royal appointees, and the major
courts [could] fairly be described as royal." Blackstone referred to the Kings'
judges as "[a] third council belonging to the king . . . for law matters. And
this appears frequently in our statutes. . . . So that when . . . the subject be
of a legal nature, then by the king's council is understood his council for
matters of law; namely his judges." To lend authority to his assertions,
Blackstone cited Lord Coke, and he actually borrowed language from the
latter's *First Institutes*.[1]

   As royal officials, judges performed a variety of roles that most modern
observers would regard as inconsistent with the judicial office. Bear in mind
that the distinctions one might make to define the function of the judiciary

under today's theories of separated governmental powers would not pertain to England in the eighteenth century and earlier. In general, "officials and institutions could not easily be compartmented into tidy groups labelled administrative and judicial, or public and private." For one thing, judges commonly occupied more than a single office. Under Charles I, for example, "most major officials were judges, and most judges were administrators. . . . The Lord Treasurer, the Master of the Wards, the Lord Privy Seal, the Presidents of provincial Councils, the Lord Admiral, the Earl Marshall, and so on—all were judges."[2] At times, judges held places on the Privy Council, which itself exercised both executive and judicial powers, and in any case they could be summoned by the council for consultations.[3] The Privy Council declined in importance during the eighteenth century, when it was replaced by an "inner" cabinet of principal ministers who served as the country's executive governing body. Judges in the eighteenth century were on occasion members of the cabinet or attended cabinet meetings.[4] From its inception, the office of the Chancellor encompassed a political dimension, and its holders were often powerful and controversial figures in government, as illustrated by the careers of such figures as Cardinal Wolsey, Lord Clarendon, Lord Hardwicke, and Lord Thurlow.[5] When the cabinet system evolved in the eighteenth century into one dominated by the inner cabinet, the Chancellor was included in its select group of members. Less frequently, Chief Justices joined in this exclusive company.[6] The Lord Chancellor typically served as speaker of the House of Lords, and common law judges might be members of the Lords if they were otherwise peers, as was true of Chief Justice Lord Mansfield.[7]

During and prior to the eighteenth century, the principal English judges also played a significant part in the ordinary administration of the kingdom. For example, judges were included on a variety of commissions formed to resolve a wide array of administrative and commercial disputes. These bodies handled somewhat weighty issues such as the prevention of fraud in collecting customs duties and the setting of rules for proceedings in certain mercantile disputes. At the same time, they dealt with more mundane matters, including administration of sewers and resolution of conflicts arising from Crown or church properties, controversies over coronation duties, regulation of the price of wine, and so on. In these positions a judge might assist in formulating a policy that later could come before him in a judicial setting. As part of their official duties, judges also supervised local government by exercising control over the officials at that level (principally over Justices of the Peace). In addition, while sitting at the biannual Assizes held throughout the country, the judges acted as royal representatives, and as such "were expected to report upon men and matters of interest, to use their influence in support of official policy, and to intervene when necessary." Grand jury charges by the judges at Assizes during the Stuart and Hanoverian eras "were designed to advertise party principles."[8]

Some critics at the time did criticize sharply the dual holding of judicial and executive offices. The influential writer "Junius," for example, accused Lord Mansfield of employing his position as Chief Justice to promote his ministerial career. As mentioned in the introduction, by the beginning of the nineteenth century the intermingling of judicial and executive roles engendered rebuke in parliamentary debates. Nevertheless, the attempt to block Chief Justice Lord Ellenborough from sitting in the cabinet failed; it produced instead a lengthy recitation of the disparate roles assumed by British judges throughout history and a defense of these practices under the constitution. Ellenborough was, however, the last Chief Justice to serve in the cabinet.[9]

EXTRAJUDICIAL ADVICE TO THE HOUSE OF LORDS

Until the end of the nineteenth century, it was accepted practice in England for the House of Lords to call the judges for consultation on legal questions. During the medieval era, "[t]he judges and the law officers of the Crown had been an integral part, indeed the nucleus of the . . . parliament." By at least the sixteenth century, however, the role of the judges and other legal officers of the Crown had been reduced from membership in the Lords to the status of advisers to the House. Blackstone described the practice in his 1765 treatise: "[The House of Lords] have a right to be attended, and constantly are, by the judges of the court of king's bench and commonpleas, and such of the barons of the exchequer as are of the degree of the coif, or have been made serjeants at law; as likewise by the masters of the court of chancery; for their advice in point of law, and for the greater dignity of their proceedings."[10]

Lord Fortescue's reports, published in 1748, stated on the authority of Coke that "[a]ll the Judges are assistants to the Lords to inform them of the common law, and thereunto are called severally by writ." The importance of the practice to the House was underscored in a 1641 speech to the Lords that presented articles of impeachment against one of the judges: "[W]hen a parliament is called, if your lordships were not assisted by them, and the house of commons by other gentlemen of that robe, experience tells us it might run a hazard of being styled *Parliamentum indoctorum*."[11] From the sixteenth to the eighteenth centuries it was common for the Lords to consult the judges, whose opinions on legal questions were afforded strong weight,[12] although the House made the final decision and on occasion disagreed with the judges. Writing late in the seventeenth century, Sir Matthew Hale said of the authoritativeness of the judges' opinions to the Lords "that though for many years last past they have had only voices of advice and assistance not authoritative or decisive; yet their opinions have been always the rules, whereby the lords do or should proceed in matters of law."[13]

Opinions from the judges to the House of Lords often pertained to cases—either appeals or trials of peers—pending before that body in its capacity as a court. Part of the explanation for calling on the judges for advice was that frequently only a few—if any—of the Lords possessed significant legal training. Compounding this problem, lay peers had the right to vote on appeals, a prerogative that persisted until 1844. During the eighteenth century, the influence of the judges on the Lords grew steadily as the volume of appeals increased: "The House was slowly being recognized by the profession as a court of law, laying down basic principles of the common law . . . and not merely as an undifferentiated political organ."[14]

Consultations between the Lords and judges were not confined to assisting the House with its adjudications; advice was frequently sought on matters pertaining to pending legislation. According to Blackstone, for example, "[i]n the house of lords, if the bill begins there, it is (when of a private nature) perused by two of the judges, who settle all points of legal propriety." In 1718, the judges were ordered to attend the House to consider the repeal of a statute, and Fortescue reports that "thereupon the Lords said it was usual to ask the Judges opinions of the consequences of repealing or making any law." Referring to the first half of the seventeenth century, a modern scholar has detailed the wide-ranging duties the judges performed as assistants to the Lords: "In parliament they assisted committees for bills, drafted amendments, explicated points of law and defended them in conferences with the House of Commons, conducted hearings, reviewed cases on writs of error, assisted with the dispatch of petitions, and performed such ceremonial functions as the House requested."[15]

Appearances by the judges before the House were mandatory, although the judges on occasion did resist giving advice. Significantly, judges occasionally declined to answer questions regarding legislative issues that could arise in adjudicated cases. The Lords themselves decided in 1718 not to ask a question because "it might come in question judicially" before the judges. In a related matter, they rephrased a query to avoid inquiring about "what might judicially come in question in Westminster-Hall."[16]

Although judges' duties varied over the years, their involvement in parliamentary affairs proved to be consistently significant and often substantial. As might be expected from the considerable influence of the judges on the course of Parliament, and the often close tie between their opinions and decisions of public policy, their advice could and did land them in the center of political controversies. At times, this situation alienated the judges from the Lords and produced serious charges against the judges from one or the other house of Parliament, or from the King.[17]

EXTRAJUDICIAL ADVICE TO THE EXECUTIVE

The judges' obligation to the King began at the same time and for the same reasons as did their service in the House of Lords. Parliament originally constituted "a royal assembly, an afforced meeting of the king's council," and "[t]he Lords was the historic nucleus" of that body. The judges, along with the King's sergeants-at-law, law officers, and masters of chancery, occupied places in the Lords "and were the official members of the King's continual or permanent council, his legal councillors." Eventually, Parliament became a bicameral institution, and the judges were reduced to a nonvoting, advisory participation. Nevertheless, their presence in the Lords continued in theory to reflect their status as royal assistants, which is evidenced by the fact that they were summoned to the Lords with writs of assistance. On some occasions when the judges refused to consult with the Lords, they justified their action by contending that the questions asked touched the royal prerogative and thus required the King's permission for them to answer.[18]

In seeking legal advice, "[t]he sovereign had many options. He could consult the Lord Chancellor, the two law officers, individual judges, or groups of judges." Monarchs conferred with judges on relatively minor matters, such as whether to postpone the opening of a session of Parliament, and more serious questions, including how to prepare the King's legislative program for Parliament and whether royal actions were legal. From at least the late sixteenth century to the early nineteenth century, judges and commentators used the term "extrajudicial" to label opinions of judges on legal questions that were given outside of the course of common law proceedings.[19]

Despite long-standing acceptance, the practice of giving advisory opinions at times proved controversial. For much of this period, the Crown employed the law as an instrument for accomplishing royal goals by restraining the people, rather than accept law as a limit on governance. Asking for advice from the judges often appeared to be a thinly disguised means of legitimizing the King's plans. Early commentators understood this pretext. Writing toward the end of the eighteenth century, Francis Hargrave remarked on Coke's statement about advisory opinions in his *First Institutes:* "[E]xtra-judicial opinions [given on demand from the King] were not favoured by lord Coke [citing example]. . . . However, it must be admitted, that there are various instances of the king's consulting the judges, and of their giving their opinions *extra-judicially*. . . . But however numerous and strong the precedents may be in favour of the king's *extra-judicially* consulting the judges on questions in which the crown is interested, it is a right to be understood with many exceptions, and such as ought to be exercised with great reserve; lest the rigid impartiality so essential to their *judicial* capacity should be violated."[20]

Coke's views on extrajudicial opinions evolved with his career, and his connection with the practice provides important insights into the place of such opinions in English political life. While Solicitor General and then Attorney General, Coke evidently favored consulting the judges for their opinions. After becoming a judge, Coke gave such opinions despite his notorious efforts to maintain judicial independence from the King and to promote the common law over royal prerogatives.[21] Hargrave's example of Coke's attitude about extrajudicial opinions in reality was not relevant. It involved a case from 1616 in which the Chief Justice resisted a command from James I to halt judicial proceedings that concerned the King's prerogative until the judges had consulted the executive on the matter. Instead of being a refusal to give an advisory opinion, this episode appears to be more an instance of resisting executive interference with an ongoing adjudication.[22]

A better illustration of Coke's attitude toward advisory opinions while on the bench comes from Peacham's Case, which arose in 1614—shortly before the case cited by Hargrave. James I took a personal interest in prosecuting Edmund Peacham for allegedly treasonous statements he had made in a written sermon found in Peacham's study. The case against Peacham was uncertain, however, not only because the sermon had never been delivered but also because there was some question as to whether the writing—which consisted mainly of derogatory comments about James—was treasonous under the existing statute. James ordered his Attorney General, Sir Francis Bacon, to find out the "feeling of the judges of the King's Bench," specifying that they should be consulted separately and enjoined to secrecy. Initially, Coke informed Bacon that it was illegal for the King to demand that the judges give their opinions separately on the issue of whether particular actions of a defendant constituted high treason. The consultation, Coke maintained, should be with the court as an entity.[23] A few days later, Bacon returned to Coke and advised the Chief Justice that the other judges "made no scruple to deliver their own opinion in private," to which Bacon added the admonition that declining would be a violation of the judicial oath, which required judges "to counsel the king, without distinction whether it were jointly or severally." Coke relented and answered James's questions, although his opinion was unfavorable to the King's interest. One of the other judges replied to the King that "every Judge was bound expressly by his oath to give your Majesty counsel when he was called; and whether he should do it jointly or severally, that rested in your Majesty's good pleasure, as you would require it."[24]

In objecting to separate opinions in Peacham's Case, Coke evidently perceived that the King was attempting to pressure the judges into unanimous views and assure the outcome of the case by ex parte consultations in advance of trial. On that score Coke's resistance may have proved somewhat successful, for in the following several decades the judges typically were consulted as a group.[25] Still, the King continued to seek individual advice from the two Chief Justices.

Coke's resistance to the King's demand for separate opinions and his refusal to halt proceedings on royal command were costly to the Chief Justice's career, albeit not to his fame. James cited these transgressions in giving his reasons for removing Coke from judicial office and membership on the Privy Council. In Coke's posthumously published *Third Institutes,* he wrote as part of a section on treason that "the Judges ought not to deliver their opinions before-hand of any criminal case, that may come before them judicially." Coke was referring to the common practice—used in Peacham's Case—of the executive consulting with the judges prior to bringing criminal charges. Fortescue's reports from 1748 show that the procedure persisted: "[I]n all criminal cases, especially high treason, the Judges met at the request of the Attorney General to advise the King in those prosecutions; as on the Restoration the Judges met to consult concerning the prosecution of the regicides, and the Attorney General made several queries, not only in framing of the indictments, but in relation to overt acts and evidence, in which all the judges gave their opinions."[26]

Coke pointed to a case from 1486 to illustrate the potential unfairness to the defendant from such advance consultation. According to Coke, the judges asked to be excused from delivering an opinion on an issue prior to trial. Noting that in a treason trial the defendant was not entitled to counsel, Coke argued that the judges' request was fair because the judges were bound to act "for the benefit of the prisoner, to see that nothing be urged against him contrary to law and right." Considering this obligation, Coke reasoned that judges should not give opinions about the case in advance of trial, "[f]or how can they be indifferent, who have delivered their opinions before-hand without hearing of the party, when a small addition, or subtraction may alter the case?"[27]

A few other judges during the early seventeenth century expressed a similar sentiment. In 1629, for example, Charles I queried the judges about whether a speech in Parliament by Sir John Eliot was censurable or privileged. In their reply, the judges expressed a "desire to be spared to give any answer to a perticular case which might peraduenture come before them judicially." Notwithstanding this reluctance, they did answer a number of other politically sensitive questions at the same time about parliamentary privileges, some of which were cited by the judges as authority in subsequent judicial proceedings. The previous year they had given answers to questions (albeit with some hedging) concerning various implications of the Petition of Right, which Parliament had asked Charles to grant. These examples illustrate that "[i]n Charles's reign [the judges] were regarded as the King's counsellors, whose opinions he might obtain in all cases of difficulty." Charles, however, was neither the first nor the last monarch to employ the practice of extrajudicial consultations with the judges. Regardless of Coke's reservations, judges gave such opinions throughout the seventeenth century, even in cases that would likely later be heard in court. As one nineteenth-century commentator pointed out, Coke needed to reach back rather far in history for a precedent, and he did not deny that extrajudicial consultations had become a regular practice.[28]

As exemplified by Charles's actions, the Stuart Kings used judicial consultations for political purposes. Whereas previous monarchs had certainly requested judicial opinions, under James I and Charles I such opinions became overt instruments for achieving the King's will. Or at least this was the prevailing contemporaneous view about the Stuart Kings. Lord Clarendon lamented the "deserved reproach and infamy that attended the judges by being made use of in . . . acts of power. . . . [I]n the wisdom of former times, when the prerogative went highest, . . . never any court of law, very seldom any judge, or lawyer of reputation, was called upon to assist in an act of power; the Crown well knowing the moment of keeping those objects of reverence and veneration with the people."[29]

Clarendon primarily was alluding to the famous case of 1637 involving the legality of a form of royal taxation known as ship money. This was a levy that had been employed since medieval times to provide armed vessels in support of the Royal Navy. In effect, ship money constituted a tax imposed as an assertion of the King's prerogative powers, and it was implemented without parliamentary approval. Earlier levies, even in the relatively recent past, had not prompted serious opposition. Intense controversy nonetheless arose when Charles I ordered, by successive writs, ship money payments as one of several ways of raising money during the eleven-year period (1629–40) in which the

King refused to call Parliament in session. In the face of mounting opposition to the measures, Charles turned to his judges for support.[30]

Lord Keeper Coventry informed the judges that the King wished them in their "Charges at the Assizes, and in all places else, where opportunity is offered," to inform the people "how just it is, that his majesty should require this for the common defence; and with what alacrity and cheerfulness they ought, and are bound in duty, to contribute unto it."[31] With popular resistance continuing to grow, Charles required separate extrajudicial opinions from each judge on the legality of the imposition, for, as he said, "the Trials in our several courts, by the formality in pleading, will require a long protraction." Charles plainly meant for the opinions to influence ongoing proceedings against subjects who had refused to pay the ship money.[32] The twelve judges signed a general answer strongly affirming the prerogative of the King to raise revenue from ship money assessments. Most of the judges also rendered separate opinions. Charles ordered these answers published throughout England and placed on the records of the central courts.[33] Shortly thereafter, the barons of the Court of Exchequer invited the judges of the other courts to join them in hearing the case of John Hampden, who had challenged the legality of ship money. The judges, who had previously given their extrajudicial opinions on this question, rendered a split decision in favor of the King.[34]

The Case of Ship Money was recognized at the time as momentous because it implicated the scope of the King's prerogative to raise taxes despite parliamentary disapproval.[35] After Charles was forced in 1640 by financial necessity to convene what became the Long Parliament, speakers in both the House of Commons and the House of Lords castigated the judges. Parliament pronounced the King's levying of ship money illegal, and it reversed the judgment against Hampden. In the course of justifying these actions, Parliament declared the "extra-judicial Opinions" to be "[i]n the whole, and in every part of them . . . against the laws of the realm." Articles of impeachment then were brought against most of the judges.[36]

In spite of the attack on the legality of the judges' opinions regarding ship money, for the most part the Long Parliament did not condemn the practice of extrajudicial consultations with the King. Rather, members complained that the judges had used the law as an instrument to oppress the people by ignoring the various parliamentary acts prohibiting this use of Crown power to raise revenues. Oliver St. John asserted in a speech before Parliament that "for now the law doth not only not defend us, but the law itself is made the instrument of taking all away."[37] Nevertheless, St. John acknowledged that the judges were "of the king's council by their oaths, [and] they are bound lawfully to counsel him; that is, when their opinions are demanded, they are to deliver them according to the law."[38] Moreover, later observers understood the judges' responsibility in these terms. Fortescue, for example, emphasized in his 1748 report that the parliamentary actions against the judges meant "no more than that their judicial as well as extrajudicial opinions were against law, not that they were against law because extrajudicial." In a leading commentary on the role of judges and the origins of the English Civil War, W. J. Jones wrote: "[i]ndividual judges were criticized rather than the law which they supervised, the procedures within which they operated, or the royal rights which they affirmed. . . . This enabled continued belief in the virtues of English law and partially accounts for the largely unchanged survival of the Justices of the central courts of common law."[39]

The use of advisory opinions for political purposes was facilitated by the ability of the King to remove or suspend judges from office, as occurred in the case of Coke and others. This weapon could be especially potent given that the twelve principal judgeships were tremendously lucrative positions for their holders. The practice of suspending, dismissing, or forcibly retiring judges appeared throughout the Stuart period, and as William Holdsworth observed, the judges' positions depended "upon court influence, and even upon bribery and other forms of corruption."[40] Under the Stuarts, "where the interests or supposed interests of the Court were concerned, the judges, almost without exception, were tools. . . . All of these were men of legal acumen and judicial fairness, except wherever the government was concerned."[41] A common perception of judges from 1640 until the end of the seventeenth century was that they "were slavish and self-interested."[42] Unquestionably there were notable examples of judicial independence in the seventeenth century, but as Howard Nenner has emphasized, "[t]he king, for the most part, controlled his judges, and for that reason alone he controlled the law." Nenner points out the importance of this control in a time of fundamental constitutional struggle, when "the law of the constitution was not yet settled" and "constitutional discourse relied more upon the language of the law than on any other political vocabulary." Throughout the century-long contest, all sides attempted to base arguments "upon their common legal heritage."[43]

The quotation above from Hargrave's notes to Coke's *First Institutes* indicates that in the eighteenth century the legality of extrajudicial opinions was accepted even by those who criticized the practice. An interesting example occurred at the death of William III in 1702, when the question arose as to whether the judges were obligated to surrender their judicial appointments, thereby leaving their tenure in the control of the next monarch,

Queen Anne. Chief Justice Holt assembled "all the Judges then in town," who proceeded to decide that their commissions expired along with the King. This advisory opinion was followed by Anne, who renewed all but two of the judicial commissions.[44]

For the Hanoverian period such opinions have not been as well documented as in the preceding two centuries, but the evidence is sufficient to confirm their use until at least 1760. In 1717, for example, the judges delivered an elaborate series of opinions on the question whether George I had the right to control the upbringing and marriages of his grandchildren. During the previous year, three judges who were to try Francis Francia for treason met with the prosecution and gave preliminary opinions about the case.[45] Another instance was the opinion given in the case of the unfortunate Admiral Byng, who had been sentenced to death by court martial in 1756 for misdirecting a naval expedition at Minorca. Following a request for advice from the King, the judges determined that Byng's death sentence had been legal, and he was accordingly executed by firing squad. Poor Byng's fate prompted a famous remark from Voltaire in *Candide:* "In this country we find it pays to shoot an admiral from time to time to encourage the others."[46]

A 1747 incident, however, does show that some judges were reluctant to confer with the Crown's law officers for the purpose of delivering extrajudicial legal advice. The substantive issue in question was whether the judges could serve along with Privy Council members on a commission to hear prize appeals from the admiralty courts. George II commanded Attorney General Dudley Ryder and Solicitor General William Murray (later Chief Justice Lord Mansfield) "to meet with the judges when they take the commission into consideration." But "[m]any of the judges thought it altogether improper to meet 'in chambers' with the law officers on such a matter." Some of the judges believed that on the merits alone it would be illegal for them to serve on the commission. For example, Justice Michael Foster reportedly protested that "it would be unbecoming the twelve judges of England to act as judges of affairs of state." By contrast, Ryder—later Chief Justice of King's Bench—expressed confidence that it was appropriate for the judges to meet with the law officers for the purpose of giving their judgment about the commission: "[T]here are many precedents of such conferences between the judges and the Attorney and Solicitor and other King's counsel, and wherein they have (certainly signed their opinion), particularly in 1702; and in 1710, when . . . all the judges and King's Attorney and Solicitor and several King's counsel joined in an opinion."[47]

Apparently the last reported instance of a formal, written extrajudicial opinion to the executive was Sackville's Case in 1760. In this matter, the King requested an opinion as to whether an army officer who had been dismissed from the service could be tried by court martial for a military offense. The judges replied that there would be jurisdiction for a court martial proceeding. Chief Justice Lord Mansfield, however, took the occasion to remark, in a letter to the Lord Keeper accompanying the opinion, that "[i]n general, they are very averse to giving extra-judicial opinions, especially where they affect a particular case; but the circumstances of the trial now depending ease us of difficulties upon this occasion." Mansfield went on to relate that the judges were "exceedingly thankful to his majesty for his tenderness in not sending any question to them till the necessity of such reference became manifest and urgent."[48]

To underscore the evident displeasure of the judges for advisory opinions, Mansfield added that they would feel free to change their views on the legal question involved if the issue came before them judicially. Actually this was a point that the judges had long insisted upon, although Mansfield's reminder may have served to deflate the usefulness of these opinions to the Crown.[49] Shortly after Sackville's Case, Mansfield's puisne colleague on King's Bench, Justice Foster, wrote a caustic account of Peacham's Case, in which he focused on James I's demand for the judges' opinions individually in advance of trial. Referring to this practice as "unbecoming the Majesty of the Crown," Foster lamented that Sir Francis Bacon had "submitted to the drudgery of sounding the opinions of the judges upon the point of law, before it was thought advisable to risque it at an open trial; that the judges were to be sifted separately and soon, before they could have an opportunity of conferring together."[50]

In spite of these admonitions against extrajudicial advisory opinions, the executive continued to consult with judges individually or as a group. Chief Justice Mansfield, for example, was a source of frequent advice—legal and otherwise—to the Crown. Furthermore, during the Gordon Riots of 1780, George III called a meeting of the Privy Council to discuss what measures should be taken to suppress the disorders. The judges were summoned to attend, along with the Attorney General and Solicitor General. At this meeting, the judges were queried specifically whether the events justified the invocation of martial law and the closing of civilian courts. Apparently most of the judges thought these actions were warranted, but one judge dissented, and in the end the administration decided not to invoke martial law.[51]

The history of judicial manipulation by the Stuarts led to a provision in the Act of Settlement of 1701 that secured the lifetime tenure of the common law judges (except that a judge could be removed by joint address of both houses of Parliament).[52] In the main, this guarantee resulted in a significant degree of independence from executive control for British judges in the eighteenth century and thereafter.[53] Nevertheless, some contemporary critics complained that insulation of the judiciary from executive control remained impaired by such practices as cabinet service by Chief Justices and the Crown's granting of "pensions to the judges, of appointments to commissionerships of the great seal . . . or of peerages." Whatever merit these charges may have had, they pale in comparison to the controversy surrounding the extensive system of royal patronage employed in the eighteenth century to influence parliamentary decision making. British judges were sufficiently secure in their offices that they could insist on restricting extrajudicial consultations only to instances of great moment.[54]

This brief review of the English practice of giving extrajudicial opinions indicates that despite the reservations of some prominent judges, and notwithstanding occasional resistance to providing this counsel to the executive, there was overall acceptance of its lawfulness prior to the nineteenth century. During this time, it was generally assumed that the judges were obligated to serve as extrajudicial counselors to the House of Lords. The next question is how the advisory function of the British judiciary fit with the overall theory of the constitution and separation of powers in this period.

THE JUDICIARY AND THE ADVISORY ROLE OF JUDGES UNDER THE BRITISH CONSTITUTION

Balanced Government and Parliamentary Supremacy

The theory of mixed or balanced government can be traced to the writings of Plato, Aristotle, and Polybius. Thomas Aquinas continued the tradition by restating it in his *Summa Theologica*. By the middle of the seventeenth century, it had become the predominant English conception of the superior form of government, the means by which both stability and liberty were preserved in society. According to this view, each form of government had its peculiar virtues and vices. Blackstone's description of the virtues was familiar, being one of several similar accounts: "Democracies are usually the best calculated to direct the end of a law; aristocracies to invent the means by which that end shall be obtained; and monarchies to carry those means into execution." A government composed solely of one form would have that form's particular advantages. So, said Blackstone, in "a democracy, where the right of making laws resides in the people at large, public virtue, or goodness of intention, is more likely to be found." Aristocracies were characterized by wisdom, whereas monarchy was distinctive in its power and unity. At the same time, each type of government entailed singular disadvantages. Charles

I's description in 1642 provided a typical rendering: "The Ill of Absolute Monarchy, is Tyranny; the Ill of Aristocracy, is Faction and Division; the Ills of Democracy, are Tumults, Violence, and Licentiousness."[55]

According to numerous writers of this period, the genius of the British constitution lay in its blending of the three estates of society in a manner that preserved the virtues of each while preventing degeneration to the states of their associated evils. The ultimate goal was to achieve an equilibrium in which none of the social orders dominated the rest—indeed, the resulting absence of domination was considered the essence of liberty. To accomplish this result required that the three estates participate in government to a degree sufficient to allow for mutual checking of political power. Consequently, the system functioned through the recognition of legal privileges in each of the three social classes, particularly in regard to their roles in government. This view of a "constitution" differed fundamentally from the form that Americans articulated by the end of the eighteenth century and championed thereafter. Instead of a written document describing the structures of government and the rights of the people, the British constitution amounted to a description of the existing social orders in the country and "that assemblage of laws, customs and institutions which form the general system."[56]

Allocation of power among the parts of British government remained central to the political history of England from the time of Charles I's collision with Parliament until the eighteenth century, with the key contest being between Crown and Parliament. One of the fundamental developments in English constitutional theory of the eighteenth century was the triumph of the Whig position that identified the supreme political authority as the parliamentary process. The sovereignty of the country resided in the interaction of the King with Parliament, as Blackstone explained at mid-century in what was considered to be a standard account of the constitution. Using the balanced constitution as the conceptual underpinning of the system, Blackstone advocated parliamentary supremacy as the most "beneficial[] as is possible for society. For in no other shape could we be so certain of finding the three great qualities of government so well and so happily united." Legislation, according to Blackstone, was the product of the three classes interacting in Parliament:

> [T]he legislature of the kingdom is entrusted to three distinct powers, entirely independent of each other; first, the king; secondly, the lords spiritual and temporal, which is an aristocratical assembly of persons selected for their piety, their birth, their wisdom, their valour, or their property; and thirdly, the house of commons, freely chosen by the people from among themselves, which makes it

a kind of democracy; as this aggregate body, actuated by different springs, and attentive to different interests, composes the British parliament, and has the supreme disposal of every thing; there can no inconvenience be attempted by either of the three branches, but will be withstood by one of the other two; each branch being armed with a negative power, sufficient to repel any innovation which it shall think inexpedient or dangerous.[57]

Placing sovereignty with "the King in Parliament" used the social orders as working units of the political structure. There was no sense, however, that the three classes should participate equally in the various parts of government, or that the three orders ought to be represented equally in what American postcolonial constitutions would describe as the separate functions of government (legislative, executive, and judicial). Nevertheless, the concept of assigning the functions of government to separate political actors was an important component of the British constitutional system. Whereas Parliament melded the three estates in the legislative function, the monarch served the independent role of executing the laws, thereby assuring that the task would be performed with "strength and dispatch," as Blackstone wrote. Participation by the monarch in legislation through the power of veto was essential, he emphasized, because otherwise the Lords and Commons "might be tempted to encroach upon the royal prerogative, or perhaps to abolish the kingly office, and thereby weaken (if not totally destroy) the executive power."[58]

Most of those in opposition to the government, whether early in the eighteenth century or later, under the reign of George III, did not disagree with the premises as stated by Blackstone. Rather, "[d]iscussions about the nature of the constitution took place within this framework, which was itself rarely questioned."[59] Opponents of the ruling party maintained that the proper balance was disturbed by a failure in practice to separate power adequately. The principal manifestation of this problem, in their view, was the excessive influence of the executive over the Parliament through such devices as patronage, the granting of financial rewards to legislators, and control of elections. Supporters of royal influence over Parliament responded by downplaying the extent of influence, and by insisting that cooperation between the executive and the legislature was essential to efficient government, and even to the monarch's independent existence.[60]

Judicial Independence Under the Theory of Balanced Government

The task now is to relate the development of judicial independence to the theories of the balanced constitution and separated powers. By doing so, one will be able to explain how the system could accommodate the advisory relationship of the courts to the executive and the House of Lords. Before reaching this ultimate issue, a more complete understanding is needed about the development of British constitutional thought regarding separation of powers during the seventeenth and eighteenth centuries. This section takes up that process with a special emphasis on the judicial function.

Arriving at a modern conception of separation of powers required a delineation of the powers of government into distinct functional compartments. During the seventeenth century in England this process was under way as part of the political history of the Civil War and the governance of the country during the Commonwealth. But the elaboration of the now familiar threefold classification of abstract functions would not be complete until the eighteenth century. Even then it would be left to Americans to employ it as the primary basis for constructing constitutions that structured governments around a system of checks and balances. In England, the idea of separated functions was grafted onto the older and analytically dissimilar theory of balanced government.[61]

Until the later part of the eighteenth century, the judicial role almost invariably was described as a component of the execution of the laws. Ordinary criminal cases of this period illustrate the accuracy of this description. Judges usually were the dominant figures in courtrooms. Attorneys for either the government or defense did not appear regularly until the 1720s and 1730s, and throughout the century most criminal cases were tried without lawyers. Judges conducted the proceedings, and although the complaining party acted as prosecutor, the judge would ask most of the questions and comment on the evidence; some judges "recommended" an appropriate verdict or otherwise coerced the jury. Under the Stuarts there was a close relationship between the monarch and the courts, which were understood as little more than "administrative adjuncts to government," with slight independence from the Crown. This was especially true in a number of notorious treason cases that made the Stuart judges the subjects of widespread condemnation.[62]

Although the courts were associated with royal control, particularly before the Act of Settlement, the highest power of adjudication resided in the House of Lords. The Lords were "the supreme court of judicature in the kingdom," both for final appeals from lower courts and as the original court for trials of peers and impeachments. Charles I again gave a succinct reason: "the Lords being trusted with a Judicatory Power, are an excellent Skreen and Bank between the Prince and People."[63]

The judicial function of the Lords derived historically from that body's role as council to the King, much as the courts' association with the monarch was rooted in the judiciary's origins as the Crown's courts. The idea of a "judicial" function in an otherwise "legislative" body, together with judicial powers in the monarch, was congenial with the medieval view of law: "Law was seen as the embodiment of the law of God in the custom of the community, and the actions of the King in his Council making formal statements of the law were seen as clarifactory acts." All government acts, whether originated by the King, the Parliament, or the courts, were thus "judicial" in that they were "aspects of the application and interpretation of the law." Perhaps more important, in an era when ultimate control of the country rested with the King, there was no conceptual barrier to the Crown's engaging in all three of the "functions" of government that are identified by modern theories of separation of power.[64]

Political writers of the mid-seventeenth century with varied ideological outlooks commonly described government as composed of two powers, legislative and executive, with the latter including the judicial function. In defending the Cromwellian Instrument of Government of 1653, for example, Marchamount Needham argued that "placing the Legislative and executive powers in the same persons, is a marvellous In-let of corruption and tyranny." Needham separated the legislative work of Parliament from what he termed "execution and administration of law and justice"; he described execution as "the peculiar Tasks of inferior Courts." At the same time, the demand for separation between the legislative function and adjudication under the laws was also a component of Leveller thought in the 1640s, as illustrated by John Lilburne's assertion that there were "multitudes of complaints of oppression" concerning the House of Commons's "determining particular matters, which properly appertains to the cognizance of the ordinary Court of Justice." Likewise, as a political radical John Milton wrote in his *Eikonoklastes* of 1649 that "[i]n all wise nations the legislative power, and the judicial execution of that power, have been most commonly distinct, and in several hands; but yet the former supreme, the latter subordinate." The middle years of the seventeenth century provided fertile ground for such political theories, as Parliament frequently wielded impeachments and bills of attainder to discipline or execute political offenders.[65]

A few of the mid-seventeenth-century commentators did articulate a more complex version of separated powers, even to the point of employing something like the now familiar tripartite classification of government functions. In *The Royalists Defense* of 1648, apparently written by the Royalist Charles Dallison, the author not only distinguished legislation as a separate category but also further subdivided execution into governing and adjudication. "The Judges of the Realme *declare* by what law the King governs, and so both *King* and *people* [are] *regulated* by a known law." At about the same time, John Sadler contended in his treatise *Rights of the Kingdom* that the English constitution had once properly observed a threefold division of legislative, executive, and judicial powers, but that these differentiations had deteriorated as the Lords became tied to the King through the royal power of granting titles. Sadler held that the judicial power properly belonged in the House of Lords, as did Henry Ireton in 1647 when he declared that "the judicial power was in the Lords principally, and . . . the legislative power principally in the Commons."[66]

Even these occasional efforts to advance beyond the twofold division of legislation and execution usually demonstrated a continuing tie to the theory of balanced government, as is indicated by the placement of the judicial function with the Lords. James Harrington's *Commonwealth of Oceana*, published in 1656 and much admired by a later generation of American revolutionaries, displayed this tendency in its depiction of an aristocratic Senate to propose laws and a body of the people's representatives to decide whether to pass them, with "a third to be executive of the Lawes made, and this is the Magistracy." As to the latter, Harrington included the "course of courts or judicatories."[67]

In spite of the tendency to overlay the concept of separated powers onto the older idea of the balanced constitution, the idea of developing distinctive functions of government had become rooted. Further, such proponents of an independent judiciary as Sadler, Lilburne, and Milton had emphasized the need to define a separate judicial power and place it in the hands of actors who were independent of the other branches. The call for greater judicial freedom—through protection for the judges from removal at the King's pleasure—was an outgrowth of experience with rule by the Stuarts, as throughout "the seventeenth century the commons charged the judges with subservience to royal influence."[68]

Although the concept of assigning discrete governmental functions to separate the political actors that emerged from the Civil War and Commonwealth period was established as a permanent feature of British political thought, the Restoration represented "a return to the theory of mixed government as the basic constitutional pattern of England." Still, the version of the balanced constitution that became dominant in the eighteenth century was modified by the principles of separation of powers that had surfaced in the mid-seventeenth century. Between the Restoration and the next century, separation of powers retained a place in political thought. John Locke incorporated it into his political theory, as did other political writers who formed the "country" opposition during the late seventeenth and early eighteenth centuries.[69]

Locke's *Second Treatise* featured the theme that the legislative and executive powers should be placed in separate hands. Like prior writers who urged such a split in governing authority, Locke's thesis reflected England's recent history, which he saw as characterized by arbitrary rule. For Locke, the danger of capricious action existed in both the executive and legislative branches because the tendency toward such abuse was rooted in human nature: "[I]t may be too great a temptation to humane frailty apt to grasp at Power, for the same Persons who have the Power of making Laws, to have also in their hands the power to execute them, whereby they may exempt themselves from Obedience to the Laws they make."[70] Locke's use of the term "executive" was broad enough to encompass almost any function associated with administering the law, including adjudication. While Locke stressed the importance of placing the execution of the laws in the control of "indifferent and upright Judges," he did not insist on the independence of judges from other executive officials.[71]

The core of Locke's ideas about separation of powers related to maintaining a distinction between legislation and execution, the purpose of which was to ensure that government would be conducted "by establish'd standing Laws, promulgated and known to the People, and not by Extemporary Decrees." By later eighteenth-century American standards, Locke's theory of separated powers seems incomplete because it emphasized the primacy of the legislature without recognizing the importance of an independent judiciary. However, Locke's ideas were not formally entwined around doctrines associated with the balanced constitution, and for that matter his outlook was consistent with a number of different types of government.[72] For example, Locke's views could support government under a monarchical executive who possessed a measure of prerogative powers and who had a share in legislation through the royal power to withhold consent to laws. Further, a government in Locke's scheme could be regarded as properly constituted even if it included such an institution as the House of Lords. At the same time, neither of these hereditary establishments was essential in Locke's view to the construction of a well-formed state.[73]

The country opponents likewise insisted on a twofold separation of governmental powers, as John Trenchard did in his influential pamphlet of 1698 on standing armies: "[A]ll wise Governments endeavour as much as possible to keep the Legislative and executive Parts asunder, that they may be a check upon one another." Trenchard and others in his circle went beyond merely separating the executive and legislative powers as Locke had done. Instead, they blended that theory with the concept of the balanced constitution by assigning distinct powers to the King and the two houses of Parliament. Trenchard wrote, for example, that "[o]ur Government trusts the King with no part of the Legislative but a Negative Voice, which is absolutely necessary to preserve the Executive. One part of the Duty of the House of Commons is to punish Offenders, and redress the Grievances occasion'd by the Executive Part of the Government." Separation of powers was achieved by assigning a portion of sovereign powers to each of the separate estates. All three—King, Lords, and Commons—participated in legislation. Execution of the laws was mainly the responsibility of the executive, whereas the House of Lords ultimately controlled the judicial power through its exercise of appellate jurisdiction.[74]

As a political movement, these opposition figures had no decisive effect on British affairs in the eighteenth century, although they produced a stream of literature during this period that for the remainder of the century influenced important sections of the movements opposed to the royal court. In terms of historical importance, their major impact was on American colonists, who incorporated the ideas of the British opposition into the theoretical framework of their demand for independence. Nonetheless, the blending of separation of powers theories with the doctrine of balanced government became the version of British constitutionalism accepted by both opponents and supporters of government in the eighteenth century. Consequently, this common understanding of the British constitution is the best conceptual starting place to explain judicial independence and the advisory relationship of judges to Parliament and Crown in this period.[75]

The easiest way to account for the advisory role of judges would be to conclude that judicial independence did not exist either in theory or in practice. When the judgment of courts may be reversed by a legislative body (particularly one whose members have scant law training) and when the judges can be summoned to give extrajudicial advice to both the executive and one house of the legislature, a lack of independence may seem obvious. Nevertheless, to appreciate how the system was justified by its contemporaries, we need to comprehend how they could have seen this situation as consistent with judicial independence. After all, Blackstone wrote: "In this distinct and separate existence of the judicial power, in a peculiar body of men, nominated indeed, but not removeable at pleasure, by the crown, consists one main preservative of the public liberty; which cannot subsist long in any state, unless the administration of common justice be in some degree separated from the legislative and also from the executive power."[76]

Blackstone's expression here must be laid against the background of more than a century of extraordinary political warfare. On the question of keeping the legislature apart from the judiciary, his position was mainly a restatement of Locke's thesis that such a separation was a prerequisite to the rule of law.

Blackstone continued in the next line: "Were [the judicial power] joined with the legislative, the life, liberty, and property, of the subject would be in the hands of arbitrary judges, whose decisions would then be regulated only by their own opinions, and not by any fundamental principles of law; which, though legislatures may depart from, yet judges are bound to observe."[77]

Notwithstanding that this statement is presented as a general principle, it was informed by the specific experiences of an earlier generation that had witnessed Parliament's combination of legislative and judicial functions. In comparison, the relationship between the judicial courts and the Lords presented a modest threat to liberty, particularly in view of the checking function played by the Commons and King. Furthermore, the judges themselves had decisive influence over the Lords' adjudications through their advisory roles in that body. Another element that apparently assuaged any concern Blackstone might have had was the deference he paid to the peerage. Describing the role of the Lords as "the last resort in matters both of law and equity," he praised it as "a court composed of prelates selected for their piety, and of nobles advanced to that honour for their personal merit, or deriving both honour and merit from an illustrious train of ancestors; who are formed by their education, interested by their property, and bound upon their conscience and honour, to be skilled in the laws of their country."[78]

Turning to the danger of a joinder of judicial and executive power in one body, Blackstone argued that "this union might soon be an over-ballance for the legislative." As an example of the potential for abuse from such a combination, Blackstone referred to the Court of Star Chamber, in which judges and Privy Council members adjudicated cases to enforce royal proclamations. The removal of "all judicial power out of the hands of the King's privy council" was justified because it "might soon be inclined to pronounce that for law, which was most agreeable to the prince or his officers." With this example in mind, Blackstone then concluded that "[n]othing therefore is more to be avoided, in a free constitution, than uniting the provinces of a judge and a minister of state." Apparently Blackstone saw no contradiction between this conclusion and his depiction elsewhere in the Commentaries of the judges' responsibility to serve as the King's "council for matters of law." This was a role with an ancient pedigree that did not carry the inherent tendencies for abuse that could be associated with such courts as the Star Chamber. Blackstone knew as well that for the ordinary run of cases, the judicial power was applied by judges who enjoyed lifetime tenure.[79]

After accepting these rationalizations for the advisory role of judges, we are nonetheless left with the fact that the mainstream political theory of this period did not regard a strict separation of either government branches or officers as essential to liberty. The minor inroads into judicial independence caused by the advisory role were inconsequential in comparison to the much more pervasive connections between the King's ministers and Parliament. Keep in mind that eighteenth-century theories did not regard advisory practices of judges as threatening to constitutional safeguards of the judiciary. The British constitution hardly consisted of a document with overarching principles explicable according to a rational plan. Instead, it was the aggregate of the community's customs, laws, and institutions that had developed over an extended period. Its success could be measured by the balance and stability it provided. Far from endangering liberty, the association of judges with other branches could have been viewed as helpful to maintaining that balance. To Blackstone and others, the key danger facing judges—subservience to the Crown—was a historical fact that had been remedied by the Act of Settlement.[80]

The constitutionality of providing judicial advice to both the Crown and the Lords would have seemed particularly unremarkable considering the explicit incorporation of customary governmental structures into the constitution. Given the lineage of the practice, and the prerogative of the King and the Lords to command such advice, it is difficult to explain why the practice of providing counsel to the executive ended after 1760. Further complicating this historical puzzle is the fact that the Lords continued to call upon the judges far into the nineteenth century. If this abandonment was not compelled by constitutional considerations, what was the explanation?

EXPLAINING THE DECLINE OF ADVISORY OPINIONS TO THE BRITISH EXECUTIVE

Sackville's Case Revisited

Further research may turn up additional advisory opinions after Sackville's Case in 1760, but the opinion by Chief Justice Lord Mansfield conveyed a decided reluctance on the part of the judges to engage in the practice. As was often true of British advisory opinions, the underlying facts of the case indicate that it was tangled in a web of personal and political disputes. Even though Lord George Sackville was not one of the most influential figures of his century, neither was he without considerable significance and notoriety.

Lord George commanded the British continental forces in 1759 during the Seven Years War. His superior in this action was the Prussian commander-in-chief of the allied forces, Duke Ferdinand, Frederick the Great's brother-in-law. The events leading to Sackville's Case transpired at the battle of Minden, where Sackville allegedly ignored Ferdinand's orders and de-layed a cavalry charge, allowing the French forces to escape a decisive defeat. Outraged at Sackville's conduct, Ferdinand complained directly to his cousin, George II, who summarily dismissed the general from military service. Regardless of whether Ferdinand's wrath was merited, the King had compelling reasons to appease him. Cooperation by the Prussians in the conduct of the war was crucial to the overall effort, and George II had a particular abiding concern for the military threat to his Hanoverian posses-sions. An additional complication was the clamor of public opinion in Lon-don, which was fueled by a battle of pamphlets that on the whole were distinctly unfavorable to Sackville. Lord George soon found himself the subject of public ridicule and deserted by his friends in the royal court, with the ministry desiring that the whole issue be forgotten.[81]

Sackville would not let the matter rest, and he took the extraordinary step of demanding a court martial in order to vindicate himself. This was a risky move for Lord George inasmuch as a conviction for disobeying orders could result in his execution, which was a realistic possibility considering the recent fate of Admiral Byng, who had been condemned for poorly handling a naval engagement. The administration saw nothing to gain from acceding to Sack-ville's request. The spectacle of a highly publicized trial could embarrass the Crown, arouse turmoil in the army, and potentially antagonize Ferdinand if Sackville were acquitted. But Sackville would not relent. Some influential figures thought that he deserved a hearing, and Sackville threatened to compel a parliamentary inquiry, which was a more unpredictable forum and one in which the opposition would have a platform to enter the fray.[82]

For a while, the administration stalled Sackville's request by pointing out that a court martial could not be held until the return of material witnesses from Germany. Then the two law officers in the administration—Attorney General Charles Pratt and Solicitor General Charles Yorke—expressed doubt as to whether Sackville could be tried by court martial in England for an offense abroad. Within a month, however, the law officers modified their opinion and allowed that the court martial could proceed if Sackville was charged with a breach of duty while under the King's jurisdiction. Shortly after the proceedings opened, the military judges discovered that Sackville held no military commission, which created a doubt as to whether the court martial had jurisdiction over Sackville as a civilian. The court martial judges then referred the matter to the King so that he might obtain the opinion of the twelve judges.[83]

George II was incensed by this development, as he had become intent on dealing harshly with Sackville. Nonetheless, Mansfield opposed convening the common law judges, insisting that to do so would interfere with the circuit Assize sessions then commencing. Mansfield wrote to the head of the government, Lord Newcastle, saying, "[B]e assured you will have no answer," and adding, "I consider it as the court martial refusing to try him." The cabinet met that night to ponder the options, and apparently Newcastle prevailed on Mansfield (who also was a member of the cabinet) to change his mind, by reminding him that the King surely would view the Chief Justice's actions as obstructionist. Mansfield then agreed to assemble the judges, which occurred the next day, and the opinion was delivered two days later. Mansfield, however, requested that his name not appear in the cabinet minute directing the referral.[84]

Four days after the judges ruled, the court martial commenced. The trial was the event of the season ("One hears of nothing else," chortled Horace Walpole). Sackville ended up being convicted, but his life was spared by a single vote—he was instead given the moderate sentence of being declared unfit for military service. Disgusted at the leniency of the military judges, King George made the most of the sentence by banishing Sackville from his court and ordering the tribunal's judgment read in all the army's regiments.[85]

This would be the end of the tale, except for a nagging detail about Mansfield's role in the proceedings. As it happens, Mansfield and Sackville were well acquainted with each other. Only about two years before these events Mansfield had written Sackville a letter that indicates a cordial relationship between the two. Some contemporaries believed that Sackville had consulted with Mansfield about the advisability of insisting on a court martial, and the Chief Justice allegedly counseled him that the proceedings would conclude favorably. Or at least that is what Sackville claimed, and for a period after the trial his relations with Mansfield were soured. They subsequently resumed their connection, perhaps on account of Sackville's remarkable political resurrection under the favor of George III. To Americans, Sackville's later career (under the new name of Lord George Germain) would be more important, for during the Revolution he served as Secretary of State for the American Colonies (1779-82) and President of the Board of Trade (1775-80).[86]

Mansfield's initial reluctance to give an opinion may have been motivated by a desire to abort the court martial, as the note to Newcastle suggests. Two factors could have influenced his change of heart on the matter. The first was his interest in averting a confrontation with George II, which Mansfield avoided while giving Sackville the forum that he wished. Furthermore, by expressly reserving the right of the judges to reverse themselves on this jurisdictional point, a safety net was left in place should the death penalty be imposed by the court martial.

Mansfield's letter expressed the judges' aversion to advisory opinions, although he implied that they could be given in exceptional circumstances. Mansfield would continue to hold the most important judicial position in the common law courts until 1788, while simultaneously wielding considerable political power both within the administration and in the House of Lords. Consequently, his reluctance to employ this device could not be overlooked by the Crown. An exploration of Mansfield's role leads us into the larger issue of cabinet politics in late eighteenth-century England. Putting these pieces of the puzzle together produces a probable explanation for the decline of advisory opinions to the British executive.

Cabinet Politics and the Role of Mansfield

The eighteenth century was a time of significant change in the processes of government in England. While the theory of the balanced constitution—the juxtaposition of the executive against the two houses of Parliament—remained constant, within the executive an important shift transpired in the relation of the King to his ministers. John Mackintosh explains in his study of the British cabinet: "In the early eighteenth century the Cabinet would have been most reluctant to suggest a measure known to be obnoxious to the King and the latter would have felt free to ignore any such advice. By 1800 it was an open matter whether the monarch could reject advice or veto consideration of a question."[87]

Historians of this period have differed concerning the extent to which, particularly under George III, either the King or his ministers had the dominant power in the administration. Without digressing into the minutiae of this debate, it is fair to say that at least after 1760—the beginning of George III's reign—the cabinet was a potent political force. Ian Christie has written: "It is evident that there was constant dialogue over policy between the king and the cabinet (as well as between the King and individual ministers); but this was more a process of participation than of direction. On some occasions George III got his way, but there were other equally significant occasions when he failed to do so or swallowed an unpalatable recommendation. The 'mixed monarchy' of the eighteenth century presupposed an active King; but it seems an exaggeration to regard the nature and extent of George III's activity in the 1760s or 1770s as justifying the description 'personal rule.'"[88]

The route by which this transformation occurred was not marked by major milestones. Rather, it was a path of gradual development that was influenced at numerous junctures by highly contingent factors, including the personalities and political strengths of various partisan players. Certain broad circumstances can be identified. One is the emergence of the small "efficient" or "inner" cabinet, which by the 1760s had eclipsed the larger cabinet council to form a ministry that was able to gain "momentum and to consolidate its position." A second circumstance, related to the first, is the transition that occurred toward the end of the 1760s from a period dominated by "personal parties (among which personal competition for power was the driving force) to one of political parties (in which the pursuit or reversal of policies was the main ground of contention). Wilkes, America, and the affairs of the East India Company gave the politicians vital issues on which to disagree." A cohesive opposition developed around a series of questions related to the central theme of the excessive power of the executive ministry. Although the executive usually was capable of securing parliamentary majorities to the end of the century and somewhat beyond, its influence was weakening, and the formation of opposition parties created noticeable political stress. To be sure, the executive exercised a substantial amount of parliamentary control through overt patronage, but its overall success depended on members of the Commons agreeing with its positions.[89]

The details accompanying many of these developments were known only to the relatively few who were active in national politics, and even for them a great deal was shrouded in confidence. Under George II, for example, the inner cabinet was a secret group; it became an openly recognized body only in the early years of George III's reign. In this environment, rather wild accusations were made by the opposition concerning the course of government. Christie explains:

> Over the whole period from the late 1760s till 1801 political conflict took on a slightly menacing tone. . . . The fundamental underlying question in debate related to constitutional propriety. By 1769, if not before, the Rockinghamite Opposition had begun to project itself as the sole champion and guardian of the constitution and of English liberties, against subversion by a supposed secret junto working behind the scenes in court and Parliament. This group was assumed to be using government patronage to overcome parliamentary resistance to its numerous nefarious activities, manipulating and coercing the ostensible ministers, and thus gradually asserting autocratic power without responsibility.[90]

Lord Rockingham characterized the clandestine influence as "unconstitutional controul and advice," whereas the Earl of Effingham's charge came with more flair, asserting that the ministers had become "subservien[t]" to an "invisible power [that] was the grand root of all the evils which have poured in upon us since the commencement of the present reign."[91]

The opposition identified several key players as preeminent in leading the conspiracy: "initially George III's early favourite, the Earl of Bute; later, the eminent lawyer Lord Mansfield, chief justice of Court of the King's Bench, who, like Bute, could be made the target of English prejudice against the Scots." William Pitt the elder, Earl of Chatham, for example, wrote in 1770 that he considered Mansfield to be effectively the Prime Minister. Edmund Burke placed Mansfield among a few names in what he regarded as the secret ministry. And the infamous writer Junius skewered Mansfield on this very theme in several of his barbed letters. In one missive published in 1770 and devoted entirely to the Chief Justice, Junius chided: "You would fain be thought to take no share in government, while, in reality, you are the main spring of the machine. . . . Instead of acting that open, generous part, which becomes your rank and station, you meanly skulk into the closet and give your Sovereign such advice, as you have not spirit to avow or defend. You secretly engross the power, while you decline the title of minister."[92]

Junius rebuked Mansfield for "continu[ing] to support an administration which you know is universally odious, and which, on some occasions, you yourself speak of with contempt." For Junius this behavior by Mansfield was not surprising; he had recently charged the Chief Justice in another letter: "I see through your whole life, one uniform plan to enlarge the power of the crown, at the expence of the liberty of the subject."[93]

There was a core of reality in both Junius's diatribe and the suspicions of the opposition, but the truth about Mansfield's role in the government was much more complicated. Modern commentators usually recall Mansfield as one of the greatest commercial law figures in English legal history. During his own day, Mansfield enjoyed a general reputation as a highly learned and forceful jurist, and as a powerful orator in the House of Lords. Like many judges of this era, he had an active life in the public arena outside the courtroom. Certainly in Mansfield's lifetime, these nonjudicial activities often were more prominently noted by observers than were his rulings on King's Bench. The Chief Justice's abiding support of the Crown's interests could not be missed.[94]

Mansfield was no stranger to executive service. He had been Solicitor General and Attorney General for George II while establishing himself as a formidable figure in the House of Commons. As Attorney General, he took a prominent role in promoting the cause of the Pelham administration. The commencement of his judicial career in 1756 (he served continuously as Chief Justice until 1788) came accompanied by a peerage and place in the House of Lords, where his legislative career again attained prominence and controversy. For a brief period at the end of George II's reign until shortly after the organization of the Grenville administration in 1763 under George III, Mansfield was an official member of the inner cabinet. He played an active part in the negotiations leading to the formation of the Pitt-Newcastle government in 1757 and had a significant advisory role to Newcastle (the Duke of Newcastle had been Mansfield's chief political sponsor). While in the cabinet he also dispensed the Scottish patronage for the government.[95]

But Mansfield's relations with the new monarch were less than harmonious. George III complained of Mansfield's absences from meetings, his "indecent language . . . , his disinclination to Government, and his own opinion of his superiority of abilitys over the rest of the world." Obviously the young King was uncomfortable in dealing with the considerably older and highly accomplished Mansfield. After one particular meeting, George grumbled that the Chief Justice displayed "so much self sufficiency concerning his own judgement, that I was glad when I got rid of him; he is but half a man[:] timidity and refinement make him unfit for the present turbulent scene. . . . I am certain [he] feels that, and therefore cries out against everything but moderation." These remarks were addressed to George's favorite, Lord Bute, whom Mansfield initially cooperated with and advised. The Mansfield-Bute relationship deteriorated early on, with Bute reportedly complaining about "the Lord Chief Justice, whom I myself brought into office, voting for me, yet speaking against me." Mansfield left the administration within the same year, a few months after the resignation of Newcastle and the collapse of the Newcastle-Bute government. Presumably Mansfield's known association with Newcastle did not improve his stature with the King; Newcastle himself complained bitterly of being shunned by George, and Bute apparently did not trust Mansfield. Nor would Mansfield's fortunes have improved when Newcastle defected to the opposition after his resignation.[96]

Although Mansfield no longer simultaneously held offices in three different branches of government, his connection with executive decision making remained, and actually increased substantially after a time. Mansfield had some dealings with the short-lived governments under the Marquess of Rockingham (1765-66) (who was Mansfield's nephew) and the Duke of Grafton (1768-70), but it was under Lord North's administration (1770-82) that Mansfield's influence reached its zenith: "Lord Mansfield, who was widely seen as the éminence grise of the Cabinet, and the true successor of Bute, played a large if unofficial part in ministerial deliberations." Thomas Hutchinson, the ill-fated Lieutenant Governor of Massachusetts, wrote in 1774 that Mansfield was one of "those Ministers who most concern themselves in American affairs." For legal advice, the North cabinet could require formal counsel from the two principal law officers, which it did on occasion. Nevertheless, Mansfield functioned as a key legal adviser to North. George III turned to him frequently for confidential advice.[97]

Mansfield's position of dominance in the House of Lords meant that he was well positioned to implement the administration's position, especially given that legislative activity increased dramatically during the second half of the eighteenth century. The Chief Justice had gained considerable experience as a legislative drafter while serving as Solicitor General and Attorney General, and he continued to propose and write legislation as a member of the House of Lords. Mansfield offered vital support for the ministry's policies at various points, most notably during the critical period of the American Revolution, from which he emerged as an unrelenting hardliner in favor of coercion. Walpole dubbed him "the chief author of the American war." A note from the King to Lord North in 1772 concerning the bill to create the Royal Marriages Act is indicative of his importance in formulating parliamentary strategy: "Your having seen Ld Mansfield will I hope enable You to give good advice to the Lords this Evening for the Management of tomorrows Debate."[98]

As Chief Justice of King's Bench, Mansfield became involved in a number of prosecutions of interest to the Crown. He presided over a series of controversial seditious libel cases, most notably the trials in 1764 of John Wilkes (and the printers of Wilkes's manuscripts) and the 1770 proceedings against publishers of the Junius letters. During these cases Mansfield received unflattering notices in the press for insisting that the issues of whether intent and sedition had been proven were questions of law for the court—not the jury—to decide. Mansfield, however, regarded his service in libel cases as one means to arrest what he regarded as the "calamitous decline" of the nation.[99]

Other cases illustrating Mansfield's association with the government include the famous 1771 controversy regarding the prosecution of the London printers for illegally publishing parliamentary debates. In that instance, the King instructed Lord North: "I am therefore clearly of the opinion that the Lord Mayor and Alderman Oliver ought to be committed to the Tower, and then a Secret Committee may be appointed to examine farther into the affair. . . . I wish you would send Jenkinson to Lord Mansfield to bring You his opinion as to the best mode of effecting this." Mansfield was also consulted regarding who should be appointed to judicial positions. He took a leading part in persuading the hapless Charles Yorke to accept the chancellorship in 1770.[100]

To state the obvious, Mansfield had managed to overcome entirely George III's early disapprobation. In 1776, the Chief Justice petitioned the King for an earldom, which was granted. Lord North remarked to George the day after Mansfield's request was received, "that Ld Mansfield wou'd think the favour greatly enhanc'd if he may be allow'd to Kiss His Majestys Hand tomorrow at the Levee." The King responded enthusiastically: "The request of Lord Mansfield after a zealous Support of near Sixteen Years without having ever asked any favour from the Crown seemed to entitle him very reasonably to ask the mark of favour he did yesterday. . . . You may send notice for him to attend tomorrow at St James's."[101]

Even considering Mansfield's numerous dealings with George III's government, the opposition exaggerated the extent of his influence, much as they overstated their theory of a secret cabal controlling the executive. Yet for purposes of this book, the actual extent of Mansfield's reach into royal concerns is not the decisive point: "If a myth is widely believed, it becomes a political reality. This is shown effectively in the [opposition's] belief that there existed a group of personal 'king's friends' (aside from his constitutional advisers) who formed a 'double cabinet.'" It is apparent from Mansfield's multifaceted political life that he was interested in playing a prominent part in the leading public affairs of his day. At the same time, he found himself accused openly of servility to the ministry. Junius addressed this theme in his first letter of 1769 by associating Mansfield with the notorious judges under the Stuarts: "A judge under the influence of government, may be honest enough in the decision of private causes, yet a traitor to the public. When a victim is marked out by the ministry, this judge will offer himself to perform the sacrifice. He will not scruple to prostitute his dignity, and betray the sanctity of his office, whenever an arbitrary point is to be carried for government, or the resentments of a court are to be gratified."[102]

A similar commentary, published under the signature "Tribunus," appeared in a 1772 London newspaper; it denounced Mansfield for having "sedulously sought, and carefully improved, every opportunity of extending prerogative, and making the King absolute." These condemnatory writings were published during a time of rising societal tensions, whose manifestations included street demonstrations and rioting that caused considerable apprehension among the elite. All sides in public life, from the administration to the opposition, concentrated on placing responsibility for these incendiary events with others. There was a common understanding of the stakes, for the very presence of widespread disruptions indicated that the balance of the constitution was degenerating: "They acknowledged that growing popular discontent and political instability were the first symptoms of a political pathology which, unless remedial measures were taken, would inexorably lead to the demise of the free constitution, and with it the society whose values, properties and liberties it protected." At a more personal level, officials associated with the government could on occasion be confronted with serious threats to their persons and properties by popular uprisings.[103]

Mansfield was at the center of some of the events that produced this unrest, and he undoubtedly understood what could happen even to himself. In 1768, crowds surrounded the Court of King's Bench as Mansfield presided over the sessions relating to John Wilkes, who was without peer in these years for inspiring popular support and mob action. Wilkes had been convicted in absentia by Mansfield four years earlier on charges of seditious libel and blasphemy. Wilkes fled to France rather than face trial, which resulted in his being outlawed for failing to appear at sentencing.[104] When Wilkes reappeared in London and petitioned for pardon, he was arrested on account of his outlawry. The hearing on this charge was preceded by a season of rioting, the last of which occurred after the fatal shootings of some of Wilkes's supporters (and several innocent bystanders) by government forces the month before the hearing. When Mansfield held court, throngs gathered outside the courthouse and throughout London, and were restrained by royal troops. It was an especially touchy case for Mansfield because he had conducted the original proceedings that convicted Wilkes. Long-standing complaints—emphasized by Wilkes in his own speech at the outlawry proceedings—held that Mansfield had severely prejudiced the first case by altering the wording of the charges on the eve of trial.[105]

Much to popular surprise, Mansfield freed Wilkes by quashing the original arrest warrant and the resulting outlawry on the slimmest of technical grounds. Mansfield found himself in the unusual position of a crowd favorite, but his popularity was short-lived, for a few days later Mansfield sentenced Wilkes to a fine and imprisonment on his prior convictions. The sentence of twenty-two months was lighter than expected, the fines were paid by Wilkes's supporters, and by all accounts Wilkes's incarceration was not only easy but also increased his renown. Wilkes appealed to the House of Lords, which affirmed the conviction after formally consulting the judges on several legal points.[106]

Mansfield's actions in the case had somewhat belied predictions, but he had warned privately that prosecution was a political mistake: "[Wilkes's] consequence will die away if you will leave him alone; but, by public notice of him, you will increase his consequence; the very thing he covets, and has in full view." As an early (and sympathetic) biographer of Mansfield noted, "[t]he singular events of the year 1768 were the causes of the public prints being, for the first time, deluged with torrents of abuse on the lord chief justice." Aware of this treatment, Mansfield responded from the bench at the first Wilkes proceeding in 1768: "I will do my duty, unawed. What am I to fear? That *mendax infamia* from the *press,* which daily coins *false facts* and *false motives?* The lies of *calumny* carry no terror to *me.*" He continued by denying party motivations: "If, during this king's reign, I have ever supported his government, and assisted his measures, I have done it without any other reward, than the consciousness of doing what I thought *right.*" Junius sneered: "The pretended neutrality of belonging to no party, will not save your reputation."[107]

The administration then orchestrated Wilkes's expulsion from the House of Commons, and subsequently the House refused to seat him despite his being elected four times (the House instead seated Wilkes's most recent opponent, who had lost decisively at the polls). Mansfield reentered the Wilkes controversy at this point, for the opposition in the House of Lords sought to overturn the action of the Commons. Speaking against the measure in the Lords, Mansfield asserted that each House must be the judge of its own elections—and added the dictum that inasmuch as Wilkes had been declared ineligible to run for Parliament, his opponent was in reality unopposed. Mansfield went on to warn about the consequences of thwarting the Commons: "The people are violent enough already, and to have the superior branch of legislation join them, would be giving such a public encouragement to their proceedings, that I almost tremble, while I even suppose such a scene of anarchy and confusion."[108]

Mansfield also presided over the trial of several of the printers of the Junius letters, proceedings in which he applied his highly unpopular (albeit legally defensible) view that the jury was limited to determining the fact of publication, which left the judges to determine the legality of the content. When juries acquitted two of the printers, "[a] crowd gathered outside Mansfield's house on Bloomsbury Square and gloated over the humiliation of the government." The Chathamite opposition in the House of Lords attempted to force a parliamentary investigation of Mansfield's rulings with the aim of producing declaratory legislation contradicting his decisions. At one point during these proceedings, Lord Camden demanded that Mansfield and the other judges answer interrogatories propounded by the House on the legal issues involved. Mansfield declined to do so, while allowing that he "had studied the point more than any other in his life, and had consulted all the judges on it, except indeed his Lordship [Camden]."[109] By invoking the opinions of the judges, Mansfield effectively caused Camden to back down from what Burke referred to as a "juridical Duel." In the end, the opposition's effort was easily defeated, but not before one of their bills to expand the power of juries was leaked to the press, where it was published with the note that the measure would "effectually skreen" Mansfield.[110]

Junius joined the debate about the jury's powers in libel cases, aiming his critical fire specifically at Mansfield: "When you invade the province of the jury, in matter of libel, you, in effect, attack the liberty of the press, and with a single stroke, wound two of your greatest enemies." Junius remarked sarcastically that he had for some time abstained from directly attacking Mansfield, and had done so not merely because the judge would preside over the resulting libel trial: "I confess I have been deterred by the difficulty of the task. Our language has no term of reproach, the mind has no idea of detestation, which has not already been happily applied to you, and exhausted.—Ample justice has been done by abler pens than mine to the separate merits of your life and character. Let it be my humble office to collect the scattered sweets, till their united virtue tortures the sense."[111]

Junius went on to call attention to Mansfield's Scottish origins and to insinuate that Mansfield was a Roman Catholic sympathizer and Jacobite. Here Junius was repeating allegations that had been the subject of serious discussions in the Privy Council and House of Lords during 1753, both of which concluded in Mansfield's favor. Throughout his career Mansfield would confront these claims, which initially stemmed from his family's Jacobite sympathies but later were fueled by various judicial rulings of Mansfield that supported religious toleration (and thus were favorable to dissenters). Unfortunately for the Chief Justice, these innuendos proved costly for him in the Gordon Riots of 1780, whose immediate cause was popular rage at a bill to lessen restrictions on Roman Catholics. Inflamed by anti-Catholic zealotry, the rioters went on a week-long rampage of physical assaults, including an attack on the carriage carrying Mansfield from which he barely escaped serious injury. The Gordon mobs burned scores of homes, one of the first of which was Mansfield's Bloomsbury Square mansion. Evidently the crowd was inspired by the Chief Justice's general reputation for supporting toleration of Catholics, inasmuch as he had not taken an active role in the passage of the relief measure.[112]

Mansfield and the Decline of Formal Advisory Opinions to the Executive

When we put these various strands of Mansfield's public life together, a picture emerges of a man wielding important power in all three branches of government, while at the same time desiring to remain outside overt scrutiny. Mansfield was highly sensitive to suggestions that his actions were a way of engendering court favoritism. In a similar vein he denied that he was in the least motivated by external opinion. During a Lords' debate in 1770, he defied Chatham "to point out a single action in my life where the popularity of the times ever had the smallest influence on my determinations." At times his voice seemed to urge pity for himself. He observed in a 1766 speech opposing repeal of the Stamp Act that "no one has had more cast upon him than myself." Given the charges that he was the real force behind the scene, Mansfield may very well have thought that the best course was to minimize scrutiny. Bernard Donoughue has made a similar observation with respect to Mansfield's role in the American Revolution: "As a member of the nominal cabinet (though outside the effective Cabinet since 1763) and as a lawyer of great eminence it was perfectly respectable that the Government should consult him. But the consultation was shrouded in considerable secrecy. This may have been at the wish of Mansfield, who had a reputation for political timidity. It may also have been expediency on the part of the Government, since Mansfield was known to be a strong supporter of the royal prerogative, and his role in the prosecution of Wilkes . . . made him unpopular with the public and a leading victim of the pen of Junius."[113]

Mansfield was regarded by some detractors as lacking courage in political confrontations, a point averred to by George III himself early in his reign and relentlessly pursued by Walpole in his writings. Contemporaries pointed to his refusals on three occasions to accept the chancellorship as key indicators of what Walpole referred to as Mansfield's pusillanimity. Taking that office would have placed him conspicuously in the administration. Although potentially more powerful, the chancellorship entailed precarious tenure. Whether politically timid or not, Mansfield had long been intent on secrecy in dealings with matters of state, as is indicated by the course of advice he gave to Newcastle in 1761 (while officially a member of the cabinet) on an important matter of army command. Newcastle pledged to Mansfield that "[i]n the first place you may be assured your name shall never be known or suspected." Only the year before, during the Sackville court martial, Mansfield had insisted that his consultation with the cabinet be left out of the official records of the meeting. On occasion, Mansfield resisted submitting a full opinion concerning a controversial question before the House of Lords by giving the excuse that the matter was pending in the Court of King's Bench.[114]

Edmund Burke remarked to Lord Rockingham that Mansfield—"Your Lordships great friend"—"interpose[d]" with the ministry "in the way to which he is best inclined, and in which he is most powerful; by a direct but private representation in the closet." Walpole needed few words to make his indictment: "Lord Mansfield, underhand, gave hot advice as long as he could secretly, and as not responsible." There is at least a measure of truth behind these obviously biased views, in that the Chief Justice often advised George III privately. Mansfield did seem more interested in asserting his influence than in holding a formal position of political leadership. Even after declining the chancellorship in 1770, for example, he was involved in the decisions of that office until 1778 owing to the inabilities of Lord Chancellor Bathurst.[115]

It is not difficult to find Mansfield's fingerprints on ministerial activities during most of the time he was Chief Justice, although his degree of involvement and influence varied with the administration in question. Still, Mansfield steadfastly insisted that apart from the period when he served on the inner cabinet, "I have had no concern or participation whatever in his Majesty's councils." This assertion rested on a fine distinction—namely, that Mansfield was not formally a member of the cabinet. For as Mansfield himself acknowledged to the Lords in 1775, he "never refused his advice when applied to" by an administration.[116]

With the departure of Newcastle from the government, and considering Mansfield's shaky start with George III, it is not surprising to find that for several years Mansfield's influence with the executive declined from what it had been while he served in the cabinet. The Rockingham, Grafton-Chatham, and Grafton administrations (1765-66, 1766-68, and 1768-70, respectively) were ministries with which Mansfield had essential disagreements, and in the case of Chatham's government the relationship was further complicated by a long and bitter personal animosity between the two.[117] An instance of this acrimony can be found from the Grafton-Chatham administration, when during a debate in the House of Lords Mansfield openly opposed Chatham's order for a corn embargo on the ground that the measure was an illegal exercise of prerogative powers. Even during periods when Mansfield was not in accord with the ministry, however, he occasionally played an active role behind the scenes. His period of greatest political influence began in 1770 with the government under North, whose political positions he generally supported.[118]

On account of Mansfield's public image, his apparent connection with a measure could be a political liability to the administration. For example, in 1771 a rumor floated that Mansfield had written the bill that was to become the Royal Marriages Act. The hint of Mansfield's involvement "produce[d] an even stronger prejudice against it in Commons," where the opposition marshaled an unusually strong resistance and lost only by a fairly narrow margin. About two months before the vote on the bill, Chatham had referred to his rival Mansfield's "political leprosy."[119]

In this environment, and considering the Chief Justice's own preferred arrangement, Mansfield and the ministries with which he worked may have perceived the greatest value in avoiding a conspicuous relationship. Formal advisory opinions could be seen as one form of a connection that did not fit with the realities of cabinet politics of this period. The taking of an advisory opinion almost inevitably would involve important matters of state. For Mansfield, there was little to gain in terms of political power, because he had several avenues to use in making his legal position known on a question. But there was always the potential for damage, personal or otherwise, by assuming a public position in cases with notoriety. Sackville's Case did not present, in the scheme of things, an issue of overriding legal significance, but it was the type of highly visible affair that Mansfield strove to avoid. Although this explanation accounts only for Mansfield's predilections, his preferences were decidedly the most important to reckon with among the judges, who apparently shared his views on extrajudicial advice. Mansfield enjoyed strong influence over the other judges, particularly those on King's Bench; with few exceptions the judges acted unanimously during Mansfield's tenure.[120]

Mansfield's ability to oppose the giving of advisory opinions was strengthened by the Chief Justice's tenure of judicial office and status as a peer—not to mention the highly lucrative income from his judgeship and his enormous private fortune. Ministries retained some influence over judges through discretionary grants of pensions (until 1799, when pensions were guaranteed by law), peerages, and titles to the judges or their relations. The Earl of Shelburne remarked in the course of a vicious exchange with Mansfield at the House of Lords in 1775 that "every noble lord in this House knows, a court has many allurements; besides even place or emolument. . . . [S]miles may do a great deal; that if he had nothing to ask for himself, he has had friends, relations and dependants amply provided for." Chatham complained in 1770, for example, that impartial justice had been impaired on account of the dependence of four judges on the ministry (Mansfield was Speaker of the House of Lords, and three other judges were Commissioners of the Great Seal, all of which were well-remunerated posts). Of course, Shelburne and Chatham were not exactly impartial observers, but the creation of Mansfield's earldom in 1776 gave credence to their point.[121]

Nevertheless, the application of raw pressure as in the Stuart days was long past, and the support of the judges could no longer be assured.[122] Notable examples of this decline in support were Chief Justice Pratt's decision declaring Wilkes's arrest a violation of parliamentary privilege and subsequent rulings disallowing general warrants used against Wilkes and his associates. Although Pratt's actions were well received in the streets, they were not appreciated by George III, who reported that Mansfield had said to him in confidence that "no man had ever behaved so shamefully as Lord Chief Justice Pratt had done." James I surely would not have tolerated such rulings. George III could not even dictate administration policies on his own terms, and he was obliged to accept cabinets against his personal views. Realistically, a judge could not be dismissed merely on account of a disagreeable decision. In any event, when the judges could be persuaded to give an opinion to the administration, the result would not necessarily be helpful.[123]

When the formal opinions of judges were needed for some reason, there remained an alternative for obtaining them (that is, aside from a litigated case). Throughout the eighteenth century, judges continued to play their role as advisers to the House of Lords, where they not only wrote legislation but also were available to give their views on contested legal points. Given that the administration usually could count on favorable votes in that House, the executive effectively was able to command an opinion on almost any pending matter. And evidence suggests that opinions were requested under precisely these circumstances. In 1758 the House of Lords required the opinion of the judges on pending legislation to extend the Habeas Corpus Act to individuals in custody for noncriminal charges. Lord Hardwicke, who opposed the measure, proposed seeking the judges' opinions on the current law and on the consequences of passing the new act. Hardwicke noted that there was "[s]carce an instance of passing such a Bill without asking the opinions of the judges, not whether it is fit upon political reasons to pass such a Bill that is a legislative consideration but to inform your Lordships in law." Horace Walpole was convinced that this maneuver was prompted by the administration: "The calling upon the judges for their solemn opinions was one of those dramatic exhibitions which had twice before been played off by the ministry with success. No man supposed that Lord Hardwicke or Lord Mansfield wished, wanted, or would be directed by the sentiments of the rest, the subordinate part of the order: but the bill was to be thrown out and the world to be amused by the gravity of the oracles that were to pronounce against it. The plan, I believe, in this, as in the former cases, was Lord Mansfield's."[124]

Regardless of whether Walpole was correct in his ultimate conclusion, the episode illustrates how easily a formal opinion could be arranged. The judges did give their views on the habeas corpus measure, albeit in a somewhat desultory fashion, with several joining Mansfield in speaking strongly against the bill. Although in the end the proposed legislation failed to pass, the Lords required the judges to draft a new bill. The judges did so, but no further action was taken on the matter until 1816.[125]

The opposition itself could move for a judicial opinion when doing so suited its purposes. This transpired in the Lords' debates over the Royal Marriages Act, a measure vehemently pushed by George III that would expand his authority to control marriages within the royal family. As was asserted by the opposition and the press, Mansfield had his hand in both the preparation of the bill and its management in the Lords. A number of opponents in the Rockingham group objected that the measure increased prerogative powers. Rockingham was able to obtain the judges' opinions, which concluded that historically the King's dominion over royal marriages was more limited than the new legislation allowed. In the end, the administration narrowly prevailed, but the opposition was highly pleased with the strong challenge it mustered.[126]

The Continuation of Judicial Advice to the House of Lords

As a practical matter, recourse to advisers trained in law was a necessity for a body whose members, although they had little legal expertise, nevertheless decided appeals, conducted trials, and drafted legislation. In theory, other sources of legal advice could have developed, but clearly the judges were a resource superior to mere attorneys. Further, long-standing tradition and regular usage sanctioned the relationship. We should not expect, then, that the Lords would have abandoned the judges unless an acceptable alternative was available. Interestingly, the mid-nineteenth century witnessed a decisive change in the House, whereby after 1844 the Lords' judicial duties were confined to Law Lords—"former Lord Chancellors or ennobled judges." Under legislation in 1873, "the judicial House of Lords . . . was no longer the same as the upper chamber of Parliament, but a court composed of professionally trained judges sitting independently of the parliamentary sittings of the House. The creation of lords of appeal rendered unnecessary the cumbrous practice of summoning the judges to give advice." Actually, the right of the Lords to call on the judges as advisers was never formally abandoned. Rather, it declined to desuetude—it was last used in 1898.[127]

In contrast to the politicized relationship that had historically existed between the courts and the executive, the presence of the judges in the House of Lords typically had not been controversial. Owing to the House's status as the highest court in the land, the connection was a fairly natural one. It would have been hard to argue that the judges' participation offended constitutional norms of separation of powers when the House itself consisted of an amalgam of legislative and judicial functions. Indeed, that was the very point the government made in defending the appointment of Chief Justice Lord Ellenborough to the cabinet.

SUMMARY

By the eighteenth century, the legitimacy of requiring the common law judges to provide advisory opinions and other forms of extrajudicial service to the King and the House of Lords rested firmly on ancient custom. In essence, both branches of extrajudicial service—to King and Lords—sprang from the same source. Judges were in theory and practice servants to the Crown, and not until 1700 did they achieve a significant measure of formal independence by way of statutorily mandated life tenure. Judicial assistance to the Lords arose from the initial conception of the peers as the King's council, of which the judges were members. Eventually, the House of Lords acquired its own institutional identity, and by the sixteenth century the judges who were not peers had lost their membership in that body. The judges continued, however, to provide expertise to the Lords on legal matters in their role as advisers to the House.

In this long history there were numerous variations on these practices, as well as resistance by the judges to certain aspects of their advisory function. Perhaps the most consistent basis for complaint was the contention that judges should not be consulted in cases that might come before them judicially. Coke objected as well to the canvassing of judges for separate opinions; he preferred that the judges be consulted as a group. Despite such reservations, judges did give opinions separately. Under the Stuarts, the taking of opinions became an infamous device for embellishing a royal position with legal authority. As such, it was part of the general practice of the Stuarts to use judges as instruments for implementing the King's will.

The advisory responsibilities of judges to the Lords continued throughout the eighteenth century and did not diminish until the nineteenth century. Judges often decisively influenced that body on account of the relatively few law-trained members of the peerage. Moreover, the membership of Chief Justices as peers in the Lords during this era heightened the influence of the judiciary in the upper house. Nevertheless, advisory opinions to the King and his ministry appear to have declined in the 1700s and eventually disappeared during the latter half of the century.

Political discourse in eighteenth-century England typically relied on appeals to long-established customs. This was true even of the various reform movements of the eighteenth century that sought increased parliamentary independence from the executive and more extensive representation in the House of Commons. In an era when innovation was distrusted and political ventures needed the justification of the past to succeed, it is not hard to explain the persistence of a traditional practice, especially when it implicates the prerogatives of the ruling elite. A more difficult task is determining the reasons behind the extinction of a privilege exercised for centuries by the Crown. To Americans, who regard the end of this period as a time of fundamental changes in the principles of separation of powers, the natural assumption may be that the decline of advisory opinions to the executive was a consequence of constitutional developments. After all, the Supreme Court Justices cited separation of powers in declining to answer President Washington's questions. But pursuing this theme for the parallel development in Great Britain—where there is no dramatic refusal by the judges even to decipher—proves fruitless.[128]

British constitutional theory from the mid-seventeenth century to the eighteenth century rested on a concept of the balanced constitution in which the three estates—King, Lords, and Commons—shared in the power of governance and checked the influence of the others. Formal separation of powers into the functioning units of executive, legislative, and judicial branches was not required by the constitution, nor was it thought necessary for individuals to occupy office in only one of the branches. It was quite common for political actors to hold places in both Parliament and the executive.

Judges could take positions in all three branches without offending constitutional principles, and occasionally they did so. Moreover, the common law judges had many duties that essentially entailed administration of the government and were unrelated to litigated cases. Then, of course, there was the Chancellor, who operated openly as a political player despite his high judicial station. Typical accounts of the judicial power placed it as part of the executive, which was a reasonably accurate shorthand description of the way courts enforced the law.

Separation of powers did become an issue in this period, but the preeminent concern in England was the extent to which the executive and legislative branches should be kept apart. Along these lines, the most important constitutional question of the eighteenth century centered on the asserted excessive influence of the executive over Parliament. Discussions about the need for judicial independence usually transpired in the context of securing judicial tenure and salaries. Constitutional protests were not provoked by the requirements that judges render advisory opinions at the behest of either the Lords or the executive.

While constitutional theory remained relatively stable in eighteenth-century England, the actual allocation of power in government became transformed as the cabinet system went through its nascent stages. By century's end, the King's ability to command his cabinet and shape policies had drastically changed. Overall—and viewed from distant hindsight—this represented a development of constitutional dimension, but it was one that took place gradually and was accommodated within the existing view of the balanced constitution. These alterations were not generated by a new vision of constitutional structure, such as that which occurred in America. Rather, the evolution of British cabinet government resulted from an intersection of events, personalities, class interests, economic pressures, and a range of other common forces associated with historical change. Constitutional custom placed limits on acceptable political moves, but the underlying constitutional order was sufficiently ambiguous that a variety of outcomes could have been possible.

Putting aside formal constitutional theory as the dominant explanation allows us to clarify why advisory opinions to the executive expired whereas they persisted in the House of Lords. This approach treats the topic of extrajudicial opinions as an aspect of the political dynamics that shaped the different administrations of the Hanoverian age. Specifically, the focus has been on the workings of cabinet government and the role of the central player in the issue of whether advice should be given by the common law courts: Lord Mansfield. Whether Mansfield actually was the clandestine force behind the ministerial scene—as opponents charged—is not the critical factor. Instead, the key is that Mansfield was viewed as such by the opposition. For reasons of his own, Mansfield wished to be known as a man outside party politics. Not only was his reputation among many to the contrary, but he also was reviled in some segments of the public for his actions regarding Wilkes, libel cases, America, Catholic dissenters, and a number of other issues. As a man who valued secrecy in dealings with the administration, and whose association with a measure could spell trouble, the best way to assert his influence would be in a manner outside scrutiny.

In the House of Lords, however, advisory opinions could be and were demanded by both opposition and administration forces. Given the work of the House of Lords as an appellate court and the need for professional expertise regarding the drafting of legislation, the presence of judges was a practical necessity. Moreover, their availability on command in effect allowed the executive to call for formal opinions whenever such were needed.

If any one source for the eventual demise of the executive's resort to extrajudicial advice were to stand out, it would be the independence of judges occasioned by the Act of Settlement. Protection for the office and livelihood of judges came not as the consequence of abstract political theory. Abuse of the judiciary by the Stuarts vividly demonstrated the need for this change, which in turn provided the impetus for enunciating a constitutional theory of an independent judicial establishment. The resulting independence provided the insulation that would enable Mansfield explicitly to discourage requests for advice from the Crown. Finally, the formal autonomy of the judges meant that their opinions were unpredictable, and hence less useful as political tools.

2

The Advisory Role of American Judges Prior to 1787

The previous chapter demonstrated that the practice of giving extrajudicial opinions grew out of a historical relationship between the judges and the Crown. The dependency of judges on the Crown and the intermingling of judicial offices with other parts of the government were not only distinctive features of that history but also potent sources for executive abuse. As a first step in analyzing advisory decision making in America, a study of the analogous judicial-executive relation on the other side of the Atlantic is essential. Two characteristics of the American experience bear emphasis. The first relates to the formal relationships among judicial, executive, and legislative processes. The second concerns the lack of tenure for judges in the colonies and their consequent subservience to royal governors. Of these two features, the second became the object of the most censure by revolutionary Americans. Both, however, were implicated in the subsequent debates over the federal Constitution.

THE COLONIAL PERIOD

In keeping with the tradition of the mother country, the American colonial governments did not separate the legislative, executive, and judicial functions of government into discrete units staffed with officials who held positions only in one branch. Instead, much like in England, there was a thorough blurring of offices and functions. The provincial council, for example, served multiple roles as an advisory panel to the governor, the upper branch of the colonial legislature, and the highest court of appeals in civil cases. Colonial assemblies went beyond legislative tasks to discharge such judicial responsibilities as hearing private petitions, granting equitable relief, and ordering appeals and new trials in cases decided by the courts. At the local level, courts did not merely resolve disputes and try criminal cases but also carried out a substantial number of everyday administrative and regulatory tasks, including tax assessments, licensing, and monitoring of public expenditures. Furthermore, multiple office-holding was common. Judges frequently were members of the provincial council, which the governor presided over during executive and judicial sessions. Council members, who typically were prominent members of colonial society, commonly were awarded other lucrative administrative and judicial offices by the governor—which in turn reinforced the dominant role of governors in the political life of the colonies.[1]

In short, judges in the colonial structure were by their very positions continually involved in the process of advising executive and legislative bodies. It is unknown whether the courts themselves were called upon regularly to give formal advisory opinions—as in England—to the governor or the assembly. In general, however, the advice would have been of limited utility given that most of the American judges of this period had no formal law training, and that one of the prominent complaints of the period was the low quality of colonial jurists. Above all else, these were colonies, and the governor was subject to instruction from home—obedience was insisted upon by the authorities in England, so the natural source for clarification lay abroad. When in doubt, opinions could be sought from the principal law officers in England.[2]

As the eighteenth century progressed, a demarcation between judicial and legislative functions was increasingly recognized. Yet there never came a point at which the colonies operated under a theory of separated branches that would have called into question the practice of judges providing advice to the executive and legislature. During the revolutionary era, the Americans did seize upon the theme of separated powers; nevertheless, the independent states found advisory opinions from judges to be compatible with their new theories of constitutionalism.[3]

THE EARLY STATE PERIOD

In spite of the relative insignificance of separation of powers to British constitutional thought in the eighteenth century and earlier, the Americans championed the theory during the Revolution. Notwithstanding (or perhaps because of) the use of the term as a slogan in revolutionary writings and in early state constitutions, the doctrine itself was burdened by the ambiguities of a still emerging ideology. In the main, Americans were reacting against the governors' abusive domination of colonial government—especially the legislature, but the courts as well. Appointments of colonial legislators and judges to plural offices, with attendant financial rewards, were perceived as a key instrument of gubernatorial manipulation. With regard to the judges, the major objections of the revolutionaries related to the lack of tenure for their judges—a right long enjoyed by judges in England—and the Crown's control over judicial salaries.[4]

James Madison observed in *Federalist No. 47* that although state constitutions were "emphatical" in proclaiming separation of powers, "there is not a single instance in which the several departments of power have been kept absolutely separate and distinct." The interference of state legislatures with their judiciaries was one of Madison's principal illustrations of a central theme in the *Federalist,* namely, that "[t]he legislative department is every where extending the sphere of its activity, and drawing all power into its impetuous vortex." Madison noted that in Pennsylvania, for example, "[t]he salaries of the Judges, which the Constitution expressly requires to be fixed, had been occasionally varied; and cases belonging to the judiciary department, frequently drawn within legislative cognizance and determination."[5]

Judicial independence was weakened in a number of states by term limitations, provisions for removal from office through legislative impeachment, and control of salaries by the legislature. Some revolutionary-era constitutions did eliminate the judicial powers of governors and their councils, turning the latter into independent upper houses of the legislatures from which judges were barred. Still, many states continued to blend the branches of state government until as late as the early nineteenth century. In New York, for example, the highest court was composed of the state Supreme Court judges and the Chancellor, along with the state Senators and the President of the Senate. Even where reforms enhanced separation of powers, legislatures continued passing private acts to carry out "functions now thought of as purely judicial or executive. They granted charters for beginning corporations, and divorces for ending marriages. They quieted title to property, declared heirships, and legalized changes of name." Moreover, they persisted in their colonial-era habits of interfering with judicial pro-

ceedings, by overturning verdicts, refusing to recognize claims established
in courts, remitting fines, passing private acts, and so on. As Alexander
Hamilton asked rhetorically in *Federalist No. 71,* "[t]o what purpose separate
the executive, or the judiciary, from the legislative, if both the executive and
the judiciary are so constituted as to be at the absolute devotion of the
legislative?"[6]

Madison and Hamilton represented a fairly advanced state of thinking
about the theoretical problem of creating an autonomous judiciary. Their
commentary shows that by the end of the 1780s Federalist thought had
overcome the earlier inclination to associate the judicial function with the
executive office. Back in 1766, John Adams had written, with words echoing
Montesquieu, that the "first grand division of constitutional powers" was
between "those of legislation and those of execution," and the judicial function resided in "the executive branch of the constitution." Gordon Wood has
argued that the developments in judicial independence during the 1780s were
a consequence of the rising distrust of legislatures and the related acceptance
of judicial review as a mechanism for assuring that enacted laws respected
fundamental rights. This endorsement of an explicit checking function for the
courts was part of the new ideology that Federalists would put forward in the
1780s: that each branch of government was ultimately responsible directly to
the people, and that no part was superior to the others.[7]

Given the still burgeoning concept of the judiciary as an independent,
coequal branch of government, it is not surprising that the states did not
limit the roles of judges merely to deciding cases brought to courts by
adversarial parties. In keeping with the long-standing British practice, state
judges acted as advisers to both executives and legislatures.

Massachusetts offers the clearest example of such practices, for the state's
1780 constitution specifically provided an advisory role for judges: "Each
branch of the legislature, as well as the governor and council, shall have the
authority to require the opinions of the Justices of the supreme judicial
court, upon important questions of law and upon solemn occasions." An
example of this procedure is a 1781 matter in which the legislature asked
the judges for their opinion on the constitutional question of whether the
House of Representatives had exclusive authority to originate an inquiry into
property valuations. The Justices appeared and gave seriatim opinions, including one by a future Associate Justice of the U.S. Supreme Court, William
Cushing, who commented that the judges were "honored" by the request.
New Hampshire copied the Massachusetts provision when drafting its own
constitution twelve years later. In both states, judges regularly were called
upon for advice, despite explicit statements in their constitutions that the

respective branches of the government "shall never exercise" any other powers assigned to the coordinate branches. The implication of this was that advisory opinions were regarded not only as a proper aspect of the judiciary's responsibilities but also as consistent with the independence of that branch.[8]

Rhode Island provides a more isolated illustration of an advisory opinion: the well-known case of *Trevett v. Weeden,* which usually is recalled primarily as an early instance of a court asserting the power to declare legislative acts unconstitutional. Newspapers in Rhode Island reported in 1786 that the five judges of the superior court had declared unconstitutional a state law imposing criminal penalties for refusing to accept paper money in payment of a debt. Upon hearing this, the legislature ordered the judges to appear before it and explain their "unprecedented" judgment, which threatened "directly to abolish the legislative authority." Three of the judges attended, and Judge Howell was recorded as saying: "He observed, that the order by which the judges were before the House might be considered as calling upon them to assist in matters of legislation, or to render the reasons of their judicial determination, as being accountable to the legislature for their judgment. That in the former point of view, the court was ever ready, as constituting the legal counsellors of the State, to render every kind of assistance to the legislative, in framing new or repealing former laws: but that for reasons of their judgment upon any question judicially before them, they were accountable only to God and their own conscience."[9]

Howell went on to insist that the judges in fact had not declared the statute unconstitutional but instead had decided against enforcement on other grounds. For the purposes of this book, the important point is that while in the course of insisting on the judiciary's right to be undisturbed by the legislature in its decision making, Howell freely granted that the judges could be called upon to assist in the process of legislation. These services, he might have added, fit precisely within the job description of a British judge commanded to assist the House of Lords in legislative affairs. Unlike Massachusetts, the Rhode Island judges' responsibilities as counselors did not derive from a constitutional text, inasmuch as the state had no written constitution at the time.

The proceedings in *Trevett v. Weeden* were publicized at the time, with accounts appearing in several newspapers, and in a pamphlet sold in Philadelphia shortly before the federal Constitutional Convention. Delegates to that convention probably would have been aware as well that the Pennsylvania judiciary engaged in advisory practices. One of the most prominent individuals in Pennsylvania at the time was Thomas McKean, a former leading figure in the Revolution, a signer of the Declaration of Independence, the President of the Continental Congress during Yorktown, and soon to be a prominent promoter for ratification of the federal Constitution. McKean had been the Chief Justice of Pennsylvania since 1777—an office he held while serving as a representative of *Delaware* in the Continental Congress. Under McKean's leadership, the Pennsylvania Supreme Court customarily provided advisory opinions, a practice that significantly enhanced the judges' influence on state law. Their opinions were given on request to the Assembly, the Executive Council, and the Continental Congress. Mostly these were written opinions, although the judges occasionally were called on to participate in oral discussions. According to a modern commentator, the opinions of the Pennsylvania judges "were not always followed . . . , but they were listened to with respect, and contributed to the national practice of having governmental agencies act in accordance with a received corpus of law, interpreted by experts."[10]

Even though he held more than one office and was willing to advise other branches of government, McKean staunchly defended judicial autonomy. His tenure on the Pennsylvania court set the foundation for an independent judiciary in the state. The keystone of that structure was a provision for life tenure added during the 1790 proceedings to revise the state constitution, in which McKean actively participated. A plausible reading of the Pennsylvania experience is that the giving of advisory opinions did not weaken the judiciary, but on the contrary seems to have augmented its political strength.[11]

Admittedly these are only examples of the acceptance of advisory opinions by eighteenth-century American courts. Yet the real surprise would be to find a rejection of the practice in general. An objection to advisory opinions presumably would have been based on some notion that in providing them courts were acting contrary to the appropriate function of the judiciary. But notwithstanding the considerable changes under way in the constitutions of state governments, the courts continued their work in the years immediately following the Revolution without substantial alterations. In the state constitutions of that era, the courts were referred to as "going concern[s]" that "needed no words of creation, let alone a direct and explicit affirmation of [their] existence." British law would remain for some time a pervasive influence on American law and legal practice. Aside from state codes, the dominant sources of law were British decisions and the works of such British commentators as Blackstone. For the "[o]rdinary lawyers [who] referred to Blackstone constantly," the model of a proper judge was at once a jurist in court and an adviser to monarchs and Lords.[12]

3

The Advisory Role of Judges During the Formation of the U.S. Constitution

SEPARATION OF POWERS AND THE JUDICIARY

Chief Justice John Jay and his colleagues on the Supreme Court referred directly to separation of powers when they refused to answer the Washington administration's questions in 1793. Although the Justices relied on "the lines of separation drawn by the Constitution between the three departments of the government," the explanation was quite vague: "The[se] being in certain Respects checks on each other—and our being Judges of a court in the last Resort—are Considerations which afford strong arguments against the Propriety of our extrajudicially deciding the questions alluded to."[1] This section addresses the general question of how the federal judiciary was affected by the Constitution's principles regarding separation of powers. Subsequent parts of the chapter consider separation of powers in the context of specific discussions at the Philadelphia Convention.

About a year before the drafting of the Constitution was completed, John Jay expressed his general views on the proper formation of a constitution in a letter to Thomas Jefferson. Jay thought that it was unwise to vest legislative, judicial, and executive powers in one body of individuals: "[T]hese three great departments of sovereignty should be forever separated, and so distributed as to serve as checks on each other." Scarcely anyone in America would have disagreed with this statement, for as Madison acknowledged in *Federalist No. 47,* by then the idea had acquired the status of a "sacred maxim of free government." As often happens with sacred principles, however, the sanctity was achieved by the opaqueness of its expression. "Separation of powers, . . . while fiercely championed by some as an article of faith not susceptible to compromise, was a mutable doctrine to others, unclear in its extent and subject, within strict limits, to practical concerns." The ideology of the Revolution had transformed a rather secondary precept into the centerpiece of a struggle to insulate the legislature and judiciary from overbearing executive influence. But state governments had gained too much legislative power in the 1780s—at least in the eyes of Federalists. Madison observed at the Convention—with a measure of hyperbole—that "[t]he Executives of the States are in general little more than Cyphers; the legislatures omnipotent."[2]

The Federalist solution did not take the form of writing the principle of separation of powers into the constitutional text. Mere "parchment barrier[s]" had proved to be "greatly over-rated," Madison argued, as evidenced by the failure of precisely that mechanism in state constitutions. Nor did Federalists follow the advice of those who insisted that it was always dangerous for one political body to possess legislative, judicial, and executive powers. Granting that "[t]he accumulation of *all* powers . . . in the same hands" would be "the very definition of tyranny," Madison denied that "these departments ought to have no *partial agency* in, or no *controul* over the acts of each other." Rather than compartmentalizing the three functions of government into separate bodies, the Constitution would prevent tyranny "by so contriving the interior structure of the government, as that its several constituent parts may, by their mutual relations, be the means of keeping each other in their proper places."[3]

For Madison and his allies, the critical question was whether the members of each branch possessed "the necessary constitutional means, and personal motives, to resist encroachments of the others. . . . Ambition must be made to counteract ambition." To accomplish this end, interbranch defensive mechanisms were inserted throughout the document. Among the most important were a legislative role in executive appointments and treaty making, presidential vetoes over proposed laws, impeachment of executive and judicial officials, and the parceling of war powers between Congress as war-declarer and the President as commander-in-chief. One could add judicial review of legislation, although that was at best an implicitly granted power. The personal motivation to use these means to check undue concentrations of power would be provided by human nature itself. A passion "for pre-eminence and power" was one of several explanations for why there existed a "propensity of mankind to fall into mutual animosities."[4]

Although the Constitution did not formally state the principle of separation of powers, the first three articles of the document did specify that the functions of government would be lodged in distinct branches. Left undefined, and consequently the source of controversy as early as the first administration of George Washington, were the meanings of the operative terms: legislative, executive, and judicial powers. For example, would a formal declaration of neutrality in an international conflict be one of the legislative powers, "all" of which must be assigned to Congress, or could the President—as Washington did in 1793—make such a proclamation without even consulting Congress? The imprecision of these terms was due in no small part to the lack of a model by which they could be interpreted. Contemporaries recognized the novelty of this situation, as Hamilton wrote: "The regular distribution of power into distinct departments—the introduction of legislative ballances and checks—the institution of courts composed of judges, holding their offices during good behaviour—the representation of the people in the legislature by deputies of their own election—these are either wholly new discoveries or have made their principal progress towards perfection in modern times."[5]

Far from being a mere issue of objective meaning, the question was normative—what should the three branches be able to claim as their responsibility and focus of political power? Having rejected the British and American state constitutions as exemplars, the next most helpful source for interpretation would be the Constitution's own internal sources of meaning. The President had certain assigned responsibilities, the Congress was accorded a list of subjects on which it could legislate, and the judiciary was supplied with a series of jurisdictional grants. In terms of legislative and judicial jurisdiction, the general purpose of the enabling clauses was apparent, for each responded to a Federalist-recognized failure of the existing systems. Diversity jurisdiction, for example, would facilitate interstate and especially international debt collection by circumventing biased state courts, thereby enhancing the business environment of the new nation. Overall, there was a distinct parallel between the jurisdiction of the Congress and federal courts. Hamilton stated in *Federalist No. 80*, "[i]f there are such things as political axioms, the propriety of the judicial power of a government being co-extensive with its legislative, may be ranked among the number."

Federalists proclaimed this as a limitation on the courts, whose "powers . . . went no further" than those of Congress, James Wilson told the Pennsylvania ratifying convention. At the same time, the scope of federal jurisdiction assured that statutes were "effectual over all that country included within the Union."[6]

For the most part, these descriptions of the allocation of powers among the branches provided only rough outlines, and they left critical questions unresolved. One issue on which the Constitution stood virtually silent was the matter of how the federal government would actually operate. Of course, the grand scheme had been prescribed—how a bill would become a law, who would preside at impeachments, whether the President could command reports from the heads of departments, and so on. At the same time, there is scarcely a word on which executive departments would exist, whether the President would have a cabinet, the rules of parliamentary procedure to be used in Congress, the size of the Supreme Court, the rules of procedure for federal courts, whether the British common law formed the basis of federal law, and so on. It surely is correct to say that a large portion of these questions could not be addressed in a constitution, lest it "partake of the prolixity of a legal code," to borrow Chief Justice Marshall's words from *McCulloh v. Maryland.* Instead, the details would be worked out through a combination of congressional action and customary arrangements established by the branches themselves without the explicit sanction of legislative grace. As John Mercer said at the Convention, "[i]t is a great mistake to suppose that the paper we are to propose will govern the U. States," because the constitutional text "will only mark out the mode and the form. Men are the substance and must do the business."[7] One thinks in this respect of the procedures that Washington instituted for the conduct of his cabinet government or the mechanisms that Hamilton set up to run the Treasury, which even in those simpler times involved a considerable amount of administration. Or, to take the case of the judiciary, the actual assignment of circuit riding duties to the individual Justices was handled initially by the Court itself.[8]

In developing the working practices of the federal government, certain existing customs provided guides. For the judiciary, just as state courts had continued operating as they had before the revolutionary-era constitutions were adopted, so too could it be expected that federal courts would at least act in the usual fashion of courts. This consistency would hold true not only for the lesser details of the office—the rules of procedure, for example—but also for concerns that were central to the conception of the judicial function. For instance, consider Madison's reaction to the motion to add "cases arising under this Constitution" to the "arising under" category of Article 3 (the Convention already had included "arising under the Laws of the United States"). According to Madison's notes, he "doubted whether it was not going too far to extend the jurisdiction of the Court generally to cases arising Under the Constitution, & whether it ought not to be limited to cases of a Judiciary Nature. The right of expounding the Constitution in cases not of this nature ought not to be given to that Department." Nevertheless, the motion passed unanimously, with Madison recording that it had been "generally supposed that the jurisdiction given was constructively limited to cases of a Judiciary nature."[9]

On the one hand, then, the new federal judiciary would follow the established routines of courts. Yet, on the other hand, there was clearly a sense that the traditional lines of demarcation among the executive, legislative, and judicial powers were being reformulated by the Constitution. Compared with the other branches, the judiciary is a less obvious example of conscious innovations. Still, alterations were under way in the conception of the role of courts, as demonstrated by the various discussions about judicial review at the Convention and during the ratification process. On many of these basic issues it is evident that the Framers failed to recognize the importance or complexity of the issues. In other places, the questions were left for later legislative solutions—the most important here being the extent of a lower federal judiciary.[10]

Reliance on legislative solutions to shape the federal courts offered a means to temporize, and thereby brush off the various antifederalist objections to the proposed federal judiciary. Concomitantly, it avoided completely the question of what limits governed Congress's potential organization of the national courts. The early history of the federal courts is marked by a series of controversies made possible by the textual silence of the Constitution on critical questions concerning the judiciary. Could Justices of the Supreme Court be assigned duties as circuit judges? Would it be appropriate for Congress to require federal judges to perform extrajudicial functions, such as serving as hearing examiners on claims for military pensions? Did the provisions of Article 3 concerning life tenure forbid Congress from repealing the 1801 Judiciary Act, which reduced the size of the federal judiciary and thereby eliminated the employment of a number of judges? Or, to take the most famous case, would it be possible for Congress to assign the Supreme Court jurisdiction in cases not clearly sanctioned by Article 3?[11]

Although the list of issues just presented involved Congress's relationship with the federal courts, several of these issues implicate the larger question of what type of institution the judiciary (and the individual judges of the system) would be. Plainly, when the Justices declined Washington's request for advice, they had some conception of their institutional role in mind in their allusion to the "lines of separation" in the Constitution and the "checks" these were supposed to provide. We know, however, that the existing vision of the judiciary in the eighteenth century easily accommodated an advisory role. That is, it did so unless something about the new constitutional order forbade that practice. But generalities about separation of powers do not satisfy this inquiry. We need to turn to more specific evidence from the Convention to ascertain whether some barrier built into the Constitution precluded extrajudicial service by the Court.

SEPARATION OF POWERS AND THE DRAFTING OF ARTICLE 3

It might be argued that the "judicial power" as outlined in Article 3 was not limited to lawsuits in which a litigant had an actual claim against another party arising from a concrete set of facts. Article 3 mandates that the "judicial Power shall extend" to enumerated "cases" or "controversies."[12] The word "case" had a range of denotations to eighteenth-century speakers, not the least of which was simply an "instance" or a "situation." Madison's Convention notes, for example, contain this entry: "The sixth Resolution stating the *cases* in which the national Legislature ought to legislate was next taken into discussion."[13] The Constitution itself repeatedly uses "case" in this manner, as where Congress is vested with power "[t]o exercise exclusive Legislation in all Cases whatsoever, over such District (not exceeding ten Miles square) as may, by Cession of particular States, and the Acceptance of Congress, become the Seat of the Government of the United States."[14] Similarly, in eighteenth-century usage, "controversy" could be taken to mean simply a matter of dispute, whether in court or not.[15]

To this it might be added that the Constitution does not explicitly say that the "judicial power" must be exercised only in a traditional court proceeding. If one recalls that courts were accustomed to rendering advisory opinions and performing a variety of executive roles outside of adjudications, it is possible to conclude that Article 3 empowers the federal courts to act "extrajudicially," by serving as official advisers to the other branches in the areas specified by Article 3.[16]

It is doubtful, however, that the Framers consciously drafted Article 3 so as to sanction explicitly such extrajudicial roles for the Supreme Court or the lower federal courts. For one thing, the argument is not convincing at the level of word usage, because in that period "controversy" commonly was used interchangeably with the word "case" in reference to litigation. The variety of possible meanings for "case" and "controversy" was most likely on Madison's mind when he suggested that Article 3 be "limited to cases of a Judiciary Nature."[17] Readers may find ambiguity in Madison's choice of words, for he seems to beg the question of whether "Judiciary Nature" encompasses only cases presented by parties in litigation. Nonetheless, although Madison's statement is inconclusive on the scope of the federal judiciary's power, he almost certainly meant that cases of a "Judiciary Nature" were lawsuits.[18]

To conclude that Article 3 was aimed at anything other than defining the scope of the federal courts' authority in litigated cases is to lose sight of both the basic context of separation of powers and the ordinary use of the term "judicial power" in the late eighteenth century. "If it be essential to the preservation of liberty that the Legisl[ative,] Execut[ive] & Judiciary powers be separate," Madison told the Convention, "it is essential to a maintenance of the separation, that they should be independent of each other." "Judiciary power" was the counterpart of the other two aspects of governmental power. When speakers referred to the three, either separately or together, they invariably did so in the sense of an ability to command or bind others,[19] for discussions about "liberty" always concerned freedom from control by others. The idea of law itself was bound up with this conception of judicial power, as Hamilton wrote in *Federalist No. 15:* "Government implies the power of making laws. It is essential to the idea of a law, that it be attended with a sanction; or, in other words, a penalty or punishment for disobedience. If there be no penalty annexed to disobedience, the resolutions or commands which pretend to be laws will in fact amount to nothing more than advice or recommendation. This penalty, whatever it may be, can only be inflicted in two ways; by the agency of the Courts and Ministers of Justice, or by military force; by the COERTION of the magistracy, or by the COERTION of arms."[20]

As with the first two articles of the Constitution, Article 3 was intended to set out the limits of the judiciary's ability to impose on the other branches —as well as to enable the courts to act independently of the legislature and executive, even to the extent of interfering with those branches. Consequently, impeding a court's legitimate exercise of authority was contrary to the exercise of judicial power. This determination would be one of the explanations given by several Justices in 1793 for why the federal circuit courts could not help administer a pension program. Noting that the courts' decisions were subject to revision by the other branches, Justices Wilson and Blair, along with Judge Richard Peters, wrote: "Such revision and control we deemed radically inconsistent with the independence of that judicial power which is vested in the courts; and, consequently, with that important principle which is so strictly observed by the Constitution of the United States."[21]

"Judicial power" was sometimes used in this period as a substitute expression for the court itself. More commonly the term referred to the exercise of the judicial function. Article 3 follows this pattern, for as Chief Justice Ellsworth observed, "[t]he Constitution, distributing the judicial power of the United States, vests in the Supreme Court, an original as well as an appellate jurisdiction."[22] References to the "judiciary power," or the similar term "judicial authority," consistently meant some type of adversarial proceeding before a tribunal, even if the body in question was not a court. According to James Wilson's subsequent law lectures, the role consisted of "applying, according to the principles of right and justice, the constitution and laws to facts and transactions in cases, in which the manner or principles of this application are disputed by the parties interested in them."[23]

The purpose of associating "judicial power" with the coercive authority of a tribunal was not inadvertent, for it specifically dovetailed with separation of powers: the American version of separated powers required the parceling of the government's authority among distinct branches. Montesquieu had warned that the "judicial power," which he defined as "punish[ing] crimes, or determin[ing] the disputes that arise between individuals," must not be united in the same person or body lest liberty be destroyed. Americans thoroughly endorsed Montesquieu's sentiments—he was "the oracle who is always consulted and cited on this subject," said Madison. History had instructed that "the power of judging, a power so terrible to mankind,"[24] was a potent source of tyranny when combined in hands that also wielded legislative or executive authority. John Jay wrote to Washington a few months prior to the Convention that "nothing very desirable" would occur unless the new constitution "divide[d] the sovereignty into its proper departments. Let Congress legislate—let others execute—let others judge."[25]

Given the purpose behind these attempts to separate power, it is hardly likely that the Framers were thinking about mere "advice or recommendation" when they invoked the term "judicial power." It is conceivable that they would have entertained concerns about separation of powers if the question had been whether the executive or legislature could command an advisory opinion from the courts. That issue is addressed in the next section. At the moment, it is enough to note that the voluntary giving of advice to other branches by the courts was not one of the considerations that informed the drafting of the scope of the judiciary's authority in Article 3.

For some readers, the conclusion just reached might demonstrate that there is a fairly certain answer to the issue of the federal courts' constitutional authority to give advisory opinions. Because the drafters apparently were not authorizing advisory opinions in Article 3, and no other section of the Constitution does so, the clear answer is that the courts may not do so. This is not a historical conclusion, however, but rather a judgment based on a constitutional theory that employs history as evidence to support its normative position. Among other things, this theory would contend that the failure of the Constitution to authorize action by one of the branches (or at least the judiciary) entails that the conduct is unconstitutional. More than a few would contest this proposition, and it does seem at odds with other modern decisions that recognize a branch's authority to act despite the absence of an affirmative assignment of power by the Constitution.[26]

Others may pursue this debate. At the level of history, there is no reason to believe on the evidence adduced so far that the Framers were averse to advisory opinions. If a practice did not menace the independence of the judiciary or arm the courts with an ability to intrude on others, it simply was not a significant concern of the drafters. Constitution drafters of this era did not include details as to how courts would operate, on the apparent assumption that the customary practices were satisfactory. At the same time, the Constitution is replete with provisions designed to avoid the perceived misallocations of power in the state constitutions.

DISCUSSIONS AT THE CONSTITUTIONAL CONVENTION ON AN ADVISORY ROLE FOR FEDERAL JUDGES

The one place where the Constitution mentions the receipt of advice is in Article 2, which provides that the President "may require the Opinion, in writing, of the principal Officer in each of the executive Departments, upon any Subject relating to the Duties of their respective Offices." Indeed, in their letter the Justices maintained that "the Power given by the Constitution to the President of calling on the Heads of Departments for opinions, seems to have been purposefully as well as expressly united to the *executive* departments."[27]

The Justices could have added that the Convention had received a proposal to require the Supreme Court to provide advisory opinions to the executive. On August 20, Charles Pickney submitted this recommendation along with several others: "Each branch of the Legislature, as well as the Supreme Executive shall have authority to require the opinions of the supreme Judicial Court upon important questions of law, and upon solemn occasions." Pickney's various suggestions were referred to the Committee of Detail, which adopted several that eventually were incorporated into the final text.[28]

No records explicitly reveal why the committee did not accept Pickney's proposal regarding advisory opinions. It is possible, however, to put together a plausible explanation by reviewing a series of proposals before the Convention to create some sort of council associated with the executive that would include judges as members. Before doing so, it should be noted that Pickney's idea was to make it mandatory for the Court to respond to executive requests for advice. His plan, in fact, was a slightly modified version of the provision in the Massachusetts constitution. On the face of it, the rejection of Pickney's idea may have reflected nothing more than disagreement with the element of requiring the courts to give advice on command of the President. Another thing to keep in mind is that the committee failed to act on several of Pickney's contemporaneously presented proposals that plainly were not considered by most to be inconsistent with the Constitution. For example, Pickney wanted to add: "The liberty of the Press shall be inviolably preserved."[29]

The Council of Revision

Pickney brought up the issue of consulting the judges only a few days after the Convention voted down for the final time the proposal to create a Council of Revision, and these events are probably connected. Edmund Randolph introduced the idea of the council to the Convention in his presentation of the Virginia Plan on May 29: "Resd. that the Executive and a convenient number of the National Judiciary, ought to compose a Council of Revision with authority to examine every act of the National Legislature before it shall operate, & every act of a particular Legislature before a Negative thereon shall be final; and that the dissent of the said Council shall amount to a rejection, unless the Act of the National Legislature be again passed, or that of a particular Legislature be again negatived by ___ of the members of each branch."[30]

The idea for a Council of Revision did not originate with the Virginians; rather, it was a feature of the New York constitution. John Jay apparently wrote a draft of the New York constitution in which the council first appeared. In any event, Jay was a proponent of this veto mechanism and may have been responsible for bringing it to the attention of the drafters of the Virginia Plan. Prior to the Convention, Jay wrote to Washington with a series of recommendations for a new constitution, including: "Might not Congress be divided into an upper and lower house—the former appointed for life, the latter annually,—and let the governor-general (to preserve the balance), with the advice of a council, formed for that only purpose, of the great judicial officers, have a negative on their acts?"[31]

Supporters of the revisionary council were motivated primarily by a desire to deflate the anticipated strength of the legislative branch. Based on his view of the states' experiences, Madison warned that legislatures were "the real source of danger to the American Constitutions; & suggested the necessity of giving every defensive authority to the other departments that was consistent with republican principles." Arming the executive and judiciary with a combined veto role over legislation "would be useful to the Judiciary departmt. by giving it an additional opportunity of defending itself agst: Legislative encroachments; It would be useful to the Executive, by inspiring additional confidence & firmness in exerting the revisionary power." Moreover, the "Community at large" would benefit, Madison insisted, because the council could serve "as an additional check agst. a pursuit of those unwise & unjust measures which constituted so great a portion of our calamities." Consultation between the executive and the judges should also improve legislation by "preserving a consistency, conciseness, perspicuity & technical propriety in the laws, qualities peculiarly necessary; & yet shamefully wanting in our republican Codes."[32]

Despite the dogged pursuit of this plan by Madison, James Wilson, Oliver Ellsworth, and Gouverneur Morris—some of the most influential delegates—opponents carried the day on four separate attempts.[33] Advocates of the council found themselves caught between two opposing forces. On one side were such delegates as Elbridge Gerry, who wished to maximize legislative autonomy and feared that uniting the judiciary and the executive would "bind them together in an offensive and defensive alliance agst. the Legislature, and render the latter unwilling to enter into a contest with them."[34] A second group wished to preserve a unitary executive unhampered by judicial participation. "[A]s the Judges will outnumber the Executive," Nathaniel Ghorum predicted that "the revisionary check would be thrown entirely out of the Executive hands, and instead of enabling him to defend himself, would enable the Judges to sacrifice him."[35]

Those championing legislative autonomy proved to be the most strident in insisting that the council was, as Luther Martin put it, "a dangerous innovation" that was inconsistent with the proper role of judges. Martin warned that "[i]t is necessary that the Supreme Judiciary should have the confidence of the people. This will soon be lost, if they are employed in the task of remonstrating agst. popular measures of the Legislature." In a similar vein, Gerry contended that the measure "was making Statesmen of the Judges" when "[i]t was quite foreign from the nature of [the] office to make them judges of the policy of public measures." Gerry added that there was peril for the Executive as well, who "standing alone wd. be more impartial than when he cd. be covered by the sanction & seduced by the sophistry of the Judges."[36]

As to the assertion that the judges would improve legislation, Martin retorted: "A knowledge of mankind, and of Legislative affairs cannot be presumed to belong in a higher . . . degree to the Judges than to the Legislature." Several opponents suggested that there were other unobjectionable mechanisms for securing the judges' opinions about legislation. Pickney allowed that although he had at first approved of the council, "[h]e had however relinquished the idea from a consideration that these could be called on by the Executive Magistrate whenever he pleased to consult them." Others agreed with this analysis, and presumably this was the source of Pickney's later proposal to require such consultation on executive request.[37]

The propriety of consulting the judges for advice was not unanimously endorsed, for several voices agreed with John Rutledge that "[t]he Judges ought never to give their opinion on a law till it comes before them."[38] Rutledge may have been rejecting all prior consultation, but other delegates seemed to be concerned only that the judges would be biased by having implicitly endorsed the policy of the legislation.[39] The interesting case is Pickney himself. Only five days before making his proposal for mandatory judicial consultation with the executive, Pickney said that he "opposed the interference of the Judges in the Legislative business: it will involve them in parties, and give a previous tincture to their opinions." Either Pickney changed his mind over the next few days, or more likely he thought that there was no problem with the executive's receiving legal advice from the judges.[40]

In the course of making these objections, speakers often invoked the principle of separation of powers. "No maxim was better established[,]" Caleb Strong insisted, than "that the power of making ought to be kept distinct from that of expounding, the laws." Madison responded with a rehearsal of an argument that would soon appear in *Federalist No. 47*, namely, that "a Constitutional discrimination of the departments on paper" was insufficient to assure their independence from each other. Rather than "blend[ing] the departments together," the council of revision would "add a defensive power to each which should maintain the Theory in practice." Madison acknowledged that "[t]he most regular example of this theory was in the British Constitution." Nevertheless, he continued, "it was not only the practice there to admit the Judges to a seat in the legislature, and in the Executive Councils, and to submit to their previous examination all laws of a certain description, but it was a part of *their* Constitution that the Executive might negative any law whatever; a part of their Constitution which had been universally regarded as calculated for the preservation of the whole."[41]

Gouverneur Morris supported Madison's statement with a similar reference to British practice, but in doing so he isolated the problem that divided the delegates on a number of questions about separation of powers. The difficulty in making the comparison with the British example, Morris granted, was that "[t]he influence the English Judges may have in the latter capacity in strengthening the Executive check can not be ascertained, as the King by his influence in a manner dictates the laws." By contrast, "[t]he interest of our Executive is so inconsiderable & so transitory, and his means of defending it so feeble, that there is the justest ground to fear his want of firmness in resisting incroachments. He was extremely apprehensive that the auxiliary firmness & weight of the Judiciary would not supply the deficiency."[42]

Morris's acknowledgment dashed any effort to draw a parallel to the British experience. The underlying difficulty lay in Madison's conception of separation of powers, under which the constitutional structure would give each branch sufficient power to resist encroachment by the others—but not so much strength as to leave one branch in a dominant position. To finely adjust the weights on the scale required visualizing the actual operation of the government under design, complete with a description of the powers that the government would wield. But there was little agreement on these basic questions, and speakers commonly resorted to sweeping claims about the possibilities for tyranny if power was added to or subtracted from one of the branches. Toward the end of the last debate on the revisionary council, Ghorum remarked in apparent disgust that he "saw no end to these difficulties and postponements. Some could not agree to the form of Government before the powers were defined. Others could not agree to the powers till it was seen how the Government was to be formed."[43]

In the end, the delegates overcame this barrier through a series of compromises, such as the agreement to give the executive a veto over legislation, subject to a supermajority congressional override. Obviously this shows some acceptance of Madison's approach to separation of powers, because several structural features of the Constitution involved an intermingling of branches. Historians, however, are left with a muddle when they try to ascertain the attitudes of the delegates toward particular issues such as whether the executive could request advice from the judges. Unraveling this history is particularly difficult when there was no actual vote on the question. A familiar illustration that emerges from the same set of debates is the constitutional propriety of judicial review. Martin and Gerry argued that placing the judges on the revisionary council would give them a "double negative" as "the Constitutionality of laws . . . will come before the Judges in their proper official character."[44] Other opponents to the council agreed—including King,

Martin, Strong, Pickney, and Rutledge. Several supporters of the council conceded that judicial review would occur, but thought that the judges should have the additional power to prevent the operation of "unjust[,] oppressive or pernicious" laws. Regardless of their explicit endorsement of judicial review, these speakers still constituted only a handful of the delegates at the Convention. And the overt backers of judicial review were somewhat counterbalanced by Mercer and Dickinson, who objected that "no such power ought to exist."[45]

The example of judicial review should remind us not to assume from the mere fact that the delegates failed to approve explicitly the advisory role of judges that the Convention decided against any such practice. At best, the rejection of the revisionary council demonstrates only a reluctance to have judges take public positions on matters of public policy. Even on that score, however, we have the recorded opinions of merely a few delegates. It is entirely possible that most were persuaded that a unitary executive, unencumbered by the judges, constituted a superior mechanism for achieving a balance of power with Congress. Neither alternative necessarily implies a rejection of consulting roles for judges, particularly if the courts could decline to give the advice.

To reiterate a theme, the delegates mainly were concerned with refining mandatory structural arrangements; if they wished to forbid a practice, they usually did so explicitly. Additional evidence for this conclusion comes from another discussion at the Convention on a topic closely related to the revisionary council—the proposal to create an executive (or privy) council.

The Proposed Executive (Privy) Council

Americans were familiar with the institution of a council to the executive inasmuch as the governors in the colonies and in the new states had advisory bodies. The colonial experience did not speak well of such councils. With councillors drawn from a narrow social elite and kept in line by gubernatorial patronage, "the governor was often able to dominate his council. He might easily convert it into an instrument for the promotion of selfish designs upon the province." In the first years of independence, however, all but two state constitutions erected councils of state that "participated in almost all executive duties and greatly diluted the independence of the governors' authority, making them (except in South Carolina) little more than chairmen of their executive boards." Whereas colonial councillors were appointed by the Crown, the states made these offices subject to election by the assemblies or the people. State constitutions drafted in the 1780s, however, reflected more wariness toward legislative autonomy and strengthened governorships by diminishing the councils' roles to an advisory status.[46]

Across the Atlantic, there was the prominent example of the British cabinet, the principal executive council for matters of state, which by the 1760s had established its position as a powerful political force. As chapter 1 explained, a major theme of the British opposition since the 1760s had been that a corrupt group of the King's cabinet ministers and other unofficial advisers dominated the government. During the Revolution, this thesis was given wide currency in America, where it became embellished with the additional proposition that the British ministry was conspiring to crush liberty in the colonies. Of special interest to the subject of this book is that one of the persons most often reviled by Americans for his advice to George III was Chief Justice Lord Mansfield, who was infamous for insisting on coercive measures against the rebellious colonists. In wickedly drawn political cartoons, and in such pamphlets as *The Plea of the Colonies,* Mansfield was accused by the colonists of "sitting in silence behind the curtain . . . guiding the political machine."[47]

The delegates in Philadelphia held varying opinions about the wisdom of setting up a council to the executive. Roger Sherman, for example, noted that councils were a customary arrangement, and thus he thought attaching one to the federal executive would prove "necessary to make the establishment acceptable to the people." Wilson, by contrast, wanted "to have no Council, which oftener serves to cover, than prevent malpractices." Tied up with this discussion over an executive council was the question of whether the executive office would be filled by a single person or by some larger number, such as Randolph's suggestion of three. Hugh Williamson contended that "[t]here is no true difference between a complex executive, formed by a single person with a Council, or by three or more persons as the executive."[48] The Council of Revision also was implicated, with delegates frequently viewing the process of vetoing legislation as merely one of the functions assigned to the executive council.[49] Nevertheless, alignments were not necessarily the same on both issues. To illustrate, Wilson favored a council for revisionary purposes but opposed the council of state. Gerry, a leader of the forces against the revisionary council, spoke warmly for a council to advise the executive.[50]

The first formal proposal for an executive council came on August 18, three days after the Convention had defeated the fourth and last effort to include a revisionary council in the draft. Oliver Ellsworth proposed that there should be an advisory council to the President consisting of the President of the Senate, the Chief Justice, and the ministers in charge of the various executive departments to be established. Two days later, Morris and Pickney introduced a more elaborate version of Ellsworth's plan. The "council of state," as they styled the body, would consist of the Chief Justice of the Supreme Court and the heads of five specifically named departments (Domestic Affairs, Commerce, Foreign Affairs, War, and Marine). These departments and their designated subject areas would have been afforded constitutional standing under the Morris-Pickney plan. Most of these officers were charged with recommending courses of action within their respective areas, and all were obliged to provide the President with consultation and written advice on request. In the case of the Chief Justice (who was to be the council's president during the President's absence), the proposal contemplated that he "shall from time to time recommend such alterations of and additions to the laws of the U.S. as may in his opinion, be necessary to the due administration of Justice, and such as may promote useful learning and inculcate sound morality throughout the Union."[51]

On the same day that Morris and Pickney advanced their council of state, Pickney submitted his own provision for requiring the Supreme Court to give advisory opinions to the legislature and the executive. Both of these proposals, along with a number of others initiated by Pickney, were sent to the Committee of Detail. The committee reported back two days later with a recommendation that was at once more elaborate and more constrained than the Morris-Pickney plan. It provided for a presidential "Privy-Council" composed of the Chief Justice, the President of the Senate, the Speaker of the House, and the chief officers of the previously named departments. Rather than defining these departments, however, the committee described them "as such departments of office [that] shall from time to time be established." As in the previous versions, this Privy Council would be purely advisory, charged with providing counsel with respect to matters that were laid before them by the President.[52]

No action was taken by the Convention on the Privy Council proposal, and instead it was referred on August 31 to a special committee of eleven members who were to report on sundry issues that had yet to be considered. That committee in turn recommended only the provision allowing the President to call for written advice from the heads of the "executive departments," which were not otherwise specified. The Convention agreed to that proposal on September 7. This determination was made on the same day that the Convention decided, after much argument, to vest the appointment of the principal figures of the executive and judiciary in the President with the advice and consent of the Senate.[53]

We have only scant information about why the committee of eleven rejected the call for the Privy Council. Speaking at the September 7 session, Morris—who had been on the committee—explained that "it was judged that the Presidt. by persuading his Council—to concur in his wrong measures, would acquire their protection for them." Earlier, when Ellsworth first brought up the question of a privy council, Gerry indicated that he opposed involving the heads of the departments "in business connected with legislation. [Gerry] mentioned the Chief Justice also as particularly exceptionable. These men will also be so taken up with other matters as to neglect their own proper duties."[54]

What emerges from this sequence of events is that the provision for requiring the heads of departments to furnish written advice to the President was the remnant of several attempts to establish an executive council. Under the more ambitious Privy Council plan of Ellsworth, Pickney, and Morris, the Constitution would have created the substructure of an executive branch. In the end, the Convention left the composition of the executive branch to later resolution by legislative and executive action. Evidently the Convention agreed with Pickney in authorizing the President "to call for advice or not as he might chuse." By specifying that advice be given to the President on demand, the Convention apparently contemplated that without this power the department heads could refuse such requests. Together with the "take care" clause for executive actions generally, the opinion provision reinforces the unitary nature of the executive. Considering the timing of the discussions on the executive council with that of the debate over appointments, it emerges that the Senate substituted as an "advisory body" for that purpose. The same is true with regard to treaties—the Senate's role there was approved on September 8.[55]

With respect to excluding the judiciary as a source of mandatory advice to the President, the most natural interpretation is that the Convention considered it inappropriate to require the judges to respond. Implicitly, the President also could not force the judges to be part of a council of advice. The Constitution, however, does not specifically forbid the President to ask either the Chief Justice or the other judges (individually or as a group) for their assistance. For that matter, it does not bar the President from asking federal judges to sit on an executive council. Nor can we assume that the silence of the Constitution implies that the President would not have such authority. There is no specific provision for an executive council or cabinet; at most, the Constitution authorizes the President to require *written* reports from the various heads. Nevertheless, President Washington almost immediately constituted a council along the lines of the Morris-Pickney plan— and he included Chief Justice John Jay in its ranks. Washington had watched all these debates from his vantage point in the Convention, and he evidently thought that the chief executive possessed inherent authority to create such a council. But before we turn to the events of Washington's administration, there is one remaining aspect of the Convention's work to consider—the matter of plural office-holding.

Plural Office-Holding Under the Constitution

From their colonial experience, Americans were deeply distrustful of plural office-holding. Looking at their home country, many Americans agreed with the British opposition's charge that the Crown was manipulating members of Parliament through patronage and other financial rewards to legislators, as well as through control of legislative elections.[56] On American shores, colonial governors used their powers to both appoint officials to and remove them from lucrative positions as a potent means to control assemblies. In varying ways, the revolutionary-era constitutions reacted to these perceived abuses by excluding from their state assemblies individuals who held other financially advantageous posts in the government. Consequently, it is not surprising to find George Mason saying that "disqualification" of legislators from other government offices was "a corner stone in the fabric" of the Constitution, as reflected in Article 1, section 6: "No Senator or Representative shall, during the Time for which he was elected, be appointed to any civil Office under the Authority of the United States, which shall have been created, or the Emoluments whereof shall have been increased during such time; and no Person holding any Office under the United States, shall be a Member of either House during his Continuance in Office."[57]

This clause of the Constitution plainly prohibits federal judges from simultaneously serving in Congress. Aside from this ban, however, the Constitution is silent about extrajudicial service: "No constitutional bar existed to judges' holding positions in the executive branch or running for political office. Nor did any provision keep them from giving advice, formally or informally, to an official of the executive branch or to a member of Congress." The failure to include a disqualifying clause specifically for judges was not inadvertent, for the Convention had been presented with two proposals to that effect. Neither reached the floor for debate, even though the Convention considered the ban on plural office-holding by members of Congress a number of times throughout the summer.[58]

Had the Convention incorporated in the Constitution a clause disqualifying judges from other offices, it is doubtful that this alone would have prevented judges from rendering advisory opinions to the other branches. Charles Pickney was the author of one of the proposed prohibitions on plural office-holding by federal judges, yet on the same day he suggested giving Congress and the executive the right to call for such opinions. This was also the moment that Pickney and Morris advocated a Council of State, with the Chief Justice serving as President of the council. There was no inconsistency here, because Pickney could consider assisting another branch to be free of the corrupting effects associated with receiving an income from offices in more than one branch. To put it another way, it "reflect[ed] a conviction that those who held judicial office had skills of statesmanship which they were obliged to put extrajudicially to the nation's service."[59]

Separation of Powers and Judicial Independence

One proposition on which virtually everyone at the Convention could agree was that the judges of the federal courts should enjoy tenure of office during "good behaviour" and protection against diminution of their salaries. At the time of the Revolution, a major complaint of the Americans had been—in the words of the Declaration of Independence—that the King had "made Judges dependent on his Will alone, for the tenure of their offices, and the amount and payment of their salaries." The first state constitutions insulated the judicial offices from gubernatorial control, but the legislatures themselves gained an upper hand over the judges through such devices as term limitations, legislative regulation of salaries, and the power to remove judges by joint address of the assembly. Then in the 1780s there came the rising revulsion against state legislative domination of the courts, and one of the themes of the movement was a demand that judges be assured their offices for life.[60]

"The Judges would be in a bad situation[,]" James Wilson warned the delegates, "if made to depend on every gust of faction which might prevail in the two branches of our Govt." Without adequate protection for their tenure and salaries, Madison stressed, the judges "might be tempted to cultivate the Legislature, by an undue complaisance, and thus render the Legislature the virtual expositor, as well the maker of the laws." These sentiments could suggest a general reluctance to allow the judiciary to become involved in political disputes. Undoubtedly the calling for an advisory opinion in the course of a heated exchange over an issue of public policy carried the potential for embroiling the judges in partisan politics. The notorious history of the Stuart monarchs' manipulation of their judges provided ample proof.[61]

There is no evidence, however, that any of the delegates—or anyone else, for that matter—believed that the furnishing of legal advice to the other branches by way of advisory opinions was fraught with peculiar dangers. In other words, it was abundantly clear that there were a variety of ways in which judges could become implicated in partisan wrangling, not the least of which might occur in lawsuits. After all, this was the very experience that was fresh in the minds of Americans. A dependence of the judges on either the legislature or the executive had "so often been productive of such calamities, and of the shedding of such oceans of blood, that the page of history seems to be one continued tale of human wretchedness." Less dramatic, but nonetheless on the minds of the Framers, were the recent attempts by judges to review the constitutionality of legislation. Such instances as *Trevett v. Weeden,* in which the judges had been called to account by the legislature when it appeared that they questioned the constitutionality of a Rhode Island statute, provided a plain demonstration of the importance of judicial independence to the future of that incipient practice.[62]

Security of tenure stood as a panacea for the historical problem of political exploitation of the judiciary. "[T]he permanent tenure by which the appointments are held," Madison wrote with evident confidence, "must soon destroy all sense of dependence on the authority conferring them." Hamilton saw "[t]he experience of Great Britain" as proof, for it "affords an illustrious comment on the excellence of the institution" of lifetime tenure. The consequence of the Stuart abuses was the tenure guarantees of the Act of Settlement of 1701, which put in place what Hamilton called an "excellent barrier to . . . encroachments and oppressions."[63]

The delegates were well aware that British judges consulted with both the executive and the House of Lords, and at least some must have known that analogous practices were occurring in their own states. Still, not a single line recorded from the Convention indicates any apprehension over such a role for the judiciary. The appropriateness of judicial advice was a matter of established custom. As to the danger that the courts could become the object of manipulation by the political branches, the threat would be avoided by the elimination of judicial dependence on the others.

4

The Advisory Role of Judges During the Washington Administration

CABINET POLITICS IN THE WASHINGTON ADMINISTRATION

George Washington entered the presidency with "the soul, look and figure of a hero united in him," to take the words of the French ambassador, whose observation was universally shared.[1] Washington brought to office immense experience as a commander of armies, together with a knowledge of political infighting derived from long years of dealing with Congress and from his own period of service in that body and the Virginia House of Burgesses. He could execute the smallest of details concerning his magnificent plantation. But the one thing he lacked was experience as an executive officer in government.

Notwithstanding all his notable accomplishments and the adoration of the public, Washington seriously considered not seeking a second term as President. In part, he was highly sensitive to criticism of his administration, which he saw as increasingly directed toward him personally. What was worse, the President accurately perceived that "discontents among the people" would be "shewing themselves more & more." Closely tied to this perception was

Washington's profound doubts about his competence for the office. In explaining to Madison why he did not wish to spend another four years as President, Washington related that "he could not believe or conceive himself anywise necessary to the successful administration of the Government; that on the contrary he had from the beginning found himself deficient in many of the essential qualifications, owing to his inexperience in the forms of public business, his unfitness to judge of legal questions, and questions arising out of the Constitution; . . . that he found himself also in the decline of life, his health becoming sensibly more infirm, & perhaps his faculties also; that the fatigues & disagreeableness of his situation were in fact scarcely tolerable to him."[2]

Always on Washington's mind was the "difficult and delicate part which a man in my situation had to act. . . . I walk on untrodden ground. There is scarcely any part of my conduct wch. may not hereafter be drawn into precedent." Believing as well "that others more conversant in such matters would be better able to execute the trust," from the very first Washington depended heavily on advisers, principally his cabinet officers.[3]

Washington's initial cabinet included Alexander Hamilton, the methodical, impetuous, and brilliant thirty-four-year-old Secretary of the Treasury, who had been General Washington's aide-de-camp and now was a leading lawyer in New York. Hamilton, unlike many men of this era, did not seek high office for personal financial gain. Other forces moved him, for he was a man whose "dominating urge . . . was for power and influence."[4]

Installed as Secretary of State was forty-six-year-old Thomas Jefferson, the restless and excitable savant who had lately returned from a five-year tour as American minister to France, an experience that had left him with a deep affection for the French people. Jefferson possessed a boundless yet sometimes desultory curiosity, which was combined with a striking tendency toward impulsive judgments. Gifted with a facility to turn a memorable phrase, Jefferson repeatedly employed his talent in harsh judgment of his fellows. A skilled state and national legislator and an accomplished diplomat, Jefferson had been an energetic governor of Virginia who paid detailed attention to the affairs of his office. But he had ended his term under strong criticism for allegedly not taking sufficiently decisive action in the closing months of his governorship, when Virginia was invaded by British forces.[5]

Edmund Randolph assumed the office of Attorney General, and although he was only thirty-five years of age, he had been attorney general and governor of Virginia, a leading figure at the Constitutional Convention, and for a time Washington's aide-de-camp. Viewed by some as a source of dispassionate advice and by others as vacillating or opportunistic, Randolph soon fell out of favor with both Hamilton and Jefferson. He continued to be heavily relied upon by Washington, however, until their terminal separation in 1795 over an allegation that Randolph betrayed his office to a foreign power for financial gain.

Washington's former general of artillery and close military adviser, Henry Knox, became Secretary of War at age thirty-nine. Knox enjoyed a reputation for intrepid soldiering: he had crossed the Delaware with Washington to capture Trenton, arrayed the cannons at Yorktown, and fought in virtually every major battle of the war. But he was regarded by Jefferson as a foolish sycophant of Hamilton, and by many as a pompous aristocrat. Knox headed an almost nonexistent army and carried little weight in cabinet deliberations.

In the early years of his administration, Washington frequently called upon two other men for counsel and assistance. James Madison, a thirty-eight-year-old member of the first Congress to whom the formation of the union was in no small part indebted, played a major role in fashioning legislation to create the new government. He functioned as a vital link to Congress, in addition to being a source of advice to Washington on political appointments. Madison shared an enduring friendship and political alliance with Jefferson, so much so that his eventual estrangement with the administration paralleled Jefferson's course. Completing the picture of presidential counselors was none other than John Jay, who at age forty-four entered the government as the carryover Secretary of State and freshly minted Chief Justice—he would hold both posts simultaneously until Jefferson's arrival to take over at State.

The formation of Washington's cabinet implemented the primary features of the Morris-Pickney proposal for a council of state, including the presence of the Chief Justice as an adviser for not only legal matters but also issues of more general importance. No serious objections were raised to the creation of executive offices and the attendant membership of the senior officers in the cabinet. For the most part, the cabinet replicated at the national level the customary manner in which eighteenth-century Anglo-American governments operated, with an executive consisting of a principal figure (a governor or the King) and a council of advisers.[6]

Procedures for consulting with the officers evolved over the first few years of the administration. In the beginning, Washington often asked the members to prepare written opinions on particular questions. Some of these requests now seem almost comical, such as his query for views on the number of levees he should hold each week (which was dutifully answered, with the respondents differing on this vital question). Frequently, he would circulate these opinions to the other officers for their comments. In 1792–93, when the country faced a series of crises regarding foreign relations, Washington regularized the convening of formal cabinet meetings, usually attended by Hamilton, Jefferson, Randolph, and Knox.[7] At these sessions, Washington was far more often a listener than a speaker; he generally did not take a position unless the group found itself evenly divided. Although Washington did not regard himself bound by the opinions of his cabinet officers, he almost invariably agreed to implement the majority view, even when it was contrary to his own.[8] This is not to say that Washington was disengaged from the issues, for he paid meticulous attention to details. When dealing with areas in which he regarded himself an expert, such as military affairs, he was more likely to trust his own judgment.[9]

The salient feature of cabinet life through the end of 1793 was the antagonism between Jefferson and Hamilton, which exploded into bitter invective on both sides. Volumes have been written on this famous feud, and only the broad outlines are needed here. The dispute was at once personal and political. In one sense it arose from entirely different aspirations for the country, and accordingly from quite divergent understandings of the form of government allowed under the Constitution. The issues that separated them were the germ of America's first national political parties. As much as anything else, Jefferson and Madison's disagreement with the government fashioned by Hamiltonian policies produced a coherent opposition party to the ruling Federalists.[10]

Jefferson was suspicious of Hamilton almost from the beginning of the administration. In mid-1791, Jefferson wrote to a protégé that Hamilton, along with Jay, Knox, and Vice President Adams, were among a group of "high names" who "desire of subverting [the present form of government] to make way for a king, lords and commons. . . . They pant after union with England as the power which is to support their projects, and are most determined Antigallicans." Early in 1793, Jefferson told the same correspondent that this "little party . . . have espoused [the Constitution] only as a stepping stone to monarchy, and have endeavored to approximate it to that in it's administration, in order to render it's final transition more easy." A growing Republican opposition to administration policies shared Jefferson's fear that a conspiracy was afoot, with Hamilton and Jay at the center, to return the country to a monarchical government.[11]

At the heart of the Jeffersonian and Republican apprehensions lay Hamilton's economic program, which was founded on his unabashed admiration of the British commercial and military state. Hamilton's financial plan bore at least a superficial resemblance to fiscal practices in England. His goal was the erection of a stable financial system that would in turn support the commercial development of America. First in priority was the creation of a stable currency, a commodity that was chronically in short supply in the American economy. As the British under Walpole had done, Hamilton fastened on the sizable public debt as the means to create a reliable currency. Not only would the federal government issue debt instruments to fund the national deficit, but the plan called for assumption of state obligations. By providing a reliable source of revenues to repay the debts when due, the paper could become a form of currency, thus turning what appeared to be a foreboding liability into an asset. The other critical components of the plan were a reliable source of revenues to fund the debt, combined with a national bank to facilitate commercial transactions and provide a rudimentary means to influence the money supply.[12]

Duties on imports would be the most significant source for funding the debt, and these would be augmented by a much smaller contribution from an excise tax on domestically produced liquor. Both measures had ramifications outside the immediate economic realm. Protest and outright rebellion greeted excise tax collectors in the back country and led directly to the Whiskey Rebellion of 1794. As to the duties, these would be sufficient to generate the required revenues only if American merchants maintained healthy levels of foreign trade. "My commercial system turns very much on giving a free course to Trade and cultivating good humour with all the world," Hamilton underscored in a 1791 message to Jefferson.[13] By necessity, Hamilton reasoned, this meant that the United States must foster links with its most important trading partner—Great Britain. Apart from the need for revenues from this trade, it was Hamilton's conviction that America's future prosperity would be best assured by expanding the country's traditional commercial ties with the British. Hence, avoiding conflict with the British became a centerpiece of Hamilton's agenda. Given that commercial and military rivalry between Great Britain and France remained a fact of life in continental politics, the concomitant for Hamilton was that America must avoid showing partiality toward France lest the British be offended.[14]

Hamilton's vision of the Constitution tracked his economic plans. It was hardly a secret that he supported a powerful and dynamic executive, as witnessed by his proposal at the Convention for a life-tenured President. In *Federalist No. 70*, Hamilton wrote that "[e]nergy in the executive is a leading character in the definition of good government," which among other things entailed a unitary executive. Forcing the President to act only with the concurrence of a council would, Hamilton opined, likely produce "an artful cabal" among its members, and it would surely be conducive to a "diversity of views and opinions [that] would alone be sufficient to tincture the exercise of the executive authority with a spirit of habitual feebleness and dilatoriness."[15]

The "immediate management" of government would of necessity be entrusted to "assistants or deputies of the chief magistrate," who "derive[d] their offices from his appointment, . . . and ought to be subject to his superintendence." To Hamilton, government administration was not a modest assignment. As he spelled out in *Federalist No. 72:* "The actual conduct of foreign negotiations, the preparatory plans of finance, the application and disbursement of the public monies in conformity to the general appropriations of the legislature, the arrangement of the army and navy, the direction of the operations of war; these and other matters of a like nature constitute what seems to be most properly understood by the administration of government."[16]

Not stated as openly, but as surely put in practice, was Hamilton's view that the legislature needed the firm leadership of the executive: "In fact the conduct of the Federalists in Congress was invariably predetermined by the decisions reached in their own secret party meetings at which Hamilton presided." Hamilton presented his economic plan to Congress in the form of a series of celebrated state papers, and he worked closely with congressional leaders in managing the bills. As J. G. A. Pocock has written, collaboration between the executive and Congress was the aspect of Federalist administrations that struck Jeffersonians "as pursuing the tradition of the Junto Whigs, Walpole and George III, which had contributed so powerfully to the belief that Britain was irredeemably corrupt." In the same way that the British Parliament was believed to be influenced by the Crown's disbursement of offices and financial rewards to members, Jefferson asserted that Hamilton had "established corruption in the legislature, where there was a squadron devoted to the nod of the Treasury, doing whatever he had directed, and ready to do what he should direct." By March 1793, Jefferson was writing that one-third of the House was "made up of bank directors and stock jobbers," and still others were "blindly devoted" to Hamilton.[17]

For his part, Hamilton held equally dire views of Jefferson and Madison. By 1792 he was warning that the pair were the *"head of a faction decidedly hostile to me and my administration, and actuated by views in my judgment subversive of the principles of good government and dangerous to the union, peace and happiness of the Country."* At about the time Jefferson was complaining to Washington about Hamilton, the latter informed the President that Jefferson was the guiding hand behind a "formed party deliberately bent upon the subversion of measures, which in its consequences would subvert the Government." In particular, Hamilton cautioned that Jefferson led a faction in Congress bent on "undoing . . . the funding system[,] . . .

which would prostrate the credit and honor of the Nation, and bring the Government into contempt with that description of Men, who are in every society the only firm supporters of government." A serious cause of concern for Hamilton was the attitude of Jefferson and Madison toward France and Great Britain, which Hamilton sneeringly called *"a womanish attachment to France and a womanish resentment against Great Britain."* Referring to Madison and Jefferson's support for retaliatory trade legislation against the British, Hamilton predicted in 1792 "that if these Gentlemen were left to pursue their own course there would be in less than six months *an open War between the U States & Great Britain."*[18]

By the summer of 1792, the relationship between Hamilton and Jefferson was defined by personal animosity and exaggerated apprehensions of sinister plots by the other. Each was bent on destroying the other's reputation and power. Hamilton in effect informed Washington that the cabinet was not big enough for both Jefferson and himself. Using a variety of pseudonyms in essays written for friendly presses, Hamilton assailed his rivals and supported newspapers sympathetic to the Federalist cause. Jefferson reserved his nastiest personal attacks for back-stabbing letters written to close associates and political supporters. For public assaults on Hamilton, he preferred to lend financial assistance to the acerbic newspaper writer Philip Freneau and his *National Gazette.* In early 1793, Jefferson sought to eliminate Hamilton from the government by drafting a series of resolutions calling for the Secretary of the Treasury's impeachment. Allegedly, Hamilton had improperly applied funds that had been raised from a loan to the government. After a congressional investigation largely exonerated Hamilton, a diluted version of the resolutions was introduced in the House, only to be defeated overwhelmingly. Jefferson professed not to be surprised by the outcome; in his judgment, a large number in the House were "voting in the case of their chief."[19]

At the outset of his administration, Washington reported that "[b]y having Mr. Jefferson at the Head of the Department of State, Mr. Jay of the Judiciary, Hamilton of the Treasury and Knox of that of War, I feel myself supported by able Co-adjutors, who harmonise extremely well together." Consequently, he watched with dismay as these relations disintegrated, a process that his own attempts at mediation could not halt. Washington did not seem bothered by their disagreement as such, for he saw the opposing points of view as reflecting different perspectives, the airing of which tended to produce more moderate decisions—some would say indecision—than did either in isolation. Jefferson's fuming about a monarchical conspiracy failed to convince Washington, who doubted that "there were ten men in the

United States whose opinions were worth attention, who entertained such a thought."[20]

On the whole, as Jefferson bitterly recounted, Hamilton prevailed in the major fights.[21] In particular, Hamilton's economic plan survived intact despite the determined efforts of the opposition, and even in the face of Jefferson's well-known opinion against the constitutionality of the national bank. Jefferson found himself with little independent room to act, given Washington's penchant for submitting all major questions to the cabinet. As a consequence, no important decision was left untouched by Hamilton's relentless energy for influencing government policy. After Jefferson became the first to resign from the administration (at the end of 1793), Hamilton was left unchallenged within the administration.[22]

Although the character assassinations and the overstated fears of conspiracy stand out in the early years of Washington's administration, there were also underlying disagreements in the respective sides' philosophies of constitutional government that would endure beyond their times. For the purposes of our discussion, the vital contradiction lay in their attitudes toward executive autonomy in both foreign and domestic affairs. It was not only Hamilton who favored a strong executive branch; this was a defining principle of most leading Federalists. Rufus King, an influential Federalist Senator from New York and a close ally of Hamilton and Jay, summarized this outlook in a letter to Hamilton: "It was never expected that the executive should sit with folded Arms, and that the Government should be carried on by Town Meetings." "Large assemblies," Jay wrote to Washington, "often misunderstand . . . the obligations of character, honour, and dignity, and will collectively do or omit things which individual gentlemen in private capacities would not approve."[23]

To Federalists of the 1790s, government was best carried out by a select group of men, as opposed to "[r]epresentative bodies," which Jay remarked "will ever be faithful copies of their originals, and generally exhibit a checkered assemblage of virtue and vice, of abilities and weakness." Fear of demagogues controlling legislatures was an ever present theme in Federalist ruminations about government, for as Jay said, "the strenuous efforts of the wise and virtuous will not cease to be necessary to frustrate their artifices and designs."[24] The composition of the Federalist leadership—lawyers, major landholders, and large-scale merchants—reflected this outlook, which was laden with class assumptions. "Virtue," Hamilton told the New York ratifying convention in 1788, was an attribute that "belongs to the wealthy. Their vices are probably more favorable to the prosperity of the state, than those of the indigent; and partake less of moral depravity."[25] Leadership accordingly fell naturally to the wealthy, who tended to have the education, experience, and personal connections necessary for the role. As John Adams wrote shortly before the Philadelphia Convention, "generally those who are rich, and descended from families in public life, will have the best education in arts and sciences, and therefore the gentlemen will ordinarily . . . be the richer, and born of more noted families."[26] Prominent Federalists traveled among the best of America's social elite, whom Federalist Judge Henry Marchant described as possessing "those easy and accommodating Manners, which consistent with Integrity and Justice to Our own Opinions, are essential to gain and preserve Esteem and Confidence."[27]

Throughout Washington's term in office, a recurring question was whether a given matter should be decided solely by the executive or referred to Congress for resolution. On almost every occasion, Hamilton favored leaving Congress out of the picture. By contrast, Jefferson in the cabinet and Madison in the House usually wished to defer to congressional judgment. As an ideological matter, both Madison and Jefferson "preferred that the balance of discretionary power be vested in the legislature, . . . and that within practical limits the president and his appointees be confined to carrying into execution the laws enacted by Congress."[28]

Madison and Jefferson watched a political scene that they perceived as dominated by executive influence, or more specifically by Hamilton, whom Jefferson regarded as "really a colossus to the anti-republican party." Madison griped to Jefferson in 1794 that "[t]he influence of the Ex[ecutive] on events, the use made of them, and the public confidence in the P[resident] are an overmatch for all the efforts Republicanism can make." The irony of this remark seems palpable, coming from one who had scarcely five years before railed against legislatures as the greatest source for political abuse in a republic. Madison may have misjudged the capacity of the executive to dominate Congress, but the constancy of his philosophy—and Jefferson's as well—lay in a deeper aversion to concentrated government.[29]

It bears stressing that this talk of executive power must be read in the context of that era. By modern standards, the power actually wielded by Washington and his administration was minuscule. For that matter, relative to the affairs of even the next century, there existed little effective government at all. America had essentially no armed forces with which to prevail upon overseas powers, a modest treasury to finance ventures, at best the beginnings of governmental influence over the economy, and little infrastructure with which to carry out commands.

From the perspective of our times, the fears of Republicans about the direction of the Washington administration seem quaint, even laughable. But we do not live in a world in which monarchy is the dominant form of government—and republicanism a mere experiment. Nor do we seriously consider the prospect that the union might dissolve into several regional blocs, perhaps in alignment with foreign princes—an entirely realistic possibility in the 1790s. No President today would anguish as Washington did over the propriety of the slightest autonomous acts. For example, at one critical juncture in June 1793, the cabinet discussed erecting four cannons on an island near Philadelphia in response to activities by French privateers. According to Jefferson's notes, Washington "did not think the Executive had a power to establish permanent guards."[30] Similarly, in a cabinet discussion later that year on creating a federal military academy, a project Washington thought important to the nation, the President nevertheless agonized over whether to include the measure in his upcoming address to Congress. Jefferson had argued that the academy was beyond Congress's enumerated powers, and Washington "did not wish to bring on anything which might generate heat and ill humor."[31]

Washington's trepidation in the instances just mentioned will be more understandable after we consider in detail the events of the year in which they occurred. The President's concern that he was acting without precedent to guide him came accompanied by an equally strong sense that every step he took would establish precedent. The antagonism between Jefferson and Hamilton arose in a setting in which there were plausible arguments to support either side's interpretation of the Constitution's allocation of power between the executive branch and Congress. It quickly became apparent to the rivals that their disagreement was not merely about the meaning of language in the text but was also rooted in basic philosophical differences on the nature of the republic. As we consider the role of Supreme Court Justices in advising the Washington administration, it is worth keeping in mind that the underlying issue of the executive's constitutional relationship with the other branches was still in a nascent state.

JOHN JAY AND THE WASHINGTON ADMINISTRATION

The Political Philosophy of John Jay

John Jay was the scion of one of New York's wealthiest and most socially prominent families, a status he enhanced by marrying a daughter of the influential Livingston clan. The Jays associated with the most fashionable figures of New York society. Jay "could be affectionate, compassionate, eloquent, fun-loving, and even ribald on occasion and in the appropriate surroundings; but to those less favored by this side of his nature, he seemed irritable, obstinate, and a stickler for the letter of the law." Hamilton observed about Jay in 1783 that "altho' [Jay] was a man of profound sagacity & pure integrity, yet he was of a suspicious temper, & that this trait might explain the extraordinary jealousies which he professed." Among the generation that founded the United States, "few . . . preferred greater distance from the 'Public,' devalued the general will so completely, and stressed the perils of lawlessness so constantly" as did Jay.[32] At the same time, Jay was a relentless opponent of slavery and thought that "all unjust and unnecessary discriminations everywhere [should be] abolished; and that the time may soon come when all our inhabitants, of every *colour* and denomination, shall be free and equal partakers of our political liberty."[33] Yet it is a curious fact that while Jay's political efforts on behalf of manumission caused him a considerable loss of public favor, he owned and even personally purchased household slaves.[34]

To Jay there was an unequivocal distinction between the judgment of reason, which he greatly admired, and "the impulse, and domination of . . . passions." "It [was] in vain to reason with those who listen only to the Dictates of their Passions and their feelings," Jay wrote. He "d[id] not believe one word" of those "modern philosophers [who] would persuade us" that "the passions and prejudices of mankind" can be "reduce[d] . . . to . . . a state of subordination to right reason." Jay thought that there was no prospect of an "age of reason, prior to the millennium, which I believe will come, though I cannot tell the precise time when. Until that period arrives I expect there will be wars, and commotions, and tyrants, and factions, and demagogues, and that they will do mischief as they may have opportunity." In grand jury addresses that were widely reprinted in newspapers at the time, Jay frankly acknowledged that it was still undecided "[w]hether any people can long govern themselves in an equal, uniform, and orderly manner."[35]

Like his two other colleagues who shared the "Publius" pseudonym, Jay was convinced that self-interest was the reigning feature of human nature. Applying this to the 1780s, Jay found his own explanation for what he saw as the nation's floundering: "Private rage for property suppresses public considerations, and personal rather than national interests have become the great objects of attention." At the same time, Jay believed that a small number of individuals were guided by reason and hence could be better trusted than the many. "The mass of men are neither wise nor good, and the virtue like the other resources of the country, can only be drawn to a point and exerted by strong circumstances ably managed, or a strong government ably administered."[36]

Jay himself was an example of an individual who enjoyed a "legendary reputation for integrity and probity." Alexander Graydon recalled that Jay "thought and acted under the conviction that there is an accountability far more serious than any which men can have to their fellow-men." Madison, who clashed with Jay over the terms of the proposed Spanish treaty in 1786-87, acknowledged later in discussing the controversy that Jay's "abilities and attachment to this country" were irreproachable. "If [Jay] was mistaken," Madison continued, "his integrity and probity more than compensate for the error."[37]

Jay's concept of human nature shaped not only his private life but his political philosophy as well. New York's constitution, which Jay took an important part in drafting, gave its governor more power than any of the other state constitutions produced around the time of the Revolution. Although he endorsed the vesting of government leadership in the hands of a select number, Jay fully expected that the elite would be blocked perpetually by those "hostile to merit, because merit will stand in their way; and being actuated by envy, ambition, or avarice, and not infrequently by them all," the opponents of virtue "will be diligently at work, while better men will take their rest."[38] Repose from public affairs was not Jay's style: for more than twenty-five years after being first elected to the Continental Congress in 1774, he held one high-level public office after another, which necessitated that he abandon his successful private law practice.[39]

Notwithstanding a career distinguished by numerous offices, Jay was like many Federalist leaders in that he preferred to work quietly outside the public eye. He thought that the same attitude of aloof governance should characterize the national administration. To Hamilton he gave this advice on responding to public criticism: "The national Govt. has only to do what is right and if possible be silent. If compelled to speake, it shd be in few words strongly evincive of Temper Dignity and self Respect. Conversation and desultory paragraphs will do the rest."[40]

In spite of his aversion to public confrontations, Jay himself was fiercely partisan and uncompromising in his political beliefs. Returning from Great Britain in 1795 to witness the outpouring of opposition to the Jay Treaty, for example, Jay saw the criticism as coming from "malcontents of various descriptions," including "the Antifederalists." Their actual concern with the treaty, Jay thought, was that it left them "disarm[ed] . . . of their affected complaints against the government on account of the posts, and commerce, etc. and by giving additional strength to the administration, etc., etc." The suppression of the Whiskey Rebellion in 1794 was a source of special pleasure for Jay. This was particularly so because he predicted that the result would lead to the "the extinction" of the newly formed Democratic-Republican societies—"these mischievous associations"—that Jay and other Federalists likened to the French Jacobin societies, and which they charged had promoted the revolt. Even though Jay was not on the bench to take part in the repression of the Republican press by federal judges later in the decade, he was quick to denounce what he termed "virulent publications." "These are political evils," Jay was convinced, which along with "factious leaders" were "as naturally as certain physical combinations [to] produce whirlwinds and meteors." In short, he was not a man to rest while "[d]emagogues . . . constantly flatter the passions and prejudices of the multitude, and . . . never cease to employ improper arts against those who will not be their instruments."[41]

The area that Jay regarded as most requiring direction by a small elite was foreign affairs. While serving as Secretary of Foreign Affairs for the confederated United States, Jay lamented to Jefferson that "although my attention to business is unremitted, . . . I so often experience unreasonable delays and successive obstacles in obtaining the decision and sentiments of Congress, even on points which require despatch." Diplomatic embarrassment was the least of the consequences that Jay feared from using a legislative body to conduct foreign affairs, for as he wrote in *Federalist No. 4*, America was entangled in relationships with European powers that went to war "whenever they have a prospect of getting any thing by it." From years of experience as a diplomat in Europe, Jay knew that "[t]he rising power of America is a serious object of Apprehension to more than one Nation, and every Event that may retard it will be agreeable to them." When diplomacy is conducted with such powers, Jay observed, "there are moments to be seized as they pass," but to do so required "*secrecy* and *dispatch*," which were attributes unlikely to be found in legislative bodies.[42]

Efficiency and confidentiality were not the only concerns that Jay had in mind when advocating a central role for the executive in foreign relations. Jay was no ideologue when he directed American foreign policy; rather, he was an advocate of pragmatic judgment. For Jay a principal benefit of centralized control over the international affairs of the United States was that the government "can collect and avail itself of the talents and experience of the ablest men." Large assemblies, however, were inclined to dissipate this advantage, because such groups "often misunderstand . . . the obligation of character, honour, and dignity, and will collectively do or omit things which individual gentlemen in private capacities would not approve." At the same time that Jay made these statements, he asserted the necessity for the three branches of government to be strictly separated in performing their respective functions. He also emphasized that when either the executive or the judiciary operated in its assigned constitutional capacities, the resulting acts "have as much legal validity and obligations as if they proceeded from the Legislature." Therefore, Jay wholeheartedly endorsed placing a major portion of the responsibility for foreign affairs in the hands of a few and excluding a direct role for Congress. His distrust of Congress arose out of practical reflection more than anything else, for Jay shared the typical Federalist perspective that blamed legislative domination of government for much of what they saw as the serious social problems of the 1780s.[43]

Although Jay was an intensely religious man, his outlook for the country remained largely secular in aim. Like other Federalists within his circle, Jay adhered to a brand of "nationalistic republicanism, . . . favored by an anglicized and cosmopolitan mercantile elite who advocated a highly centralized government, an active commercial life, and a deferential social order."[44] "[O]ur individual prosperity depends on our national prosperity," Jay told a grand jury in 1790, and "our national Prosperity depends on a well organized vigorous Government, ruling by wise and equal Laws, faithfully executed." Jay was an early proponent of the view that "[a] continental national Spirit should pervade our Country," so that America could present a united front to the Europeans. Upon becoming Chief Justice, he lectured the citizenry in grand jury charges on the importance of "avoid[ing] those Jealousies and Dissensions which often springing from the worst Designs frequently frustrate the best Measures."[45]

Along with the rest of the Federalists in Washington's administration, Jay had an affinity for British culture and government. As he remarked in 1796, "[i]t certainly is chiefly owing to institutions, laws, and principles of policy and government, originally derived to us as British colonists, that, with the favour of Heaven, the people of this country are what they are." Jay was somewhat defensive in saying this, for he was "recognized as one of the high priests in the Federalist party," whose adherents were being lambasted by Jeffersonian Republicans for their partiality to Great Britain in its ongoing conflict with France. It was not forgotten that Jay had been among the last to support American independence from the British empire. Jay personally became the target of a torrent of popular abuse for his role in negotiating the Jay Treaty, an agreement that was denounced by Republicans as a betrayal of American interests to the British.[46]

It was unfair to accuse Jay, as Jefferson did, of longing for a national reunion with the former mother country. Jay actually thought that "all foreign interference in our counsels [wa]s derogatory to the honour and dangerous to the best interests of the United States." "In my Opinion," Jay recorded early in his diplomatic career, "we should endeavor to be as Independent on the Charity of our friends, as on the Mercy of our Enemies." Along with Hamilton, Jay appreciated the virtues of patterning the American economy after the commercial empire of the British. Moreover, he saw that the financial integrity of the country, and its future economic development, could best be advanced by developing trade relations with the British.[47]

Still, Jay had no feeling that the British possessed a superior society, and he knew this from direct observation. Writing to his wife from London in 1783, Jay reflected that "I shall probably return to America fully persuaded that Europe collectively considered is far less estimable than America." Of the British, he commented: "This People is immersed in Pleasure, and yet very far from being happy." It also was true that Jay had little regard for the French, particularly after the execution of Louis XVI in 1793. "[The French] revolution did not give me pleasure," Jay wrote in 1796, inasmuch as it "has caused torrents of blood and of tears, and been marked in its progress by atrocities very injurious to the cause of liberty and offensive to morality and humanity." He lamented "the disastrous fate of a prince who (from whatever motives) had done us essential services, and to whom we had frequently presented the strongest assurances of our attachment and affection."[48]

Forming a nation on republican principles was an "[e]xperiment," Jay reminded the public, and he counseled that the people must "by Experience . . . discover and correct its Imperfections."[49] This dose of pragmatism in Jay's thinking tempered somewhat his tendency toward rigidity in ethical and legal judgments. Personally, he had long shown a willingness to be flexible in interpreting the strictures of his office. While on diplomatic assignments, for example, Jay readily exceeded the specific lines of his instructions when he thought it necessary in order to accomplish the overall objective.[50] Upon becoming Chief Justice, Jay exhibited a similar willingness to interpret his role in order to serve what he perceived to be the best interests of the nation.[51]

Chief Justice Jay's Extrajudicial Service to the Washington Administration

John Jay left a meager paper trail for later generations reconstructing his service to the Washington administration. The scarcity of documentation was not an accident. In an era when the mails could be leaky vessels, Jay warned that "letters by *ordinary conveyances* should contain nothing which in case of publication would produce inconveniences. Between friends slight hints are often intelligible, though not to be understood by others."[52] Few documents exist that provide an inside view of Jay's attitude about his role as

Chief Justice. Nevertheless, a fair amount of objective evidence allows a reasonably complete picture of Jay's thoughts concerning the propriety of extrajudicial service by judges to the executive.

In general, Jay regarded separation of powers as one of several areas of the Constitution that were in the process of formation, rather than already set as rigid doctrine. During his first grand jury address in 1790, Jay commented that among "[w]ise and virtuous men" there was unanimous agreement on the necessity for the division of powers "into three distinct, independent departments." Nevertheless, he continued, "how to constitute and ballance them in such a Manner as best to guard against Abuse and Fluctuation, & preserve the Constitution from Encroachments, are Points on which there continues to be a great Diversity of opinions, and on which we have all as yet much to learn."[53]

The one apparent guiding principle behind Jay's career with the federal government was that he considered it imperative for the executive and judiciary to work closely together in advancing the Federalist view of America's future. However strongly Jay may have asserted the necessity for a strict separation of powers, he evidently saw no incompatibility in a judge's providing advice to the executive branch or facilitating coordinated action by the two branches. Nor did he object to a judge's performing functions that were plainly executive in nature, even to the extent of holding a formal office in another branch. This view is not surprising; Jay had long advocated the joint participation of executive and judicial officers in a council of revision.[54]

Jay was comfortable with serving as Chief Justice while holding an office outside the judiciary—in fact, he simultaneously served as both Secretary of State and Chief Justice. Plainly this was a temporary arrangement founded on expediency: Jefferson would not arrive for some months to assume the office, and Jay was clearly the American figure most experienced in foreign affairs.[55] No disapproval was heard at the time over Jay's holding office concurrently in two branches of the federal government. By contrast, separation of powers would be the basis for Republican attacks on Jay in 1794 for remaining on the Court while negotiating the treaty with England that eventually would be known by the Chief Justice's name. Even within the administration, Edmund Randolph protested Jay's dual service, "because it was a bad precedent that a chief-justice should be taught to look up for *executive* honors, flowing from the head of it, while he retained his judicial seat."[56]

Under various statutes, the Chief Justice was officially assigned additional responsibilities in other departments. Thus Jay served as an inspector of the coins produced by the Mint—a relatively minor position, yet one that was essential to establish the value of the country's coins. Of considerably more importance was his designation as a commissioner of the Sinking Fund. Ostensibly set up to retire the public debt with surplus post office revenue, the fund actually was closely tied to Hamilton's plan for central management of the economy. Timely purchases of public securities with assets of the fund could operate to stabilize the market and thereby help the overall effort to establish public credit. For example, in the New York panic of March 1792, which was occasioned by William Duer's collapsing financial fortunes, the commissioners made such purchases to calm the market.[57]

Membership in both the group of coin inspectors and the commissioners of the Sinking Fund consisted by law of several principal cabinet officers, along with one other senior official and the Chief Justice. In Hamilton's report proposing a plan for the Mint, he explained that in England the Lord Chancellor took part in the process of inspecting coins to establish that they contained the requisite quantity of gold. With regard to the Sinking Fund, the British counterpart included a judicial officer, the Chancellor of the Exchequer. No controversy seems to have been sparked in the United States over the designation of a sitting member of the judiciary to serve in a similar capacity. Future conflicts over administration of the fund might have been anticipated given the substantial sums involved and the investment discretion afforded the commissioners. Indeed, controversy regarding management of the fund erupted within a short time after its creation as part of a broader attack on Hamilton's economic plans.[58]

Inclusion of the Chief Justice on these extrajudicial bodies likely was intended to enhance public confidence in their handling of the consequential business involved.[59] It should not be overlooked, however, that their composition was consistent with the process of executive governance in Washington's administration. That is, the critical affairs were entrusted to a small group of advisers. Asking Jay to do duty as an inspector or as a commissioner fell in line with the general way that he was employed within the administration. In part, his role was to provide authoritative legal advice. For example, when deciding to take action during the panic following Duer's financial ruin, the commissioners of the Sinking Fund were divided equally on the legality of their contemplated action. They requested that Jay (who was away on circuit assignment) come "as speedily as possible" to Philadelphia as his counsel was "indispensable" to resolving the legal questions. Jay declined the invitation, which would have interfered with his circuit court duties. Remarking that the issue involved appeared to be "a meer law Question," Jay instead promptly sent a written legal opinion, which apparently satisfied the commissioners.[60] Jay said in his letter to the other commissioners that while he regarded his "Duty to attend the Courts as being in point of legal Obligation *primary,* and to attend the Trustees as *secondary,*" he could "conceive that the Order would be sometimes inverted, if only the Importance of the occasion was considered."[61]

In the opening years of the Washington administration, Jay had been afforded a considerable voice in executive affairs of state. Until July 1790, when the capital moved from New York to Philadelphia, Jay joined with Madison, Hamilton, and Knox as Washington's main advisers. "To put it another way, Washington's principal advisers were his former general of artillery and Publius." Prior to March of that year, Jay's continuing work as Secretary of State accounted for much of his involvement with the cabinet. At the outset, Jay received a request from Washington for his written report of the business at the State Department in order to give him a "distinct *general idea* of the affairs of the United States, so far as they are comprehended in or connected with that Department." On such foreign relations, Washington would have "Secretary Jay prepare drafts which he reviewed and perhaps changed in small particulars." Consultations on other department matters also occurred, as when Jay was asked by Washington in February 1790 for advice on how to handle the case of an American sea captain being held by the Portuguese.[62]

Jefferson's assumption of the post of Secretary of State in March 1790 did not end Jay's association with the other cabinet officers on foreign policy, including the most sensitive of issues. A prime illustration occurred in July 1790, when Washington received a written report from Hamilton on the latter's discussions with Major George Beckwith, a British agent who had been dispatched to reconnoiter in America and establish informal relations with key Americans. Beckwith expressed to Hamilton the interest of Great Britain in having the United States join forces with it against Spain. Washington was skeptical of British intentions, and this feeling was reinforced by his conviction that they were evading existing treaty obligations with the United States. But he added: "However, I requested Mr. Jefferson & Colo. Hamilton, as I intend to do the Vice-President, Chief Justice & Secretary at War, to revolve this Matter in all its relations in their minds that they may be the better prepared to give me their opinions thereon in the course of 2 or three days."[63]

Jay was absent from New York City, so at Washington's direction Hamilton wrote to him, relating that the President had "a strong wish" for Jay to come to New York to consult on matters "of a delicate nature. . . . *They Press.*" A few days later, Washington recorded: "Had some further conversation to day with the Chief Justice and Secretary of the Treasury with respect to the business on which Majr. Beckwith was come on. The result—

To treat his communications very civilly—to intimate, delicately, that they carried no marks, official or authentic; nor, in speaking of Alliance, did they convey any definite meaning by which the precise objects of the British Cabinet could be discovered." Hamilton's contacts with Beckwith became regular, and the British agent sent his Foreign Office notes penned by Hamilton, Jay, and Washington. Because of the secrecy of these discussions, the leading actors were assigned code numbers. Jay was number 12.[64] From the British perspective, of course, the Chief Justice's active participation in foreign policy would not have seemed out of the ordinary, for they were accustomed to high-ranking jurists taking part in affairs of state (Mansfield's service was of recent memory).

The natural explanation for involving Jay at such moments was his indisputable expertise on foreign affairs. Nevertheless, the Chief Justice was often called on for his legal opinion in conjunction with his political judgment. Jay's experience as a common lawyer was rather slight, but he had acquired considerable knowledge of the law of nations. For the administration, abiding by the law of nations was indispensable—and not merely because of an abstract commitment to the rule of law. More important, it reflected the status of the United States as a weak nation with virtually no military and a struggling economy. If the international politics of the previous few centuries were any guide, the country could expect its fortunes to be tied to the struggles over the European balance of power, in which warfare was a traditional tool of territorial and commercial expansion. Given the professed desire of that generation of Americans to avoid such international entanglements, it was critical to obey international law: violation of the law of nations might give another nation just cause for declaring war. A principal reason for holding the Philadelphia Convention centered on concern that individual states were risking war with their transgressions of the law of nations.[65]

The first real international crisis to command the administration's attention came in 1790 when war appeared imminent between Great Britain and Spain. This episode arose when the Spanish captured two British trading vessels on Nootka Sound in the Pacific Northwest, allegedly for violating Spain's treaty rights to the area. Washington was convinced that the British would use the incident as a pretext to seize New Orleans and the Spanish posts on the Mississippi. If successful, this would place "the British on both our flanks and rear, with their navy in front," with consequences "too obvious to need enumeration," Washington wrote to Jefferson, Hamilton, Knox, Vice President Adams, and Jay. Washington anticipated that the British attack would originate from Detroit and proceed down the Mississippi; it either would be preceded by a formal request for permission to traverse American territory, or would happen without leave. Washington wanted advice on how to answer an application from the British, as well as counsel on what course to take should the British advance without permission.[66]

As did the other recipients of Washington's request, Jay responded promptly with a written opinion. With the exception of Adams's statement, all of them included discussions of the law of nations, including citations to treatise writers and recitations of established principles. These opinions did not, however, rest entirely on their legal conclusions. Instead, the authors blended their treatment of international law with a candid assessment of the Realpolitik surrounding the episode. Jay cautioned, for example, that although Washington probably would have grounds under the law of nations to refuse the British request, "it will be adviseable to calculate the Probability of their being restrained by such a Refusal." Taking the hypothesis that the British would cross American territory even in the face of a refusal, Jay pointed out that this would leave the country with two unattractive alternatives: "opposing their Progress by Force of arms, and thereby risque being involved in the War; or of submitting to the Disgrace and Humiliation of permitting them to proceed with Impunity." Considering the alternatives, Jay thought it better to consent if asked—provided Washington thought it likely that the British would ignore an American rebuff. Jay himself did not venture an answer on this question of probabilities. He did suggest that Washington consider how Europe would react if the British took "Possession of the Floridas," which required an assessment of whether the continental powers would regard this event as upsetting their "Idea of preserving a Ballance of Power."[67]

On several of the occasions that Washington sought Jay's legal advice, the subject related to the President's powers under the Constitution. A typical instance occurred in February 1790, when Washington was deliberating over whether to commission someone to negotiate with the Creek Nation for the purpose of averting war. Considering the expense involved in treating with the Creeks, Washington thought that there was a doubt about the *"Powers of the President,"* and he contemplated whether he should make the appointment "without laying the matter before the Senate." Washington ordered Knox, the Secretary of War, "to take the opinion of the Chief Justice of the United States and that of the Secretary of the Treasury on these points and let me know the result." A similar situation transpired in April of the same year, when Washington wanted to know whether it was the prerogative of the President or the Senate to prescribe the accreditation rank of diplomatic officers; another question was whether the Senate selected the place where the officer would be stationed. Jefferson gave his written opinion to the effect that the President had a right to determine these questions and that the Senate could only reject or approve the person named. Washington's diary notes indicate that he had discussed this question with Madison, and that Madison's "opinion coincides with Mr. Jays and Mr. Jeffersons."[68]

Prior to the opening of Congress in December 1790, Washington wrote to Jay seeking his ideas for matters to bring up in the coming session: "If any thing in the Judiciary line, if any thing of a more general nature, proper for me to communicate to that Body at the opening of the session, has occurred to you, you would oblige me by submitting them with the freedom and frankness of friendship." As if anticipating Washington's wish, Jay had six days earlier drafted a letter to the President that contained a number of suggestions for legislative revisions. Some of these appear to be answers to specific questions, for example, whether Congress could outlaw counterfeiting of foreign coins. Others were comments on policy issues, such as recommendations for the establishment of military posts, preservation of timber masts, creation of a uniform inspection system for meat exports, and so on. After receiving Washington's solicitation in the mail, Jay quickly wrote back that he had taken "the Liberty of suggesting some Hints on Subjects of wh. a few appeared to me, to merit, *present,* and others *future* Regard."[69]

Washington returned to Jay for help a year later in preparing for the December congressional session, asking that "your ideas . . . not be confined to matters merely Judicial, but extended to all other topics which have, or may occur to you as fit subjects." As requested, Jay's response covered a wide range of topics, many of which were unrelated to the judiciary. In 1793, Jay became actively involved in the administration's formulation and execution of a neutrality policy. That subject will be taken up at length in the next chapter, as it relates directly to the Justices' refusal to answer Washington's questions during the summer of 1793 concerning the impact of the law of nations on American neutrality. It should be added that Jay's mission to negotiate a treaty with the British, while not strictly speaking an advisory function, evidences Jay's willingness to play a major role in carrying out the executive's responsibilities.[70]

Jay and Washington's relationship was such that the Chief Justice showed no hesitation in advising the administration on any of a number of topics, whether legal or not. By 1790, Jay felt comfortable proffering advice without a specific request. Undoubtedly, the ease with which the two related was a product of their long and cordial association. Each made a point of professing his cordial feelings for the other. Washington closed one letter in which he sought Jay's counsel by writing that "[t]o add assurances of my regard and friendship would not be new, but, with truth, I can declare etc." Jay, in return, told Washington that he "rejoice[d] in opportunities of manifesting" his "attention" to Washington's invitation for candid advice. Of the two, Jay was the more effusive in praising Washington, to the point where he became involved in a project to erect a monument—at public expense—honoring Washington and the Revolution. He was moved to do so, Jay explained, by "the effect which this measure would naturally have on the President's feelings. . . . It is only while he lives that we can have the satisfaction of offering fruits of gratitude and affection to his enjoyment; posterity can have only the expensive pleasure of strewing flowers on his grave."[71]

With such strong sentiments expressed, it may seem odd that the number of times Jay advised Washington declined significantly after 1790. There is no indication that this reflected a diminution in Jay's feelings for either Washington or the administration's programs. To the contrary, Jay remained an enthusiastic promoter of the Federalist cause throughout Washington's tenure. After the government was moved from New York to Philadelphia in 1790, "Jay seldom visited it without a long conference with the President."[72]

Some have speculated that the administration called on Jay less frequently after he became the Chief Justice because there was concern that he might be asked to give advice about matters that could come before him in litigated cases.[73] But this supposition is contradicted by the record. The administration turned to Jay for counsel a number of times after he went on the bench, and no evidence suggests that either Washington or his cabinet hesitated in seeking his advice. The best indication of this is the incident mentioned in the introduction to this book, when the administration asked Jay and the other members of the Court to answer the series of questions in the summer of 1793. Jay's rebuff of that approach remains to be explored, but there is no suggestion that he personally saw any difficulty in continuing to play an advisory role (as opposed to the Court's doing so). And many of the issues Jay gave opinions on were ones that might become the subjects of litigation. As it happens, the Jay Treaty itself involved questions that could be brought within the Court's jurisdiction.[74]

A much more prosaic explanation can be found for Jay's diminished role as an adviser to the executive after 1790: he was no longer resident in the capital, which had moved to Philadelphia, and much of his year was spent on the exhausting circuit rides away from his family and friends. The twice-yearly Supreme Court sessions in Philadelphia afforded some opportunity to confer directly with members of the administration, but the sessions in these early years lasted only a few days or weeks. It goes almost without saying that communications were such that Jay and the other members of the Court could not have been involved in the policy discussions that took place in cabinet meetings. At the most, the Justices might be called upon in circumstances that presented unusually significant issues.[75]

The Collaboration of John Jay and Alexander Hamilton

Jay and Alexander Hamilton established a warm personal association during the Revolution, and their friendship endured until Hamilton's death. Their political perspectives were closely aligned, and often they worked together to achieve public objectives, as is illustrated by their collaboration on the *Federalist Papers*. At the New York ratifying convention, Jay and Hamilton, along with Chancellor Livingston, were the principal speakers for the Federalists. Each promoted the other man's career at a number of turns. Hamilton nominated Jay as an additional delegate to the federal Constitutional Convention from New York, although his motion lost.[76] It was Hamilton who urged Washington to appoint Jay as envoy to England in 1794.[77] During 1795 Hamilton managed the Federalist campaign for New York state offices, which resulted in Jay's election as governor.[78] Governor Jay offered to appoint Hamilton as Senator from New York in 1798.[79]

During the Washington administration, Hamilton continually turned to Jay for advice. In November 1790, for example, Hamilton wrote to Jay regarding resolutions, passed by the Virginia House of Delegates under the influence of Patrick Henry, that condemned Hamilton's plan for assumption of state debts. "This is the first symptom of a spirit which must either be killed or will kill the constitution of the United States," Hamilton asserted. "I send the resolutions to you that it may be considered what ought to be done. Ought not the collective weight of the different parts of the Government to be employed in exploding the principles they contain?" Jay responded by calmly suggesting to let it pass: "To treat them as very important might render them more so than I think they are." Jay then relayed some political intelligence and offered several suggestions regarding pending policy questions unrelated to the judiciary.[80]

In the summer of 1791 in western Pennsylvania, the first stirring of resistance to the collection of the federal excise tax on distilled spirits began. The opposition escalated during the ensuing year. Distillers who complied with the tax felt the force of public intimidation, a collector was tarred and feathered, and an arson threat resulted in the closing of a house designated for use as a collection office. Protest meetings were held in the dissenting counties to denounce the Excise Act and Hamilton's general economic policies. The Secretary of the Treasury, along with many others in the administration, was greatly aroused by these acts of noncompliance. Hamilton became especially concerned about the results of a meeting in Pittsburgh in late August. Participants agreed to organize committees of correspondence, to "withhold all the comforts of life" from collectors and "treat them with that contempt they deserve." They also resolved "to persist in our remonstrances to Congress, and in every other legal measure that may obstruct the operation of the Law, until we are able to obtain its total repeal."[81]

In early September, Hamilton wrote to Jay, asking his views on the turmoil, with a particular focus on these resolutions, a copy of which he enclosed. "You will observe," Hamilton pointed out, "an avowed object is to—'*obstruct* the *operation* of the law.' This is attempted to be qualified by a pretence of doing it by 'every legal measure.' But [the qualifier] is a contradiction in terms. I therefore entertain no doubt, that a high misdemeanor has been committed." Specifically, Hamilton wanted to know from Jay if the circuit court scheduled to meet at York on October 11 should be "noticing the state of things." He further asked whether the President should issue a proclamation stating the criminality of the proceedings and warning of prosecutions. Planning ahead, Hamilton queried: "[i]f the plot should thicken and the application of force should appear to be unavoidable, will it be expedient for the President to repair in person to the scene of commotion?" Jay was urged to consult with Senator Rufus King, as "[h]is judgment is sound he has caution and energy." Hamilton also wrote to Washington that day to outline his responses to the crisis, but he did not mention that he was consulting Jay.[82]

Jay responded to Hamilton within a week, indicating that he had conferred with King. Through Jay's letter, the two counseled a prudent course, concurring that "neither a Proclamation nor a *particular* Charge by the Court to the G. Jury would be adviseable at present." Instead, they suggested that the matter be broached first in Washington's speech opening the next session of Congress in early November. On the advisability of "strong Declarations," Jay said that they should not be made unless there is "ability & Disposition to follow them with strong measures," but that "it is questionable whether such operations at this Moment would not furnish the antis with Materials for decieving the uninformed part of ye. Community, and in some measure render the operations of administration odious." One line in this letter succinctly summarized the Chief Justice's view that there was no contradiction between separation of powers and cooperation among the branches in achieving national objectives: "Let all the Branches of Govt. move together, and let the chiefs be committed publickly on one or the other Side of the Question."[83]

Before Jay's letter reached Philadelphia, Washington decided to follow the recommendation of Hamilton (who had conferred with Knox and Randolph) to issue a proclamation denouncing "all unlawful combinations and proceedings whatsoever having for object or tending to obstruct the operation of the laws." Subsequently, Washington did take the step of including the issue in his address to Congress on November 6. Widespread resistance to the excise tax in western Pennsylvania and elsewhere continued, as the Whiskey Rebellion of 1794 demonstrates. Moreover, the federal courts would be dragged into the controversy, a matter that will be explored later.[84]

Jay wrote to Hamilton twice during November and December 1792 in regard to Congress's consideration of revamping the judiciary system. Excusing himself for not answering either letter earlier, Hamilton laid the blame on the burdens of his work, but lamented that the worst distraction was the multiple attacks he had been enduring from Congress, the press, and Jefferson: "[T]he malicious intrigues to stab me in the dark, against which I am too often obliged to guard myself, that distract and harass me to a point, which rendering my situation scarcely tolerable interferes with objects to which friendship & inclination would prompt me." On the subject of the judiciary, Hamilton reported that "[n]othing material has happened since" the Senate appointed a committee to consider the issue.[85]

Jay answered with soothing words: "The Thorns they strew in your way, will (if you please) hereafter blossom, and furnish Garlands to decorate your administration." Urging perseverance, Jay implored him "not to be driven from your Station; & as your Situation must it seems be militant, act accordingly." Concluding, Jay turned to the recent victory of John Adams over George Clinton for the vice presidency: "I rejoice with you in the Re-Election of Mr. adams—it has relieved my mind from much Inquietude—it is a great Point gained, but the unceasing Industry and arts of the Anti's, render Perseverance, union, and constant Efforts necessary."[86]

Shortly after this exchange took place, the country was thrust into the midst of an international crisis precipitated by the outbreak of war in Europe. During 1793 Jay and Hamilton would work closely on formulating and enforcing the administration's response. The series of events that transpired led directly to the request for advice from the Supreme Court. Before we turn to that subject, one remaining topic needs to be addressed: the extrajudicial activities of other Justices and federal judges in this period.

EXTRAJUDICIAL ACTIVITIES OF JUSTICES AND FEDERAL JUDGES
DURING THE WASHINGTON ADMINISTRATIONS

The Partisanship of Federal Judges

"Washington chose his judges carefully. . . . [A]ll those he appointed were ardent supporters of the national government and the powers it derived from the federal Constitution." Considered in the aggregate, they had far more experience as political operatives than as judges. Gordon Wood has pointed out that "[o]f the twenty-eight men who sat on the federal district courts in the 1790s only eight had held high judicial office in their states; but nearly all of them had been prominent political figures, having served in notable state offices and in the Continental Congress." Washington expected that they would form the "department which must be considered as the Key-stone of our political fabric," and he was not far off the mark.[87]

The federal judiciary figured prominently in the political struggles of the 1790s: "the first federal judiciary was deeply compromised, both responsive and submissive to the needs and demands of the ruling Federalist party." Federal courtrooms promoted national economic policies by serving as fo-rums for debt collection. This function was particularly important with re-spect to claims by British creditors, because the failure of state judicial enforcement persisted as a major irritant to Anglo-American relations. The Supreme Court advanced this effort by interpreting the terms of the treaty with Great Britain against state efforts to relieve debtors. An action for debt was also the occasion for the best-known case of the 1790s, *Chisholm v. Georgia,* in which the Court trumped state autonomy with federal sover-eignty. Likewise, federal courts provided the underpinning for the revenue laws, through both prosecution of tax evaders and uncompromising punish-ment of the Whiskey rebels. In the first court case testing the constitution-ality of a federal law, the Court upheld the national assessment on carriages against the attack that it constituted an invalid direct tax under Article 1.[88] When the Washington administration decided in 1793 on a policy of strict neutrality in the ongoing war among the European powers, the federal courts played a substantial role in the enforcement effort. During the Adams administration, the federal courts tried dissenters under the common law crime of sedition and under the Sedition Act of 1798: "all but one of the leading opposition papers were prosecuted."[89]

Throughout the 1790s, the Justices roamed the country to conduct circuit sessions, and following the model of their British counterparts, they used grand jury charges—reprinted widely in newspapers—to explain and defend national policies. At first these charges were mild civic lessons on the nature of the new government and its laws, and on the responsibilities of citizens in the new federal order. As the 1790s unfolded, however, and the Federal-ists increasingly were the subject of harsh attacks from opposition groups, the charges "became more specifically political rather than general, more emphatic in their warnings of danger to the new republic from abroad and from enemies within." Typifying this tone, Justice Cushing denounced "the

clamors of faction, the unaccountable rage of PRETENDED PATRIOTS to subvert the government and general interest of this country, by subjugating all
to the political will and pleasure [of] a foreign ONE; slandering all REAL
PATRIOTS with whom the constitution and the people have entrusted the
management of their affairs."[90]

Extrajudicial Contacts with the Administration and Congress

Owing to their personal backgrounds, federal judges in the 1790s were well
connected with the political elite, and they regularly exchanged correspondence with political figures on a variety of topics. Not infrequently, the
judges conveyed political intelligence gained during circuit rides or at home.
Justice Iredell, for example, carried on a chatty political dialogue over the
years with his brother-in-law, Senator Samuel Johnston, which included
informally lobbying the Senator for reforms in the circuit riding system.[91]
Similarly, Federal District Judge Henry Marchant of Rhode Island kept in
contact with both Hamilton and Washington, and with members of Congress. Hamilton, for example, asked Marchant to suggest names of candidates to fill a vacant U.S. Attorney's post in his state. Marchant responded
with a lengthy list of possible candidates, accompanied by commentary
replete with references to political ramifications.[92]

Most of the federal judiciary resided at a distance from the capital, which
precluded regular direct contacts with national leaders. Not surprisingly, then,
it appears that the bulk of formal contacts between federal judges and either
the administration or Congress occurred in the form of written pleas for
legislative action of interest to the courts. The outstanding instance of this
was the Justices' effort to convince Congress to overhaul the circuit riding
system. Almost from the beginning, the Justices complained, at times bitterly,
about the provision in the Judiciary Act of 1789 that required them to participate in twice-yearly circuit courts held in the three judicial circuits.[93]

All the Justices had a standing request from Washington to provide him
with information they obtained while riding circuits. At the commencement
of the first circuit assignments in 1790, Washington wrote to each of them,
introducing the subject by saying that "the stability and success of the national Government . . . would depend in a considerable degree on the Interpretation and Execution of its Laws," and that "therefore, it is important,
that the Judiciary System should not only be independent in its operations,
but as perfect as possible in its formation." Remarking that "many things
may occur in such an unexplored field" during the circuit tours, Washington
came to the point of his letter: "I think it proper to acquaint you, that it will
be agreeable to me to receive such Information and Remarks on this Sub-

ject, as you shall from time to time judge expedient to communicate."[94] As with Washington's formation of a cabinet, the practice of judges' providing the executive with information learned while on circuit duty paralleled the way British judges gathered intelligence for the Crown from Assize sittings.

At the August 1790 session of the Court, the Justices concurred on the general lines of a letter that Jay was to write on their behalf to the President. Jay did so, and circulated the draft among the Justices. The thrust of the letter was that the provision in the Judiciary Act of 1789 requiring circuit riding by Justices was unconstitutional, the implication being that Washington should ask Congress to cure this defect. It is unclear whether a final version of this letter was sent to the President.[95] Nonetheless, it is apparent that the Justices' concerns about circuit riding were communicated in one way or another to Congress. During the session of the Court in which the Justices agreed to write to Washington, Congress resolved to require the Attorney General to report at the next session about whether the judicial system needed modifications. Randolph immediately requested assistance from Justice James Wilson, with whom he had served on the Committee of Detail at the Convention. In his resulting report to Congress the following December, Randolph recommended abolition of circuit riding, but Congress did not act on his proposal.[96]

By 1792 the Justices were desperate to eliminate their circuit assignments. As a group they signed a letter of protest to Washington: "[W]e cannot reconcile ourselves to the idea of existing in exile from our families, and of being subjected to a kind of life, on which we cannot reflect, without experiencing sensations and emotions, more easy to conceive than proper for us to express." They appended a letter of remonstrance, addressed to Congress, and requested that Washington lay it before that body for consideration, which he did. While Congress was considering this matter, Jay wrote to Justice William Cushing: "I have heard that some Members of Congress doubt the Expediency of adopting our Plan—You will have many opportunities of conversing with them on the Subject, and I flatter myself it will be in your power to remove their Objections."[97]

Justice Cushing thought that there was "a favorable prospect of a radical alteration of the present Itinerant System for the better." His political prognostication proved false, as Congress provided only partial relief in 1793. Consequently, the Justices wrote Washington again in 1794 with a request similar to the first one; Washington sent their enclosed letter to Congress. No relief was given, however, until the Judiciary Act of 1801—which abolished circuit riding temporarily, until the Act was repealed the following year when the Republicans gained control of Congress in the first year of Jefferson's administration.[98]

The Justices also employed Washington as an intermediary to make other suggestions for reforms in the judicial process. For example, Justice Iredell wrote Washington in 1792, and after making specific reference to the President's letter two years earlier, proceeded to detail two procedural problems that the circuit courts had encountered that required legislative revisions. Iredell mentioned that he regarded his contact with Washington as "not only proper for a single Judge, but his express duty when he deems it of importance to the public service." At a subsequent cabinet meeting, Washington brought up Iredell's concerns; the Justice's views were forwarded to Congress, which enacted legislation dealing with the questions raised. On other occasions, individual Justices worked directly with friendly members of Congress to achieve legislative action.[99]

Extrajudicial Duties

By statute, a number of extrajudicial responsibilities were assigned to the federal courts. Typically, these statutory schemes employed judges on account of their presumed expertise at determining facts. For example, a 1792 enactment required district judges to make arrangements for salvaging French vessels. Under another law, judges investigated contested congressional elections, reporting their findings to Congress, which in turn resolved the dispute. A similar reporting arrangement was contained in a 1790 law providing that judges would hear petitions for remission of customs fines; their factual conclusions were sent to the Secretary of the Treasury for final administrative disposition. Congress also gave federal judges the task of ascertaining—in a nonadversarial proceeding—whether immigrants met the standards for naturalization, including the requirement that the applicant possess "good moral character."[100]

At times, these statutory arrangements could require the judges to decide controversial questions. One illustration is the Militia Act of 1792, which authorized the President to summon the militia only if a federal district judge or Justice certified that laws of the United States were being opposed "by combinations too powerful to be suppressed by the ordinary course of judicial proceedings, or by the powers vested in the marchals by this act." At the outbreak of the Whiskey Rebellion in 1794, Justice Wilson was asked to review various documents concerning the insurrection in order to determine whether such a certificate should be issued. The issue was hotly contested by state officials, including the Chief Justice of Pennsylvania, Republican Thomas McKean, who believed "that the [state] judiciary power was equal to the task of quelling and punishing the riots, and that the employment of a military force, at this period, would be as bad as anything that the Rioters had done—equally unconstitutional and illegal." Edmund Randolph, now Secretary of State, wrote that the evidence was not sufficient to justify certification inasmuch as "the certificate specifies no particular law, which has been opposed." "This defect I remarked to Judge Wilson," Randolph reported, although Wilson went ahead and signed the necessary authorization. After peace negotiations failed, the administration dispatched thousands of troops to western Pennsylvania, where they encountered no organized resistance but did arrest a number of participants in the uprising.[101]

A determination of the sort made by Wilson under the Militia Act involved a question that could very well be at issue in a subsequent judicial proceeding. Twenty-four persons were accused of treason in the affair, ten were brought to trial, and two were convicted. Justice Paterson's charges to the grand jury and to the trial jury defined treason as encompassing those "who by numbers and open force *in a violent and forcible manner* resist and prevent the *regular administration of justice,* and due execution of the laws." Wilson's earlier certification at least implied that treasonous activities were transpiring through a conspiracy that was beyond the judiciary's ability to control.[102]

The Invalid Pension Cases

Congress enacted a measure in 1792 to provide relief for veterans who were disabled as a result of service during the Revolution. Under the Invalid Pension Act of 1792, applicants were to petition the circuit court in the district of their residence with proof that they met the terms of the statute. After an appropriate fact-finding inquiry, the court would inform the Secretary of War of its recommendation. In turn, the Secretary could withhold the pension if "the said Secretary shall have cause to suspect imposition or mistake," in which case the matter would be reported to Congress. The Act further mandated that the circuit court remain open "five days at the least from the time of the opening the sessions," so that the petitioners "may have full opportunity to make their application for the relief proposed by this act."[103]

This new responsibility for the Justices—added to the existing burdens of circuit riding—was poorly received, to say the least. Justice Iredell lamented to his wife: "The Invalid-business has scarcely allowed me one moment's time, and now I am engaged in it by candle-light, though to go at three in the morning."[104]

In April 1792 Justices Jay, Cushing, Wilson, and Blair, along with two prominent federal district judges (James Duane and Richard Peters) sitting with the Justices in two separate circuits, wrote the President to protest their new duties under the pension law. Justice Iredell and District Judge John

Sitgreaves did the same in June. The writings were so similar that some discussion about their contents must have occurred among the Justices. Essentially, the Justices contended that their assignments under the Pension Act violated constitutional principles of separation of powers. According to Jay, Wilson, and Duane, "neither the *legislative* nor the *executive* branch can constitutionally assign to the *judicial* any duties but such as are properly judicial, and to be performed in a judicial manner." In their view, these assignments were extrajudicial because any judgments they reached would be subject to revision by both the Secretary of War and Congress. A separate reason was stated ambiguously, namely, that the tasks assigned to the judges under the pension law were not of a judicial nature. This second point, however, was not developed in the letter—it is unclear why the judges thought that the fact-finding tasks assigned to them under the Pension Act diverged either from customary judicial responsibilities or from their other extrajudicial duties under the various statutes mentioned above.[105]

In spite of their reservations about proceeding with pension cases while sitting as a court, Jay, Cushing, and Duane nevertheless declared that they were willing to act as commissioners for purposes of executing the pension law, and would carry out this business "in the same court room, or chamber" as the circuit court. Iredell and Sitgreaves voiced reservations about whether the statute authorized them to proceed "personally in the character of commissioners during the session of a court," but Iredell put these doubts aside and performed the work. In contrast, Wilson, Blair, and Peters declined to examine pension applications in the Circuit Court for the District of Pennsylvania. Their opinion was the only one of the three that arose from a pension application; the other two gave their views despite the lack of any pending case.[106]

The proceeding involving Wilson, Blair, and Peters became known as Hayburn's Case. It represented the first occasion that a federal court declared an act of Congress unconstitutional, and this development was noted contemporaneously in Congress and elsewhere. The case could have afforded the Supreme Court an opportunity to decide the constitutionality of the pension law, along with the fundamental question of whether the Court possessed the power of judicial review over congressional enactments. However, before the Court could decide these issues, Congress amended the Pension Act by eliminating the role of circuit courts.[107]

Notwithstanding the absence of an authoritative ruling by the Supreme Court, it is clear that the Justices refused on constitutional grounds to make deliberative judgments that would be subject to reversal by the other branches. At the same time, a significant number of them were amenable to adopting the guise of "commissioners" and thereby performing what they considered to be a nonjudicial function in their own courtrooms. Furthermore, they were willing to express their views on these matters not only in the context of an actual pension application but even without a pending case, through the route of extrajudicial letters of opinion to the President. Moreover, it was obvious that concrete cases would soon arise to present the identical issue. As modern commentators have pointed out, "[t]he letters were, in the most classic sense, advisory opinions."[108]

Of the three groups who wrote letters to Washington, only Iredell and Sitgreaves broached the question "as to the propriety of giving an opinion in a case which has not yet come regularly and judicially before us." After raising this doubt, they proceeded to justify their action:

> None can be more sensible than we are of the necessity of judges being, in general, extremely cautious in not intimating an opinion, in any case extra-judicially, because we well know how liable the best minds are, notwithstanding their utmost care, to a bias which may arise from a preconceived opinion, even unguardedly, much more, deliberately, given. But in the present instance, as many unfortunate and meritorious individuals, whom Congress have justly thought proper objects of immediate relief, may suffer great distress even by a short delay, and may be utterly ruined by a long one, we determined at all events, to make our sentiments known as early as possible, considering this as a case which must be deemed an exception to the general rule upon every principle of humanity and justice.[109]

Plainly, their doubts on the wisdom of volunteering an extrajudicial opinion did not rise to the level of a constitutional objection. Iredell and Sitgreaves's letter limited the proper occasions for extrajudicial opinions to unusual situations. In doing so they restated the common understanding of British judges and commentators about the limitations on advisory opinions. As had their British counterparts, the Justices left an escape for themselves, by reserving the right to change their view "in case an application should be made, . . . and if we can be convinced this opinion is a wrong one."[110]

Ironically, the resolution of the Invalid Pension Act issue in the 1790s has been interpreted by the modern Supreme Court as part of the foundation for the requirement that federal courts proceed only in live "cases or controversies." Among other things, this has come to mean that the federal judiciary may not issue advisory opinions. An additional irony is that the Justices would, only a little more than one year later, refuse to give an advisory opinion when the Washington administration requested it under urgent circumstances.[111]

Another oddity with respect to the Pension Act issue is that Justices Jay,

Cushing, and Iredell could have waited to decide the question in the context of a real pension application. Why did the Justices act in such haste? Perhaps the most obvious answer is that they apparently were not convinced that there was any constitutional bar to rendering an extrajudicial opinion on the subject. Nor did they see a contradiction in refusing to proceed as circuit courts to handle the Pension Act applications—this position, after all, derived from their view that the work was not judicial in nature. Iredell and Sitgreaves did think that advisory opinions should be rendered only in compelling circumstances. But what was so compelling about this situation, when an actual case surely could have been anticipated?

The answer is provided partially in the opinions themselves. As Iredell and Sitgreaves reflected, even "a short delay" could have "utterly ruined" some of the applicants. Pension applicants often appeared before them in desperate circumstances. One newspaper described a session involving a pension applicant: "To see the lame and emaciated, war-torn soldier, the decrepit and almost naked seaman the best years of whose life had been spent in the service of his country, humbly supplicating the scanty morsel to save him from perishing was a sight which affected every benevolent and generous heart present. . . . But the attention of the Hon. Judges was commensurate with the necessities of the wretches who applied." In a similar vein, the *National Gazette* warned that "[o]ur poor, starving invalids have at length some provision made for them by Congress; and as the distress of many of them are urgent in the extreme, it is to be hoped that not a moment's delay will be made by the public officers who are directed to settle their accounts."[112]

Those Justices who refused to proceed even as commissioners stated pointedly that their objections might be cured by appropriate legislative action. Alerting the President about their rulings could hasten the process of producing remedial legislation, and in fact Washington promptly forwarded the letters to Congress. Writing directly to Washington himself may have seemed essential given the President's obvious interest in the welfare of his former troops.

The Justices undoubtedly could perceive that turning away the pension applicants would provoke rebuke from the Congress and the public. Censure did come, although interestingly enough, mostly from Federalists. A leading Federalist, Rep. Fisher Ames of Massachusetts, wrote from Philadelphia: "The decision of the Judges, on the validity of our pension law, is generally censured as indiscreet and erroneous. At best, our business is up hill, and with the aid of our law courts the authority of Congress is barely adequate to keep the machine moving; but when they condemn the law as invalid, they embolden the States and their courts to make many claims of power, which otherwise they would not have thought of."[113]

Calls for impeachment of the noncomplying judges soon were heard, as a Republican organ, the *General Advertiser*, noticed with astonishment: "The high-fliers in and out of Congress, and the very humblest of their humble retainers, talk of nothing but impeachment! impeachment! impeachment! As if, forsooth, Congress were wrapped up in the cloak of infallibility which has been torn from the shoulders of the Pope; and that it was damnable heresy . . . to doubt the constitutional orthodoxy of any decision of theirs." Opposition Republicans generally commended the judges for asserting the power to declare an act of Congress unconstitutional, and urged them to do likewise with other federal programs, such as the national bank. Although the impeachment stirrings bore no results, they did mark "the first time the justices found themselves in the middle of public controversy."[114]

The Justices did have other concerns involving congressional relations that could have prompted their advisory commentary. During the same period that the Pension Act events were transpiring, several Justices "entertained high hopes that Congress would soon lift their burdensome circuit duties." Yet on April 13, 1792, only three weeks after passage of the pension law, Congress enacted the Circuit Court Act of 1792. The new law mandated rotation of circuit court assignments among the Justices, assuring that all would take a turn on the strenuous Southern Circuit, a duty that most had avoided previously. This measure might have been styled the "James Iredell Relief Act," in that it resulted from his indignant complaint over being assigned permanently the Southern Circuit.[115]

Far from resolving the Justices' objections to circuit riding, the Act of 1792 worsened the lives of most of them. Adding insult to injury, the Invalid Pension Act contained a statutory mandate for the circuit courts to remain open "five days at the least" during each session for the purpose of processing claims. At the same time, the Pension Act must have seemed a poor precedent to the Justices. If this law was constitutional, Congress could design any number of other programs to be administered by federal judges at ever-lengthening circuit sessions. By insisting that judicial decisions could not be subject to review by the other branches, the Justices set an important limit on Congress's ability to treat the courts as if they were executive agencies. They also underscored that their extrajudicial service could only be requested, not commanded—federal judges were "at liberty to accept or decline that office."[116]

At the next meeting of the Supreme Court, in August 1792, the Justices signed the previously mentioned letter to Washington complaining about the circuit court system and asking him to bring the matter to Congress's attention. This was not, therefore, the best time to offend Congress. Two of the Justices' statements on the pension law praised the good intentions underlying the relief measure. According to Jay, Cushing, and Duane, for example, "the objects of this act are exceedingly benevolent, and do real honor to the humanity and justice of Congress," and the judges would thus proceed in the capacity of commissioners in order "to manifest . . . in every proper manner their high respect for the national Legislature."[117]

Jay had a personal reason for avoiding criticism over the pension law. Somewhat more than a month before his action on the pensions, the Chief Justice agreed to accept the nomination as the Federalist candidate in the New York gubernatorial election. Although Jay refused to campaign on his own behalf, others were actively doing so for him, and the newspapers regularly printed commentary on the candidates.[118]

Chapter 3 explored the challenges posed to the delegates at the Philadelphia Convention by the lack of a model or precedent for a form of government that would be at once republican and federalist. Nevertheless, certain propositions generally were accepted that relate to the themes in this book. To start with, it would be impossible to duplicate the British constitutional system, whose cornerstone was the achievement of a balance among the leading social classes in the nation. Americans liked the idea of balanced government, but in the United States there existed neither a hereditary aristocracy nor any serious prospect for creating a monarchy. An additional point of agreement was that separation of powers must be integrated into the fundamental structure of the constitution. Whatever separation of powers meant, it did not involve setting up another version of the British political system, in which the executive could dominate the other branches. For all this antipathy toward the British form of government, however, the delegates often found lessons and guides in the political order of their ancestors. Delegates appreciated the virtues of such features of the British constitution as judicial independence. And they incorporated many of these in the Constitution—lifetime tenure for judges being a prime example.

When the initial federal government took shape under President Washington, the essential features of its operations were patterned along British lines. Throughout this chapter, examples have proved this point: the cabinet system, Hamilton's financial plan, a strong role for the executive in foreign affairs, and the use of the Chief Justice as an adviser to the executive. Congress contributed toward this emulation of British ways through a variety of laws, not the least of which were those implementing Hamilton's economic proposals and the overall plan of the national administration. Similarly, Congress adapted British practices in organizing the judiciary. Circuit riding, for example, bore more than a casual resemblance to the Assizes. As in Great Britain, judges were placed on commissions and assigned administrative responsibilities. For its part, the judiciary relied heavily on British traditions to guide almost every aspect of the court system. While on their circuits, judges delivered circuit grand jury charges laced with civics lessons and partisan declarations; these same judges saw no problem with passing along political news and policy recommendations to the other branches. Most were willing to accept administrative responsibilities as "commissioners." When the Supreme Court finally began to hear cases in 1792, Chief Justice Jay ordered that "the practice of this Court" would follow "the practice of the Courts of Kings Bench and of Chancery in England."[119] Certainly this made sense, considering that the substantive law used by the Court—all American courts, for that matter—depended heavily on British law.

Given the many ways the British legal system became replicated in the new federal judiciary, what remains to be explained is why the Supreme Court declined to assist the Washington administration. Unlike some aspects of British constitutional theory that had been rejected by the Framers, an advisory relationship of the type sought by Washington in 1793 was not inconsistent with the text of the Constitution or the views of the Philadelphia Convention. To understand why the Justices seemingly turned away from this aspect of their British legal heritage, a thorough investigation of the events leading to the refusal must be undertaken.

5

Declining Washington's Request:
The Events of 1793

In April 1793, Washington wrote to a British correspondent: "I believe it is the sincere wish of United America to have nothing to do with the political intrigues, or the squabbles of European Nations; but on the contrary, to exchange commodities and live in peace and amity with all the inhabitants of the Earth." Despite the professed desire of the American leadership during the early 1790s to remain aloof from the political affairs and military conflicts of Europe, the hard fact was that potentially hostile powers encircled the country: the British in Canada, and the Spanish in Louisiana and the Floridas. For European powers, the American continent since colonial days had been a piece in the geopolitical web that formed the international balance of power. "Territories changed hands thanks to wily schemes and skillful intrigues." American territories were both the object of imperial aspirations and the scene of armed conflicts throughout the century. It would have been folly for Americans to assume that the Revolution had changed this reality—rather, it was one more event in the continual reshuffling of power.[1]

The diplomatic climate with Britain remained frosty owing to a number of unresolved issues from the revolutionary period. According to Jefferson's assessment in June 1793, "Gr. Britain holds back with the most sullen silence and reserve. . . . Our correspondence with her consists in *demands* where she is interested, & *delays* where we are." Even in the face of long-standing American protests, the British continued to occupy military posts on the frontier, effectively holding the Northwest Territories south of the Great Lakes. The British also had begun to give active support to that region's Native American nations, whose leaders had been pressing territorial claims against the United States. Another source of friction was the continuation of Britain's restrictive navigation acts, and its refusal to negotiate a treaty of commerce, which together seriously hampered American trade. Impressment of American sailors by British warships likewise persisted, notwithstanding American complaints.[2]

For the British, these policies were part of a general strategy to realize geopolitical advantages from American military and political weaknesses. Part of their aim was to encourage territories on the frontier to seek independence from the United States and form alliances with Britain. Maintaining their forts along the western frontier served this end, and in any event provided bases to support valuable trade with the Native Americans. With regard to the tribes, the British policy was aimed at creating an Indian buffer state to constrain American frontier expansion, thereby insulating British Canada. Lest it be forgotten, the Native Americans of these regions presented a formidable military threat, especially because they banded together in united fronts to counter expansion by the United States. Great Britain encouraged this resistance by supporting Indian claims that the American presence in the Old Northwest was illegal.[3]

Relations between the United States and Spain were hardly better. Spain resented American bids for navigation rights on the Mississippi; these rights had been the subject of discussions since John Jay's unsuccessful negotiations with Madrid on the subject in the early 1780s. Given the generous support Spain had provided the colonies during the Revolution, the Spanish regarded the American position as the demand of "a spoilt, selfish and spiteful child." Soon after taking office, the Washington administration found that the Spanish were inveigling to further their strategic objectives by influencing Native American tribes in the Southwest Territory. Jefferson assessed the problem in a letter of November 1792 to the American commissioners in Madrid. According to Jefferson, the Spanish governor of Louisiana and West Florida "has undertaken to keep an Agent among the Creeks, has excited them, and the other Southern Indians to commence a war against us; has furnished them with arms and ammunition for the express purpose of carrying on that war, and prevented the Creeks from running the boundary, which would have removed the source of differences from between us." During early 1793, the administration accumulated reports of what Jefferson referred to as "Murders and Depredations" by Creeks and other Indian nations, the blame for which he laid on the Spanish, who had "undertake[n] . . . to support them with their whole power."[4]

Aside from some blunt protests to the Spanish, however, the administration was unwilling to do more than authorize defensive actions against Indian attacks in the Southwest. In part this was due to their recognition that American settlers in Georgia were provoking many of the problems by incursions into Native American territories. More important, caution was needed to avoid a total rupture in American-Spanish relations. As these events unfolded, the American representatives in Madrid were attempting to reach agreement on the larger questions of the southern boundary, American access to the Mississippi, and a commercial pact with Spain.[5]

Regardless of the diplomatic concerns, few military resources were available to deal with the Indian conflict in the Southwest, particularly given parallel developments in the North. Secretary of War Knox advised William Blount, the governor of the territory south of the Ohio River, that the administration "view[ed] an Indian War in any event of it as unproductive either of profit or honor, and therefore to be avoided if possible. . . . [T]he President . . . for great political reasons ardently desires a general tranquility in the Southern quarter. He is exceedingly apprehensive that the flame of War once kindled in that region upon the smallest scale, will extend itself, and become general." Finally, the administration was unwilling to engage the country in a full-scale war on the frontier without authorization from Congress, which had taken no action in the prior session despite being advised of the serious clashes occurring between settlers and Indians.[6]

Taken separately, Great Britain, Spain, and the Native American nations each presented the United States with formidable foreign policy challenges. A further complication was posed by the relationship between these two traditional European rivals. Each of them eyed the other through the lens of the international balance of power, and both were suspicious of their counterpart's intentions on the American continent. During the 1790 Nootka Sound incident, Pitt's government was willing to risk war against Spain over the Pacific Northwest, and such a conflict almost surely would have spread throughout the American frontier. The administration feared that Britain would use the clash as an occasion to wrest Louisiana and the Floridas from the Spanish. Spain was having its own problems holding down internal revolts in Spanish America—a situation that the British were quite willing to foster. The consequence of having the British, as John Adams put it, "in our rear, and on both our flanks, with their navy in front, are very obvious." Although the Nootka Sound affair was resolved by Spain retreating from the confrontation, the weakness thus demonstrated merely encouraged British designs on Spanish America, and an Anglo-Spanish war undoubtedly would embroil the United States.[7]

France added a third and highly unstable element to the dynamics. Despite the revolution already under way in 1790, "France [wa]s the intimate ally of Spain," Hamilton noted, due to the Family Compacts that still tied the Bourbon monarchs of both countries. As Knox predicted, "[t]he probability therefore is that France will be combined with Spain" in the event of an Anglo-Spanish war. Events in France soon clouded this picture. Louis XVI still retained his head at this point, but the escalating civil war in France left Spain without a dependable ally in the event of a conflict with Britain. Likewise, the turmoil in France and Spain's apparent vulnerability led Britain to believe that the Americans could not count on their former allies if war occurred. By 1793 the British appeared willing to push the United States even to the point of war, and in any event they saw no reason to settle grievances given their current strength. To the British, the French Revolution provided an ideological justification for action inasmuch as the French example raised the specter of a revolutionary upheaval spreading to Spanish America, thereby producing a new set of independent republican states.[8]

As much as the United States might have wished to remain unaligned in the struggle among the three European players, a prior chapter in American history could not be erased: the treaties of 1778 between France and the United States. Although the treaties were designed initially to be the basis for French support of the American Revolution, they contained mutual and perpetual pledges to guarantee the territorial possessions of the other. In practical terms, this meant that the United States had promised to provide military assistance to protect the French West Indies from attack. The actual extent of the American obligation, however, was subject to interpretation and would require reference to the law of nations. This topic will be explored in detail shortly, because the letter from the Washington administration to the Supreme Court requested a legal opinion explicating certain terms of these treaties.[9] Plainly, a war between France and Great Britain would present the risk of engulfing the United States in the conflict. Apart from the treaty obligations, many Americans would expect the United States to aid France in a clash with the British. Washington reportedly said to Jefferson at the end of 1792 that "there was no nation on whom we could rely, at all times, but France; and that, if we did not prepare in time some support, in the event of rupture with Spain and England, we might be charged with a criminal negligence." Jefferson recorded that he "was much pleased with the tone of these observations. It was the very doctrine which had been my polar star."[10]

THE NEUTRALITY CRISIS OF 1793

On January 21, 1793, Louis XVI was executed. Shortly thereafter, France declared war on Great Britain, Spain, and Holland (France already had been at war with Austria and Prussia since April 1792). "Not only were all the great maritime powers now at war, but also the major colonial powers of the New World." News traveled slowly in those times, and it was not until the end of March that the administration began to advise American diplomats abroad of "a probability of very general war in Europe," which necessitated them "to be particularly attentive to preserve for our vessels all the rights of neutrality, and to endeavor that our flag be not usurped by others to procure to themselves the benefits of our neutrality." Washington wrote to Gouverneur Morris, the American minister to France, that it would be "unwise . . . in the extreme to involve ourselves in the contests of European Nations, where our weight could be but small; tho' the loss to ourselves would be certain."[11]

In the first week of April 1793, Hamilton and Jefferson each sent letters to Washington in Mt. Vernon, advising the President that the rumored war among the European powers was confirmed. Hamilton noted with "great satisfaction" that so far the British had acted "unexceptionally" toward American shipping. A prompt response came from Washington, informing them that he would leave for Philadelphia the next day. In Washington's view, "immediate precautionary measures ought . . . to be taken . . . to maintain a strict neutrality" on the part of the United States. Washington also "ha[d] reason to believe (from some things I have heard) that many Vessels in different parts of the Union are designated for Privateers and are preparing accordingly." Stressing that it was "incumbent on the Government of the United States to prevent, as far as in it lies, all interferences of our Citizens" in the conflict, Washington requested that "[t]he means to prevent it" be "seriously thought of," so that a plan of action could be implemented upon his arrival in the capital.[12]

Hamilton did not need the President's reply to take action. On April 9—the day after he wrote to Washington—Hamilton sent two letters to John Jay. The first dispatch concerned the anticipated arrival of the new ambassador from the French Republic to the United States, Edmond Charles Genêt. The question posed by Hamilton to Jay was whether Genêt should be received without reservation, as it was predictable that in the wake of Louis's decapitation a regent "will arise . . . acknowledged and supported by the powers of Europe almost universally, . . . and who may himself send an Ambassador to the United States." If the United States were to "receive one from the Republic and refuse the other, shall we stand on ground perfectly neutral?" Notwithstanding the dilemma presented by the possible appearance of rival ambassadors, Hamilton perceived the situation as ripe with opportunity. It presented a perfect occasion to suspend American obligations under the treaties: "What the Government of France shall be is the very point *in dispute.* 'Till that is decided the *applicability* of the Treaties is suspended. When that government is *established* we shall consider whether such changes have been made as to render their continuance incompatible with the interest of the U[nited] States. . . . [T]ill the point in dispute is decided[,] I doubt whether we could *bona fide* dispute the ultimate obligation of the Treaties."[13]

An unqualified reception of Genêt, Hamilton worried, might imply acceptance of the Franco-American treaties: "If it will ought we so to conclude ourselves?" Hamilton reminded Jay that "[w]hen we last conversed together on the subject we were both of opinion that the Minister expected from France should be received," a conclusion that Washington, Randolph, and Jefferson also had reached. "I would give a great deal for a personal discussion with you," Hamilton said in closing. In the second letter to Jay, Hamilton asked whether a proclamation of neutrality from the administration would not be advisable and whether it should prohibit American citizens from taking commissions on either side. Hamilton urged Jay to draft such a proclamation.[14]

Jay was in New York at this time, but he was able to reply two days later, enclosing a "hastily drawn" proclamation, which "says nothing of Treaties — it speaks of neutrality, but avoids the Expression, because in this country [it is] often associated with others." Ever the diplomat, Jay gave the advice he often tendered in such circumstances: "I think it better at present that too little sh[oul]d be said, than too much." Regarding the Genêt question, Jay advocated caution: "I w[oul]d not receive any Minister from a Regent until he was Regent *de facto;* and therefore I think such intention should be inferable from the proclam[atio]n." As the Chief Justice would travel to Richmond in May to convene a session of the circuit court, Jay informed Hamilton that he would stop at Philadelphia on the way.[15]

Upon arriving in Philadelphia, Washington sent the cabinet a list of thirteen questions that would be discussed at a meeting the following morning.

Although the questions were in the President's handwriting, they apparently were conceived or at least strongly influenced by Hamilton—a fact Jefferson immediately perceived. Most of the questions related to the ones that Hamilton had posed to Jay in his letters of April 9, namely, whether a declaration of neutrality should be promulgated and whether the French minister should be received without qualification. These new questions were more elaborate, however, and showed signs that their author had been studying the law of nations. For example, they asked if the American obligation to guarantee French possessions was "applicable to a defensive war only, or to War either offensive or defensive?" The next question then asked whether France's declaration of war should be characterized as offensive or defensive.[16] Hamilton would argue in a newspaper essay in early July (under the pseudonym "Pacificus") that the United States had no obligation to the French because they were engaged in an offensive war. For authority, he cited two distinguished commentators on the law of nations, Vattel and Burlamaqui.[17] A final question, which may be attributable to Jefferson, asked if it were "necessary or advisable" to convene Congress "with a view to the present posture of European affairs."[18]

At the meeting on April 19, the cabinet decided unanimously that a proclamation should be issued forbidding American citizens from taking part in the ongoing war, including transporting contraband to the parties. They also resolved to receive the French ambassador, although the question of imposing qualifications on the reception was debated but not decided. That issue, along with the remainder of the thirteen questions, was postponed "to another day." Hamilton and Knox did take the position at this meeting that the United States could declare the treaties void, and that receiving an ambassador without qualification might compromise that position. Jefferson advanced the contrary opinion, with which Randolph reportedly concurred, "but on Hamilton's undertaking to present to him the authority in Vattel (which we had not present) and to prove to him, that if the authority was admitted the treaty might be declared void, Randolph agreed to take further time to consider." All the cabinet officers, Knox excepted, were to prepare written opinions for Washington's review.[19]

On April 22, a proclamation was released under Washington's name reciting an intention on the part of the United States to "adopt and pursue a conduct friendly and impartial toward the belligerent Powers." A specific warning was given to American citizens:

[W]hosoever of the citizens of the United States shall render himself liable to punishment or forfeiture under the law of nations, by committing, aiding, or abetting hostilities against any of the said Powers, or by carrying to any of them, those articles which are deemed contraband by the modern usage of nations, will not receive the protection of the United States, against such punishment or forfeiture; and further, that I have given instructions to those officers, to whom it belongs, to cause prosecutions to be instituted against all persons, who shall, within the cognizance of the courts of the United States, violate the law of nations, with respect to the Powers at war, or any of them.[20]

Randolph had drafted the proclamation, which caused Jefferson to write to Madison: "I dare say you will have judged from the pusillanimity of the proclamation, from whose pen it came." Whether Randolph had the benefit of Jay's draft proclamation is unknown.[21] Substantively, the Randolph and Jay versions are similar in their warnings to American citizens against involvement in the war. Jay's contribution, however, raised several points avoided by the official proclamation. For one thing, Jay would have "enjoin[ed] all magistrates and others in authority to be watchful and diligent" in enforcing the neutrality, and in particular would have urged that they "cause all offenders to be prosecuted and punished in an exemplary manner." Jay also suggested declaiming that "the misfortunes, to whatever cause they may be imputed, which the late King of France and others have suffered in the course of that revolution, or which that nation may yet experience, are to be regretted by the friends of humanity, and particularly by the people of the United States to whom both that king and that nation have done essential services." With respect to receiving an ambassador from the French Republic, Jay recommended that the Washington administration regard the "new form of government" as "the act of the nation until that presumption shall be destroyed by fact." Accordingly, the Chief Justice concluded, "it is proper that the intercourse between this nation and that should be conducted through the medium of the government in fact."[22]

For all that appeared to the public, Jefferson was agreeable to the proclamation. Yet if his account to Madison in a letter of June 23 is credited, Jefferson voiced reservations about at least the wording of the statement. According to Jefferson's recollection, he had insisted that the word "neutrality" not be used because "a declaration of neutrality was a declaration there should be no war, to which the Executive was not competent." More fundamentally, Jefferson thought that a declaration of neutrality was "a thing worth something to the powers at war, that they would bid for it, & we might reasonably ask as a price, the *broadest privileges* of neutral nations."[23]

Jefferson's remarks came, it should be noted, only after a Republican organ—the *National Gazette*—launched a series of essays by one "Veritas," upbraiding Washington severely not only for issuing the proclamation without congressional assent but also for a policy that in practice amounted to a repudiation of treaty obligations to France. Jefferson's friends, Madison among them, were pressing him for an explanation of his support of a policy that seemed to spurn the French. Madison wrote Jefferson on June 10:

> Every Gazette I see . . . exhibits a spirit of criticism on the anglified complexion charged on the Executive policies. I regret extremely the position into which the P[resident] has been thrown. The unpopular cause of Anglomany is openly laying claim to him. . . . The proclamation was in truth a most unfortunate error. It wounds the National honor, by seeming to disregard the stipulated duties to France. . . . And it seems to violate the forms & spirit of the Constitution, by making the executive Magistrate the organ of the disposition the duty & interest of the Nation in relation to war & peace, subjects appropriated to other departments of the Government.[24]

Prior to this onslaught of criticism, Jefferson himself on a number of occasions had alluded to the nation's "neutrality" policy. Six days after the proclamation was issued, for example, Jefferson wrote to Madison: "I fear that a fair neutrality will prove a disagreeable pill to our friends, tho' necessary to keep us out of the calamities of a war." Actually, neither Jefferson nor any other responsible person inside or outside the administration was interested in introducing American military forces (such as they were) into the conflict. "It is very necessary for us then to keep clear of the European combustion, *if they will let us,*" Jefferson wrote toward the end of May.[25] What divided the opposing camps were the terms of American neutrality. According to Jefferson, the country should pursue a "manly neutrality, claiming the liberal rights ascribed to that condition by the very powers at war." Jefferson was referring to rights of neutral parties under the law of nations in the eighteenth century, which afforded neutral nations the right to take almost any action short of engaging in combat. In effect, Jefferson and Hamilton were vying to interpret the rights of neutrals under the law of nations in harmony with their respective partisan interests.[26]

Rapidly unfolding events in the spring and summer of 1793 produced a series of questions whose prompt and proper resolution was essential to avoid giving any of the warring powers a basis for charging that the United States was taking sides in the conflict. Unfortunately, "[u]ntil the latter part of the eighteenth century the mutual relations of neutral and belligerent states were, on the whole, the subject of the least determinate part of international usage." Notwithstanding that the members of the Washington administration purported "to give effect to the obligations then incumbent upon neutrals," the rules worked out during those months "represented by far the most advanced existing opinions as to what those obligations were."[27]

The first opportunity to formulate the American position on neutrality came in preparing position papers in response to the still unanswered questions on Washington's list of April 18. Hamilton issued a characteristically prolix opinion urging that the reception of Genêt be accompanied by a declaration that "[t]he United States . . . reserve[d] to future consideration and discussion, the question whether the operation of the Treaties . . . ought not to be deemed temporarily and provisionally suspended." For support, Hamilton cited various treatise writers on the law of nations, most importantly Vattel, who stated that a party to a treaty may renounce it when the counterpart nation undergoes a change of government that "renders the alliance *useless, dangerous*, or *disagreeable*." Moreover, as a practical matter, the United States would be in a quandary if it were to answer a call for assistance from France and if thereafter a serious attempt were made to restore the monarchy. "The most prevailing practice," Hamilton went on to assert, "has been to assist the *ancient sovereign*." At the very least, he insisted, respecting the treaties was merely an option, the election of which "would be to pass from a *state* of *neutrality* to that *of being an ally*—thereby *authorising* the Powers at War with France to treat us as an enemy."[28]

Jefferson had little difficulty in dispatching Hamilton's argument, which he termed in a letter to Madison "the boldest and greatest that ever was hazarded, and which would have called for extremities, had it prevailed." Turning to the law of nations, which he said rested in this instance on "the Moral law of our nature," Jefferson urged in a written opinion to Washington that treaties between nations were "obligatory on them by the same moral law which obliges individuals to observe their compacts. . . . For the reality of these principles I appeal to the true fountains of evidence, the head and heart of every rational and honest man. . . . He will never read there the permission to annul his obligations for a time, or for ever, whenever they become 'dangerous, useless, or disagreeable.'"[29]

Head and heart aside, Jefferson took up Hamilton's reliance on Vattel. To begin with, Jefferson asserted, Vattel was in disagreement with other writers on the question of breaking treaties if they prove "*useless* or *disagreeable*." Vattel's own position was less than clear. Jefferson pointed to other parts of his treatise indicating that treaties can be abrogated only where "the absolute *ruin* or *destruction* of the state" is threatened. Considering Vattel as a whole, Jefferson observed somewhat sardonically, "[w]e should hardly have expected that, rejecting all the rest of his book, this scrap would have been culled, and made the hook whereon to hang such a chain of immoral consequences." Just as Hamilton had claimed, Jefferson warned that the decision could lead to war, but France would be the one to have a "cause of war" if the United States failed to honor its commitments: "An injured friend is the bitterest of foes, and France has not discovered either timidity, or overmuch forbearance on the late occasions." Finally, on the specific subject of receiving Genêt, Jefferson professed not to see a connection between doing so and declaring the treaties invalid: even after receiving Genêt, the United States would retain its right to revoke agreements *"ruinous* or *destructive* to the society."[30]

While the administration was pondering how to treat the new French minister, Genêt was en route to Philadelphia from Charleston, where he had landed on April 8. Taking the scenic route via Richmond, Baltimore, and Camden, Genêt was greeted and fêted by enthusiastic crowds throughout the journey. Noting Genêt's expected arrival, Jefferson remarked that it would be an "occasion for the *people* to testify their affections without respect to the cold caution of their government." Jefferson was not disappointed, for he reported that "a vast concourse of the people attended" the new French ambassador's welcome to Philadelphia on May 16. Flushed by this outpouring of public sentiment, Jefferson wrote of Genêt's prospect: "It is impossible for any thing to be more affectionate, more magnanimous than the purport of his mission." For his part, Hamilton downplayed the size of the crowd and opined about the dangers of such demonstrations. Those organizing the greeting "were the same men who have been uniformly the enemies and the disturbers of the Government of the UStates," and they represented "a curious *combination* growing up to controul [the Government's] measures, with regard to foreign politics, at the expence of the peace of the Country—perhaps at a still greater expense." In a similar vein, Jay had suggested that the proclamation contain a "recommend[ation]" to "fellow-citizens in general to omit such public discussions as may tend not only to cause divisions and parties among ourselves, and thereby impair that union on which our strength depends, but also give unnecessary cause of offence and irritation to foreign powers."[31]

Washington formally received Genêt the day after the new ambassador's arrival. Although Genêt's credentials were accepted without qualification, the President carried out his intention not to show "too much warmth or cordiality."[32] From the French side, however, came the assurance from Genêt that his country would not "reclaim the obligations imposed on the United States, by the treaties she had contracted with them." According to Jefferson, Genêt specifically disclaimed any intention to call for American assistance in defending French possessions in the Caribbean. Genêt went on to communicate France's decision to open its ports to Americans on the same terms enjoyed by French citizens, and stated that he had authority from his government to negotiate "a true family compact." Jefferson conveyed Genêt's announcements to Madison with an enthusiastic endorsement—one that the Secretary of State perhaps soon regretted: "In short he offers every thing and asks nothing."[33]

The relative coolness of Washington's greeting to Genêt reflected a less sanguine view of the French minister's mission than Jefferson's view. Purely at the level of protocol, Genêt's failure to sail directly to Philadelphia to present his credentials was unusual and had been compounded by the new French ambassador's five-week overland journey. Of greater concern to Washington were Genêt's activities since alighting on American soil. Genêt came to the United States with three hundred blank commissions for authorizing privateers to capture prizes on France's behalf. Prior to leaving Charleston, he sent four privateers to sea, which were busily capturing British prizes as Genêt made his way to Philadelphia. By October, Genêt was able to inform his government that "14 Privateers mounting between them all 120 guns, manned with Americans, have gone forth from all the ports and have taken from our enemies more than 80 richly laden ships."[34] Genêt also was organizing Americans to participate in assaults on Spanish possessions in East Florida and Louisiana, including a planned takeover of New Orleans.[35]

News of French privateering against British shipping reached the administration during April and May. French-commissioned vessels, sailing with mainly American crews, were bringing prizes into ports along the Atlantic.[36] In late April, for example, the French frigate *L'Embuscade*—the ship that had transported Genêt from France to Charleston—captured the British vessel *Grange* within the Bay of Delaware. Jefferson described to Monroe the scene in Philadelphia when the *Grange* was brought into port: "Upon her coming into sight thousands & thousands of the *yeomanry* of the city crowded and covered the wharfs. Never before was such a crowd seen there, and when the British colours were seen *reversed*, and the French flying above them they burst into peals of exultation."[37]

The British government was not amused by these incidents. George Hammond, the British ambassador to the United States, immediately dispatched a protest to the administration, demanding the release of the *Grange* on the ground that its capture within American territorial waters was "in direct violation of the Law of Nations."[38] A few days later Hammond sent an additional set of protests over fresh reports of privateers operating out of Charleston with predominately American crews. In the same memorial, the

British minister complained that the French consul in Charleston was condemning seized British ships and placing them for sale. Hammond objected as well to the procurement of a "considerable quantity of arms and military accoutrements" by French agents, who were in the process of exporting the matériel from New York to France.[39] Grievances were also received from the owners of captured ships.[40] Other inquiries came from customs collectors in various American ports, who desired instructions on how to deal with captured prizes, and on what action to take with regard to vessels being fitted out as privateers in their ports.[41]

To respond to these protests and requests, and to others that would occur in the coming months, the administration needed to formulate rules for dealing with the various activities of Genêt and his recruits for the French cause. Initially, the administration handled the incidents on an ad hoc basis, but it soon became clear that a general set of regulations was necessary. This in turn produced the question of whether the executive, as opposed to Congress, was authorized by the Constitution to promulgate such rules. For reasons to be discussed, the cabinet decided to proceed with rule making and took a number of steps before eventually seeking an advisory opinion from the Justices of the Supreme Court on various aspects of the legal issues involved.

The administration did not await Genêt's arrival in Philadelphia to resolve most of the issues raised by Hammond's protest. On May 15, Jefferson sent letters to Hammond and to Jean Baptiste Ternant, Genêt's predecessor, explaining the administration's resolution. In the case of the French consular activities, Jefferson wrote that the consul had no lawful authority to act as a prize court, and thus the condemnation was "a mere nullity." With respect to the *Grange,* an investigation by Randolph had shown the capture "to have been unquestionably within [American] jurisdiction, and that according to the rules of neutrality [the government] is bound to see that the crew be liberated and the vessel and cargo restored to their former owners." The government, however, would not prevent the sale of arms and other military supplies to the belligerents: "[O]ur citizens have been always free to make, vend, and export arms: that it is the constant occupation and livelihood of some of them. . . . The law of nations . . . has not required from them such an internal derangement in their occupations. It is satisfied with the external penalty pronounced in the President's proclamation, that of confiscation of such portion of these arms as shall fall into the hands of any of the belligerent powers on their way to the ports of their enemies. To this penalty our Citizens are warned that they will be abandoned."[42]

Regarding the issue of the French using American ports to outfit privateers, and the employment of American seamen on these vessels, the administration took a diplomatic stance. Unquestionably it was impermissible for American citizens to be involved in these enterprises, and Jefferson wrote that the government "express[ed] our highest disapprobation" of such actions, and that "we will exert all the means with which the Laws and Constitution have armed us, to discover such offenders and bring them to condign punishment." As to the equipping of privateers in American ports, Jefferson temporized, claiming that all the facts had not been received.[43]

Genêt promptly supplied the necessary facts by acknowledging that "several vessels have been armed at Charleston; that they have received from me commissions of the republic, . . . and that these vessels, dispatched to sea with great celerity, have made many prizes." According to Genêt, the privateers "belong to French houses," and he "believed no law existed which could deprive the French citizens in the ports of the United States of the privilege of outfitting their vessels . . . and of serving their country by causing them to cruise out of the United States, on the vessels of their enemy." To this he added the somewhat insulting note that the governor of South Carolina had been consulted on the legality of this operation, and Genêt said "[h]is opinion appeared to correspond to mine, and our vessels put to sea." With respect to bringing prizes back to American ports for condemnation, Genêt appealed to the French-American treaty, which only days before he had suggested would not be relied upon by France. Genêt now claimed that the treaty gave the French "the right of bringing our prizes into the American ports, and of there doing with them as we please, as property on the validity of which the civil or judiciary officers of the United States have nothing to do." Moreover, he continued, the treaty expressly required the United States to deny the same privilege to nations at war with France.[44]

Given Genêt's admission and the arrival of a Charleston-equipped privateer (re-christened the *Citoyen Genêt* and commissioned by Genêt himself) in Philadelphia with a prize, the administration was unable to evade this issue any longer. Through the intermediary of Jefferson, Washington informed Genêt on June 5 "that the arming and equipping [of] vessels in the Ports of the United States to cruise against nations with whom they are at peace, was incompatible with the territorial sovereignty of the United States; that it made them instrumental to the annoyance of those nations, and thereby tended to compromit their peace." More specifically, the President ordered "that the armed vessels of this description should depart from the ports of the United States."[45]

Letters had already been sent by the administration in late May to the governors of the states, instructing them to employ their militia to stop "all cases of hostility committed between the belligerent parties within the protection of your state," and to prevent privateers from arming. After several ships were seized by such militia action, U.S. Attorneys were told to commence "proceedings at law against the vessel and her appurtenances as may place her in the custody of the law, and may prevent her from being used for purposes of hostility against any of the belligerent powers." Customs collectors in American ports were instructed to admit French privateers and their prizes to American ports, provided that customs duties were paid on the captured vessels and cargoes. The same privilege would not be granted to powers at war with France, however, because the treaty with France obligated the United States to refuse such permission.[46]

The federal judiciary was enlisted as well to prosecute individuals engaged in illegal privateering activities. Early in May, Washington asked Hamilton whether it would not be advisable to communicate to the district attorneys "requiring their attention to the observance of the Injunctions of the Proclamation." Shortly thereafter, indeed on the same day that Genêt presented his credentials to Washington, the United States Attorney in Philadelphia (William Rawle) ordered the arrest of one Gideon Henfield and another man for privateering actions contrary to the President's Neutrality Proclamation. Henfield was an American citizen who had shipped out of Charleston on the privateer *Citoyen Genêt*. The crew of the privateer promptly captured the British ship *William*, and Henfield was appointed prize master in order to bring the vessel into Philadelphia, where he was arrested and held for trial. Meanwhile, the administration instructed the U.S. Attorney in New York to institute prosecutions against "all persons, citizens or aliens" employed in arming or equipping vessels for privateering.[47] Later in the summer the administration authorized prosecutions in Boston against other Americans who were privateering for the French, and against the French consul in Boston, who had forcibly reclaimed a prize that had been detained by the U.S. Marshall.[48]

At almost the same time as Henfield's arrest, Chief Justice Jay delivered a strongly worded charge to the grand jury for the circuit court in Richmond, in which he stated that Americans who took part in the ongoing war would be prosecuted in federal court for violation of the law of nations. Foreigners were to receive the same treatment: "[T]he subjects of belligerent powers, are bound while in this Country, to respect the Neutrality of it, and are punishable in Common with our own Citizens for Violations of it. . . . [F]oreign Recruiters are hanged immediately, and very justly, as it is not to be presumed that their Sovereign ordered them to commit the Crime." Jay went out of his way to endorse the Neutrality Proclamation itself by remarking that Washington's promulgation was "exactly consistent with and declaratory of the Conduct enjoined by the Laws of Nations." If this statement were not clear enough, it would become even more obvious in the months to come that "as far as the justices were concerned, the administration's neutrality policy was their judicial policy as well."[49]

Genêt vehemently protested the Philadelphia arrests: "The crime laid to their charge, the crime which my mind cannot conceive, and which my pen almost refuses to state, is the serving of France, and defending with her children the common and glorious cause of liberty." Pressing for the President to order the "immediate releasement" of the imprisoned sailors, Genêt asserted that there existed no "positive law, or treaty, which deprives Americans of this privilege." Genêt's contention was arguable, inasmuch as the United States had no statute prohibiting citizens from engaging in actions contrary to official neutrality.[50] But the administration was unmoved by this posture, as it had concluded that such actions as Henfield's were "indictable at the common law, because his conduct comes within the description of disturbing the peace of the United States." Jefferson merely told Genêt, however, that the matter was out of the hands of the administration: "Mr. Henfield appears to be in the custody of the civil magistrate, over whose proceedings the Executive has no controul. The act with which he is charged will be examined by a Jury of his Countrymen, in the presence of Judges of learning and integrity."[51]

Left unresolved by the administration was the issue of whether to order the return of prizes captured by French privateers. Genêt agreed to relinquish the *Grange,* saying that he accepted Randolph's conclusion that the capture had occurred in American waters. The more difficult question concerned the fate of ships seized on the high seas by French privateers outfitted from American ports. Hammond was pressing for restitution of several such ships—including one named the *Little Sarah*—that allegedly had been seized in open sea by a privateer originally outfitted in Charleston and operated in part by American sailors. On this question, Washington requested written opinions from the cabinet.[52]

Jefferson opened his memorandum by stating that the French activities were "an act of disrespect to the jurisdiction of the US." Moreover, the British could claim injury as well. Under the treaty with France, the United States was prohibited from allowing those warring with the French to outfit privateers in American ports. "We ought not therefore to permit France to do it, the treaty leaving us free to refuse, and the refusal being necessary to preserve a fair and secure neutrality." Nonetheless, Jefferson urged that nothing more than a "very moderate apology" be tendered to the British government, accompanied by the explanation that the incident occurred early in the war at a distant port and before the United States could take preventive measures. As to restitution of the ship and its cargo, Jefferson would leave it to the courts to decide whether the seizure was valid. If the executive simply caused the return of the property without a judicial resolution, when in fact the capture had been lawful, then the French could regard it as an act of war. In any event, "the powers of the Executive are not competent by the constitution" to take such action. Randolph gave a separate opinion substantially agreeing with Jefferson.[53]

Hamilton took a much harder line toward the French. Their actions in equipping privateers and in recruiting personnel for military service ("whether by land or sea") constituted "an injury and affront of a very serious kind" to American sovereignty. Worse, "they make us an instrument of hostilities against Great Britain." As a neutral nation, the United States had an obligation to prevent its territory from being used as a staging ground by one of the belligerents, and it followed that there was a duty to redress injuries that had occurred. It might be true, Hamilton conceded, that the capture was lawful "as between the parties at War." This did not excuse the United States—the executive, that is—from granting reparation, because "we have been made accessory" to the French actions. A "refusal to cause restitution to be made," Hamilton concluded, would be the "equivalent to our becoming an accomplice in the hostility. . . . Hence we shall furnish a cause of War." Recourse to the courts was out of the question, Hamilton asserted: "[T]hey are not competent to the decision. The whole is an affair between the Governments of the parties concerned—to be settled by reasons of state, not rules of law. Tis the case of an infringement of our sovereignty to the prejudice of a third party; in which the Government is to demand a reparation, with the double view of vindicating its own rights and doing justice to the suffering party."[54]

Jefferson and Randolph's pleas to turn the issue of restitution over to the courts carried the day. To the British ambassador it was explained that the outfitting had occurred in "the first moment of the War, in one of their most distant ports," and was thus "impossible to have been known, and, therefore, impossible to have been prevented by the Government." For the future, "the Executive Government of the United States would pursue measures for repressing such practices. . . , and for restoring to their rightful owners any captures, which such privateers might bring into the ports of the United States." With respect to British ships already captured, if the seizures violated the "laws of wars," then "the case would have been cognisable in our Courts of Admiralty, and the Owners might have gone thither for redress."[55]

Instructions were given to the U.S. Attorney in New York to institute "proceedings at law" to determine whether a particular vessel had been captured by the French inside American territorial waters, "and for redelivering her to the owners, if it be so decided." Shortly thereafter, the British owners of at least two captured ships instituted admiralty actions in federal district courts to obtain restitution.[56]

While the administration was grappling with these questions concerning privateering activities, another problem was brewing. A number of the captured British vessels were being converted into privateers for the purpose of cruising on behalf of France. Governors had been alerted to use their militia to prevent such arming from occurring. In early June, the administration was informed by Governor Clinton of New York that his militia had seized such a vessel.[57] Again, the government decided to employ the courts as a first resort. The U.S. Attorney in New York was instructed to take actions "against the vessel and her appurtenances as may place her in the custody of the law, and may prevent her being used for purposes of hostility against any of the belligerent powers."[58]

Notwithstanding these resolutions, there was concern within the administration that the federal courts would refuse jurisdiction over these cases on the ground that a provision in the French-American treaty forbade either side "mak[ing] examination concerning the Lawfulness" of prizes seized from their enemies. To the warring powers, nonetheless, the government emphasized that the courts were the appropriate recourse. The British were told that it was "much more desirable" for the courts to handle these matters, as the "Executive['s] . . . functions are not analogous to the questions of law and fact produced by these cases, and whose interference can rarely be proper where that of the Judiciary is so." Genêt was given much the same line: "The functions of the Executive are not competent to the decision of Questions of property between Individuals. These are ascribed to the Judiciary alone, and when either persons or property are taken into their custody, there is no power in this country which can take them out. You will therefore be sensible, Sir, that . . . the President is not the Organ for doing what is just in the present case."[59]

Neither France nor Great Britain was satisfied with this resolution. For the British side, Hammond pointed out on June 14 "in strong terms," Washington recorded, "that the privateers were yet in our Ports waiting the departure of british vessels." Hammond soon followed this complaint with an additional inquiry as to whether the privateers ordered to depart would be allowed to return to American ports with their prizes. The administration stalled on these points, saying that the departure of the privateers "would obviate the inconveniencies" that concerned Hammond. As to the question of what would happen if these vessels returned with prizes, the administration refused to take a position. Washington wrote in his diary that "the Government were too much employed to go into a discussion of hypothetical questions; but would be always ready to meet & decide with justice, cases as they actually arose."[60] At the same time, the administration turned the tables on Hammond by asking when the United States would receive a reply to a year-old request for a decision "on the articles still unexecuted of the treaty of peace between the two nations," in particular the question of when the British would evacuate the western posts.[61]

Whereas Hammond was coolly diplomatic, Genêt responded to the administration's decisions about privateering activities with outright furor. "Let us explain ourselves as republicans. Let us not lower ourselves to the level of ancient politics by diplomatic subtleties," Genêt admonished Jefferson. Lambasting the Secretary of State for "excus[ing] infractions committed on positive treaties," he added a pointed note: "It is not thus that the American people wish we should be treated." Turning to specifics, he protested the seizure of French prizes in New York and Philadelphia, as well as the decision to ask the courts to determine the lawfulness of their captures. Jurisdiction over the vessels "belongs exclusively to the consular tribunals," and accordingly Genêt demanded "immediate redress of these irregularities." As to the arming of privateers, Genêt was equally adamant: "It is incontestable, that the treaty of commerce (art. xxii) expressly authorizes our arming in the ports of the United States, and interdicts that privilege to every enemy nation." Finally, he made a renewed plea for Americans who wished to enlist in the French cause, as Henfield had done: "Do not punish the brave individuals of your nation, who arrange themselves under our banner, knowing perfectly well, that no law of the United States gives to the Government the sad power of arresting their zeal by acts of rigor."[62]

On June 22, the day Genêt wrote to Jefferson, the *National Gazette* published the opinion of Judge Richard Peters of the federal district court in Philadelphia regarding the vessel that Henfield had commanded as prize master, the *William*. Peters ruled that his court had no jurisdiction over the matter, even on the assumption that the vessel had been captured inside American waters. Peters did acknowledge that such a capture would constitute "a flagrant violation of the rights of neutrality" and "a proper subject of enquiry on the part of our government, or in a court of the country of the captor." The courts of a neutral country have no business inquiring into the lawfulness of prizes, Peters concluded; rather, "the affair must be treated by negotiation, and not through the instrumentality of their courts of justice."

In the February 1794 term, the Supreme Court would rule to the contrary in another case involving a British ship captured by the *Citoyen Genêt*.[63] During the interim, however, the administration was faced with the problem of taking action regarding the mounting number of disputed prizes being brought to American ports. For the moment, the pressing issue was keeping the captured vessels in question from leaving port before the administration could decide whether the prizes had been taken in violation of American sovereignty. Initially, Washington requested that Pennsylvania Governor Thomas Mifflin "place a guard of Militia on board to avoid this consequence," but shortly thereafter Genêt was asked to detain the disputed vessels "under the orders of yourself, or the consuls of France in the several ports, until the Government of the united States shall be able to inquire into and decide on the fact."[64]

Almost at the moment these events took place, the administration received a communication from Governor Mifflin with information that the captured British brigantine *Little Sarah,* newly renamed *Petite Democrate,* was being fitted out as a privateer in the port of Philadelphia. Washington unfortunately was obliged to depart for Mt. Vernon immediately thereafter to deal with the impending death of his estate manager, which left his cabinet to deal with the *Little Sarah*.[65]

Relations with Genêt rapidly deteriorated. Governor Mifflin informed the administration on July 6 that the number of cannons on board the *Petite Democrate* had increased from four to fourteen, at least two of which had been purchased in Philadelphia. Mifflin thought that the freshly equipped privateer was ready to sail, as it had a full complement of 120 men, a number of whom were Americans. At Mifflin's request, the Pennsylvania Secretary of State Alexander Dallas—a prominent Philadelphia lawyer with Republican sympathies—asked Genêt to detain the vessel. According to Jefferson's secondhand account of this interview, Genêt "flew into a great passion, talked extravagantly, and concluding by refusing to order to vessel to stay." To make matters worse, Genêt purportedly told Dallas "that he would appeal from the President to the people."[66]

Jefferson then approached Genêt personally on July 8 and "told him it would be considered a very serious offence indeed if she should go away." Specifically, Jefferson asked that the privateer be kept in port for the few days remaining before Washington's anticipated return to the capital. As he had done with Dallas, Genêt "took up the subject instantly in a very high tone, and went into an immense field of declamation and complaint." The thrust of Genêt's argument was that the United States had "violated the treaties between the two nations," while at the same time the Americans "suffered our flag to be insulted and disregarded by the English," as when the British confiscated French property in transit on American ships. Jefferson actually sympathized with Genêt's position regarding British transgressions, but he nevertheless emphasized that the administration's resolve on the issue of the privateers was firm. To this Genêt asked that if the President "decides against a treaty, to whom is a nation to appeal?" Jefferson answered that "the constitution had made the President the last appeal." Continuing his description of this interview, Jefferson said that "[Genêt] made me a bow, and said, that indeed he would not make his compliments on such a constitution, [and] expressed the utmost astonishment at it, and seemed never before to have had such an idea."[67]

In the end, Genêt refused to promise Jefferson that he would prevent the *Petite Democrate* from sailing, yet he did give the Secretary of State the impression—"by look and gesture"—that the vessel would not be ready to leave until after Washington returned.[68] Jefferson passed on this account to Hamilton and Knox at a meeting the next day. Both Hamilton and Knox wished to take military measures to keep the privateer from departing, including erecting a battery of cannons "under cover of a party of militia" to block its movement. Jefferson, however, dissented from this proposal, although all three agreed that the Americans on board should be referred to the U.S. Attorney for prosecution. Hamilton and Knox insisted that "not taking effectual measures to prevent, when known, *the fitting out of privateers*, in our ports, by one of the belligerent powers to cruise against any of the others is an unequivocal breach of neutrality." They predicted that allowing the *Petite Democrate* to sail would be a "just cause of complaint against the United States" by the British, and could lead the country into the war. Moreover, they added, Genêt appeared to be following "a *regular plan to force the United States into the War.*"[69] Disagreeing, Jefferson opined that erecting the battery might itself provoke the privateer to escape. More seriously, firing on the *Petite Democrate* would surely lead to "bloody consequences," as its crew would certainly resist. "At this moment," Jefferson added, "we expect in the river 20. [French] ships of war, with a fleet of from 100. to 150. of their private vessels, which will arrive at the scene of blood in time to continue it, if not to partake in it."[70]

This quarrel soon became moot, as the *Petite Democrate* slipped to a point on the river where it would be impossible to stop her. Genêt then informed Jefferson of his intention to let the privateer sail at will: "When treaties speak, the agents of nations have but to obey." Arriving to this state of affairs on July 11, Washington was aghast: "Is the Minister of the French Republic to set the Acts of this Government at defiance, *with impunity?* and then threaten the Executive with an appeal to the People. What must the World think of such conduct, and of the Governmt. of the U. States in submitting to it?"[71]

Washington called a cabinet meeting for July 12. At that session, discussions began about whether to request Genêt's recall—a conversation that culminated a few weeks later in a resolve to ask the French government to replace its minister. The more urgent issue was the need to arrive at a comprehensive set of policies on the myriad questions posed by the intersection of American neutrality and the obligations of the French-American treaties. Although agreement prevailed on some points (for example, that France could be prohibited from arming vessels in American ports), there was sharp discord on numerous items (such as whether France could recruit its own citizens on American soil as seamen). This was not an academic exercise, as the *Petite Democrate* affair dramatically demonstrated. An improvident answer to these questions could drag the country into war.[72]

It was in this context that the administration resolved to seek the advice of the Supreme Court Justices. On July 12, the cabinet agreed to send "letters . . . to the Judges of the Supreme court of the US. requesting their attendance at this place on Thursday the 18th. instant to give their advice on certain matters of public concern which will be referred to them by the President." The British and French ambassadors were to be informed that "the Executive of the US., desirous of having done what shall be strictly conformable to the treaties of the US. and the laws respecting the said cases has determined to refer the questions arising therein to persons learned in the laws." During the interim, "it is expected" that the several privateers and prizes involved in the dispute would "not depart till the further order of the President."[73] Despite this request, Genêt dispatched the *Petite Democrate* to sea shortly thereafter.[74]

THE REQUEST FOR ADVICE FROM THE JUSTICES

Letters were sent on July 12 to Chief Justice Jay and Justices Iredell and Paterson, asking for their appearance in Philadelphia on the 18th. It is unclear why only these three were sent these requests, but most likely it was a matter of the Justices' locations and schedules. Justice Wilson may still have been away on circuit duty, whereas Iredell resided in Philadelphia. Both would be in Philadelphia by July 22 for the special session of the circuit court trying the *Henfield* case, at which they would preside along with Jay. The Court's regular term would begin on August 5. In any event, Jay called on Washington on the 17th to learn "at what time he should receive my communications." Washington professed to Jefferson that he was "embarrassed" as the "business wch. it was proposed to lay before them, was not fully prepared," apparently because the cabinet had been waiting for the arrival in Philadelphia of Attorney General Randolph to complete a list of questions. During this conversation, Jay evidently broached the subject of whether it would be appropriate for the Justices to answer the administration's queries. Washington explained this in a note to Jefferson the same day: "And as the Judges will have to decide whether the business wch., it is proposed to ask their opinion upon is, in their judgment, of such a nature as that they can comply, it might save time if you were to draft something . . . that will bring the question properly before them."[75]

Jefferson prepared the letter Washington requested, and copies were sent to all the Justices on July 18. Alluding to the fact that the ongoing war "produces frequent transactions within our ports and limits, on which questions arise of considerable difficulty, and of greater importance to the peace of the U.S.," Jefferson noted that "[t]hese questions depend for their solution on the construction of our treaties, on the laws of nature & nations, & on the laws of the land." Regrettably, he explained, the questions "are often presented under circumstances which do not give a cognisance of them to the tribunals of the country." Moreover, "their decision is so little analagous to the ordinary functions of the Executive, as to occasion much embarrasment & difficulty to them." Consequently, "the President would therefore be much relieved if he found himself free to refer questions of this description to the opinions of the Judges of the supreme court of the US. whose knolege of the subject would secure us against errors dangerous to the peace of the US. and their authority ensure the respect of all parties."[76]

Knowing that the Justices might be reluctant to participate in such an endeavor, Jefferson asked for a meeting "of such of the judges as could be collected in time for the occasion" to consider a preliminary issue: "Whether the public may, with propriety, be availed of their advice on these questions? and if they may, to present, for their advice, the abstract questions which have already occurred, or may soon occur, from which they will themselves strike out such as any circumstances might, in their opinion, forbid them to pronounce on."[77]

On the same day that Jefferson's letter was sent to the Justices, July 18, the cabinet (minus Randolph) agreed to address twenty-nine questions to the Court, which were to be delivered the following day. The initial twenty-one questions followed Hamilton's draft; Jefferson supplied the next seven, and Washington added the final one. All of them concerned specific issues, and many had subparts. None of the questions referred to actual incidents, although the context undoubtedly was clear to their readers. The general topic areas included:[78]

- Could France or the other powers arm vessels in U.S. ports, and if so, what types of vessels and under what circumstances? (questions 1-5 and 11-16) What could be done with vessels armed in U.S. ports prior to the Proclamation, and what action could be taken regarding their prizes made before and after its issuance? (24)

- Could powers at war with France use American ports (privateers excepted), including for purposes of trade? (6-7)

- Could the French sell their prizes in U.S. ports or erect consular courts to condemn prizes? (8-10 and 17-18)

- If an armed vessel were to take a prize within U.S. jurisdiction, did the United States have a right or obligation to cause restitution of such property? (19)

- How far offshore could the United States exclude the belligerents from engaging in hostilities? (20)

- Could the warring powers recruit seamen or soldiers within American territory, whether U.S. citizens or not? (21)

- What articles (by name) were to be prohibited to either party? (22-23)[79]

- Could Americans sell ships, warships included, to the belligerents? If so, where? (25-26)

- Was the principle that free bottoms make free goods, and enemy bottoms make enemy goods, a part of the law of nations? (27) If not, could nations with which the United States had no treaties remove enemy noncombatants and their baggage from American vessels? (28)[80]

- Could an armed vessel of any belligerent follow immediately a merchant vessel of an enemy for the purpose of making it a prize? (29)

Whether these questions actually were delivered to the Justices remains unknown. According to the editors of the *Documentary History of the Supreme Court*, they apparently "were never officially sent. . . . [N]o appropriate cover letter has been found, nor a copy of the questions received by any of the justices." Jefferson's letter of the 18th did not contain them; rather, it indicates that the President wished to know preliminarily whether the Justices would answer *any* questions. On July 20 the four Justices then in

Philadelphia (Jay, Wilson, Iredell, and Paterson) responded to Jefferson's letter with an exceedingly polite note that acknowledged the "difficulty as well as importance" of the request. "The occasion which induced our being convened is doubtless urgent," the four wrote, and they were "solicitous to do whatever may be in our power to render your administration as easy and agreeable to yourself as it is to the country." Nevertheless, because the administration's summons "affects the judicial department, we feel a reluctance to decide it without the advice and participation of our absent brethren." They were willing to "immediately resume the consideration of the questions, and decide it," should "circumstances . . . forbid further delay." Washington answered this letter three days later, declining to "press a decision whereon you wish the advice and participation of your absent brethren."[81]

Even if it is true that the Justices never formally received the questions, it hardly seems plausible that they were unaware of their general content. Given the close relationship of Hamilton and Jay, the basic issues, if not the precise questions, surely must have been shared in the days prior to the Court's refusal to answer them. Furthermore, a number of events in the period following the cabinet's initial resolution to consult the Justices indicate that a considerable number of people were aware of their content.

Apparently the administration made little or no effort to keep the referral to the Justices out of the public eye. Private correspondents conveyed quite accurate accounts of what was occurring. William Bradford, a Justice on the Pennsylvania Supreme Court, wrote on July 14: "I understand that some differences in the construction of the treaty has taken place among the President's advisers, & that expresses have been sent to Mr. Jay & all the other Judges to summon them to the Council. The question I believe is, Whether there is not an implied permission given by it to the fitting out of *French* privateers. All other nations are expressly excluded—& whether that exclusion does not implicate the right which Genet contends for, is the doubt. If it does not—Equality being Neutrality, they must be prohibited as well as the British."[82] Some writers with Republican leanings were concerned about the substance of the answers that the Justices would produce. Governor Thomas Mifflin said in a letter of July 17: "[T]he Judges of the U S are convened, to meet here To Morrow to give their Opinions on the 22d Article [of the treaty]. Their Decision will produce I fear Effects not favorable to America." [83]

News of the request to the Justices also promptly appeared in newspapers throughout the country. The Philadelphia *General Advertiser* published a piece on July 17, which was rapidly reprinted by other papers up and down the coast, indicating that the "federal executive, we understand, have sent for two of the United States' judges, to take their opinions on some part of our treaty of amity and commerce with France." On the 20th, the Philadelphia *National Gazette* updated the story by reporting that four judges had been asked to consult on the treaty. Both the *General Advertiser* and the *National Gazette* generally were strongly partisan in their denunciations of administration actions, and their editors had a close association with Jefferson.[84] An acidic letter was printed in the *National Gazette* on July 27, criticizing the call for the judges, and again it quickly reappeared in other presses. The writer, one "Juba," thought that "[i]t is a little strange that lawyers alone should be supposed capable of deciding upon common sense and plain language, for such is the treaty." If the executive had any doubts on the subject, Juba continued, "the *voice of America* would be the best interpretation of the treaty, and surely this is not to be obtained from a few interested individuals buzzing in the sunshine of court favour . . . or from a bench of judges, who can speak their own sense of it, but not the sense of the people." Juba further opined that "[i]f instead of *legislating* himself, the President had convened Congress, the people would not have beheld the arbitrary use of power which has excited alarm, and he would have escaped the censure which has been so generally bestowed."[85]

Meanwhile, on June 22, the *Henfield* trial opened at the federal circuit court sitting in Philadelphia, with James Wilson delivering the grand jury charge. Wilson's prose was erudite and flowery, and probably hard for many in his audience to follow, as he quoted learned authorities and alluded to obscure historical references in the course of explaining a citizen's obligation to respect the President's Neutrality Proclamation. But the main point was clear: "That a Citizen, who, in our State of Neutrality, and without the Authority of the Nation, takes an hostile Part with either of the belligerent Powers, violates thereby his Duty and the Laws of his Country, is a Position so plain as to require no Proof, and to be scarcely susceptible of Denial."[86]

Wilson could have stopped here, as he had stated squarely that it was an indictable offense for an American citizen to serve on board a French privateer. But he went on to discuss the central point of dispute between Genêt and the administration: whether France had a right under the treaty to outfit privateers in American ports. His answer was an unequivocal negative. The treaty obligated the United States to deny permission for such activities to the enemies of France, yet it did not affirmatively grant the right to equip privateers. As of that time, Wilson explained, the United States had not elected to open its ports to French privateering activities, and "private Citizens are certainly unauthorised and unwarranted" to do so for the government. To the contrary, Wilson admonished, the United States was obligated by the law of nations to punish those citizens whose actions were contrary to the country's official neutrality. The logic of Wilson's argument was not airtight, but he did answer directly several of the questions formulated by the cabinet only four days earlier.[87] Julius Goebel remarked that it is "difficult to believe that Wilson's charge was not a partial reply to some of the queries." As was common in this period, the charge was reprinted within days in newspapers in Philadelphia, Boston, Newport, Baltimore, and Charleston.[88]

On July 26, *Dunlap's Daily American Advertiser* in Philadelphia reprinted the grand jury charge delivered May 22 by Jay in Richmond. Jay had asked the clerk of the court to send copies to Hamilton the previous month. Of course, when he delivered the Richmond charge, Jay probably did not anticipate that the President would solicit the Justices for advice. All the same, it is interesting that the charge dealt with the subject areas of several subsequent questions from the administration. Jay firmly declared that neither citizens nor foreigners could aid or abet hostilities against any of the belligerent powers. This statement included a prohibition on recruiting activities. Albeit a more general declaration than Wilson's, the charge by Jay dispatched Genêt's contention that the French had a right under the treaty to stage military operations from American soil. Jay went on to address the question of what kind of trading activities Americans were permitted consistent with neutrality.[89]

The grand jury in Philadelphia indicted Gideon Henfield on July 24 for his privateering escapades. The indictment had been drafted by U.S. Attorney William Rawle and Attorney General Randolph, with assistance from Hamilton and William Lewis, a Federalist lawyer in Philadelphia and former federal judge for the Eastern District of Pennsylvania. Henfield was charged with violating a number of treaties between the United States and France's enemies in Europe, and these acts in turn were alleged to constitute infringements of the law of nations. The trial itself was held on July 27 before Justices Wilson and Iredell and District Judge Richard Peters. Rawle and Randolph prosecuted the case at trial. Genêt reportedly financed Henfield's defense by three prominent lawyers associated with Republican causes—Peter Du Ponceau, Jared Ingersoll, and Jonathan Dickinson Sergeant.[90]

Justice Wilson instructed the jury, opening with a warning that "[u]pon your verdict the interest of four million of your fellow-citizens may be said to depend." Wilson minced no words in informing the jury of the "joint and unanimous opinion of the court" that Henfield's "acts of hostility . . . [were] an offence against this country, and punishable by its laws." Emphasizing again the importance of the case, Wilson highlighted the consequences of an acquittal: "If one citizen of the United States may take part in the present war, ten thousand may. If they take part on one side, they may take part on the other; and thus thousands of our fellow-citizens may associate themselves with different belligerent powers. . . . And will not a civil war, with all its lamentable train of evil, be the natural effect?"[91] One of Henfield's principal defenses asserted that his actions were not proscribed by any existing law. Wilson was unimpressed: "It has been asked by his counsel, in their address to you, against what law he offended? The answer is, against many and binding laws. As a citizen of the United States, he was bound to act no part which could injure the nation; he was bound to keep the peace in regard to all nations with whom we are at peace. This is the law of nations; not an ex post facto law, but a law that was in existence long before Gideon Henfield existed."[92]

After a day of deliberations, the jury returned a verdict of not guilty on Monday, July 29.[93] A correspondent to the *National Gazette* was one of many who praised the "independent jury" that had "firmly withstood the violence of the aristocratic torrent, whose sluices were opened upon them. . . . [T]hey have set bounds to the declamation of an attorney general, and to the sophisticated pleadings (for pleadings they were) of an arbitrary judge."[94] Predictably, the Republican press trumpeted the result in *Henfield* as having determined that Americans were entitled to serve on French privateers.[95] Genêt himself made the same point, and proceeded undeterred to recruit Americans to the French cause, including placing advertisements in newspapers for this purpose.[96] Both the administration and the judges were roundly condemned by Republicans for what they termed the persecution of Henfield and the judges' misinterpretation of the treaty with France. *Dunlap's American Daily Advertiser* carried a typical letter, from one "Pluckamin," who targeted Randolph's presentation at the trial: "It appeared that the whole of that gentleman's discourse was intended to intimidate and frighten the jury into a condemnation of the defendant, merely to appease the rage of Briton, which, he seemed to think, would fall on us in the case of an acquittal." A writer to the Charleston *State Gazette* reflected a common view that the judges were beholden to the executive:

> The President directed a prosecution, evidently *unwarranted* by the constitution, and without the authority of any *known* law of the land. Whether such an act could be justified in a person whose *sole* duty it was, to *execute*, and *not* to *make* laws, was *afterwards* to be determined by judges *of his own creating*, upon whose decision, in the eyes of the world, he would be either exculpated, or censored. Was it to be supposed, when we consider the weaknesses and propensities of human nature, that these judges would give such an opinion as would fix a censure

on the conduct of the President, to whom, they owe their political importance? An answer in the negative, will be pronounced by every unbiased man.[97]

Opposition writers used the *Henfield* result as an occasion for insisting that it was the right of the citizenry to reach its own conclusions about American treaty obligations. Referring to Wilson's grand jury charge, the *National Gazette* "presumed that the Freemen of these States, feel the degree of independence as to dispute the infallibility of opinions, however sanctioned by office." Others sarcastically commented on the interpretation given to treaties by the federal judges: "Since the strong arm of presidential *power* has extended itself to the *imprisonment* of a *free citizen,* for *changing his allegiance,* it has become a subject of serious enquiry, from what source, *this power* is derived. From the constitution it is not, neither is it, from the law of the land. It must then have its origins in the fertile imaginations and creative minds of federal judges, whose wonderful sagacity in the construction of *treaties,* and of the *law of nations,* place their discoveries in the science of law, beyond the comprehension of common capacities."[98]

The administration took immediate steps to refute the claim by Genêt and other Republicans that the acquittal in *Henfield* left Americans free to participate in armed activities on the side of France. Randolph argued in the *Federal Gazette* that the court had unmistakably held Henfield's conduct to be a violation of law. "[A]s the law is so undeniably clear and explicit, it may be presumed, it must be presumed, that [the verdict] was owing to some deficiency in point of fact, or some *equitable* circumstances attending this case, which are the points of consideration for the jury." Hamilton had a blunter explanation: "The Judges who tried the cause were united in their opinion of the law. The Jury was universally believed in this city to have been selected [by the U.S. Marshall] for the purpose of acquittal; so as to take off much of the force of the example and to afford no evidence that other juries would pursue the same course."[99]

Randolph also announced that fresh prosecutions would ensue should additional violations occur, and this threat was carried out later in the month by a prosecution against the French consul and others in Boston for activities relating to privateering. This was the official administration stance, as Jefferson detailed in instructions to Gouverneur Morris, the American minister to England. Jefferson forwarded copies of Jay's and Wilson's grand jury charges and related Randolph's "official Opinion" on the case, all of which showed that such actions as Henfield's were "punishable by law." As to the acquittal, Jefferson explained that the jury apparently believed that "the crime was not knowingly and wilfully committed; that Henfield was ignorant of the unlawfulness of his undertaking; that in the moment he was apprised of it he shewed real contrition; that he had rendered meritorious services during the late war, and declared he would live and die an American." Jefferson neglected to mention that upon his acquittal Henfield had been fêted by Genêt at a victory feast, during which he re-enlisted on another French privateer.[100]

On the same day that the *Henfield* trial ended, the cabinet met to begin formulating a set of rules for the nation's conduct with respect to the belligerents. Over the next several days the cabinet came to an agreement on a formal list of rules, and in turn applied those rules to resolve the cases of a number of privateers and their prizes that had accumulated in recent months. During the same time, on August 1–2, the cabinet was debating the question of Genêt's future, which culminated in a decision to seek the French ambassador's recall. Jefferson recorded in his diary that at the August 2 meeting Washington had been in a fury over the virulent press attacks on him. Knox provoked him with what Jefferson termed "a foolish, incoherent sort of speech, [that] introduced the pasquinade lately printed, called the funeral of George W——n, and James Wilson, King and Judge, &c., where the President was placed on a guillotine." Jefferson described Washington's reaction: "The President was much inflamed; got into one of those passions when he cannot command himself; ran on much on the personal abuse which had been bestowed on him; defied any man on earth to produce one single act of his since he had been in the government, which was not done on the purest motives; . . . that *by God* he had rather be in his grave than in his present situation; that he had rather be on his farm than to be made *Emperor of the world;* and yet that they were charging him with wanting to be a King."[101]

Washington wrote to his cabinet members on August 3 to urge that the drafting of the rules be completed without delay: "Fresh occurrences, but communicated through private channels, make it indispensable that the general principles which have already been the subject of discussion, should be fixed and made known for the government of all concerned, as soon as it can be, with propriety. To fix rules on substantial and impartial ground, conformable to treaties, and the Laws of Nations, is extremely desirable."[102] Precisely what "fresh occurrences" Washington had in mind is unknown, but there are several possibilities. One involved a new dispute involving the British vessel *Jane,* which Genêt had alleged was arming in Philadelphia as a privateer.[103] A second prospect was a decree of the French National Convention of May 9, which authorized French vessels to seize cargoes on neutral ships en route to enemy ports. This decree constituted a plain violation of the French-American treaty of commerce. By late July, Americans were discovering that the French had seized a number of American vessels and their cargoes pursuant to the decree.[104] Rufus King referred to the decree in a letter to Hamilton on August 3, and Washington mentioned it in correspondence to Jefferson the following day; newspaper accounts of the decree also appeared in early August.[105] Washington's reference also could have been to the new report that the French warship *L'Embuscade* had defeated the British frigate *Boston* off Sandy Hook, New Jersey, after a two-hour cannon duel witnessed by a crowd of spectators. The cabinet discussed the battle on August 3. Jefferson reported that Hamilton and Knox "showed the most unequivocal mortification at the event."[106]

Related to this last point was the news that a French fleet of fifteen warships had sailed into New York harbor during the battle, where they were greeted by thousands of celebrants. The fleet had arrived in the Chesapeake during mid-July, with a convoy carrying some ten thousand French refugees from Saint Dominique in more than one hundred merchant ships. The refugees were fleeing a rebellion by blacks that had resulted in the end of white domination on the island. Writing to James Monroe on July 14, Jefferson spoke passionately of "the St. Domingo fugitives (aristocrats as they are)," whose situation "calls aloud for pity and charity. Never was so deep a tragedy presented to the feelings of man." Jefferson thought that the revolt was a harbinger of future black uprisings in his own country: "I become daily more and more convinced that all the West India islands will remain in the hands of the people of colour, and a total expulsion of the whites sooner or later take place. It is high time we should foresee the bloody scenes which our children certainly, and possibly ourselves (south of Patowmac) have to wade through, and try to avert them."[107]

Taken together, these incidents heightened the tension and urgency under which the cabinet deliberated on the rules respecting America's neutrality. Washington personally had other worries on his mind. On July 31, Jefferson communicated his intention to resign at the end of September. Unknown to Jefferson was the fact that in the previous month Hamilton had voiced a similar intention to leave the cabinet. In discussing Jefferson's resolve, Washington told the Secretary of State about Hamilton's own decision and "again expressed his repentance at not having resigned himself, and how much it was increased by seeing that he was to be deserted by those on whose aid he had counted; that he did not know where he should look to find characters to fill up the offices."[108] Compounding the seriousness of the situation were the ongoing disputes with the Spanish and Native American tribes, which at any moment could deteriorate into open warfare.[109] So concerned was Washington about the mounting troubles that he asked his cabinet on August 3 for written opinions on the advisability of convening Congress early.[110]

At some point between the end of July and August 3, it became apparent that the Justices were not going to assist the administration with a formal advisory opinion. In a letter to Washington on July 29, Jefferson returned "the copy of questions which had been destined for the judges." A few days later, on August 3, Jefferson wrote to Madison that *"the judges . . . however will not agree* I believe *to give opinions."* The administration's process of formulating rules respecting neutrality had commenced by July 29 and was completed on August 3, well before the rejection letter was sent by the Justices on August 8.[111] These rules were communicated to Collectors of the Customs on August 4, and to Genêt and Hammond on the 7th. Moreover, the administration proceeded on August 5 to apply these rules to decide the outstanding disputes concerning a number of privateers and their prizes. Needless to say, the rules covered the same ground as the unanswered questions to the Justices.[112]

The Supreme Court held its regular session on August 5 and 6. Justice William Cushing missed the entire proceeding, whereas Justice William Paterson sat with his brethren for the first time. Only one significant action was taken, namely, to carry over further proceedings in the momentous case of *Chisholm v. Georgia* until the next term in February. Chief Justice Jay apparently left Philadelphia immediately, as evidenced by a letter he wrote to Justice Cushing from New York dated the 6th, explaining the circuit assignments agreed upon that morning by the Court. The letter to Washington declining the consultation bore the date of August 8 and was signed by all the Justices except Cushing.[113] As the letter was in Jay's handwriting, he may have left it in Philadelphia for the other Justices to sign after his departure for New York.

DENOUEMENT: JOHN JAY'S CONTRIBUTION TO GENÊT'S POLITICAL DEMISE

Several days after returning to New York following the August 1793 session of the Court, John Jay joined with Senator Rufus King to publish a remarkable newspaper announcement: "Certain late publications render it proper for us to authorize you to inform the Public, that a report having reached this City from Philadelphia, that Mr. Genet, the French Minister, had said he would appeal to the People from certain decisions of the President; we were asked on our return from that place, whether he had made such a declaration—we answered, That He Had, and we also mentioned it to others, authorising them to say that we had so informed them."[114] This statement related to the allegation circulating since July that, during the *Little Sarah* incident, Genêt had threatened to take Washington's decisions regarding French privateers directly to the American people. According to a version of the story told by Jefferson to the President at the time, Genêt had made this declaration to Alexander Dallas. Upon hearing the original account, Jefferson quickly recognized that Genêt's tempestuous remark could "enlarge the circle of those disaffected to his country." Jefferson was furious at Genêt for the damage done to American relations with France—"His conduct is indefensible by the most furious Jacobin," Jefferson wrote Monroe in July. To make matters worse, Jefferson knew that Hamilton, "sensible of the advantage they have got," was "urging a full appeal by the government to the people," which "would manifestly endanger a dissolution of the friendship between the two nations."[115]

In early August, shortly before the Supreme Court officially declined the President's request for counsel, the administration determined to seek Genêt's recall. Jefferson reported this development to Madison, with the additional note that *"Hamilton presses eagerly an appeal* to the *people* . . . . *I hope we shall prevent it* tho the *President is inclined* to it." Convinced that the country was in the midst of a "crisis whereon the continuance of the government or it's overthrow by a faction depended," Hamilton urged in July that the administration place "the whole proceedings before the public in order that the great body of the people could be kept on the right side by proper explanations." For his part, Jefferson felt that publication of Genêt's correspondence with the administration would be "a fatal stroke at the cause of liberty." At a cabinet meeting, Jefferson warned that Hamilton's proposal "was calculated to make the President assume the station of the head of a party, instead of the head of a nation." Notwithstanding that Washington was "manifestly inclined to the appeal to the people," he determined to proceed with the recall request, and "perhaps events would show whether the appeal would be necessary or not." Months later, in December, the Genêt correspondence was presented to Congress as part of the administration's explanation of the recall.[116]

Hamilton was not content with merely maneuvering inside the cabinet. At the end of July, he published the first of his "No Jacobin" essays, the opening line of which read: "It is publicly rumored in this City that the Minister of the French Republic *has threatened an appeal from The President of the United States to the People.*" In the same paper, Hamilton went on to argue that Genêt already had "begun the appeal" through a series of essays appearing in newspapers under the signatures of "Juba" and "A

Jacobin." With Hamilton's encouragement, Federalists throughout the country held public meetings and issued declarations of support for Washington and the proclamation. Senator Robert Morris told Washington that he was prepared to use all his connections in aid of the President against Genêt.[117] Jefferson himself recognized that the tide had turned against the French minister: "The indications from different parts of the continent are already sufficient to shew that the mass of the republican interest has no hesitation to disapprove of this intermeddling by a foreigner, and the more readily as [Genêt's] object was evidently, contrary to his professions, to force us into the war."[118]

No direct evidence has surfaced to show that the Jay-King declaration came at the urging of either Hamilton or Morris, but its publication was at least consistent with the overall effort to discredit Genêt. Hamilton and Knox did acknowledge publicly in November—in a statement approved by Washington—that they were the ones who had communicated "the particulars" of the Genêt story to Jay and Knox, and furthermore that his threat to "appeal to the people" was reported to them by Jefferson.[119] As might have been expected, Genêt responded to the accusation with furious denunciations, and opposition writers demanded that Jay and King come forward with their evidence.[120] A writer in Boston, for example, asked "to know the time, place, manner, when and where [Genêt's] crime was committed," and insisted that "Mr. JAY, would not conceive he was authorized to condemn a man in his judiciary capacity, upon the evidence he has given respecting the conduct of Mons. GENET."[121]

In November, Genêt formally requested that Attorney General Randolph prosecute the Chief Justice and Senator for the "scandalous falsity of the charge against me." To defend themselves, Jay and King published a narration of their basis for the original allegation. They insisted that Genêt had announced to Alexander Dallas his intention of "appealing to the people." Dallas in turn had relayed the story to both Governor Mifflin and Jefferson. They incorporated into their statement a copy of the declaration by Hamilton and Knox, which affirmed that they were the source of the information. Jay and King did not seem in the least embarrassed that their assertions rested on multiple hearsay. Instead, they took the occasion to argue that Genêt's subsequent denials of the statement were equivocal. Explaining their motivation for coming forward on the matter, the pair maintained that such "an appeal by a foreign minister from the President to the People, appeared to us to be a serious, and alarming measure," for history had shown that "foreign influence is the most subtle and serious poison, that can be communicated to a nation." "[E]very well policed State forbids foreign ministers from so acting," they continued, as such behavior would "evidently and necessarily [be] productive of parties, practices, and intrigues, highly detrimental to the peace and independence of the country."[122]

A few days later, Alexander Dallas weighed into the controversy with his own newspaper notice. Dallas, whose Republican leanings were well known, denied that Genêt had used the precise words alleged by Jay, King, and others. Nevertheless, Dallas did admit that Genêt had made the following statement: "that, if, after the business was laid before Congress, Mr. Genet did not receive satisfaction on behalf of his nation, he would publish his appeal, withdraw, and leave the governments themselves to settle the dispute." Jefferson issued no public announcements on this subject, although he had privately given almost precisely the account published by Jay and King. To Madison, for example, Jefferson wrote in September: "You will see much said & again said about G[enêt]'s threat to appeal to the people. I can assure you it is a fact." Jay was particularly irked at Jefferson's lack of cooperation with a request to produce documents from the State Department supportive of his and King's position. Writing to Hamilton in November, Jay observed with apparent understatement that "[i]t is generally understood that you and Mr Jefferson are not perfectly pleased with each other." "[B]ut surely," Jay continued, "Jefferson has more magnamity than to be influenced by that consideration to suppress Truth, or what is the same Thing refusing his Testimony to it. Men may be hostile to each other in politics and yet be incapable of such conduct."[123]

Publicly, Washington treated Genêt's request for prosecution formally, and he appointed Randolph to investigate the charges. The mere referral of the question to Randolph produced a bit of tension between Washington on the one side and Jay and King on the other, which was resolved in a private conference by the three. Randolph engaged in a brief inquiry, only to announce that there were no grounds for prosecution. Genêt's days as a public minister were numbered. Although he attempted to pursue his complaint against Jay and King as a private action, the affair ended with the February. 1794 arrival of Genêt's replacement, Jean Antoine Fauchet. Along with his credentials of appointment, Fauchet brought a warrant for Genêt's arrest, together with a warning that Genêt's family in France would be held accountable should the proceedings continue.[124]

Isolating the effect of Jay's involvement in Genêt's downfall is a daunting task, given that Genêt's personal fate was sealed through a string of impudent diplomatic maneuvers. Yet it was one thing for the administration to replace Genêt and quite another to convince the public that this step was appropriate. For this purpose, the certification by the Chief Justice of the United

States that Genêt had threatened to make a public appeal might have had
some significant impact on popular opinion. Unquestionably, Jay's personal
involvement heightened the resentment toward the Chief Justice among
Republican sympathizers, who lambasted Jay and King in the press for their
public accusation against Genêt. One writer thought it ironic for Jay and
King to denounce Genêt in a newspaper announcement when their own
publication on the issue constituted a similar plea to the public. Another
dissenter urged readers to treat the "clamours" of *"Jay the great judge* and
the *Senator King* . . . with Sovereign Contempt." A "Uniform Federalist,"
writing in the *Virginia Gazette,* was "naturally led to enquire how far it
comports with the *official* characters of the Chief Justice, and a Senator of
the United States to become the trumpeters of such intelligence? . . . The
object indubitably was, to transfer the honest affections of the American
people from the cause of France, to the cause of Britain. The operating
motive must have been, a preference of Britain, to France, of British, to
French political principles."[125]

6

Explaining the Supreme Court's Refusal to Assist the Washington Administration

Prior to hearing from Chief Justice Jay on July 17 and thereafter from other members of the Supreme Court, the President and most of his cabinet apparently anticipated that the Justices would be willing to offer their assistance. It seems doubtful that the administration would have made the request without assuming that some degree of cooperation might be forthcoming. Not only did the cabinet go to the ultimately futile effort of framing the questions, but it announced to the foreign countries involved that the consultation would occur. And the referral was known throughout the country.

Writing on August 11 to Madison, Jefferson remarked that "I mentioned to you that we had convened the judges to consult them on the questions which have arisen on the law of nations. [T]hey declined being consulted. In England you know such questions are referred regularly to the judge of Admiralty." Jefferson's expression was not explicitly critical of the Court's action, yet it shows that to a lawyer in his era the idea of the executive consulting formally with the Justices as a group was not out of the question or even exceptional. Considering the evidence marshaled in the earlier portions of this book, such an assumption would have been entirely warranted.[1]

In Great Britain, centuries of practice and the conclusions of such learned commentators as Blackstone supported an advisory role for the judges to both the executive and the House of Lords. Similar consultations occurred in the American states. Discussions at the Constitutional Convention in 1787 included several references to the practice. Nothing in the Constitution's text explicitly forbade such a role, and in fact federal judges were not precluded from active service in other branches, whereas service by executive officers in Congress was specifically prohibited. The debates at the Convention suggest that in rejecting the creation of a formal executive (or privy) council, the Framers nevertheless preserved the option for the later creation of a cabinet, whose members could be required to give written advice to the President. No similar provision allowed the President to command opinions from federal judges, but the evidence suggests that the Framers assumed that such advice could be requested from the courts.

Perhaps more important, the theory of separation of powers as developed through the 1780s did not preclude advisory opinions, much less a cooperative relationship on other official matters between the judiciary and the political branches. The numerous contacts between the Justices, particularly Chief Justice Jay, and the executive in the early 1790s support the view that it was not inappropriate for federal judges to give legal advice to other branches outside the confines of litigated cases. Under the then prevailing constitutional understanding of the role of the judiciary in the operation of government, the Court easily could have justified answering the administration's questions. Especially given Jay's close association with Washington and the overall Federalist leanings of the Justices, why did they shun the assignment?[2]

The usual interpretation of the Justices' action takes their explanation at face value: "The Lines of Separation drawn by the Constitution between the three Departments of Government—their being in certain Respects checks on each other—and our being Judges of a court in the last Resort, are considerations which afford strong arguments against the Propriety of our extrajudicially deciding the questions alluded to."[3] Even if we accept that the Justices wished to refine the principle of separation of powers to preclude advisory opinions, it remains to be explained why they came to this conclusion. The answer lies within the tangled political history of the early 1790s, and this chapter pieces together the evidence into a coherent explanation.

Before proceeding to this discussion, it bears emphasizing that the Justices may not have meant to rule out all future advisory opinions to the executive. In their letter the Justices specifically declined to answer "the questions alluded to"; they did not reject advisory opinions in a more general way. This may seem an academic distinction, but consider that only the year before—during the controversy over the Invalid Pension Act—most of the Justices had given Washington extrajudicial opinions on the constitutionality of their service in administering the pension law. Furthermore, these opinions were issued not by individual jurists but by federal judges and Justices sitting as circuit courts. Justice Iredell, along with Judge Sitgreaves, professed to be "extremely cautious in not intimating an opinion, in any case extra-judicially," but nevertheless thought "an exception to the general rule" was warranted "upon every principle of humanity and justice."[4] It is entirely possible that the Justices did not consider the circumstances of the treaty an appropriate exception. John Jay's subsequent career, in fact, indicates that he was not averse to courts providing advisory opinions in a proper setting.

In 1801, Jay, as governor of New York, became embroiled in a constitutional crisis. Political parties in the state were split over the question whether the governor had the exclusive right to nominate individuals for various state offices, or whether that power resided with the state's Council of Appointment. Jay maintained that as governor he had the exclusive right of appointment (that is, selection of the candidates), with the council possessing only the right to reject or approve his recommendations. Most of the members of the council insisted that the powers of both nomination and appointment rested in their body under the New York constitution.[5]

Governor Jay requested an advisory opinion from the Chancellor and the Chief Justice and judges of the Supreme Court of New York, "unless a mode of having it judicially determined should occur to you, and in that case, that you will be pleased to indicate it." Averring to the "sense of respect due to the sentiments of the Judicial Department, on questions arising from the constitution or laws of our country," Jay asked for their views on the proper construction of the relevant section of the state constitution. Despite referring pointedly to the importance of "divid[ing] the powers of Government into three distinct and independent departments," Jay nevertheless believed it was proper for the judges to assist the Governor: "Aggregately considered, [the three branches of government] possess the whole power of Government, and are always in capacity to defend their respective authorities against improper assumptions of power. As this mutual security is not less important to the welfare of the State, than to the orderly and proper discharge of the trusts reposed in them, there results in my opinion a natural and mutual reliance on each other, to support their respective constitutional rights; and to do it by such interpositions as the nature of the case, and the circumstances of the occasion, may render advisable."[6]

In response, Jay received much the same reply as he had himself given to Washington's similar plea some eight years earlier. Four of the judges acknowledged that "[n]o mode occurs to us, to be adopted by your Excellency, to have the question judicially determined." In any event, the lack of a procedure made no difference, for the judges believed that they could not "comply with your Excellency's request, inasmuch as any opinion from us on the question, unless in a judicial procedure, or in the Council of Revision, . . . would be without effect." Unlike Jay in his 1793 letter, however, the New York judges expressly stated that there might be situations in which an advisory opinion would be proper: "We cannot therefore view the present as one of the cases (for we will not pronounce there cannot be any) in which the Governor may require the advice of the Chancellor and Judges of the Supreme Court, on the laws and constitution, in the execution of his office."[7]

Considering that this incident in New York occurred some eight years after the summer of 1793, it does not definitively demonstrate Jay's views on advisory opinions in the earlier period, nor does it illuminate the attitudes of the other Justices. Yet Jay's remarks about separation of powers in the letter to the New York judges accorded with his long-standing philosophy of cooperative action among the branches—that is, cooperative action tempered by a pragmatic judgment that recognized the need to assign certain powers to particular branches (such as foreign affairs to the executive). At the very least, we should pause before concluding that the 1793 letter represented a flat rejection of advisory opinions on the grounds of separation of powers. Rather, it demonstrates that the issue of providing extrajudicial advice remained in flux at the turn of the century.

Certainly some Justices continued to provide advice to members of the executive. In 1796, for example, a furious controversy erupted when the House of Representatives passed a resolution demanding copies of Jay's instructions for negotiating a treaty with the British, and all related correspondence. Threats of impeachment were heard on the House floor to buttress the demand. According to his own account, Chief Justice Ellsworth advised Senator Jonathan Trumbull that it was as "unwarranted as it is dangerous" to allow the House to "participate in or control the treaty-making power."[8] In 1798, Ellsworth furnished Secretary of State Timothy Pickering with a private opinion supporting the constitutionality of the Sedition Act. Pickering indicated to Rufus King in 1796 that he relied on advice from Supreme Court Justices on "weighty points" concerning the law. A more minor episode took place in 1800, when Secretary of War James McHenry wrote to Justice Samuel Chase asking for his legal opinion as to whether the President could appoint a public printer without the advice and consent of the Senate (President Adams had solicited opinions from his cabinet on this point). Chase gave an opinion to McHenry on this constitutional question with no apparent hesitation.[9]

Chief Justice Ellsworth went on to serve as a special envoy to France in 1799. Some members of Congress were wary of again sending the Chief Justice on a diplomatic mission. One congressman observed that many Senators felt caught in a dilemma. On the one hand, it was critical to improve relations with the French during the Quasi-War of the late 1790s. Federalist Senators were anxious to have Ellsworth at the negotiations, given his strongly Federalist leanings. On the other hand, there was concern that such appointments tended to "destroy[] the independence of the Judiciary inasmuch as it makes the Judges dependent upon the Executive for additional honors & favors." These reservations, however, did not prevent Ellsworth's nomination from being approved by a margin of twenty-three to six. Thereafter, in 1801, John Marshall remained as Secretary of State for the first month after he became Chief Justice.[10]

It is doubtful that we will ever know for certain whether the Justices in 1793 intended to foreclose all future consultations with the executive. The best that we can accomplish with available information is a reconstruction of the probable reasons why the Justices declined Washington's plea. What follows is an effort to put together the fragments of the story into a recognizable picture.

WHY THE JUSTICES REFUSED WASHINGTON'S REQUEST

The Issue of Executive Power and the Foreign Policy Crisis of 1793

As the year 1793 unfolded, it was apparent to any knowledgeable observer in the United States that the country was in the midst of the most serious crisis it had faced since the inception of the nation. In March, Hammond wrote to Lord Grenville with the assessment that the U.S. government was "in a moment of crisis, and that a very short period will be requisite to ascertain its fate." Jefferson was convinced that "[t]his summer is of immense importance to the future condition of mankind all over the earth: and not a little so to ours. For tho' its issue should not be marked by any direct change in our constitution, it will influence the tone and principles of it's administration so as to lead it to something very different in the one event from what it would be in the other." "Our situation," Jefferson wrote to the

American ministers in Spain, "is critical." This anxiety on Jefferson's part was rooted in a conviction that leading Federalists and their newspaper allies intended to subvert the republic and reestablish a monarchical form of government, including a reunion with Great Britain. Among those "here in favour of this doctrine," Jefferson wrote, were "Adams, Jay, Hamilton, Knox. Many of the Cincinnati. The second [Jay] says nothing. The third [Hamilton] is open. Both are dangerous."[11] In Jefferson's mind, there was a close association between the likelihood of this subversive activity succeeding and the current turmoil in France. Writing to a leading French Girondist on May 8, Jefferson said: "I continue eternally attached to the principles of your revolution. I hope it will end in the establishment of some firm government, friendly to liberty, and capable of maintaining it. If it does, the world will become inevitably free. If it does not, I feel the zealous apostles of English demi-despotism here, will increase the number of it's disciples."[12]

On the whole, Jefferson was sanguine about the country's future, feeling that in the end "we shall still remain free," even though "[a] germ of corruption indeed has been transferred from our dear mother country, and has already borne fruit." Despite his simmering anger over Hamilton's having prevailed on many issues in cabinet discussions, Jefferson was convinced that "the ardent spirit of our constituents" would prevail: "All the old spirit of 1776 is rekindling. The newspapers from Boston to Charleston prove this; and even the Monocrat papers are obliged to publish the most furious Philippics against England." From Jefferson's angle, the social conflict that flared during these months reflected a deeper division in American society: "The line is now drawing so clearly as to shew, on one side 1. the fashionable circles of Phila., N. York, Boston & Charleston (natural aristocrats), 2. merchants trading on British capitals, 3. paper men, (all the old tories are found in some one of these three descriptions). On the other side are 1. merchants trading on their own capitals, 2. Irish merchants, 3. tradesmen, mechanics, farmers, & every other possible description of our citizens."[13]

Republicans routinely labeled supporters of a strict neutrality as British sympathizers, who were opposed to the revolutionary principles driving the French cause. A typical expression of the period is found in a letter from an anonymous Philadelphia writer, dated July 24, 1793, which was published in a Boston newspaper. The author described Philadelphia as replete with

> every ancient enemy to the free principles which illuminated the dawn of our revolution. Among this description you find, . . . every halfway, timid, hesitating whig of the eleventh hour, joined and incorporated with the train-band of Speculators (with some exceptions) and the Merchants in the British trade, in about the same proportion. . . . Do you not see in Boston the same leaven at work,

openly or secretly, as will best suit their designs? Under the plausible exterior of national independence of foreign connections, do you not perceive the English influence in full operation, to vilify the only European power, that from principle, interest and inclination, can wish well to American liberty. . . . REMEMBER the freedom of North-America can be lost only in France, and the dissolution of the Gallic republic, will renew the convulsive struggle for our rights.[14]

An unusual feature of the previous congressional elections (1792) had been the appearance of such overt partisanship for the first time in the young nation's history. Based on the results of those elections, the next Congress would have considerable Republican representation, including a majority in the House. Jefferson, who followed these elections closely, was predicting that the coming session of Congress would be "strongly republican," and thus "actuated by a very different spirit from that which governed the two preceding Congresses."[15] Some viewed the political scene as a "struggle between the Treasury department and the republican interest," and others perceived it to be a contest between "republican & . . . the aristocratical candidates," but regardless of the labels it was plain that a significant opposition had arisen to counter Federalist governance. Against this backdrop, in cabinet debates Hamilton and Knox argued strongly against convening Congress early to take up the controversies arising from neutrality. By contrast, Jefferson recommended that Washington assemble Congress a month ahead of schedule to deal with Spanish incitement of the Creeks and to legislate with respect to the "incidents and perplexities" that arose from the European war.[16]

Many other observers shared Jefferson's analysis of the widening split in American political society but interpreted the resulting social conflict in a far more threatening light. After all, it had long been a tenet of republican philosophy that partisanship was toxic to the body politic. The painter John Trumbull, who had spent considerable time in France and was acquainted with many leading Americans on account of his portraiture work, gave this description of the political scene in 1793:

> In America, the artful intrigues of French diplomatists, and the blunders of the British government, united to convert the whole American people into violent partisans of one or the other;—to such a degree did this insanity prevail, that the whole country seemed to be changed into one vast arena, on which the two parties, forgetting their national character, were wasting their time, their thoughts their energy, on this foreign quarrel. The calm splendor of our own Revolution, comparatively rational and beneficial as it had been, was eclipsed in the meteoric glare and horrible blaze of glory of republican France; and we . . . learned to admire that hideous frenzy which made the very streets of Paris flow with blood.[17]

Washington, deeply troubled by the turmoil that had erupted, feared the "danger of anarchy being introduced," which could result in "rending the Union asunder."[18] As a man who had been uniformly adored by his public for so many years, Washington despised the personal attacks against him that appeared regularly in the press.[19] Federalists saw with alarm the rising number and intensity of crowd actions targeting the administration and its policies, as well as the appearance in the cities of Democratic Societies, seeming imitations of Jacobin groups in France.[20] According to Hamilton, "[o]pen and *ardent* demonstrations of attachment to the cause of France and opprobrium of the most offensive kind against the Powers at War . . . hold us up to the jealousy and resentment of those Nations and after all statesmen are but men and far more actuated by their passions than they ought to be. . . . If we run a risk [of war] 'tis probably chiefly on this score. Yet one may as well preach moderation to the Winds as to our zealots."[21]

As Hamilton often did in moments of intense public controversy, he brought his pen to action through a series of essays in newspapers that summer, using the pseudonyms "Pacificus," "No Jacobin," and "Philo Pacificus." In these writings, which were readily identified as Hamilton's, he defended the Neutrality Proclamation, minimized American obligations under the French treaties, assailed Genêt's activities, and generally lambasted the administration's critics. In *Pacificus No. 1,* published on June 29, Hamilton argued that the President must interpret the treaties in order to carry out the responsibility of executing the laws: "He who is to execute the laws must first judge for himself of their meaning." For the executive to determine the proper course of its conduct "in reference to the present War in Europe," the President had no choice but to interpret "the law of nations combined with our treaties," in order "to judge for himself whether there was any thing in our treaties incompatible with an adherence to neutrality."[22]

Hamilton granted that Congress also might have to interpret treaties and the law of nations, as, for example, when it exercised its power to declare war. Although it was true that "[t]he Legislature is free to perform its own duties according to its own sense of them," the executive, in wielding its "*concurrent* authority," "may establish an antecedent state of things which ought to weigh in the legislative decisions." Moreover, it was the executive, and not Congress, that had constitutional responsibility to be "*organ* of intercourse between the U States and foreign Nations." It followed from this that the legislature was "not naturally that Organ of Government which is to pronounce the existing condition of the Nation, with regard to foreign Powers, or to admonish the Citizens of their obligations and duties founded upon that condition of things."[23]

For Hamilton it was even more evident that in the present crisis the federal judiciary had no role in determining American rights and responsibilities arising from the intersection of treaties and the law of nations: "The province of [the Judiciary] Department is to decide litigations in particular cases. It is indeed charged with the interpretation of treaties; but it exercises this function only in litigated cases; that is where contending parties bring before it a specific controversy. *It has no concern with pronouncing upon the external political relations of Treaties between Government and Government.* This position is too plain to need being insisted upon." These views were consistent with Hamilton's long-expressed opinions on the necessity for strong executive control in government, especially over the conduct of foreign policy. For that matter, Hamilton's articulation of these points reflected a bedrock view of Federalists—especially John Jay. "It is one thing," Hamilton had written in *Federalist No. 71,* for the executive "to be subordinate to the laws, and another to be dependent on the legislative body."[24]

Jefferson readily perceived that Pacificus's forceful presentation hit directly at the heart of his vision of republican government. "Nobody answers him," Jefferson wrote to Madison on July 7, and consequently "his doctrines will therefore be taken for confessed. For god's sake, my dear Sir, take up your pen, select the most striking heresies, and cut him to pieces in the face of the public." Madison attempted to do so, with the first of his five "Helvidius" essays appearing on August 24. Whereas Pacificus was logical and systematic in argument, Helvidius seemed brooding and forewarning. Conceding a limited role for the executive in determining American obligations under the law of nations, Madison insisted that Congress was assigned the prerogative to define neutrality and related treaty obligations: "The executive must . . . execute the laws of neutrality whilst in force, and leave it to the legislature to decide, whether they ought to be altered or not." Madison would not even concede that the President had the authority to recognize foreign governments. Most important, he insisted that the Constitution "confide[d] the question of war or peace to the legislature, and not to the executive department."[25]

It is in the context of this Federalist aim to maintain executive control over foreign policy that the Supreme Court's refusal of Washington's request must be analyzed. Chief Justice Jay's attitude is crucial to this inquiry, for he more than the other Justices had unparalleled experience in foreign affairs. Jay's orientation in foreign policy was guided by pragmatism, as opposed to ideological conviction. Above all else, his diplomatic career had taught him the necessity of unitary action in the conduct of foreign affairs, which was essential if the nation was to "move on uniform principles of policy." Unquestionably for Jay, the leadership in foreign affairs had to be firmly in the control of the executive.[26]

Jay's insistence on executive direction of foreign relations was coupled with another judgment born from practice, to "regard all foreign interference in our country as derogatory to the honour and dangerous to the best interests of the United States." In his grand jury address in Richmond at the end of May, Jay combined this point with a plea to present a united front to the European belligerents. Emphasizing that the United States could still become involved in the war, he urged that the most important preparation was to instill "Union and Harmony among ourselves. It is very desirable, that [a war] do[es] not find us divided into Parties, and particularly into Parties in favor of this or that foreign nation. Should that be the Case, our Situation would be dangerous as well as disgraceful. . . . [I]t is sincerely to be wished that our Citizens will cheerfully and punctually do their Duty to every other Nation, but at the same Time carefully avoid becoming the Partizans of any of them."[27]

Quite apart from the abhorrence with which Jay and other Federalists regarded the developments in France since the beheading of Louis XVI, from a pragmatist's perspective it also made little sense at this juncture to show partiality toward the French. Among Federalists in 1793, it was widely expected that the French would be defeated by the British and that eventually the French throne would be restored. Communications from France since the spring of 1793 depicted numerous military setbacks for the French, a serious possibility of famine, and a picture of general complexity and uncertainty. Rufus King gave a Federalist outline of the situation that summer in France: "[t]he late accounts from Europe may teach moderation, and cannot fail to inspire the Government with Caution—every thing seems to be changing; distrust, defeat, confusion & Dejection, are manifest in the affairs of France. It seems as if their past Fortunes had suffered almost a total change. . . . [I]t can scarcely be doubted that the French army must fall. . . . The Paris accounts up to the 1st. Ap[ri]l shew the alarming situation of that Metropolis and render it probable that they were at the point of another massacre." Jay and the other Justices assembled in Philadelphia surely would have been aware of these developments. In any event, they had demonstrated, and would continue to show, firm support for the President's Neutrality Proclamation.[28]

So far, the administration had followed policies regarding the interpretation of the French treaties that were either urged by Hamilton or consistent with his outlook. The real problem that prompted the cabinet to consult the Justices was Genêt's intransigence, and as Jefferson's letter to the Justices emphasized, the administration expected that the Supreme Court's "authority [would] ensure the respect of all parties." But it was unlikely that Genêt would be affected by anything the Court said about the treaties. Not only was Genêt stubbornly convinced of the correctness of his position, nurtured as it was by revolutionary fervor, but he had already shown a willingness to defy openly the orders of the President. Furthermore, Wilson's jury charges at the *Henfield* trial had answered the leading questions at issue, by holding that French vessels could be precluded from arming in American ports and that U.S. citizens violated the law if they participated in hostilities against France's enemies. If even this judicial declaration were to have no effect on Genêt—and it did not—then answering the remaining questions would be of dubious value in changing the French minister's attitude. It also may have seemed to the Justices that the administration's decision to seek Genêt's recall (which occurred while they were deliberating about whether to answer) was a much more direct way of handling the confrontation. Finally, a number of other issues covered by the questions that were unresolved by *Henfield* would be open to resolution if the federal courts accepted jurisdiction over the claims made by owners of seized vessels. As it happens, in the February term of the Supreme Court, the Justices would hold that such cases were justiciable in *Glass v. Sloop Betsey*.[29]

All these considerations taken together merely show why the Justices might have regarded their intervention as futile or unnecessary. Another factor for them to weigh in considering their reply was the negative ramifications to providing such overt assistance on this occasion. For Jay in particular, the request created a difficult dilemma. On the one hand, he had long given similar advice without reservation, and on occasion he had even offered it without being expressly asked. Given his personal relationship with Washington, he must have been unhappy to decline. On the other hand, from the standpoint of his diplomatic experience and views on executive prerogatives, Jay was loathe to do anything that might interfere with the President's independence in foreign affairs. In effect, the request amounted to the administration's publicly announcing that it was seeking the counsel of the Court on the French treaties. As Jay knew from long experience, including the recent Nootka Sound episode, these issues did not exist in a vacuum but rather were tied to practical political considerations. Had the administration received the advice, it would have been hard pressed to act contrary to the Justices' answers. A precedent would have been set by which the Justices' involvement in interpretations of treaties and the law of nations would be expected upon request by the other branches. It was one thing for the administration to have the counsel and participation of Jay and the other

Justices personally on such issues, and quite another to have to deal permanently with the influence of the Supreme Court.

Once these larger concerns for executive independence are taken into account, the Justices' letter may be seen in a different light. The letter referred to the "Lines of Separation drawn by the Constitution between the three Departments" as "being in certain Respects checks on each other" and stated that the Constitution specifically allowed the President the privilege of "calling" for opinions only from the "*executive* Departments." As to separation of powers, the actual intent may have been to decline advice under the circumstances presented, namely, the interpretation of treaties in a time of fast-evolving crisis. Arguably, the letter itself was an advisory opinion, not only on why the Court would not answer but also on the President's authority over the issues involved. Jay's letter concluded with a flourish of rhetoric expressing the Justices' confidence that "your Judgment will discern what is Right, and that your usual Prudence, Decision and Firmness will surmount every obstacle to the Preservation of the Rights, Peace, and Dignity of the united States." In a sentence, this affirmed Pacificus's assertion that the President was assigned full authority under the Constitution to interpret treaties and any related questions concerning the law of nations. Jefferson had asked the Justices for an opinion so that "the public may . . . be availed of their advice on such questions," but doubtless he was not anticipating the reply to be an affirmation of the President's power to interpret treaties.[30]

On this reading of the letter, the Justices might not have been rejecting their involvement—either as individuals or as a group—in future advisory opinions. Instead, it would depend on the situation. Certainly Jay himself concluded eight years later that it was perfectly appropriate for an executive to seek an advisory opinion from the New York Supreme Court. This tends to indicate that Jay found advisory opinions to be consistent with his overall conception of separation of powers. Jay surely understood that the constitutional text did not explicitly prohibit advisory opinions. In an earlier commentary on the Constitution, Jay remarked: "Silence and blank paper neither grant nor take away anything."[31]

Agreeing to the consultation with Washington would not only pose risks to the executive's independence in foreign affairs but would contain drawbacks for the Court as well. Already the mere announcement of the referral had set off adverse commentary in opposition newspapers, not to mention the reaction in the press to the *Henfield* rulings. From their perspective, the Justices may have felt themselves being drawn directly into the controversy, in a way somewhat reminiscent of the manner in which the Stuart monarchs used their judges to provide helpful advisory opinions. Moreover, the Justices could have perceived the advance announcement of the referral as in effect a *command* rather than a voluntary consultation. For important reasons of the moment, the Justices would have seen this type of development as against the Court's best interests. To that question—our final one—we now turn.

The Court's Interest in Avoiding Public Controversy

"The fœderal Courts have Enemies in all who fear their Influence on State objects," Jay wrote to Rufus King in December 1793. The statement was written during the first month of the new congressional session and came in the course of a letter mentioning a number of reforms in the federal judiciary that Jay thought Congress should consider.[32] Although most of the issues Jay mentioned were minor, his primary target was the circuit riding system: "When it is considered that the important Questions expected to arise in the Circuit Courts have now been decided by them, I can conceive of no Reason for continuing to send the Sup[reme] Court Judges to preside in them, of equal weight with the objections which oppose that measure."[33] Nevertheless, Jay urged caution when approaching Congress on such subjects: "it is to be wished that their Defects should be corrected quietly—if those Defects were all exposed to public View in striking Colors, more Enemies wd. arise, and the Difficulty of mending them encreased." Jay's sensitivity to the Court's political vulnerability reflected a long-standing concern on his part. Three years earlier, Jay had counseled Washington that the subject of altering the judicial system must be raised in Congress in a manner so "as to cause as few Questions or Divisions as possible."[34]

Abolishing circuit riding was not an idle topic for Jay and the other Justices. It had become a matter of intense and continual preoccupation for them. Justice Thomas Johnson already had resigned owing to his unwillingness to take circuit assignments. Jay himself decided in 1792 that he would leave the Court if changes were not made in the circuit system; purportedly he said that "almost any other Office of suitable Rank and Emolument was preferable" to continuing as Chief Justice.[35] When Jay decided to make his ultimately unsuccessful bid for the New York governorship in that year, his decision to enter the race came after learning that Congress had failed to abolish circuit riding. Jay changed his mind thereafter, concluding that remaining on the Court now was tolerable enough on account of the partial relief granted by Congress in the previous session—reducing the number of Justices required at circuit sessions to one. Nevertheless, he remained sufficiently disgruntled with the status quo that in December 1793 Jay told political supporters in New York that he would "certainly acquiesce" to a second gubernatorial nomination in the next election, "and if elected would accept." History shows, of course, that Jay was so nominated and elected during his absence in 1795, when he was in England negotiating the treaty that eventually became known by his name.[36]

At the root of the opposition to the federal judiciary was the very nature of the system established by Article 3. Theodore Sedgwick, a Federalist congressman from Massachusetts, advised in 1791 that it might be better "*at present* to do nothing" about the federal courts, "because the greatest embarrassments seem to be inherent in the nature of the subject. They arise from an administration of justice by two distinct & independent sovereignties over the same persons, in the same place and at the same time; and [from] the necessity which will exist for the national government, if it shall provide for a compleat execution of its laws, of extending its courts thro' the whole extent of country and multiplying its officers without number." Sedgwick feared that proposals for extensive changes "may excite all the agitations of federal and antifederal passions which now seem to lie dormant thro' all the northern and eastern states." This remark was an allusion to the Antifederalist charge brought out during the ratification debates in 1788, that the federal judiciary "must in time take away the business from the state courts entirely."[37] Closely associated with this attack was the Antifederalist claim that, under the proposed Constitution, the states would be powerless to resist lawsuits by British creditors, and further that states would be "carried to the Federal Court" and forced to honor depreciated continental currency at face value.[38] A parallel Antifederalist apprehension had been that individuals would be abused by federal revenue collectors, who could enforce oppressive tax laws in federal courts. In rebuttal, leading Federalists had denied flatly the claim that states could be forced into the federal courts without their consent. Among those Federalists giving such assurances were Madison, Hamilton, and John Marshall.[39]

During the February 1793 term, the Supreme Court decided *Chisholm v. Georgia,* holding that a state *could* be sued without its consent in federal court over a debt owed to a citizen of another state. Edmund Randolph, the Attorney General, served as private counsel for the plaintiff before the Supreme Court. Condemnations of *Chisholm* reverberated throughout the country, starting the day after the decision with a resolution in the Senate for a remedial constitutional amendment. Newspapers predicted disaster if the holding was allowed to stand, because the states would be at the mercy of "refugees, Tories, etc., that will introduce such a series of litigation as will throw every State in the Union into the greatest confusion." Worse, the Court's ruling represented a frontal assault on the sovereignty of the states.

A writer in the Boston *Independent Chronicle* opined on July 25 that "a nation surrenders its sovereignty, as far as it relinquishes the right of final judgement—and if in all cases, we have done it, we have made by the adoption of the Constitution, a complete surrender of it to the federal judiciary: as the power of final decision is the essence of sovereignty." Finally, what made *Chisholm* all the more galling to its many critics was that during the ratification period the possibility of a state's being sued "was denied peremptorily by the Federalists as an absurdity in terms."[40]

Suits against state governments were only part of a larger issue concerning debt actions brought in federal courts on the basis of diversity of citizenship. Private debtors in the various states owed staggering sums to British creditors—the total reached upward of five million pounds *sterling*—which exceeded the nation's total foreign debt and was equal to almost a quarter the amount of the overall public debt. The principal debtors were planters and yeoman farmers in Southern states; Virginians, who topped the list, owed almost half of the overall debt due to British creditors. Another third of the debt was owed by citizens of South Carolina, Maryland, North Carolina, and Georgia.[41] Prior to the adoption of the Constitution, these debts essentially were uncollectible, as many states had erected legal barriers effectively blocking suits by British creditors, notwithstanding a provision of the Treaty of Paris requiring that no legal impediments would prevent repayment of all bona fide debts in sterling money. Failure of the states to enforce such debt obligations had been a major topic of discussion at the Philadelphia Convention because it was perceived that state recalcitrance over this matter could endanger the peace with Great Britain. One of the primary reasons for creating the federal courts had been to provide a neutral forum to enable creditors to collect such debts, which in turn would add stability to the national economy.[42]

In this instance, the intent of the Framers was somewhat fulfilled inasmuch as lawsuits seeking to enforce American debts owed to British subjects were among the first cases brought in the new circuit courts. Federal judges soon found themselves embroiled in controversy as they issued decisions siding with British creditors. This did not mean that the British were satisfied with these results. Ambassador Hammond remonstrated to Jefferson in June 1793 about the failure of British creditors "to procure legal redress in *any* of the courts of law in one or two of the southern states," and he averred that this obstacle was delaying Great Britain's fulfillment of obligations under the Treaty of Paris.[43]

As Chief Justice, Jay had taken the lead in lecturing the public through grand jury addresses and circuit court opinions on the importance of honoring treaty obligations—including the responsibility to settle delinquent accounts owed to British creditors. One such occasion took place during the circuit court session in Richmond in late May and early June 1793, at which Jay and Iredell sat with District Judge Cyrus Griffin. In *Ware v. Hylton*, the circuit court dismissed all but one of the defenses offered by Virginia debtors to an action by a British creditor for recovery on a bond from 1774. The critical questions in the case revolved around two Virginia statutes enacted during the war. One statute provided that the debt obligations would be discharged to the extent that payment was made to the Virginia treasury (under this law, the payment could be in paper money, although the bond specified repayment in sterling). Another Virginia act barred the recovery of any British debt unless assigned to a citizen by a certain date in 1777. The creditor denied the validity of these statutes on the ground that they conflicted with the guarantee of the Treaty of Paris against legal impediments to repayment. In response to this argument, the debtors maintained that the treaty was effectively suspended owing to British violations of several important provisions.[44]

Writing separate opinions in *Ware*, both Iredell and Jay rejected this last defense on the ground that the judiciary was not competent to hold a treaty void due to infractions by a foreign party. "[T]he judiciary are not authorized to annul a treaty," wrote Jay. Great Britain, however, could regard a court's failure to enforce the treaty's provision on debts as an infringement on its sovereignty: "Every judgment . . . against a subject . . . is a judgment mediately against the sovereign or moral person with whom the treaty was made, and which moral person is composed of all the people or nation collectively considered."[45]

On the remaining defense in *Ware*, namely, that the defendants were not responsible for that portion of their debt that had been paid to the state, Iredell and Griffin disagreed with Jay. In upholding this defense, Iredell wrote that the debt remained valid but that Virginia had substituted itself "in the place of the debtor." Dissenting, Jay insisted that the Virginia statute was invalid because it was contrary to the treaty and thus could not prevent recovery by the plaintiff. Jay's indignation at the defense undoubtedly was heightened by his own part in negotiating the treaty in question. For Jay the issue was one of simple equity. Under the treaty, "all American creditors are secured," and so accordingly, it was "but fair that all British creditors should be so likewise." Besides, Jay reminded the Virginians, "Britain neither sequestered nor confiscated any of our property; she interposed no lawful impediments to the recovery of debts."[46]

Some three years later, when the Justices reviewed *Ware*, the Supreme

Court would agree with Jay's position. During the interim, the circuit court's majority decision upholding the statutory defense proved to be of little consequence—only a small number of debtors had satisfied their debts by way of payments to the state treasury. A long line of creditors stood waiting for the outcome of *Ware* before filing collection cases, and now the circuit court had rejected all the other major defenses to repayment. Adding insult to injury, Jay instructed the circuit court jury that it should bring in a verdict for the principal and full interest. In requiring interest, Jay touched a raw nerve among Virginians, who like many Americans widely believed that the revolutionary conflict had made repayment impossible, and hence debtors had no moral obligation to bear interest charges.[47]

Needless to say, Jay was hardly a popular man in Virginia or the other debtor states, as evidenced by the heated denunciations of the Chief Justice that appeared in Republican newspapers. Edmund Randolph, during a trip through Maryland and Virginia shortly after the circuit court session, wrote to Washington reporting widespread dissatisfaction with the administration over the Neutrality Proclamation and the prosecution in *Henfield*. Much of this dissension Randolph attributed to misinformation on the part of critics. In Virginia, he found that "[t]he late debates concerning British debts have served to kindle a wide-spreading flame. The debtors are associated with the antifederalists and the discontented federalists; and they range themselves under the standard of [Patrick] Henry, whose ascendancy has risen to an immeasurable height. . . . Mr. Jay is considered here by some under very unfavourable aspects." A letter from Richmond appeared in the *National Gazette* during early July, taking note of Jay and Iredell's opinions "on the payment of the old British debts in favour of the British," adding that the city was "full of patriots, and no enemy to the French Revolution among them dares to open his mouth to vent his pestiferous principles."[48]

Another of the original Antifederalist contentions—that the federal courts would become instruments for administering onerous federal taxes—also was resurfacing. By this time agitation against the excise tax on distilled spirits had commenced in various parts of the country. Protesters already had warned that the federal courts would be used to drag tax resisters to trials in distant cities, in a manner not unlike British measures instituted before the Revolution. Jay had been asked by Hamilton in 1792 for advice on using the circuit court in Pennsylvania to take action in response to allegedly illegal agitation against the revenue tax in that state.[49] An element of class relations lay behind these events. Arrayed against the administration and the Federalist establishment generally were farmers at the lowest levels of society, who depended on distilling whiskey for their meager livelihoods.

These were the types of ordinary folks who would form the popular backbone of the Jeffersonian ascension to national leadership.

Abundant evidence documents the Justices' awareness of the political mood concerning the judicial establishment. Yet all this documentation taken together does not prove a link between those events and the Justices' declining to give advice to Washington. Still, to ignore this material would be to lose sight of the context in which the Justices acted. The question then becomes, What is the most likely explanation for the Justices' actions given the information we have about the political climate of the times?

Jay and his brethren were seasoned political actors, and they were not the type to squander political capital unnecessarily. Their actions in the Invalid Pension Act cases—in which most of them agreed to work as commissioners while declaring mandatory administrative assignments unconstitutional—show an adeptness at political maneuvering. Even so, they had brought down upon themselves the wrath of many in Congress—Federalists, no less—by questioning their duties under the Act. In fact, it is possible that one of the reasons for rebuffing Washington and his cabinet was a desire on the part of the Justices to show that they would consistently claim the right to turn down extrajudicial assignments from the other branches. In declining to extend judicial jurisdiction to encompass the handling of Pension Act applications, they had based their argument for unconstitutionality in large part on the ground that their actions would be subject to revision by both the Secretary of War and Congress. Perhaps they felt that reviewing the treaty-related issues presented by the administration would be perceived by Congress and the public in the same way, as the executive was under no formal duty to agree with their advice.[50]

No direct proof exists, however, to show that the Justices in 1793 recognized the parallels between Washington's questions and their work on the pensions. Nor is there any good reason to conclude that they were concerned about their advice being ignored in this instance. Surely the Justices realized that the chances of the Washington administration's disregarding their interpretations of the treaties (particularly Jay's views) were slim to none. The very fact that all the parties involved (the public included) knew that the Justices had been consulted as "persons learned in the laws" almost assured that their views would be treated with deference. One of the major concerns of the administration, after all, was to have authoritative support for the cabinet's judgments. Furthermore, given the ideological closeness of the Justices to the Federalist outlook on the European conflict, it is doubtful that the administration would have been disappointed by the answers.

Nevertheless, in politics it is the perception that counts, not necessarily the reality. What the Justices knew to be true was that they had "enemies" at large, and more than a few of these were in Congress. Considering the Justices' awareness of the need for legislative action on issues central to the future of the judicial branch, it made little sense to become entangled unnecessarily in a public debate that they could very well influence in other ways. Through a combination of informal advice, grand jury charges, dictum in opinions, and decisions in actual cases, the Justices were able to render similar assistance in a fashion less obviously tied to administration objectives. In chapter 1, we found that Chief Justice Mansfield apparently reached a similar conclusion about the utility of advisory opinions versus other means by which he might have an impact on national affairs.

This is not to say, however, that someone such as Jay or Mansfield was timid in the face of possible adverse public reaction. On the contrary, their records in office show them to be men who used their influence astutely and at times fearlessly. Only days after turning down Washington's request, Jay joined with Rufus King in an open effort to discredit Genêt. Inevitably, the Republican press denounced the pair's published charge that Genêt had threatened an "appeal to the people." Presumably Jay believed that his own involvement in this affair did not directly implicate the Court. An additional element—honor—was at work in Jay's mind, because Genêt was perceived as having crossed the line from representing his government to insulting Jay's friend, the President. Jay explained that his motive in issuing the declaration with King arose from "Indignation" at the manner in which Genêt's "Improprieties . . . affected our Contry, Governmt and the President, for whom we both entertained the most cordial Respect Esteem and attachment." Moreover, after Jay had rebuffed Washington with his letter, the Genêt incident afforded Jay an opportunity to express his devotion to the Federalist cause and to the President personally.[51]

Throughout this narration of the national political scene in 1793, we have witnessed the intersection of three powerful personalities: Jay, Hamilton, and Jefferson. On the basic outline of separation of powers and the essential role of the executive in foreign affairs, Jay and Hamilton were ideological twins. Jefferson could not have disagreed with them more thoroughly. In both camps, the ultimate stakes were seen as nothing short of the survival of the nation. Hamilton and Jefferson already had tried to destroy each other politically, and Jay plainly was capable of striking at another man personally when the occasion called for it. So ardent was the mutual dislike of Hamilton and Jefferson that even Washington could not mediate their quarrel.

Jay and Hamilton were together in Philadelphia throughout the time the Justices were considering Washington's inquiry. It would have been most unusual had the two of them *not* conversed about the events unfolding around them. Both were accustomed to cooperating in pursuit of the Federalist cause, and neither had any compunctions against doing so confidentially, even outside the President's view. From their point of view, such maneuvering did not amount to disrespect for a man whom both of them revered. Whatever other strengths President Washington possessed, his knowledge of the relevant law—whether constitutional law or the law of nations—was minimal. From the perspective of Jay and Hamilton, they simply were acting in the best interests of the President and the Federalist cause. Viewed objectively, however, Washington's dependency on the collective judgments of his cabinet made the situation open to political manipulation.

Hamilton and Jay played their hands masterfully. Throughout 1793, Jefferson steadily lost ground within the administration over the course of American relations with France and Great Britain. Jefferson found himself checked by Hamilton's facility with invoking learned authorities on the law of nations to support his position regarding American neutrality. Washington scarcely was capable of resolving the differing legal opinions by his key cabinet officers. Turning to the Justices for help—especially for advice from the President's friend and confidant, Jay—would have seemed to Washington a perfectly reasonable move considering the Justices' prior extrajudicial service to the administration. Hamilton appears to have gone along with this effort, to the extent of drafting many of the questions, despite his recent insistence as Pacificus that the executive and not the courts must take the lead in resolving legal disputes having a bearing on foreign policy.

This does not mean that Hamilton had changed his mind about the role of the courts. Rather, it indicates that the Secretary of the Treasury was acting in his characteristic way, attempting to take charge whenever an important issue was before the administration. Within the administration, Hamilton had been urging for months that the courts should play no role in public disputes over treaty obligations. Consequently, he may have acceded to Washington and Jefferson's desire for an outside opinion, while cautioning that the Court would not cooperate. It is quite likely that Hamilton had learned directly from Jay that he opposed answering the request; indeed, the two could have discussed the matter together in advance of Jay's meeting with Washington on July 17. Even if this understanding did not come straight from a conversation with Jay, Hamilton certainly was intimately familiar with Jay's overall interest in furthering a strongly unified executive branch on foreign affairs.

As events transpired, the entire affair worked out precisely in accordance with Hamilton and Jay's outlook on a range of issues. By declining the consultation, Jay and his brethren left the executive in primary control of the controversies spawned by the European war, knowing full well that the Federalist judiciary would be able to influence the interpretation of the law of nations through the avenue of litigated cases and grand jury charges. Leaving the cabinet with the responsibility for formulating rules to deal with the belligerents meant that Hamilton would prevail on virtually every issue. Jefferson knew this, as he already had complained forcefully that his great rival was dominating cabinet debates relating to the overseas conflict. Urging Madison to answer Pacificus produced a fine series of essays from Helvidius, but they failed to blunt Hamilton's assault. With his President at a loss regarding the law applicable to this affair, the Secretary of State had little hope of prevailing within the administration. Calling for an opinion from the judges, even with Jay on the Court, offered at least the prospect that some of Jefferson's positions would be vindicated.

At the end of this episode, Hamilton and Jay's philosophy favoring unified executive control over foreign affairs prevailed decisively. Not only that, Hamilton was vindicated in his position that the courts had no business addressing these questions. Jefferson found himself thwarted, if not embarrassed, by the Court's reply, which aligned perfectly with Hamilton's assertions as Pacificus. In a way, the affair resembled the clash between Hamilton and Jefferson on the constitutionality of the Bank of the United States, another occasion in which the ambitious Secretary of the Treasury had prevailed over the Secretary of State. As in the former case, Hamilton had once again shown the President that his interpretation of a central constitutional question was correct and Jefferson's was wrong.

Jefferson, thoroughly frustrated by these developments, informed Washington at virtually the moment the Court's declination became known to the cabinet that he intended to resign within a few months.[52] Hamilton and Jay then seized the opportunity presented by Genêt's tactless maneuvers to deal a strong blow to French diplomacy, a result that could only rebound to the benefit of British and Federalist interests. Persuading the President not to convene Congress early added the final flourish to the rout of Jefferson, inasmuch as it assured executive dominance of relations with European powers in the critical months to come.

The political history of the 1790s evinces a period fluid with change, and the alteration of a small set of facts might have affected profoundly the outcome of the Justices' deliberations over the questions. If the country had been less divided over the conflict, if circuit riding had never been instituted, or if Genêt had acted with more judgment—to mention several possibilities among many—it is conceivable that the Justices would have decided to play the historically acceptable role of formal advisers to the executive. Pondering how history might have been altered by the occurrence of contingent circumstances such as these may be an interesting exercise, but it does little to assist us in understanding why these long-ago events transpired in the way they did.

By untangling this complicated web of events, we may appreciate nevertheless how easy it is to be misled by the superficial explanations that public officials often offer to justify their actions. For most of American constitutional history, courts and commentators have taken the Justices' words in 1793 as an authoritative and literal depiction of the limitations on the advisory role of American judges. From the abstract language chosen by Jay when he penned the letter, an observer might think that the Justices felt bound by the inherent strictures of their office as set out in the text of the Constitution. Once we discover that no such structural or textual barriers prevented an advisory role for the nation's judges, we then are compelled to wind through the contorted passages of early American politics to explain the outcome. Keeping in mind the historical context of these events is essential to this inquiry. Above all else, the summer of 1793 seemed momentous to those involved because a decisive juncture had been reached in the nation's brief history—a juncture that implicated not only the future of the country but republicanism itself.

Conclusion

The Supreme Court has singled out the "case or controversy" requirement of Article 3 as "defin[ing] with respect to the Judicial Branch the idea of separation of powers on which the Federal Government is founded," and thus "stat[ing] fundamental limits on federal judicial power in our system of government." According to the Court's own historical analysis, "the oldest and most consistent thread in the federal law of justiciability is that the federal courts will not give advisory opinions."[1] At the same time, the Court has acknowledged that "historical antecedents of the case-and-controversy doctrine" are uncertain, noting that "the power of English judges to deliver advisory opinions was well established at the time the Constitution was drafted." Consequently, it is "not history alone [that] impose[s] the rule against advisory opinions on federal courts." Rather, the ban rests on "the implicit policies embodied in Article III," as the Court articulated in *Flast v. Cohen:* "When the federal judicial power is invoked to pass upon the validity of actions by the Legislative and Executive Branches of the Government, the rule against advisory opinions implements the separation of powers prescribed by the Constitution and confines federal courts to the role assigned them by Article III." *Flast*, nevertheless, did not ignore the influential events of 1793, as the opinion cited the correspondence between the Justices and the Washington administration.[2]

Whether the rule against advisory opinions "has been adhered to without deviation,"[3] as the Court at times claims, is a matter of interpretation. Those disagreeing with a decision of the Court, particularly dissenting Justices, commonly pin the charge of "advisory" on opinions that address issues not directly implicated by the facts presented in a given lawsuit. Nonetheless, there is general agreement that the 1793 incident provides the source for not only the prohibition against advisory opinions but an entire constellation of doctrines falling under the label of "justiciability": mootness, standing, ripeness, political questions, the doctrine of independent state grounds, the principle that constitutional questions are reached only as a last resort, and its related doctrine favoring a narrow basis for decision. All have been explicitly associated by the Court with the rule against advisory opinions. Similarly, the Court has linked its refusal to give advisory opinions to the principle in Hayburn's Case, that "'executive or administrative duties of a nonjudicial nature may not be imposed on judges holding office under Art. III of the Constitution.'"[4]

Why is so much reliance placed on a single episode, especially when the historical circumstances turn out to be far more complicated and contingent than usually has been assumed? The answer is, as much as anything else, inherent in the language forms of our culture. To demonstrate almost any principle, we invoke an archetypal case, a straightforward illustration of the point we are making. Asked to define a word, we often resort to descriptive examples when answering. Not any example will do, either, for the archetypal case must have some characteristic quality that is found in the general class of things we are discussing. Never mind that Plato (among others) demolished reasoning by example as a means of arriving at a definition—we still do exactly that in ordinary discourse, as well as in legal discussions.

In this instance, the archetypal case is the Court's exchange with Washington and his cabinet during the summer of 1793. The rationale outlined in the letter signed by Jay and his colleagues depicts a model of judges properly limiting themselves to a role as passive adjudicators of claims in contested court proceedings. In a 1984 case, *Allen v. Wright*, the Court explicitly acknowledged the kinship among "all of the doctrines that cluster about Article III—not only standing but mootness, ripeness, political question, and the like," namely, that they all "relate in part, and in different though overlapping ways, to an idea, which is more than an intuition but less than a rigorous and explicit theory, about the constitutional and prudential limits to the powers of an unelected, unrepresentative judiciary in our kind of government." Central to this conception of the proper role for judges is an understanding that the judicial branch does not have primary responsibility for executing the laws. "The Constitution after all," the Court has explained, "assigns to the Executive Branch, and not to the Judicial Branch, the duty to 'take care that the Laws be faithfully executed.'"[5]

Considering that Chief Justice Jay's letter to Washington specifically referred to the "Lines of Separation drawn by the Constitution between the three Departments of Government," and to "our being Judges of a court in the last Resort," it may seem to follow that the Court's refusal to give an advisory opinion was based on the same concerns about separation of powers that are delineated in modern cases. This is an unfounded assumption, for the concept of separated powers espoused in that earlier era was far less complex in its theoretical content and application than is the modern set of doctrines organized under the same rubric. Depending on the perspective of the observer in 1793, the actual implications of accepting the need for separation of powers under the Constitution differed markedly. Partially responsible for these variations in interpretation was the novelty of the situation in which early Americans found themselves. They had few models to draw upon: the British constitution relied on an entirely different conception of separated powers, and the distributions of powers in the various state constitutions were seen as having contributed greatly to the problems of government under the Articles of Confederation.

The approach taken in this book has been to set aside contemporary attitudes about advisory opinions and separation of powers generally. Working from the perspective of 1793, the Court's disinclination to provide an advisory opinion can be seen as a point occurring in a line of historical development that began centuries ago.

During the seventeenth century, early conceptions of separation of powers emerged from the struggle between Parliament and Crown. The abuses of the judiciary by the Stuart monarchs led to the view that judges needed insulation from political pressures. Life tenure for judges became the institutional solution to the problem. Under the constitutional theory prevailing in Great Britain through the nineteenth century, separation of powers was grounded on a division of power among three class-defined institutions: Lords, Commons, and Crown.

American theory of separation of powers as developed during the Revolution and thereafter depended upon maintaining a balance among three functionally defined branches of government (executive, legislature, and judiciary). Each branch had a core function, but no significant constitutional power could be exercised by one branch without some possibility of a check by another branch. These separate branches were expected to develop discrete political cultures, each with its own distinguishing characteristics, and to be directed by individuals who would be likely to resist the assertion of countervailing power by another branch.

In developing conceptions of separation of powers, Americans preserved many of the practices employed by British constitutional theory, including the structure of three branches, each with core responsibilities, and the protection afforded by life tenure for judges. The actual operation of government took place along traditional lines, with the British experience serving as the primary exemplar: the executive operated under a cabinet structure, the judiciary handled cases using the same procedural forms employed in the colonial period, and the legislature was divided into two houses. Even a semblance of the aristocratic elements of British government continued under the U.S. Constitution, as national offices were expected to be occupied by a relatively small segment of the population, distinguished by their wealth and social position.

At the federal Constitutional Convention, the theory of separation of powers was implemented mainly by parceling out power between the executive and the legislature. Comparatively little time was spent by the delegates on the judiciary. Critical questions regarding the courts were left unresolved or unconsidered, including such issues as the existence and scope of federal common law, the legitimacy and nature of judicial review, and the extent of federal judicial jurisdiction.

During the first years of the federal judiciary's existence, numerous points of dispute emerged regarding the federal courts' autonomy vis-à-vis the other branches. Hayburn's Case represents one early example of how the judiciary reacted when Congress attempted to exert its institutional power at the expense of the federal courts, and in its response the Court enunciated an interpretation of legislative limits over the judiciary. At the same time, both the executive and Congress were asserting their supposed prerogatives over different aspects of governance. Much uncertainty existed as to the proper allocation of powers. Among the unresolved issues were the questions of which branch had authority to declare neutrality, to recognize foreign governments, and to interpret treaties. New political coalitions—the seeds of the first national political parties—grew from this struggle to distribute power at the national level and from the parallel process of determining the boundaries between federal and state lawmaking authority.

The Justices were not constrained by an explicit constitutional rule against assisting Washington in interpreting the French treaties. Furnishing the requested advice would have been consistent with centuries of Anglo-American practice. Given the early stage of the development of the American theory of separation of powers, there was no inherent constitutional barrier to the Court's providing extrajudicial advice on appropriate occasions. Suitable restrictions could have been imposed to reduce the Justices' concerns for institutional autonomy—for example, the Court could have insisted, as the British judiciary had, on the right to change its opinions should the issue arise in a litigated case.

To explain the probable reasons why the Justices declined the request, it is necessary to study both the political events of these years and the personal outlooks of the key actors. The year 1793 presented an acute moment of crisis for the young country—a crisis that was perceived as threatening the very existence of the nation as a republican government. All the contending sides focused their arguments on interpreting treaty provisions and obligations to other countries under the law of nations. From the standpoint of Hamilton, Jay, and many other Federalists, it was essential to maintain executive dominance over these issues—a view that was based not only on ideological outlook but also on the practical lessons gained from their earlier experiences in foreign affairs. Two other related factors of importance were the Justices' ardent desire to prevail upon Congress to alter the judiciary system by abolishing circuit riding and their consistent determination in establishing the right of federal judges to decline extrajudicial assignments. Injecting the Courts' voice into the fray over the interpretation of the French treaties almost certainly would have engendered hostility in Congress, which was all the more troubling in light of the expected electoral gains by Republicans in the next session.

Another way of reaching the same conclusion is to keep in mind that the Justices were veteran political players, as well as loyal Federalists. At the very moment they were called upon to assist Washington, the immediate source of the controversy—the conduct of Edmond Genêt—was nearing resolution through the expedient of recalling the French ambassador. Jay himself would contribute to Genêt's demise through his joint statement with Rufus King concerning the foreign minister's threat to take his complaints regarding the administration's construction of the treaties straight to the American people. Pragmatic judgment loomed large on this occasion: the Justices avoided tying the Court directly to Washington's policies, but Jay and his colleagues were well aware that they had other avenues by which they might lend a decisive hand of support for the key aims of the administration.

Entwined in these events was the bitter rivalry among the key cabinet officers. This was a deeply personal affair of mutual animus so intense that the parties could not set aside their differences in spite of their recognition that the turmoil of 1793 constituted a turning point in the country's history. They were unable to do so for the simple reason that nearly everyone involved linked the actions of rivals to the fundamental question of whether the United States would continue as a republic or return to some version of monarchy. In this regard, the clash among the European powers that grew out of the French Revolution represented an epochal struggle that would determine the future of republicanism. Whether this was true or not makes no difference, for these were the stakes as perceived by the people at the time. When embroiled in any highly personal clash, the participants often lose sight of the larger dimension, which in this instance happened to be the best interests of the country. So intent were the protagonists in this drama at vanquishing their rivals that it becomes impossible to describe this episode without taking into account the human elements that influenced the actions of the major players.

It is on this note that a final comparison can be made between the experience of the Americans and their counterparts in Great Britain. In carefully reconstructing the centuries in which British judges were considered servants to monarchs and Lords, we continually found ourselves exploring the personal nature of major events. Whether it was the chronic tension in the relationship between the judges and their Stuart kings or Chief Justice Lord Mansfield's desire to affect public policy from behind the scenes, the human drive for power and influence shaped the struggle as much as any other factor.

As Washington himself predicted, every action taken by his administration would become a precedent. By invoking separation of powers as the rationale for not providing the advisory opinion, the Justices would be interpreted as implying that federal courts were authorized to take official action only in the course of actual judicial cases. A string of other issues that bore a resemblance to this earlier theory of the limits of proper judicial authority were encountered by future Justices. These various doctrines, arrayed under the general heading of justiciability, may not have followed inevitably from the 1793 incident, but they would be influenced strongly by the archetypal conception of courts as solely adjudicators of claims arising in the context of adversarial disputes.

Unless we take the time to look below the surface, almost any constitutional development can be depicted as a conflict over competing ideologies. By stripping the human dimension from an account of the past, we are left with an abstract conception of the question involved. The letter from the Justices in 1793 is such an abstraction. It presents a model of the proper judge under the Constitution—a normative archetype that serves as a guide for resolving other questions about when judges may exert their influence in a public controversy. In this case at least, the model has little to do with what actually occurred in history. Power grows from particular circumstances, rather than abstract principles.

Appendix

Letter from the Justices of the Supreme Court to President George Washington

Philadelphia 8 Aug. 1793

Sir

We have considered the *previous* Question stated in a Letter written to us by your Direction, by the Secretary of State, on the 18th of last month.

The Lines of Separation drawn by the Constitution between the three Departments of Government—their being in certain Respects checks on each other—and our being Judges of a court in the last Resort—are Considerations which afford strong arguments against the Propriety of our extrajudicially deciding the questions alluded to; especially as the Power given by the Constitution to the President of calling on the Heads of Departments for opinions, seems to have been purposely as well as expressly limited to *executive* Departments.

We exceedingly regret every Event that may cause Embarrassment to your administration; but we derive Consolation from the Reflection, that your Judgment will discern what is Right, and that your usual Prudence, Decision and Firmness will surmount every obstacle to the Preservation of the Rights, Peace, and Dignity of the united States.

We have the Honor to be, with perfect Respect,

Sir, your most obedient and

most h'ble Servants.

(signed)

John Jay

James Wilson

John Blair

Ja. Iredell

Wm. Paterson

Abbreviations

Adair & Evans	Adair & Evans, *Writs of Assistance, 1558–1700,* 36 Eng. Hist. Rev. 356 (1921).
Adams	G. Adams, Constitutional History of England (R. Schuyler ed. 1934).
Annual Register	The Annual Register, or a View of the History, Politics, and Literature for the Year 1806 (1806).
Anson	W. Anson, The Law and Custom of the Constitution (4th ed. 1935).
ASP-M & ASP-F	1 American State Papers (W. Lowrie & W. Franklin eds. 1834) (Miscellaneous & Foreign Relations).
Bailyn	B. Bailyn, The Ideological Origins of the American Revolution (1967).
Baker	J. Baker, An Introduction to English Legal History (3d ed. 1990).
Banning	L. Banning, The Jeffersonian Persuasion: Evolution of a Party Ideology (1978).

Blackstone	Commentaries on the Laws of England (1765).
Boyd	J. Boyd, Number 7: Alexander Hamilton's Secret Attempts to Control American Foreign Policy (1964).
Bramston	J. Bramston, The Autobiography of Sir John Bramston, K.B. (1845).
Brown	P. Brown, The Chathamites (1967).
Buel	R. Buel, Securing the Revolution (1972).
Burke	The Correspondence of Edmund Burke (G. Guttridge ed. 1961).
Campbell, Chancellors	J. Campbell, Lives of the Lord Chancellors (1880).
Campbell, Justices	J. Campbell, The Lives of the Chief Justices of England (1881).
Carroll & Ashworth	J. Carroll & M. Ashworth, George Washington— First in Peace (1957).
Casto	W. Casto, The Supreme Court in the Early Republic (1995).
Charles	Charles, *Hamilton and Washington: The Origins of the American Party System,* 12 Wm. & Mary Q. 217 (2d ser.) (1955).
1 Christie	I. Christie, Myth and Reality in Late-Eighteenth-Century British Politics (1970).
2 Christie	I. Christie, Stress and Stability in Late Eighteenth-Century Britain (1984).
1 Coke	E. Coke, The First Part of the Institutes of the Laws of England (18th ed. 1823, notes by Charles Butler and Francis Hargrave; originally published 1628).
2 Coke	E. Coke, The Second Part of the Institutes of the Laws of England (5th ed. 1671; originally published 1642).
3 Coke	E. Coke, The Third Part of the Institutes of the Laws of England (1644).
4 Coke	E. Coke, The Fourth Part of the Institutes of the Laws of England (reprint ed. London 1797; originally published 1644).
Collectanea	Collectanea Juridica (F. Hargrave ed. 1791).
Combs	J. Combs, The Jay Treaty—Political Battleground of the Founding Fathers (1970).
DeConde	A. DeConde, Entangling Alliance (1958).

DHR	The Documentary History of the Ratification of the Constitution (M. Jensen ed. 1976).
DHSC	The Documentary History of the Supreme Court of the United States, 1789-1800 (M. Marcus ed. 1985-).
Dickinson	H. Dickinson, Liberty and Property (1977).
Duman	D. Duman, The Judicial Bench in England, 1727-1875 (1982).
Elkins & McKitrick	S. Elkins & E. McKitrick, The Age of Federalism (1993).
Ellingwood	A. Ellingwood, Departmental Coöperation in State Government (1918).
Elliot's Debates	The Debates in the Several State Conventions on the Adoption of the Federal Constitution (J. Elliot ed. 1863).
Ernst	R. Ernst, Rufus King (1968).
Farrand	The Records of the Federal Convention of 1787 (M. Farrand ed. 1911).
Federalist	The Federalist (J. Cooke ed. 1961).
Fletcher	Fletcher, *Exchange on the Eleventh Amendment,* 57 U. Chi. L. Rev. 131, 133 (1990).
Flexner	J. Flexner, George Washington: Anguish and Farewell (1793-1799) (1972).
Flexner, New	J. Flexner, George Washington and the New Nation (1970).
E. Foster	E. Foster, The House of Lords, 1603-1649 (1983).
M. Foster	M. Foster, Crown Cases (3d ed. 1809).
Freeman	D. Freeman, George Washington (1954).
Gardiner	S. Gardiner, History of England from the Accession of James I to the Outbreak of the Civil War, 1603-1642 (reprint ed. 1965; originally published 1883-84).
Goebel	J. Goebel, Antecedents and Beginnings to 1801 (1971).
Gough, Fundamental	J. Gough, Fundamental Law in English Constitutional History (1955).
Gough, Locke	J. Gough, John Locke's Political Philosophy (1956).
Graves	M. Graves, The House of Lords in the Parliaments of Edward VI and Mary I (1981).

Graves & Silcock	M. Graves & R. Silcock, Revolution, Reaction and the Triumph of Conservatism (1984).
Gwyn	W. Gwyn, The Meaning of the Separation of Powers (1965).
Hale	M. Hale, The Prerogatives of the King (D. Yale ed. 1976, from 1660s manuscript).
Hamilton Papers	The Papers of Alexander Hamilton (H. Syrett ed. 1961–).
Havighurst	Havighurst, *The Judiciary and Politics in the Reign of Charles II*, 66 Law Q. Rev. 62 (1950).
Hoffman	R. Hoffman, The Marquis—A Study of Lord Rockingham, 1730-1782 (1973).
Holdsworth	W. Holdsworth, A History of English Law (1922–).
1 Holt	Holt, *"To Establish Justice": Politics, the Judiciary Act of 1789, and the Invention of the Federal Courts*, 1989 Duke L. J. 1421.
2 Holt	Holt, *"The Federal Courts Have Enemies in All Who Fear Their Influence on State Objects": The Failure to Abolish Supreme Court Circuit-Riding in the Judiciary Acts of 1792 and 1793*, 36 Buffalo L. Rev. 301 (1987).
3 Holt	Holt, *"Federal Courts as the Asylum to Federal Interests": Randolph's Report, the Benson Amendment, and the "Original Understanding" of the Federal Judiciary*, 36 Buffalo L. Rev. 341 (1987).
House Journal	Journal of the House of Representatives of the United States (Gales & Seaton eds. 1826).
1 Jay	Jay, *Origins of Federal Common Law: Part I*, 133 U. Penn. L. Rev. 1003 (1985).
2 Jay	Jay, *Origins of Federal Common Law: Part II*, 133 U. Penn. L. Rev. 1231 (1985).
Jay Papers	Correspondence and Public Papers of John Jay (H. Johnston ed. 1891).
Jefferson, Anas	T. Jefferson, Anas (E. Sawvel ed. 1970).
Jefferson Papers	The Papers of Thomas Jefferson (J. Boyd, et al., eds. 1950–).
Jefferson Works	The Works of Thomas Jefferson (P. Ford ed. 1904).

Jefferson Writings	The Writings of Thomas Jefferson (P. Ford ed. 1892–).
1 John Jay	John Jay: The Making of a Revolutionary (R. Morris ed. 1975).
2 John Jay	John Jay: The Winning of the Peace (R. Morris ed. 1980).
Jones	W. Jones, Politics and the Bench (1971).
Judson	M. Judson, The Crisis of the Constitution (1949).
Junius Letters	The Letters of Junius (J. Cannon ed. 1978).
Keir	D. Keir, The Constitutional History of Modern Britain Since 1485 (9th ed. 1969).
Kenyon	J. Kenyon, The Stuart Constitution, 1603–1688 (1986).
King	Life and Correspondence of Rufus King (C. King ed. 1894).
Labaree	L. Labaree, Royal Government in America (1930).
Langford	P. Langford, A Polite and Commercial People: England, 1727–1783 (1989).
Life of Jay	The Life of John Jay (W. Jay ed. 1833).
Link	E. Link, Democratic-Republican Societies, 1790–1800 (1942).
Lint	Lint, *The American Revolution and the Law of Nations*, 1 Dipl. Hist. 20 (1977).
Locke	J. Locke, Two Treatises of Government (P. Laslett ed. 1960).
Lycan	G. Lycan, Alexander Hamilton and American Foreign Policy (1970).
Mackintosh	J. Mackintosh, The British Cabinet (3d ed. 1977).
Madison Papers	The Papers of James Madison (R. Rutland & T. Mason eds. 1984–).
Madison Writings	The Writings of James Madison (G. Hunt ed. 1900–1910).
Maitland	F. Maitland, The Constitutional History of England (1908).
Malone	D. Malone, Jefferson and the Ordeal of Liberty (1962).
McDonald, Hamilton	F. McDonald, Alexander Hamilton: A Biography (1979).
McDonald, Washington	F. McDonald, The Presidency of George Washington (1974).

Miller	J. Miller, The Federalist Era, 1789-1801 (1960).
Montesquieu	Montesquieu, The Spirit of the Laws (G. & A. Ewing & G. Faulkner eds. 1751).
Morris, Nation	R. Morris, John Jay, The Nation & the Court (1967).
Morris, New England	Morris, *John Jay and the New England Connection*, 80 Proceedings of the Massachusetts Historical Society 29 (1968).
Namier	L. Namier, Crossroads of Power (1962).
Ogg	D. Ogg, England in the Reign of Charles II (1955).
O'Gorman	F. O'Gorman, The Rise of Party in England—the Rockingham Whigs, 1760-82 (1975).
Oldham	J. Oldham, The Mansfield Manuscripts and the Growth of English Law in the Eighteenth Century (1992).
Plucknett	T. Plucknett, A Concise History of the Common Law (5th ed. 1956).
Pocock	J. G. A. Pocock, The Machiavellian Moment: Florentine Political Thought and the Atlantic Republican Tradition (1975).
President's Journal	The Journal of the Proceedings of the President, 1793-1797 (D. Twohig ed. 1981).
Randolph	M. Conway, Omitted Chapters of History Disclosed in the Life and Papers of Edmund Randolph (1889).
Rudé	G. Rudé, Wilkes and Liberty (1961).
Senate Journal	Journal of the Senate of the United States of America (Gales & Seaton eds. 1820).
Setser	V. Setser, The Commercial Reciprocity Policy of the United States, 1774-1829 (1937).
Spedding	J. Spedding, The Letters and Life of Francis Bacon (1869).
State Trials	Cobbett's Complete Collection of State Trials (T. Howell ed. 1809).
Stevens	R. Stevens, Law and Politics: The House of Lords as a Judicial Body, 1800-1976 (1978).
Stewart	D. Stewart, The Opposition Press of the Federalist Period (1969).

Stourz	G. Stourz, Alexander Hamilton and the Idea of Republican Government (1970).
Tachau	M. Tachau, Federal Courts in the Early Republic: Kentucky, 1789-1816 (1978).
Thomas	C. Thomas, American Neutrality in 1793 (1931).
Treaties	Treaties and Other International Acts of the United States of America (H. Miller ed. 1931).
Turner	E. Turner, The Privy Council of England in the Seventeenth and Eighteenth Centuries, 1603-1784 (1927).
Valentine	A. Valentine, Lord George Germain (1962).
VanBurkleo	VanBurkleo, *"Honor, Justice and Interest": John Jay's Republican Politics and Statesmanship on the Federal Bench,* 4 J. Early Republic 239 (1984).
Vile	M. Vile, Constitutionalism and the Separation of Powers (1967).
Walpole, Correspondence	H. Walpole, Horace Walpole's Correspondence with Sir Horace Mann (W. Lewis, W. Smith, & G. Lam eds. 1960).
Walpole, Final	H. Walpole, The Last Journals of Horace Walpole (A. Steuart ed. 1910).
Walpole, George II	H. Walpole, Memoirs of King George II (1985).
Walpole, George III	H. Walpole, Memoirs of the Reign of King George III (G. Barker ed. 1894).
Warren	C. Warren, The Supreme Court in United States History (1947).
Washington Diaries	The Diaries of George Washington (D. Jackson & D. Twohig eds. 1979).
Washington Writings	The Writings of George Washington (J. Fitzpatrick ed. 1939).
Watson	S. Watson, The Reign of King George III, 1760-1815 (1960).
Wheeler	Wheeler, *Extrajudicial Activities of the Early Supreme Court,* 1973 Supreme Court Rev. 123.
White	S. White, Sir Edward Coke and "The Grievances of the Commonwealth," 1621-1628 (1979).
Williams	B. Williams, The Whig Supremacy, 1714-1760 (1939).

Wood	G. Wood, The Creation of the American Republic (1969).
Yorke	P. Yorke, The Life and Correspondence of Philip Yorke, Earl of Hardwicke (1913).

Notes

INTRODUCTION

1 Thomas Jefferson to John Jay and the Associate Justices of the Supreme Court (July 18, 1793), reprinted 26 Jefferson Papers, 520; 7 Jefferson Works, 451; John Jay, James Wilson, John Blair, James Iredell, & William Paterson to George Washington (Aug. 8, 1793) (original in National Archives, RG 59, M179, roll 10, Misc. Letters), reprinted 15 Hamilton Papers 111 n.1 & Jay Papers, 488. The Jay Papers version is based on a draft of the letter and varies slightly from the final form. A reprint of the original letter appears in the appendix of this book. The sixth and remaining member of the Court, William Cushing, was not present in Philadelphia for the August 1793 Term and thus would not have been able to sign the letter. See 1 DHSC, 217 n.143.

2 Morris, Nation, 46; T. Sergeant, Constitutional Law 363 (1822); 2 J. Story, Commentaries on the Constitution § 1571, 362 (2d ed. 1851).

3 1 Goebel, 626 n.68; McDonald, Hamilton, 280; Thomas, 150; see Elkins & McKitrick, 352 ("The justices, however, were reluctant to assume extra-judicial functions in passing upon these questions, and on constitutional grounds politely declined to do so."); R. Hendrickson, The Rise and Fall of Alexander Hamilton 394 (1981) ("The Supreme Court . . . established an important new constitutional

doctrine by holding that the court would refuse all requests to issue advisory opinions. . . . It firmly underscored the constitutional doctrines of separation of powers, checks and balances, and the independence of the executive branch."). By contrast, William Casto's book, *The Supreme Court in the Early Republic,* provides a more realistic account of this episode. See Casto, 75–82.

4 1 Warren, 111.

5 Marcus & Van Tassel, 42; Wheeler, 152.

6 Annual Register, 28 & 29–30 (1806) (summary of remarks of opposition speakers in the House of Commons, March 3, 1806); see 2 Anson, 118; F. Fletcher, Montesquieu and English Politics (1750–1800) 147 (1939).

7 Attorney-General for Australia v. The Queen and Boiler Makers' Society of Australia, 2 W.L.R. [1957] 607, 619 (H.L. 1957) (Austl.).

8 Muskrat v. United States, 219 U.S. 348, 354, 357 (1910); Gouriet v. Union of Post Office Workers, 3 W.L.R. [1977] 300, 332 (H.L. 1977) (C.A.); H. Hart & H. Wechsler, The Federal Courts and the Federal System 78 (1953); see P. Bator, et al., Hart and Wechsler's The Federal Courts and the Federal System 68 (3d ed. 1988).

9 Allen v. Wright, 468 U.S. 737, 750 (1984), quoting Vander Jagt v. O'Neill, 699 F.2d 1166, 1178–1179 (D.C. Cir. 1983) (Bork, J., concurring); see Valley Forge Christian College v. Americans United for Separation of Church and State, Inc., 454 U.S. 464, 471–476 (1982); H. Hart & H. Wechsler, supra note 8, at 78; P. Bator, et al., supra note 8, at 68.

10 This does not deny that American judges now perform "legislative" functions, as when they promulgate court rules or draft sentencing guidelines, see, e.g., United States v. Mistretta, 488 U.S. 361 (1989), but these are narrow exceptions justified in part by the courts' long-standing presence in certain fields (e.g., courts have always had inherent authority to make procedural rules; sentencing guidelines are a codification of what judges do in individual cases). Similarly, *individual* federal judges may perform nonjudicial functions, such as serving on the Warren Commission, for example, but the Supreme Court has refused to permit such assignment to federal *courts* since Hayburn's Case, 2 U.S. 409 (1792). In England there has been a much more expansive employment of individual judges for such extrajudicial purposes. During modern times, British judges often have served on Tribunals of Inquiry (special fact-finding bodies that investigate controversial matters, such as alleged government corruption) and Royal Commissions (bodies formed to investigate specific problems and recommend changes in the law, such as in the area of labor-management relations). See F. Morrison, Courts and the Political Process in England 174–91 (1973). Judges in Britain may be members of the House of Lords, where they participate in debates on changes in substantive law, although in theory "the law lords abstain from debate on other issues of political contention, even though they may involve important constitutional questions." Id., 192. Many of these "extrajudicial" tasks are adjudicative in nature, albeit outside a formal case in court. See id., 176–77 & 184. As chapter 1 demonstrates, there is only a distant relationship between these isolated instances

and the practices of British judges prior to the nineteenth century. It may be the case, however, that the greater willingness of Great Britain than America to use judges in such roles is derived from that country's long tradition of requiring judges to serve as advisers to the executive and the House of Lords.

11 "Executive" is a shorthand expression to distinguish advice given to the Crown or its ministers, as opposed to the House of Lords. For purposes other than those of this book, the term "executive" may be inappropriate when referring to early British government. Applied to the eighteenth century, for example, it hinders differentiating between the monarch and the cabinet as distinct political powers. In eighteenth-century vernacular, "executive" referred to a function of government (to execute the laws), rather than a particular branch of government.

12 There are other complications as well, such as the continuation in modern times of the chancellorship as a political office. See N. Underhill, The Lord Chancellor 173-201 (1978).

13 Cannadine, *No Entrance* (Book Review), N.Y. Rev. Books, Dec. 20, 1984, at 64 (quoting Lawrence Stone).

CHAPTER ONE: JUDGES IN GREAT BRITAIN

1 Blackstone, 221, 257, 260; see Hale, 106-7, 177-90; Jones, 27. Regarding the period before Henry III, G. O. Sayles emphasized that "the courts [were] the king's courts and the justices [were] the king's justices: it was their duty to watch over his interests and vindicate his rights . . . and we have good reason to believe that those who sat on the bench were expected to make arrangements for the prosecution of the king's business and actively intervene during the hearing of cases." G. Sayles, 5 Select Cases in the Court of King's Bench—Edward I, Edward II and Edward III, xxx (1958) (Selden Society, vol. 76); see J. Edwards, The Law Officers of the Crown 17 (1964). Writing in the mid-seventeenth century, Sir Matthew Hale described the King's "concilium ordinarium, or legal council," as "bound to advise the king in such questions as concern law or government." Members of the council included "the great officers of state and justice. . . , viz. the Chancellor, Treasurer, Keeper of the Privy Seal, Chancellor of the Exchequer, Justices of both Benches, Barons of the Exchequer, Master of the Rolls, King's attorney and serjeants, Masters of the Chancery, and . . . the Chancellor of the Duchy." 2 Anson, 77-78. Coke wrote in the *First Institutes* that "[t]he fourth councell of the king are his judges of the law for law matters; and this appeareth frequently in our bookes: and must be intended, when it is spoken generally by the councell, it is understood *secundum subjectam materiam;* for example, if it be legall, then by the king's councell of the law, viz. his judges." 1 Coke, 110a, § 164 (the *First Institutes* was originally published in 1628).

2 Jones, 17. A prime example of officials with multifaceted roles were the provincial Councils, which "united what would now be called administrative and judicial duties within the single concept of controlling geographical areas." Id., 16-17. These examples were part of a common pattern, according to John Brewer:

"Many corporate bodies combined what we today would distinguish as political and judicial functions. The House of Commons, for example, enjoyed a judicial as well as legislative capacity. . . ; aldermen both ruled and dispensed justice in their boroughs; and grand juries, as well as determining whether indictments were true bills, were seen as the proper body to initiate the petitioning process that brought political grievances to the attention of those at Westminister." Brewer, *The Wilkites and the Law, 1763-74: A Study of Radical Notions of Governance,* in An Ungovernable People 133 (J. Brewer & J. Styles eds. 1980).

3 On the judicial functions of the Privy Council, see J. Dawson, A History of Lay Judges 172-74 (1960); 5 Holdsworth, 155-56; 1 Turner, 180-90; 2 id., 157-66, 416-17; Dawson, *The Privy Council and Private Law in the Tudor and Stuart Periods,* 48 Mich. L. Rev. 393 & 627 (1950). On membership by judges on the council, see Ellingwood, 5; Plucknett, 242; 1 Turner, 20, 52, 73-74, 77, 98, 107, 375, 429; 2 id., 18, 25-26, 32, 38, 212-15, 228, 235, 266, 272, 273, 407, 434, 438. On legal advice by judges to the council, see Ellingwood, 5, citing J. Fortescue, The Governance of England, ch. 15, 148 (rev. ed. 1885; written 1471-76); Havighurst, 66; see, e.g., T. Barnes, Somerset, 1625-1640, 174 n.4 (1961) ("legal points connected with the suppression of Irish vagrancy and poor relief"). The membership of the Court of Star Chamber, which was abolished in 1641, included some or all of the Privy Council, and the Lord Keeper or Lord Chancellor (presiding), who were assisted by the two chief justices, and occasionally the puisne judges of Common Pleas and Kings Bench. See W. Hudson, A Treatise of the Court of Star Chamber, in 2 Collectanea Juridica (F. Hargrave ed. 1792) (written by William Hudson, a leading Star Chamber practitioner, circa 1621, and available only in manuscript until 1792); Barnes, *Star Chamber Mythology,* 5 Am. J. Legal Hist. 1, 4-5 (1961). One of the important functions of Star Chamber was the enforcement of royal proclamations, a jurisdiction that contributed heavily to the court's unpopularity in its final years. See J. Kenyon, The Stuart Constitution, 1603-1688, 106 (1986); Phillips, *The Last Years of the Court of Star Chamber, 1630-41,* 21 Transactions Royal Hist. Soc. 103, 116-17 (1939).

4 On the development of the inner cabinet, see Mackintosh, 52-63. The inner cabinet also was referred to as the "efficient," "effective," or "confidential" cabinet, among other terms. With a membership of ten to twelve, it became the principal executive council for matters of state by the 1760s. See Christie, 56. The larger cabinet, with a membership of thirteen to twenty under the Georges, included Chief Justices and Chancellors, but its powers became largely formal. Id.; 10 Holdsworth, 468-81, 629, 720; Williams, 38 & n.2; "Lord Ellenborough CJ was (in 1806) the last of many chief justices to serve in the Cabinet." Baker, 193; The Annual Register, 29-30 (summary of remarks made by government ministers in the House of Commons, March 3, 1806, reciting numerous examples of judges serving in executive positions). Two prominent examples cited by the last source were Lords Mansfield and Hardwicke. Mansfield's cabinet service is described later in this chapter; see 10 Holdsworth, 720; 12 Holdsworth, 473. Hardwicke's principal cabinet service occurred during his time as Lord Chancel-

lor from 1737 to 1756, but he was an active member of the inner cabinet and an influential member of the House of Lords while serving as Chief Justice of King's Bench from 1733 to 1737. See 1 Yorke, 143-156. Judges also served on the Council of State during the interregnum; see 1 Turner, 248-52, 353, & 363.

5 "[The Chancellor] was the first judge of the realm, the head of the Court of Chancery, a cabinet member, was always given a peerage with his office, and sat on the woolsack as speaker of the House of Lords. . . . Between 1714 and 1801 the Lord Chancellor was a member of the government but his office did not depend on the life of the government. He was in practice as well as in theory responsible only to the King." Duman, 20 & n.39, quoting Brown, 235-36. See Baker, 114 ("Some chancellors, notably Cardinal Wolsey (1515-29) and Lord Clarendon (1658-67), were prime ministers in all but name."). Maitland commented: "[i]t is curious that one who is the highest of judges is a member of the cabinet, a politician actively engaged in party warfare. . . . [I]t is a reminder that in the past judicial and governmental functions have been much blended." Maitland, 413; see 2 Anson, 164-69; 6 Holdsworth, 523-48; P. Langford, A Polite and Commercial People: England, 1727-1783, at 708 (1989). Lord Hardwicke, who was Chancellor from 1737 to 1756, "enjoyed vast political influence." Id. Hardwicke's biographer commented: "It would be misleading, however, to imagine that there was any such distinction in reality between his [Hardwicke's] political and judicial functions. The artificial, but convenient and indeed necessary separation of judicial office from political activity, maintained in modern times, was not then invented and would have been impracticable." 1 Yorke, 143; see also Campbell, Chancellors, 73-236; 12 Holdsworth, 237-54. On Thurlow, who was Chancellor from 1778 to 1792, see R. Gore-Browne, Chancellor Thurlow (1953); 12 Holdsworth, 318-27.

6 See 2 Anson, 111-18; 1 Christie, 63; 10 Holdsworth, 479-80; Williams, 38-39. Chief Justice Mansfield was a member of the inner cabinet under Newcastle (1757-62) and Bute (1762-63); 3 J. Campbell, The Lives of the Chief Justices of England 351 (1881). Christie, 57 & n.5. Early in the Grenville ministry (1763-65), the inner cabinet meetings were attended by both the Chancellor and Chief Justice Mansfield. 2 Anson, 113. Mansfield left the inner cabinet in 1763, after the resignation of his political patron Lord Newcastle, but thereafter Mansfield indicated that he was ready to give advice when requested. See id., 115; 1 Christie, 61. Mansfield's subsequent role with regard to advising the King and ministry is detailed later in this chapter.

7 1 Blackstone, 174 ("speaker of the house of lords is the lord chancellor, or keeper of the king's great seal"); E. Foster, 28. Foster also notes that under the early Stuarts, if the Chancellor was unable to preside over the House of Lords, the King designated a "substitute, often one of the judges." Mansfield became a peer (a baron) in 1756, at the same time that he was appointed Chief Justice of King's Bench. See Plucknett, 249; 12 Holdsworth, 472. Prior to Chief Justice Lord Raymond, who was made a peer in 1731, only two chief justices had been raised to peerages—George Jeffreys (King's Bench, 1683-89) and Thomas Parker

(King's Bench, 1710-18). See 3 Campbell, Justices, 84 n.2. Thereafter, the practice became more common; see 13 Holdsworth, 499; Williams, 445; Duman, 21. In the House of Commons, "[j]udges of the three Common Law courts were declared to be disqualified [from membership] by a resolution of the House in 1605, they being attendants as Judges in the Upper House." 1 Anson, 74; see 1 E. Porritt, The Unreformed House of Commons 220 (1903). Nevertheless, the judges in the early seventeenth century were in some instances present on behalf of the Lords at conference meetings with the House of Commons; at times, the judges took charge of these meetings for the Lords. See E. Foster, 74, 78-79, & 82. Judges were not barred by statute from serving in the Commons until 1875. See The Supreme Court of Judicature Act, 38 & 39 Vict. c. 77 § 5. Outside the common law courts, three judicial officers were allowed to sit in the Commons: the Master of the Rolls, the judges of the Court of Admiralty, and the judge of the Prerogative Court of Canterbury. See Duman, 21.

8 See Havighurst, 66; B. Abel-Smith & R. Stevens, Lawyers and the Courts 9 (1967); 4 Holdsworth, 68-69 & n.1. The blending of administrative, legislative, and judicial roles was most apparent in the local Justices of the Peace, who in the eighteenth century had wide-ranging and often unreviewable authority over rural and urban governmental administration, including levels of taxation. The Justices tried minor criminal and civil actions and acted as magistrates in preparing more serious criminal cases for Assize trials. See J. Dawson, A History of Lay Judges 143-44 (1960); 10 Holdsworth, 155-56, 243-56, & 720. Control was exercised by the judges at the twice-yearly Assizes, in which "the judges instructed the justices [of the Peace] in the niceties of the law and, in cooperation with the justices, issued orders of local administration." N. Landau, The Justices of the Peace, 1679-1760 (1984); 6-9, see id., 19-46; 1 S. Webb & B. Webb, English Local Government From the Revolution to the Municipal Corporations Act 533-50 (1906); Watson, 42-47; Williams, 49-51; Jones, 16. The impact of the common law judges' authority over local Justices of the Peace declined substantially in the eighteenth century; at the same time, the power of the Justices over their respective communities grew markedly. See id.; Landau, 7-8, 39-45, & 60; Watson, 47.

9 See 13 Holdsworth, 503.

10 See Baker, 163 & n.32; Ellingwood, 18-19; Stevens, 12; Veeder, *Advisory Opinions of the Judges in England,* 13 Harv. L. Rev. 358 (1900); Graves, 126; E. Foster, 70; Adair & Evans, 360; 1 Blackstone, 162.

11 Reports of Select Cases in All the Court of Westminster-Hall; also the Opinion of All the Judges of England Relating to the Grandest Prerogative of the Royal Family, and Some Observations Relating to the Prerogative of a Queen Consort, 92 Eng. Rep. 902 (1748). Fortescue was a judge of the Court of Common Pleas.

12 See Ellingwood, 26; E. Foster, 70-86 ("Their influence on legislation had long been profound, both in and out of parliament."); Graves, 132 (mid-Tudor period: "Throughout the legislative process their learning and expertise were prominent, even the pre-eminent, formative influences."); 10 Holdsworth, 610; Plucknett,

233; Williams, 23; Havighurst, 66; Lovell, *The Trial of Peers in Great Britain*, 55 Am. Hist. Rev. 69, 77 (1949) (attributing the near unanimity of decisions in peer trials during the seventeenth and eighteenth centuries to "increasing influence of the advisory royal justices"). Fortescue's reports contain a number of instances of judicial advice to the House of Lords; see 21 Eng. Rep. at 902-8. By the end of the seventeenth century, the judges' attendance was less than regular, despite the Lords' insistence on their attendance. For example, in 1694 the judges were admonished by the Lord Keeper: "I am commanded, by the House, to tell you, you have the Honour to be Assistants here; and the House takes Notice of your great Negligence in your Attendance: You have had sometimes Warning given you, though not with so much Solemnity as I am directed now to do it. If this Fault be not amended for the future, the House will proceed with greater Severity against you." 1 Journals of the House of Lords, 364 (Feb. 9, 1694); 10 Holdsworth, 610; Adair & Evans, 360. The reprimand was on account of the judges' failure to attend the House of Lords daily. Adair and Evans write that "during the 18th century the attendance of the judges became more and more spasmodic." They also contend that "throughout this period [1558-1700] the part they play [in legislation] seems to be rapidly decreasing in importance." Id., 362-63. Holdsworth maintained that the practice of consulting judges "was grow- ing less frequent" by the end of the eighteenth century. 10 Holdsworth, 610. Nevertheless, as the sources cited in this note and elsewhere indicate, the judges continued to give opinions throughout this period. For example, in 1758 the judges were consulted by the Lords on a proposed revision to the Habeas Corpus Act; at the Lords' request they drafted a bill, although it was not adopted until 1816. Indeed, the practice of consulting the judges was continuing when Adair and Evans wrote in 1921. See id., 362.

13 See Ellingwood, 23-24; Veeder, supra note 10, at 359. The judges had no formal vote, and "they were not even to speak unless asked for their opinion." Maitland, 84 & 176. Early in English history, during the reign of Edward I, the judges were members of Parliament, but at some point, perhaps in the reign of Richard II, they no longer voted and acted only as assistants to the Lords. E. Foster, 70 & 75; M. Hale, The Jurisdiction of the Lords House 158-59 (F. Hargrave ed. 1796).

14 On the influence of judges over the lay peers, see Ellingwood, 18-22; 10 Hold- sworth, 610; Plucknett, 232-33. There were occasions when the Lords had only a single law-trained peer in its membership, as occurred during a nineteen-year period in the early eighteenth century. Williams, 58. In addition to the problem of legal expertise, Robert Stevens points out that the "dry fare" offered by most appeals would hold little interest to the typical lay peer. See Stevens, 79. On the increase in appeals and the corresponding rise in the judges' importance to the House, see id., 9-12 (quote in text at 10-11).

15 1 Blackstone, 175-76; 21 Eng. Rep. 903 (1748). See Ellingwood, 25-28; E. Foster, 70-86; Graves, 120-40; Stevens, 7 & 12; Adair & Evans, 362. Many judges had substantial experience in drafting legislation prior to taking judicial office. Judges often were drawn from the ranks of law officers to the Crown; since the

sixteenth century, "it had been a very frequent practice . . . to offer chief justice-ships when vacant to government law officers." Baker, 192. A principal duty of the two major law officers—the Attorney General and the Solicitor General—was the drafting of legislation on behalf of the Crown for consideration by Parliament. 1 Oldham, 16.

16 Attendance in the House of Lords took precedence over the judges' circuit duties; if conflicts arose, special leave was required in order to be absent because of court work. See Ellingwood, 27-28 & 82. During the mid-eighteenth century, the two Chief Justices and the Chief Baron were often listed in official notices as absent from the Lent Assizes in order to attend to the House of Lords. See 1 Oldham, 129. On resisting advice, see E. Foster, 79-82; see, e.g., 1 Coke, 110a, § 164 n.5 (notes by Francis Hargrave, giving instances when the judges declined to give advice to the House of Lords); Jones, 62 (examples). For the 1718 incident, see 21 Eng. Rep. 903 (Fortescue's reports).

17 Michael Graves indicates that in the sixteenth century "the judges and law officers of the Crown were needed to assist the Lords in the business of drafting, revising and amending legislation." Graves, 120. He also demonstrates that the judges served on conciliar committees that put together the legislative programs for coming sessions of Parliament. Id., 132. Elizabeth Foster writes that judges in "all periods . . . explicated statutes," and in the seventeenth century "their advice was sought on proposed legislation before a parliament was summoned and they did preliminary work on bills." E. Foster, 72. Referring to the period from 1558 to 1700, Adair and Evans concluded that "[i]n addition to providing the lords with advice on technical legal points, the judges . . . sometimes sat on committees of the lords when law bills were under discussion, or sometimes had bills com-mitted to them for examination, though after 1600 the more usual custom was to summon them to attend on the lords' committee; they were also sometimes called upon to draft the amendments the lords proposed to a bill or even the whole bill itself, and it was the duty of two of them to carry to the commons all messages relating to bills which concerned the Crown or royal family." Adair & Evans, 362. On charges against judges, see E. Foster, 76-82.

18 Graves, 120 & 125-26. See Ellingwood, 2-7 & 19; 1 Turner, 1-15; Foster, 70; Adair & Evans, 357 n.1 & 360; Jones, 59 & 72.

19 Jones, 50; see, e.g., Graves, 131-32 (Queen Elizabeth, 1559). Mansfield's role in assisting George III with his legislative strategy is discussed later in this chapter. On assisting with legislative programs, see E. Foster, 82; Graves, 132. As to advising the monarch on the legality of royal actions, there are numerous exam-ples cited in this section and in sources listed in notes. Advising the King could be a perilous business, as is illustrated by a case in 1387 during the turbulent reign of Richard II, when Parliament agreed to create a council of Lords Appel-lant to curb the King. In answer to Richard's questions, the judges gave a series of opinions condemning Parliament's action as treasonous. M. Foster, Crown Cases 394-96 (3d ed. 1809). Parliament responded by impeaching several of Richard's councillors for treason; among the charges was that the defendants had

procured the questions from the judges. One of those convicted and executed
was Chief Justice Robert Tresilian. 1 State Trials, 106-8; For uses of "extrajudicial," see, e.g., The Case of Corporations, 76 Eng. Rep. 1052, 1053 n.(a) (1599);
Beckman v. Maplesden, 124 Eng. Rep. 468, 478 (Common Pleas 1662); Sackville's Case, 28 Eng. Rep. 940, 941 (1760) (certificate of the judges); Sackville's
Case, 2 Eden's Ch. 371, 372 n. (1760) (Eden's notes, published in 1818). Other
examples can be found in passages quoted in text or notes to this chapter.

20 1 Coke, 110a, § 164 n.5 (Hargrave's notes). Hargrave's observations tracked fairly
closely Chief Justice Mansfield's reservations about the use of advisory opinions
expressed in *Sackville's Case* (1760).

21 See Maitland, 270; Jones, 50-51; 5 Spedding, 114-20 (citing an instance of Coke's
participation in a meeting with the King's counsel prior to a prosecution; on this
case, involving John Owen, see note 25, infra). Coke's "[r]eports are laced with
resolutions, many of them fanciful and only off-the-cuff remarks [of the judges]
with which he agreed. He had affirmed that a resolution of all the judges was of
the highest authority next unto the court of Parliament." Jones, 51, quoting 2
Coke, 218.

22 Known as the *Case of Commendams,* the controversy arose out of a suit pending
in the Court of Common Pleas during the reign of James I that involved the
King's prerogative to make royal grants of benefices to a bishop. See 72 Eng.
Rep. 982 (Moore's Reports; Law French); 80 Eng. Rep. 290 (Hobart's Reports,
English trans.); 81 Eng. Rep. 600 (Rolle's Reports; Law French) (1616). James
commanded through his Attorney General, Sir Francis Bacon, that the proceedings stop until the judges had consulted with the King on the course of the action.
Initially, the judges refused the request, upon which all twelve were commanded
to appear before the King and Privy Council, where they were "severely repri-
manded" by the King in person. 1 Coke, 110a, § 164 n.5 (Hargrave's notes).
Francis Hargrave wrote that "after his majesty's declaration, all the judges fell
upon their knees and acknowledged their error of form" in disobeying the King's
command. Case of Commendams, in 1 Collectanea Juridica 14 (F. Hargrave ed.
1791). But Coke persisted in arguing that the judges had been right to refuse
delaying the case, which prompted James to demand the judges to answer
whether they would continue to contest his decree. According to Hargrave, all
the judges except Coke swore to honor "at any time" the King's command that
they stay proceedings and consult with the King "in a case depending before the
judges, which his majesty conceived to concern him, either in power or in profit."
Coke, however, replied "that when the case should be, he would do that [which]
should be fit for a judge to do." Id., 17. 3 Gardiner, 13; 5 Holdsworth, 439-40;
Maitland, 271; H. Woolrych, The Life of the Right Honourable Sir Edward Coke
110 (1826). Hargrave also explained that the justification given for the King's
order was a purported statute that "expressly requires them to *counsel the king
in his business.*" The oath in question originated in 1344, and it read: "Ye shall
swear, that well and lawfully ye shall serve our lord the King and his people in
the office of justice, and that lawfully ye shall counsel the king in his business,

and that ye shall not counsel nor assent to any thing which may turn him in damages or disherison by any manner, way, or colour." The Oath of the Justices, 1344, 18 Edw. 3 stat. 4. Coke denied that this was a statute; rather he said it was "simply the form of an oath" to the King. 1 Coke, supra (Hargrave's notes), citing 3 Coke, 146 & 224. In any event, Coke said that the oath required them not to delay proceedings, and that "the judges knew well amongst themselves that the case (as they meant to handle it) did not concern his majesty's prerogative of grant of commendams." Case of Commendams, supra, 14–15. James replied that the judges' decision to consider the matter "peremptorily . . . without consulting with his majesty first, and informing his princely judgement, was a thing preposterous." Id. Although the example illustrates Coke's willingness to challenge royal authority, it does not demonstrate that, when pushed, Coke refused to provide an extrajudicial opinion. In fact, in the main the example shows the judges bending to the King's demand that they follow his dictates. See Keir, 200 & n.4.

23   On James's order to Bacon, see Francis Bacon to James I (Jan. 27, 1614), reprinted 5 Spedding, 100. Bacon reported to James that Coke had objected "that Judges were not to give opinions by fractions, but entirely according to the vote whereupon they should settle upon conference; and that this auricular taking of opinions, single and apart, was new and dangerous; and other words more vehement than I repeat." Francis Bacon to James I (Jan. 31, 1614), reprinted id., 107; see also Francis Bacon to James I (Jan. 27, 1614), reprinted id., 100; 2 State Trials, 871–72. On the statutory problem of prosecuting Peacham, see Hamburger, *The Development of the Law of Seditious Libel and the Control of the Press*, 37 Stan. L. Rev. 661, 666–667, & n.11 (1985).

24   See Francis Bacon to James I (Feb. 11, 1614), reprinted 2 State Trials, 873; Francis Bacon to James I (Feb. 14, 1614), reprinted 5 Spedding, 121; 2 State Trials, 875; see also 5 Holdsworth, 438. Peacham was later convicted of treason but was not executed. See 79 Eng. Rep. 711 (King's Bench 1615); 2 State Trials, 869. The other judge's statement is by Dodderidge, J., and is quoted by Sir Francis Bacon in a letter to James I. Francis Bacon to James I (Jan. 27, 1614), reprinted 5 Spedding, 101; 2 State Trials, 872.

25   See Jones, 51. Shortly after *Peacham's Case,* in a case involving John Owen, who was accused of declaring it lawful to kill the King, the Justices were consulted as a group in advance of the trial. Although James suggested taking separate opinions, Bacon counseled otherwise: "that the same course might be held in the taking of opinions apart in this, which was prescribed and used in Peacham's cause, yet both my Lords of the Council and we amongst ourselves, holding it in a case so clear not needful, but rather that it would import a diffidence in us, and deprive us of the means to debate it with the Judges (if cause were) more strongly, (which is somewhat), we thought best rather to use this form." Francis Bacon to James I (Feb. 11, 1614), reprinted 5 Spedding, 119. After receiving the documents in the case, the other judges asked for time to consider, but Coke launched into a discussion of the issues. See id.

26   See White, 7. Francis Hargrave identified Coke's obstinacy in refusing James's

demand to halt proceedings in the *Case of Commendams* as the immediate reason for his removal. Coke was suspended from office two weeks after his confrontation with the King, during which Coke refused to promise obedience to similar orders in the future. See Case of Commendams, in 1 Collectanea Juridica, 3–4. For quote from *Third Institutes,* see 3 Coke, 29. On criminal consultations, see 92 Eng. Rep. at 905 (Fortescue's reports). See 2 Ogg, 522; Jones, 71 (Five Knights' Case); J. Pollock, The Popish Plot 284–85 (1944) (consultations under Charles II). In the famous case of John Eliot, in which Charles I had ordered the arrest and confinement of Eliot and a number of other parliamentary opponents, the judges advised the King in a letter that they would be forced to grant bail, and that Charles might release the prisoners himself in order to claim credit for the act. Charles, however, refused to produce the prisoners, and instead moved them to various jails to avoid the writ. Eliot subsequently was convicted in King's Bench (the court refusing to accept his plea of parliamentary privilege; see infra note 28 and accompanying text) and died in the Tower, never having been released. Bramston, 57–8; Jones, 79–80; 3 Gardiner, 92–96.

27 3 Coke, 29. As Fortescue notes, Coke cited the case of Hugh Stafford, a peer who was attainted of high treason by parliamentary act. In 1485, during the reign of Henry VII, Stafford fled to a sanctuary, where he was seized by the King's forces. The question arose whether the seizure was in violation of the right of sanctuary; the Attorney General asked the judges for an opinion, explaining that the King wished to know "before hand" if the sanctuary would save Stafford, because in that event the judicial proceedings would not take place. Chief Justice Hussey "went to the King and requested the favour that he would not desire to know their opinions; for, he supposed it would come into the King's bench judicially, and then they would do that which was right, and the King accepted of it." 92 Eng. Rep., at 905. Fortescue was paraphrasing Coke's account; see 3 Coke, 29. Coke also cited a case from 1535 in the period of Henry VIII involving the treason trial of a peer before the Lords, in which "it was resolved by all the judges in England" that they would hold no conferences with the Lords trying the case; if a question arose in which the Lords "shall doubt of any matter," they should consult with the judges "openly in Court, and in the presence, and hearing of the Prisoner." Coke called this "a just resolution: for when the Lords should put a case, and ask advice thereupon, the prisoner ought by law to be present, to see that the case or question be rightly put." Considering this precedent, Coke returned to the issue of executive consultations in criminal cases: "[I]f the Peers of the Realm, who are intended to be indifferent, can have no conference with the Judges . . . in open Court in the absence of the prisoner: à fortiori, the kings learned Counsell should not in the absence of the party accused, upon any case put, or matter shewed by them, privately preoccupate the opinion of the Judges." Id., 29–30.

28 Bramston, 48–54, 59, reprinted in Jones, 51–52, 81, 164–65, & 168, quoted in 5 Holdsworth, 351, 352 n.2. The judges added, however, that "they all disliked manie parts of the speech, and did conceaue it to be not accordinge to a parlia-

mentarie proceedinge." Id. A few other instances of refusals are collected in Holdsworth, id., 352. There were two sets of questions and answers, the first given by the Chief Justices and the Chief Baron, and the second by all the judges. 7 Gardiner, 89-91. These questions and answers are reprinted in Bramston, 48-49, and in Jones, 164-68. On the expansive scope of the judges' answers, see id., 60; on the use of answers in later proceedings against John Eliot and other members of Parliament, see Bramston, 59. That the judges withheld a complete answer is indicated by their response to the question whether the Petition would "conclude [the King] from committing or restraininge a subject for any tyme or cause whatsoeur without shewing cause." The judges replied that the answer would depend upon the precise case at issue, "which cannot perticularly be discerned vntil such case shall happen." Nevertheless, they added that should Charles grant the Petition of Right, "there is noe feare of conclusion, as in the question is intimated." "King's counsellors" quote in text is from Gardner, 294-96; see, e.g., Memorandum of the Justices, Hutton's Reports, 61-62, 123 Eng. Rep. 1101-2 (1623), reprinted id., 157-58 (a resolution on whether Parliament had on a previous occasion been properly assembled); G. Aylmer, The King's Servants — The Civil Service of Charles I, 1625-1642, at 108 (1961). On consistent use of advisory opinions in the seventeenth century, see Adams, 276; Ellingwood, 12; Kenyon, 395 (examples from the reign of Charles II); Wade, *Consultation of the Judiciary by the Executive,* 46 Law Q. Rev. 169, 181-82 (1930); 5 Spedding, 116-18.

29 Adams, 277; 8 Gardiner, 207; 5 Holdsworth, 351; Judson, 144; Ogg, 522; 1 E. Hyde (1st Earl of Clarendon), The History of the Rebellion and Civil Wars in England 88-89 (W. Macray ed. 1888). Id., x-xiii, xvii (editor's introduction). W. J. Jones comments: "Their [the judges'] opinions were solicited by the King to clarify the strands of policy, and as such used for propaganda in a fashion which was intended to nullify, but in fact compelled, resentment." Jones, 19-20; id., 49.

30 See 6 Holdsworth, 49-50; Keir, *The Case of Ship Money,* 52 Law Q. Rev. 546, 551-53 (1936). For a comprehensive history of the legal proceedings in the ship money controversy, see Keir, 369-91; 8 Gardiner, 79-105, 199-210, 269-81, 383; 9 id., 7, 75, 107-14, 130, 140, 153, 188, 245, 264, 383, 415. Traditionally, ship money had been exacted only from coastal towns on the theory that they benefited most from the protection offered by the naval forces. The opposition to Charles's ship money scheme arose vigorously after the second imposition of the tax, when he demanded ship money from inland counties as well. See Keir, supra, 551-55.

31 Address of Thomas Lord Coventry, in the Star Chamber (June 17, 1635), reprinted 3 State Trials, 825, 838. In a later address to the judges, Lord Coventry reported that "his majesty received satisfaction, in that you made a full declaration thereof in your circuits." Address of Thomas Lord Coventry, in the Star Chamber (Feb. 14, 1636), reprinted id., 839, 842. Oliver St. John asserted in the Long Parliament in 1640 that "most of them [the judges] declared their opinions [on ship money] in their circuits." Address of Oliver St. John (conference of both

houses of Parliament, 1640), reprinted 3 State Trials, at 1262, 1279. One of the articles of impeachment brought against Chief Justice John Finch of Common Pleas and Justice Robert Berkeley of King's Bench by the Long Parliament was based on their grand jury charges on circuit supporting the legality of ship money (Berkley called the levy "a lawful and inseparable flower of the crown for the king to command."). Articles of Impeachment of Sir Robert Berkely (1641), reprinted 3 State Trials, 1283 & 1286; T. Barnes, supra note 3, at 226 & n.43 (Finch).

32 Charles I to the Judges (Feb. 2, 1636), reprinted 3 State Trials, 842 & 843; 2 Historical Collections 354-55 (J. Rushworth ed. 1721). Charles's concern about dilatory process was not without cause, as "slow justice in the courts [w]as the central judicial problem of the age." Flemion, *Slow Process, Due Process, and the High Court of Parliament: A Reinterpretation of the Revival of Judicature in the House of Lords in 1621,* 17 Hist. J. 3, 3 (1974). That actions were pending was emphasized by Lord Coventry's address to the judges when he delivered the King's letter demanding their opinions. Address of Thomas Lord Coventry, in the Star Chamber (Feb. 14, 1636), supra note 31, at 842; 8 Gardiner, 207. Charles did tell the judges to "let all know" that his orders were not intended "to stop, or check, the actions or suits which any have brought, or shall bring, concerning this [ship money]." Coventry, supra, 845.

33 As a group, the judges issued at least two extrajudicial opinions concerning ship money. The first occurred in December 1635, a few months after the second writ was ordered, which for the first time demanded exactions from both inland counties and seaports. Apparently all but two of the judges signed an opinion stating that the charges could be imposed on the whole kingdom, and that "his Majesty is the sole judge" of the necessity for the measure. Opinion of the Judges (Dec. 1635), reprinted The King v. John Hampden in the Case of Ship Money (Ex. 1637), 3 State Trials, 1266, & in Bramston, 68; 8 Gardiner, 94. According to Oliver St. John, the judges had been consulted separately for this opinion and were sworn to secrecy. See Address of Oliver St. John, supra note 31, at 1262 & 1264. By early 1637, substantial opposition had arisen to ship money in influential circles, see 8 Gardiner, 205, and Charles wrote to the judges saying that "out of his princely love, to avoid all mistakes," he required a second opinion. Charles I to the Judges (Feb. 2, 1637), reprinted 3 State Trials, 842 & 843. The judges signed an opinion that was stronger than the first, using language suggested by the King's letter. The opinion said in part that "your Majestie is the sole judge, both of the dainger, and when and how the same is to be preuented and auoided." The Judges to Charles I (Feb. 7, 1637), reprinted 3 State Trials, 844; Bramston, 67-68. Then, on "command from his majesty," the various answers were published and entered in the records of the courts of Chancery, Kings Bench, Common Pleas, and Exchequer, and the judges were further ordered to "declare and publish this general Resolution of all the Judges of England, through all parts of the kingdom, that all men may take notice thereof." Address of Thomas Lord Coventry, in the Star Chamber (Feb. 14, 1636), supra note 31, at 839 & 845. Chief Justice John Finch claimed in his opinion for the *Case of Ship Money* that

Charles issued the first writ only after consulting with the barons of the Exchequer on the legality of ship money. Finch further asserted that prior to taking the opinions of the three benches, Charles twice received favorable opinions from the Chief Justices of the Court of Common Pleas (Finch) and Court of King's Bench, as well as from the Lord Chief Baron of the Exchequer. He also contended that the judges' second opinion was agreed upon "not singly, nor any one in a corner," but only after they had "advise[d] together." Argument of Sir John Finch, Kt. Lord Chief Justice of the Court of Common Pleas, The King v. John Hampden in the Case of Ship Money (Ex. 1637), 3 State Trials, 1219. Finch's account is not entirely trustworthy; for example, he does not mention the judges' first opinion in 1635. Moreover, Finch was accused of taking a more active role in obtaining the opinions than he described. During subsequent parliamentary deliberations on the matter of ship money, Oliver St. John told a session of both houses that the separate opinions were "procured by the solicitation of my lord Finch," who kept them secret for more than a year, after which he "liked them so well, as that he presumed to deliver them to his majesty." Address of Oliver St. John, supra, 1262 & 1264. There were also allegations that Finch resorted to bribes, threats, and misrepresentations to induce the judges to give their signatures. See 5 Holdsworth, 351-52 n.11; Jones, 125-26. Chief Justice Bramston's son wrote that Justices Hutton (Common Pleas) and Crooke (King's Bench) disagreed with the majority in the second opinion "and subscribed only for conformitie." Chief Justice Bramston (King's Bench) purportedly wished to say that the King had the power to exact ship money "duringe such necessitie only" (as opposed to "such tyme as your Majestie shall thinck fitt," used in the answer). Bramston signed, however, when "he was told by the antiente Judges that it was euer the vse for all to subscribe to what was agreed by the major part." Bramston, 68. See generally 8 Gardiner, 199-209 & 270-81.

34 The King v. John Hampden in the Case of Ship Money (Ex. 1637), reprinted 3 State Trials, 1215 & 1218-19 (opinions of the judges). The vote was 7-5 in favor of the Crown, but three of the dissenters relied on technical grounds that did not challenge the King's power. See 8 Gardiner, 279; Jones, 127. Until the decision of the Exchequer Chamber was overruled by Parliament, the opinion was cited in later cases as conclusively settling the lawfulness of ship money. See id., 128.

35 See Gough, 69-76; D. Hanson, From Kingdom to Commonwealth 315 (1970); Jones, 129; Judson, 269-73. Chief Justice Finch's view of the prerogative powers highlighted the constitutional claim at stake: "No act of parliament can bar a king of his regality. . . . [T]herefore acts of parliament to take away his royal power in the defence of his kingdom, are void." Argument of Sir John Finch, supra note 33, at 1235. The speeches in Parliament attacking the course of events in the Case of Ship Money recognized that the issue went beyond the tax to the entire question of parliamentary rights. St. John asserted, for example, that "here the endeavour was at once, not to blow up one act of parliament, but all; and these not introductive, but declaratory of the common law; as was the Petition of Right, the statutes there mentioned, and the resolutions." Address of Oliver St. John,

supra note 31, at 1280. For Charles, the case was immediately important because of his need for revenue; the *Case of Ship Money* was one of a series in which the Crown "looked increasingly to the judges to endorse its extraparliamentary devices. [T]he judges were forced to reach judicial verdicts which also had wide political and constitutional implications. It made life uncomfortable for them, but it was yet another reason why, in 1629, Charles I could contemplate governing without recourse to Parliament." Graves & Silcock, 167.

36 The quoted language is from the resolutions of the House of Commons, which are reprinted in 3 State Trials, 1261–62; the House of Lords' resolves, which were similar, are reprinted in id., 1299. The various speeches before Parliament are reprinted in id., 1260–1306. The King assented to Parliament's acts in August 1641. See Maitland, 308. Parliamentarians also condemned the judges' actions in imprisoning and denying bail to those refusing to pay the ship money levies. See Jones, 138, 139. As to impeachment charges, with the exception of the elderly Justice Croke, "every judge who had been involved in the ship-money decision was either dead or under attack." Jones, 139. Ultimately, however, none of the judges were convicted; one fled the country, and as to the others, the House of Commons "did not fear these men, and therefore felt no compulsion to destroy them. In the second place they did not believe that they could persuade the Lords that the . . . legal opinions of these men were crime." C. Roberts, The Growth of Responsible Government in Stuart England 101 (1966). Some of the judges even managed to rehabilitate themselves with Parliament. See G. Aylmer, supra note 28, at 386.

37 Address of Oliver St. John, supra note 31, at 1275. Similarly, Lord Falkland said that "those persons who should have been as dogs to defend the sheep, have been as wolves to worry them. . . . [A] most excellent prince hath been abused by his judges telling him, that, By policy he might do what he pleased." Address of Lord Falkland, before the House of Commons (Dec. 7, 1640), reprinted id., 1260–61. The speeches directed against the judges are strident in tone: "the attack upon the judges in 1640–1 sustained by an intensity of conviction which makes it a central episode of the period." Jones, 147.

38 Address of Oliver St. John, supra note 31, at 1276. "[W]hen Lord Keeper Finch protested [in 1640 to the House of Commons] that the judges by their oath had a duty to advise the King . . . he was enunciating a truth that no one attempted to deny. Instead, it was insisted that they had deliberately betrayed their trust by proffering pernicious advice." Jones, 20. Still, some parliamentarians criticized advisory opinions. John Pym, for example, in his 1640 speech to the Short Parliament listed the following as one of his grievances: "*Extrajudicial Judgments* and Impositions of the Judges without any cause before them, whereby they have anticipated the judgment which is legal and publik and circumvented one of the parties of just remedies, in that no writ of Error lyes, but only upon the Judicial proceedings." Speech of John Pym (Parliament, Apr. 17, 1640), reprinted 4 Historical Collections, supra note 32, at 1135; Kenyon, 187.

39 21 Eng. Rep. at 905 (Fortescue's reports). Hargrave quoted Fortescue to this

effect in his notes to Coke's *First Institutes;* 1 Coke, 110a, § 164; Jones, 13. On the later Stuarts, see H. Nenner, By Colour of Law 64 (1977): "[I]t could never in truth be said that the Stuarts operated in disregard of the rules. Instead, they used the law and, with the help of a dependent judiciary, maneuvered their way toward an interpretation of the constitution that was becoming ever more politically menacing."

40   See 5 Holdsworth, 351-52; Maitland, 312-13. On lucrative judgeships, see Jones, 37. "With [Coke's] dismissal, opposition from the Bench ceased, though an occasional reminder proved necessary in later years that the judges must be careful not to check or oppose any points of sovereignty." Keir, 200. Chief Justice Ranulph Crewe was dismissed in 1626 for refusing to acknowledge the legality of coerced loans to the sovereign. 6 Gardiner, 149; T. Barnes, supra note 3, at 164. Gardiner commented that although the other judges declined to submit to the loan, "it would be remembered that [the judges] were no longer disinterested umpires, and that the highest of their number had been dismissed from office because he refused to say that to be legal which he believed to be illegal." Id., 150. A subsequent proceeding, the *Five Knights' Case,* arose out of refusals by some seventy gentlemen to pay the loans; when five of these who were held without charges applied to the Court of King's Bench for writs of habeas corpus, relief was denied, with Crewe's successor (Chief Justice Nicholas Hyde) presiding. Id., 213-17; Jones, 37, 39, 68-69. Hyde commented in his opinion that "if no cause of the commitment be expressed it is to be presumed to be for matter of state, which we cannot take notice of." 3 State Trials, 59. Dismissals or suspensions of judges did not stop with Charles I: "Charles II removed eleven judges between 1676 and 1682, James II twelve in the four years of his reign." Graves & Silcock, 238. Although the dismissals and suspensions by Charles I and James I often are emphasized, "the later Stuart period was to see more dismissals than the early part of the century." Jones, 39; see Adams, 346.

41   2 Ogg, 522. David Keir writes that insecure tenure was only part of the explanation for the judges' support for the King; in addition, the legal rules regarding royal prerogatives "usually told strongly on the side of the King." Keir, 197. David Hanson writes similarly that the basic problem for those opposing royal authority on legal grounds was the difficulty in denying the lawfulness of prerogative powers: "there were abundant precedents for Stuart actions." D. Hanson, supra note 35, at 307; see generally id., 281-308; Judson, 115-16.

42   Jones, 148. See G. Davies, The Early Stuarts, 1603-1660, at 80 (1937) (Under Charles's prerogative government, "the judges, like the bishops, were popularly regarded as the willing instruments of despotism."); Graves & Silcock, 238 ("[R]oyal power over the judiciary was responsible for many of its unpopular decisions. The bullying of witnesses and intimidation of juries in political trials reflected the belief that it was the judge's duty to get a conviction in such cases."); D. Hanson, supra note 35, at 299 (After Coke's removal, in the pre-civil war period, "the bench was a supine instrument of the crown."); Black, *The Courts and Judges of Westminster Hall During the Great Rebellion, 1640-1660*, 7 J.

Legal Hist. 23, 23-24 (1986) (In contrast to the "high degree of practical independence from political interference" of medieval and Tudor judges "the Stuart
monarchs came more and more to look upon the courts and judges as instruments
of political policy.").

43 H. Nenner, supra note 39, at 108, 64, & 198. See Jones, 14-15, 137; Judson,
    107-70. J. P. Kenyon argues, however, that "until 1681 there is no sign that the
    Crown was using its wide powers, and the authority of the judges, against its
    opponents in any systematic way." Kenyon, 393. Moreover, he contends: "Nor is
    it a fact that insecurity of tenure weakened the resolve of the judges," and he
    cites several examples of judicial firmness in the face of royal pressure and
    dismissals. Id., 394. Similarly, J. W. Allen writes that following Coke's dismissal
    "the support of the judges became more steady. But it was never entirely reli-
    able." J. Allen, English Political Thought, 1603-1644, at 39 (1938).

44 Address of the Earl of Hardwicke to the House of Lords (Mar. 3, 1761), reprinted
    15 The Parliamentary History of England 1009 n.° (T. C. Hansard ed. 1813)
    (Lord Hardwicke presented a summary of Chief Justice Holt's opinion in a speech
    to the House of Lords in 1761). The issue was complicated by the Act of Settle-
    ment of 1701, which arguably granted the judges lifetime tenure during good
    behavior. The judges apparently decided, however, that the Act did not prevent
    the expiration of their offices with the demise of the monarch. By statutory
    change in 1761, the judges thereafter retained their offices notwithstanding royal
    transitions.

45 The Grand Opinion for the Prerogative Concerning the Royal Family, 92 Eng.
    Rep. 909 (1717) (Fortescue's reports). By a 10-2 vote, the judges concluded that
    the King possessed the prerogative power to control his grandchildren. Id.,
    924-25. On the background of George I's strained relations with his son, see
    Williams, 160-61. On the Francia prosecution, see 92 Eng. Rep. 734, 905 (For-
    tescue's notes). Fortescue was the solicitor general and reported that he was
    personally present at the meeting. Id. M. Foster, 241.

46 See D. Pope, At Twelve Mr. Byng Was Shot 298-99 (1962). 2 Walpole, George
    II, 210-11. The defeat at Minorca and the issue of Byng's responsibility for the
    matter were the source of considerable controversy and even rioting at the time.
    A long-standing view has been that Byng's court martial and sentence were
    ordered to deflect attacks on the ministry. See D. Pope, supra, at 204-42 &
    283-316. Prior to the proceeding, Chief Justice John Willes of Common Pleas
    wrote to the Duke of Newcastle (who, as First Lord of the Treasury, was head
    of the government), remarking that "I never found all sorts of people so uneasy,
    and so dispirited, as they are at present. . . . Mr Byng must be very severely
    punished; otherwise the clamour will be so very great that it will be impossible
    to put a stop to it." Willes advised Newcastle that there were two possible
    methods of trial, impeachment and court martial. Willes acknowledged that
    impeachment would "better satisfy the minds of the people" but that "there is I
    think one objection against it, which I cannot answer—it is that . . . he cannot be
    capitally convicted on an impeachment." John Willes to Duke of Newcastle (Aug.

21, 1756), quoted in id., 211. The court martial convicted Byng of negligence and imposed death, which the admirals trying Byng considered the only possible penalty, but they recommended mercy. When it became apparent that the sentence would be carried out, several of these admirals commenced a campaign for Byng's life; this included an effort to have Parliament lift the admirals' oaths of secrecy so that they could testify as to what occurred at the court martial. The House of Commons approved this measure, but it failed in the House of Lords. In the Lords, the admirals were questioned by Lord Mansfield (recently made a peer and Chief Justice; he had already given the King his opinion with the other judges on the legality of the sentence), with Lord Hardwicke taking a major role. According to one Byng supporter, Capt. Augustus Hervey, Mansfield and Hardwicke "'seemed like two attorneys at assizes pleading for the blood of a man.'" See id., 284-316 (Hervey quotation is at 313, quoting Augustus Hervey's Journal 241 [D. Kimber ed. 1953]). On the Byng proceedings, see 1 State Trials, 96-138. For Voltaire's original words, see Candide (ch. 23): "[D]ans ce pays-ci il est bon de tuer de temps en temps un amiral pour encourager les autres." Thanks to John Orth for this point.

47 For the background of this controversy, see Oldham, *The Work of Ryder and Murray as Law Officers of the Crown,* in Legal Record and Historical Reality 161-64 (T. G. Watkin ed. 1989); R. Pares, Colonial Blockade and Neutral Rights, 1739-1763, at 101-2 (1938). Regarding command from the King, see Diary of William Ryder (Dec. 1, 1747; Dec. 10, 1748) (quoting a letter from Chancellor Hardwicke; Dudley Rider reporting what Chief Baron Parker had stated to be Foster's view), quoted in Oldham, supra, at 162-63. Evidently the meeting between the judges and the law officers did not take place, although the evidence is conflicting as to why (the judges claimed the law officers had canceled, whereas the law officers thought that only a postponement had been requested). The question of the commission's legality was resolved by passage of a statute. Id., 164.

48 Sackville's Case, 28 Eng. Rep. 940-41 (1760). The reporter to *Eden's Chancery Reports* (1818 ed.), Robert Henley Eden, stated in a note to the case, 2 Eden's Ch. 371, 372 n. (1760), that "[t]his is the last time the crown has taken the opinion of the judges extrajudicially, there being no instance of it in the present reign." *Sackville's Case* is discussed in greater detail later in this chapter.

49 See, e.g., The Case of Corporations, 76 Eng. Rep. 1052, 1053 n.(a) (1599) ("The opinion in this case is extrajudicial, and therefore not entitled to the same consideration as if it had been adjudged upon a case regularly debated before the Court."); Beckman v. Maplesden, 124 Eng. Rep. 468, 478 (Common Pleas 1662) ("[I]t was an extrajudicial opinion; and though I must give reverence to the opinions of the Judges, yet I make a difference between cases adjudged upon open debate and having counsel on both sides, and resolution upon a case reported or referred to them."). Chief Justice Finch wrote about the 1637 *Case of Ship Money* that "we did not deliver our opinions as binding, nor were they so required by his majesty." The Argument of Sir John Finch, reprinted 3 State Trials, 1221. Finch also stated "that when judges singly deliver their opinions to the king, . . . we ought

to see very good and pregnant reasons to vary from that opinion, though it is not binding." Id., 1220. In assessing Finch's caveat, it should be remembered that his opinion was in favor of the King's prerogative powers. See id., 1235 ("[A]cts of parliament to take away his royal power in the defence of his kingdom, are void."). In 1711, when the judges were asked by Queen Anne for an opinion concerning a proceeding for heresy, eight of the judges indicated that inasmuch as "this being a matter which, upon application for a prohibition, . . . may come in judgment before [some] of us . . . in places of judicature, we desire to . . . reserve an entire freedom of altering our opinions, in case any records, or proceedings, which we are now strangers to, shall be laid before us, or any new considerations, which have not occurred to us, be suggested by the parties, or their counsel, to convince us of our mistake." Resolution of the Judges, reprinted 15 State Trials, 706. This opinion was joined by the Attorney General and Solicitor General. Id., 706–7. The judges' reservation is noted in the report to *Sackville's Case*, 28 Eng. Rep. 940, 941 n. (1760) (note describing the 1711 case). See also G. Burnet, Burnet's History of His Own Time 868 (1875) (Memoirs of Gilbert Burnet, Bishop of Salisbury, 1643–1715). Advisory opinions could still serve a purpose in cases where there was little or no prospect that the issue could come before the courts in a justiciable controversy. One thinks in this regard of the fate of Sir John Fenwick, who was attainted by Parliament in 1696 for plotting to assassinate William III. Fortescue records Fenwick's fate and the extrajudicial role of the judges in the proceeding: "[A]ll the judges met, Holt, Treby, &c. and also the Attorney General, to consider of the King's pardoning the judgment; and were all of opinion that the King could pardon all or any part of the judgment; and in this case all the judgment in high treason was pardoned, except severing his head from his body, and he was beheaded accordingly." 92 Eng. Rep. 734, 903 (Fortescue's reports). Bills of attainder were useful precisely in cases where the courts could not be employed to convict the attainted person. Fenwick's case, for example, did not meet one of the prerequisites for a conviction in court: that two witnesses be available to testify to the overt acts. See Maitland, 386.

50 M. Foster, 199. Foster mentioned this incident to deflate the use of *Peacham's Case* as a precedent on the definition of treason. Id. Mansfield and Foster had a "particularly close" relationship, and Mansfield "turned to [him and Judge Wilmot] for advice and training." 1 Oldham, 53.

51 See J. De Castro, The Gordon Riots 171–73 (1926); 2 Walpole, Final, 310–11 (the Gordon riots are discussed later in this chapter). Walpole believed that neither of the Chief Justices were in attendance at this meeting on June 7, 1780, but the *London Evening Post* reported that all the judges were present. See London Evening Post, June 8–10, 1780, quoted in De Castro, supra, at 171–73. Chief Justice Mansfield himself said, however, that "I never was present at any consultation upon the subject." Speech to the House of Lords (June 19, 1780), reprinted in J. De Castro, supra, at 205. Mansfield could have been absent because his house had been burned to the ground by a mob the day before the Privy Council meeting; he narrowly escaped with his life from the attack. See 2

Walpole, George III, 310. On questioning of judges at this session, see 2 id., 310-11; De Castro, supra, 171-73. The dissenter was Justice Henry Gould of the Court of Common Pleas. The *London Evening Post* reported that Gould "dared to stand single in his opposition to a measure which he stated as unnecessary in the present instance, as a precedent in the last degree dangerous to the liberties and constitution of the country. . . . The name of Gould will be dear to Englishmen." London Evening Post, June 8-10, 1780, quoted in De Castro, supra, 172. Walpole had a typically cynical interpretation of these events: "The Lord President [Henry] Bathurst, though then fuddled [by Gould's declaration], persuaded the King not to make Gould too popular by contradicting him; on which it was determined not to shut up the courts nor proclaim martial law, but to empower the military to act at their discretion." 2 Walpole, George III, 311.

52 12 & 13 Will. 3, ch. 2, § 3 (1700). The Act "made statutory the practice [regarding judicial tenure] regularly followed by William III." Keir, 269. "From the earliest patents down to the Long Parliament, [the] tenure [of the judges of King's Bench and Common Pleas] was practically invariable during the pleasure of the king." McIlwain, *The Tenure of English Judges*, 7 Am. Pol. Sci. Rev. 217, 219 (1913). Charles I agreed to the Long Parliament's petition in 1640-41 that the common law judges should enjoy tenure during good behavior. Charles II and James II, however, returned to the older practice of making judges subject to removal at the pleasure of the King. Id., 222-23; see Black, supra note 42, at 24. The situation of the Barons of the Exchequer was more complicated, but under the Stuarts their tenure was similarly precarious. See McIlwain, supra, 220-223. The Lord Chancellor remained a political figure accountable to the King for continuation of his office.

53 See 1 B. Bailyn, Pamphlets of the American Revolution 250 (1965); 6 Holdsworth, 234; 10 Holdsworth, 416-17 & 644-49; Williams, 56; E. Williams, The Eighteenth Century Constitution, 1688-1815, at 383-86 (1960); Black, supra note 42, at 24 & 46 n.7. The Act of Settlement left one loophole, namely, that judges' commissions expired six months after a monarch's death, thus allowing the royal successor to choose new judges. A few months following his ascension to the throne, George III in 1761 agreed not to insist on the right to appoint his own judges upon succession. See An act . . . relating to the commissions and salaries of judges, 1 Geo. III, ch. 23 (1761); Williams, 57 n.1. George III remarked, on the occasion of recommending to Parliament that this agreement be placed in a statute, that "their [the common law judges'] Offices have [terminated] upon the Demise of the Crown, or at the expiration of Six Months afterwards, in every Instance of that Nature which has happened." Address of George III (House of Lords, March 3, 1761), reprinted Journals of the House of Commons 1094 (1761). Lord Hardwicke noted that George I had refused to give new commissions to three judges in 1714 when he ascended the throne; George II refused only one. Address of the Earl of Hardwicke to the House of Lords (Mar. 3, 1761), supra note 44, at 1010 n.°; see McIlwain, supra note 52, at 224 ("[I]n 1714 and 1727, a number of judges failed of reappointment on the acces-

sion of the new king."). Horace Walpole thought, however, that George III's concession made no practical difference but was promoted for political purposes. See 1 Walpole, George III, 31.

54 10 Holdsworth, 419 (paraphrasing the argument of the Duke of Richmond). Others denied that there was any serious impairment to judicial autonomy, a conclusion with which Holdsworth agreed. See id. The Earl of Shelburne referred to Chief Justice Mansfield's membership in the cabinet as "repugnant" to the constitution: "For my part, I always imagined, according to the true principles of this constitution, that it was the great pervading principle and excellence of it, to keep the judicial and executive powers as separate and distinct as possible, so as to prevent a man from advising in one capacity what he was to execute in another." 18 Journal of the House of Lords 281 (1775).

55 See Gwyn, 24; Vile, 35-37 (1967); C. Weston, English Constitutional Theory and the House of Lords, 1556-1832, at 10-23, 34 (1965). Corinne Weston notes that the practice of mixed government was interrupted by the Interregnum, yet the theory persisted. After the Restoration, it "spread steadily in the reign of Charles II and after, and in the second half of the 18th century received its perfected form in the writings of Montesquieu, Sir William Blackstone, John Louis De Lolme, William Paley, and Edmund Burke." Id., 87. However, "it became the twofold task of the supporters of court and church to rescue the king from membership in the three estates by restoring him to the more appropriate position at their head and to bring back the bishops to parliament as one of the three estates." Id., 42-43. For example, Hale referred to Parliament as "the high and supreme court of this kingdom, being a convention of the commons by their proxies, the lords or peers together with the king, by virtue of his Majesty's writ or summons. . . . It anciently consisted of the king [being] the head, and the three estates of this realm, viz. the peers, the commons [and] the clergy; and that these were the three estates of the realm appears most plainly by the act of [listing statutes], and by divers other records. Therefore it is a great mistake and injury to the frame of government of this kingdom to make the king the third estate of the realm." Hale, 135. For quotations in text, see 1 Blackstone, 49-50; Answer to the Nineteen Propositions, reprinted 4 Historical Collections, supra note 32, at 731.

56 This description closely follows that in Bailyn, 67-77, but the account is standard; see Gwyn, 23-24; Weston, supra note 55, at 87-137; Wood, 18-20, 198, & 261; Dickinson, 44-45 (1977); C. Inglis, True Interest of America 18 (1776), quoted in Wood, 261; see Bailyn, 67-68.

57 See Vile, 39; 1 Blackstone, 50-51; see C. Weston, supra note 55, at 126-28.

58 Bailyn, 71-73; 1 Blackstone, 50-51. Montesquieu's account of the British constitution as based on balanced powers did not differ essentially from Blackstone's, whose writing on this subject depended heavily on Montesquieu. Vile, 102-6. However, in *The Spirit of the Laws*, Montesquieu more sharply emphasized than would Blackstone the importance of separated powers by demarcating a threefold classification of legislative, executive, and judicial functions, each of which must be placed in distinct hands in order to protect liberty. W. Fletcher, Montesquieu and

English Politics (1750-1800) 136-37 (1939); Gwyn, 109-10; Vile, 102-3. Montesquieu distinguished a legislative power that "enacts temporary or perpetual laws," an executive power over foreign relations and national defense, and a "judiciary power" that "punishes crimes, or determines the disputes that arise between individuals." Uniting any of these powers in the same person was inimical to liberty. A combination of legislative and executive powers would result in "tyrannical laws . . . execute[d] . . . in a tyrannical manner." The Spirit of the Laws, bk. 11, ch. 6, at 185-86 (G. & A. Ewing & G. Faulkner eds. 1751). As Locke had done before him, Montesquieu based his theory of separated powers on the need to uphold the rule of law. See Gwyn, 108. Nevertheless, Montesquieu did not regard a separate judicial establishment as decisive in maintaining the constitutional balance of power; of the three functions of government, Montesquieu wrote, "the judicial is in some measure next to nothing." Montesquieu, supra, bk. 11, ch. 6, at 190. The reason for this view was that Montesquieu regarded "[t]he judiciary power" as residing in juries, "persons taken from the body of the people, at certain times of the year . . . in order to erect a tribunal that should last only as long as necessity requires." Id., bk. 11, ch. 6, at 187; see Gwyn, 103 & 111; A. Cohler, Montesquieu's Comparative Politics and the Spirit of American Constitutionalism 107 & 111 (1988); see Montesquieu, supra, bk. 11, ch. 6, at 190; Gwyn, 110-11.

59 Vile, 69 & 13. See Pocock, 480-81. For example, Lord Bolingbroke, a Tory but nonetheless a leader of the opposition in the reign of George II, gave a well-known rendition of the constitution: "A king of Great Britain is that supreme magistrate who has a negative voice in the legislature. He is entrusted with the executive power, and several other powers and privileges, which we call prerogatives, are annexed to his trust. The two houses of Parliament have their rights and privileges; some of which are common to both, others particular to each. They prepare, they pass bills, or they refuse to pass such as are sent to them. They address, represent, advise, remonstrate. The supreme judicature resides in the lords. The commons are the grand inquest of the nation, and to them it belongs likewise to judge of national expences, and to give supplies accordingly." Remarks on the History of England (Letter VII, 1730), reprinted 1 The Works of Lord Bolingbroke 332 (1841).

60 See Bailyn, 48-51; 1 Christie, 296-98; Dickinson, 146-47, 169-75, 196, 225, & 229; 10 Holdsworth, 577-84 & 629-35; Namier, 88; Vile, 72-73; Wood, 33 & 143-45. Although "influence" was a common theme among opponents to the government, it has been contended by a leading British scholar of this period that: "'[i]nfluence' in the sense of corruption was of little account in the House of Commons of the later 18th century. . . . The distribution of patronage doubtless helped to cement support for the government, but with most of its supporters political opinions and the commonly current attitude of respect and loyalty towards the king's administration counted for more than the mere enjoyment of place. Often place was clearly a consequence, not a cause of political behavior . . . particularly the case after 1765, when Wilkes and America had brought great controversial questions back into politics." 1 Christie, 309-10.

61 See Gwyn, 37-65; Vile, 38-51. This is not meant to imply that there is anything
     timeless or universal about the notion of separation of powers, or that the move-
     ment in the direction of tripartite structures in modern Western countries was
     inevitable. Separation of powers (in current usage) is consistent with or at least
     congruent with current structures of democratic capitalism, but the entire devel-
     opment has been dependent upon historically specific and contingent factors.
62 See Gwyn, 5, 87, & 101; Vile, 28. In the later seventeenth century, the terms
     "executive" and "judicial" were employed interchangeably. Id., 30. On criminal
     proceedings, see J. Beattie, Crime and the Courts in England, 1660-1800, at
     268-79, 342-47, 352-62, & 406-49 (1986); Beattie, *Scales of Justice: Defense
     Counsel and the English Criminal Trial in the Eighteenth and Nineteenth Cen-
     turies,* 9 Law & Hist. Rev. 221 (1991); Landsman, *The Rise of the Contentious
     Spirit: Adversary Procedure in Eighteenth-Century England,* 75 Cornell L. Rev.
     498 (1990); Langbein, *Shaping the Eighteenth-Century Criminal Trial: A View
     From the Ryder Sources,* 50 U. Chi. L. Rev. 1, 126-127 (1983); Langbein, *The
     Criminal Trial Before the Lawyers,* 45 U. Chi. L. Rev. 263, 282-314 (1978).
     Over the course of the eighteenth century, the role of counsel increased, as did
     the adversarial nature of the proceedings. Nevertheless, Landsman has shown,
     with evidence from sessions papers for Old Bailey (London's principal criminal
     court), that even by the end of the century counsel did not appear in most
     criminal cases; likewise, prosecution attorneys were rare throughout the period.
     See Landsman, supra, 607; see also Beattie, supra, 9 Law & Hist. Rev., at
     226-30; Langbein, supra, 50 U. Chi. L. Rev., at 124-27; but see 1 Oldham,
     137 (citing a letter written by Chief Justice Mansfield in 1758, saying that at a
     recent Assize session all the defendants had counsel). Serious criminal cases
     were prepared by a local Justice of the Peace, a magistrate whose "task was to
     ensure that . . . the strongest evidence of [a defendant's] guilt would be con-
     tained in the depositions and examination that they were required to send in
     to the court. . . . The magistrate was more a policeman than a judge." J. Beattie,
     Crime and the Courts, supra, 222-24, 230-31, 271, 357. This pretrial process
     changed during the eighteenth century, so that by the beginning of the nine-
     teenth century the magistrate's proceedings were akin to a judicial hearing for
     determining whether evidence supported the charges. Id., 272-77. At the Assize
     trial, where the judge theoretically was acting as counsel for the accused, "the
     greater reality of the trial was that the prisoner (at least in offenses against
     property and other felonies) was mainly in a weak and disadvantageous position
     that was not fundamentally altered by [the] occasional examples of judicial be-
     nevolence and humanity." Id., 347. Landsman, supra, 497; Langbein, supra, 50
     U. Chi. L. Rev., at 123. Even when lawyers participated in eighteenth-century
     criminal trials, judges continued to insist "that the accused . . . speak for them-
     selves in court. . . . [L]awyers acting for accused felons were allowed in effect
     to do what the judge had always done for the defendant: to examine and cross-
     examine witnesses and to speak to rules of law. Counsel . . . were not allowed
     to speak to the jury on their client's behalf or to offer a defense against the

facts put into evidence." "Administrative adjuncts" quote is from S. Stimson, *The American Revolution in the Law* 4 (1990).

63 3 Blackstone, 56; 1 Holdsworth, 351–94; 10 id., 610–12; Vile, 54 & 69; Williams, 23 & 58; Beven, *Appellate Jurisdiction of the House of Lords,* 17 Law Q. Rev. 155–70, 357–71 (1901); Lovell, supra note 12; see E. Foster, 207–8; Answer to the Nineteen Propositions, reprinted 4 Historical Collections, supra note 32, at 731. On appeals to the Lords from various courts, see 3 Blackstone, 43 (King's Bench; this court also served as the appellate court from Common Pleas, and subsequent appeals went to the Lords); id., 46 (Court of Exchequer); id., 55 (Court of Chancery); id., 56 (Court of Exchequer Chamber). Regarding the Lords' role in impeachments and the trial of peers for felonies and treason, see 4 id., 256–62.

64 See Vile, 24; 1 Holdsworth, 363–64; Gwyn, 30. The trial of peers in the House of Lords, however, was actually a right that the peers had insisted on for centuries as a means to avoid trial in the King's courts. For a history of the Lords' efforts to secure this independence of trials, see Lovell, supra note 12, at 141.

65 On twin powers of government, see Gwyn, 30–33; Vile, 28–32; M. Needham, A True State of the Case of the Commonwealth 10 (1654), quoted in Vile, 48–49. Needham's work apparently had the approval of the Cromwell government. See id., 48. Needham elaborated on the themes in this tract in a 1656 work, *The Excellence of a Free State,* which John Adams described as being familiar to colonial Americans. See Vile, 50; Gwyn, 131–33 (partial reprint). For Adams's critique of Needham's work as providing insufficient separations of powers, see J. Adams, Defence of the Constitutions of Government of the United States of America (1787), reprinted 6 Adams Works, 44–50; Gwyn, supra, at 118–21; see Lilburne, The Earnest Petition of Many Free-born People, in A Declaration of Some Proceedings 28–29 (1648), quoted in Vile, 44; J. Milton, Eikonoklastes (1649), reprinted 1 J. Milton, Prose Works 363 (Bohn ed. 1848), quoted in Gwyn, 52. On parliamentary abuses, see C. Roberts, supra note 36, at 92–102 & 124–33; A. Woolrych, Commonwealth to Protectorate 258–69 (1982).

66 C. Dallison, The Royalist Defense A2 (1648), quoted in Vile, 31 & 46. On Dallison's authorship, see id., 32; J. Sadler, Rights of the Kingdom; or Customs of Our Ancestors 87–92 (1649), cited in Gwyn, 54–56; Address of Henry Ireton (Putney Debates, Oct. 28, 1947), reprinted Puritanism and Liberty 119 (A. Woodhouse ed. 1951).

67 J. Harrington, Commonwealth of Oceana (1656), reprinted The Political Works of James Harrington 174, 185 (J. Pocock ed. 1977), quoted in Vile, 29 & 51. As to impact on Americans, see Pocock, *Machiavelli, Harrington, and English Political Ideologies in the Eighteenth Century,* 22 Wm. & Mary Q. (3d ser.) 549, 551 & 558 (1965).

68 See Robbins, *The English Republicans,* in Two English Republican Tracts 46–47 (C. Robbins ed. 1969). Quotation is from Gough, 99.

69 Vile, 51; see Gwyn, 66–69. Opponents of Charles II and James II frequently invoked the theory of the mixed constitution as stated in Charles I's *Answer to*

the Nineteen Propositions in order to argue for limitations on the King's powers and to advance parliamentary causes. Royalists, in turn, condemned the theory as denigrating the King's rights with its assertion that the royalty shared power with the two houses of Parliament. As Corinne Weston explained, the "maxims [of the theory of mixed monarchy] were too radical for the years in which the doctrines of passive obedience, nonresistance, and the divine right of succession were ascendant." Weston, supra note 55, at 111. The "doctrine of the three estates triumphed. . . . The language of mixed monarchy was frequently employed in tracts published at the time of the Revolution and afterwards its maxims became commonplace." Id., 113; see id., 92-113. On the "country" opposition, see Bailyn, 48-50; Wood, 14-15 & n.34; Pocock, 349-552; C. Robbins, The Eighteenth-Century Commonwealthman (1959).

70 See, e.g., The Second Treatise of Government, §§ 137, 143, 159, in Locke, 377, 382, & 392 (first edition published in 1690 but revised substantially in three additional editions, the fourth published posthumously in 1713) ("[T]he Legislative and Executive Power are in distinct hands . . . in all moderated Monarchies, and well-framed Governments."). See Gough, Locke, 36 & 99. "In view of the contest for power between king and parliament, which was the dominant feature of English history at that time, and the constant efforts of parliament to check and oppose the actions of the king and his ministers, the distinction between executive and legislature was an obvious one, and it can be found in a number of writers before the publication of Locke's Treatises." Id., 98-99. In one of a number of passages about arbitrary rule, Locke wrote: "Absolute Arbitrary Power, or Governing without *settled standing Laws,* can neither of them consist with the ends of Society and Government, which Men would not quit the freedom of the state of Nature for, and tie themselves up under, were it not to preserve their Lives, Liberties and Fortunes; and by *stated Rules* of Right and Property to secure their Peace and Quiet." Locke coupled this point with the argument that a separation between executive and legislative powers was necessary to maintain government according to standing laws.

71 See R. Grant, John Locke's Liberalism 74-75 (1987); see also Gough, Locke, 97; M. Seliger, The Liberal Politics of John Locke 332 (1968).

72 Locke, § 131, at 371. For Locke, the ability of a people to appeal to known laws and established judges determined whether a civil society existed; see id. § 87, at 342, § 136, at 376, & § 149, at 385; R. Grant, supra note 71, at 77-78, 96; Gough, Locke, 94.

73 In the preface to the *Two Treatises,* Locke announced that the works were intended in part *"to establish the Throne of our Great Restorer, Our present King William; to make good his Title."* Locke, 155. Locke noted that a commonwealth may be organized with "the *Executive* . . . vested in a single Person, who has also a share in the Legislative." Id., § 151, at 386. See Gough, Locke, 102-3 (noting the similarity between this theory and the English constitution of Locke's period); J. Dunn, The Political Thought of John Locke 148-56 (1969); R. Grant, supra note 71, at 83-98; W. Von Leyden, Hobbes and Locke 143-50 (1982).

74 J. Trenchard, A Short History of Standing Armies in England (1698), quoted in Gough, Locke, 85; see Gwyn, 85-89, 109; Vile, 67-69.

75 See Bailyn, 51; C. Robbins, supra note 69, at 3-4.

76 1 Blackstone, 259.

77 Id.

78 3 id., 60.

79 1 id., 260. At the time Blackstone wrote, however, the Privy Council continued to hear appeals from colonial courts. See J. Smith, Appeals to the Privy Council from the American Plantations (1950); Goebel, *Ex Parte Clio* (Book Review), 54 Colum. L. Rev. 450, 462 (1954); Schlesinger, *Colonial Appeals to the Privy Council II,* 28 Pol. Sci. Q. 433 (1913).

80 It is important to keep in mind that the strict separation of governmental branches is a modern construct, just as "judicial independence" is a modern ideal. Although these concepts were being formed in this earlier period, people of those times did not hold them out as norms against which to evaluate such practices as judicial advisory opinions.

81 Except where indicated, the events described in this section rely on the following sources: P. Mackesy, The Coward of Minden (1979); P. Mackesy, George III and Lord Bute (1973); Valentine, 49-70.

82 Sackville's primary motivation for persisting was that he had become the subject of "universal denunciation," a "pariah in Society." Valentine, 54 & 57. Another impetus for the venture was the financial disaster he faced from the loss of the various military positions that were associated with his former office. See Horace Walpole to Sir Horace Mann (Sept. 13, 1759), reprinted 21 Walpole, Correspondence, 328.

83 See Lord Holdernesse to Lord George Sackville (Sept. 10, 1759), reprinted 1 Report on the Manuscripts of Mrs. Stopford-Sackville 316 (1904); Valentine, 56. On January 22, 1760, Sackville was informed that the King had agreed to a court martial. See Lord Holdernesse to Lord George Sackville (Jan. 22, 1760), reprinted 1 Report on the Manuscripts, supra, at 317. The court martial commenced on February 29. See Charles Gould to Lord George Sackville (Feb. 24, 1760), reprinted id., 318. An indication of the unusual nature of these events is that Sackville was asked *by the administration* to specify the charges to be preferred against him. See Lord Holdernesse to Lord George Sackville (Jan. 15, 1760), reprinted id., 317. Sackville replied with "astonishment" and indicated that he assumed Prince Ferdinand must have specified the offense; he "request[ed] that his Majesty . . . direct him to be prosecuted for whatever crime he is supposed to be guilty of." Lord George Sackville to Lord Holdernesse (Jan. 17, 1760), reprinted id.

84 Lord Mansfield to Lord Newcastle (Feb. 29, 1760), quoted in Mackesy, Coward, supra note 81, 181-82.

85 Horace Walpole to Sir Horace Mann (Mar. 26, 1760), reprinted 21 Walpole, Correspondence, 384.

86 See Lord Mansfield to Lord George Sackville (Jan. 1, 1758) (Germain Papers,

Vol. 1, William L. Clements Library, University of Michigan). On the Sackville-Mansfield connection, see Mackesy, Coward, supra note 81, 182 & 233. Horace Walpole noted this relationship in his memoirs. See 3 Walpole, George III, 93; Valentine, 55–56 ("It was currently believed that Lord George consulted Lord Mansfield and received that distinguished authority's opinion that a court martial would exonerate him, and the story is supported by the facts that after the court's adverse decision Lord George was very bitter toward Lord Mansfield."); 3 H. Walpole, George III, 95 (originally published 1757–60) ("It was pretended [apparently by Sackville] that Lord Mansfield had assured him he could not be convicted—but do general officers weigh legal niceties in the scales of Westminster Hall?"). Sackville wrote prior to the trial (and long before the judges gave their formal opinion): "I flatter myself, I must be acquitted. . . . Many people conceive it impossible for me to be tried, now I am absolutely out of the army, but I believe the best authorities in the law think I may." Lord George Sackville to Lord Viscount Bateman (Sept. 18, 1759), reprinted G. Coventry, A Critical Inquiry Regarding the Real Author of the Letters of Junius 282 (1825); Valentine, 93 ("Lord George . . . re-established a working amity with Lord Mansfield, whom he had attacked only four years earlier."); Lord Mansfield to Lord Sackville (Jan. 4, 1763), reprinted 1 Report on the Manuscripts, supra note 83, at 58 (discussing legislative matters); Lord George Sackville to John Irwin (Jan. 5, 1768, reprinted 1 id., 126 ("I had the pleasure of a long conversation with Lord Mansfield on Saturday last.").

87 Mackintosh, 69.

88 See, e.g., 1 Christie, 12–13, 84–108 & 209; Namier, 137; R. Pares, King George III and the Politicians (1953). To generalize, Namier tended somewhat to downplay George III's power, whereas Pares argued that he had a decisive role, particularly in Lord North's administration. Christie criticizes at length these two works and contends that a "more balanced assessment" is needed, one that falls somewhere in between Pares and Namier. 1 Christie, 107. A summary of Christie's views appears in the next few passages of text.

89 Id., 14–15, 38–39, 108, 296–310. On the transition to political parties, see A. Foord, His Majesty's Opposition, 1714–1830 (1964); Hoffman; Mackintosh, 63–65; O'Gorman; K. Perry, British Politics and the American Revolution 96–127 (1990); 2 Christie, 38–39.

90 See Mackintosh, 59–62; Christie, 39.

91 20 Parl. Hist. 1029 (1779) (Marquess of Rockingham); 19 id. 917 (1778) (Earl of Effingham), quoted in G. Guttridge, English Whiggism and the American Revolution 104 (1963).

92 Christie, 39, 44; see also J. Brooke, The Chatham Administration, 1766–1768, at 284 (1956); Hoffman, 274–75; D. McCracken, Junius and Philip Francis 65–66 (1979). On Pitt's view of Mansfield as Prime Minister, see Hoffman, 254. For Burke's understanding, see Edmund Burke to the Marquess of Rockingham (Jan. 5, 1775), reprinted 3 Burke, 89–90. Burke admitted that this was merely a supposition, remarking that "[i]t would conduce greatly to our acting with some

regularity if we knew who the Ministry were." Id., 89; The Plea of the Colonies (1776), quoted in G. Guttridge, supra note 91, at 104; To the Right Honourable Lord Mansfield (Letter XLI, Nov. 14, 1770), reprinted Junius Letters, 215. On the unusually wide circulation of the Junius writings, see J. Brewer, Party Ideology and Popular Politics at the Accession of George III, 154–55 (1976). Horace Walpole likewise asserted that in 1774 Mansfield was a key figure in a "secret junto, who, though really the confidential Ministers, were very distinct from the Administration." 1 Walpole, George III, 415.

93 To the Right Honourable Lord Mansfield (Letter XLI, Nov. 14, 1770), reprinted Junius Letters, 208.

94 See 1 Oldham, 5–7, 30.

95 See 12 Holdsworth, 468–71, 473; Brown, 236. Horace Walpole recorded that Mansfield, along with the Duke of Newcastle and Lord Hardwicke, "governed entirely" the Lords, whom Walpole described as a powerful but "tame, subservient, incapable set of men." 3 Walpole, George II, 18; 3 Campbell, Justices, 239–40, 349–50, 352 (quoting letters of Lord Waldegrave and Lord Mansfield); E. Heward, Lord Mansfield 77–83 (1979). On the Mansfield-Newcastle connection, 1 Walpole, George II, 109 (describing Mansfield as Newcastle's "creature").

96 See George III to Lord Bute (July 1762), reprinted Letters from George III to Lord Bute, 1756–1766, at 131 (R. Sedgwick ed. 1939) ("I long to hear whether Ld. Mansfield has been at Council [which he had not been], if he has not it is the greatest mark of disrespect ever showed to my Commands."); see also Letters of Jan. 13, 1763, & Nov. 4, 1762, reprinted in id., 157 & 184. Quotation from Bute is in J. Adolphus, The History of England 109 (4th ed. 1817) (citing "private information"), quoted in 3 Campbell, Justices, 361. On the earlier Mansfield-Bute relationship, see id., 257–360; Namier, 99; J. Brewer, supra note 92, at 126. According to Horace Walpole, Mansfield pleaded in vain with Bute to retain Newcastle as head of Treasury. See Walpole, George III, 132–33. Walpole indicated that Bute did not trust Mansfield. Id., 156. On Newcastle in opposition, see Hoffman, 38–65.

97 See 3 Campbell, Justices, 370. Mansfield said in a 1775 speech to the Lords that "he had lived with every administration on equal good terms; and never refused advice when applied to; that particularly the noble marquis [Rockingham] must recollect giving him every assistance his poor abilities were capable of affording; nor was it his fault that noble duke [Grafton] did not experience the same; for had he been applied to, he would have cheerfully rendered him every assistance in his power." 18 Parl. Hist. 275 (1775); Langford, 522, 708; also 3 Campbell, Justices, 356 (no individual had more influence than Mansfield in the first fifteen years of George III's reign). Many examples could be cited, but a characteristic one involves the attempt by the cabinet in 1775–76 to form a conciliation commission to resolve the crisis with America. Certain fundamental issues, such as whether to require the Americans to declare their submission to Parliament as a prelude to a treaty, divided the administration to the point of near dissolution. "North saved the situation—and perhaps his ministry—by bringing in the vener-

able Mansfield to arbitrate." O'Gorman, 339. "Mansfield's decision was accepted: that the colonies should be invited to make proposals for negotiation. Those which did not, would be recognised to be at war with Britain." Id., 606 n.13. Interestingly, one of the chief players in this affair was Lord George Germain, formerly Lord George Sackville, who urged demanding submission. Hutchinson quoted in B. Donoughue, British Politics and the American Revolution 46 (1964). On receiving advice from law officers, see 1 Christie, 76 & 209. Regarding Mansfield's advising George III, see 1 Oldham, 30.

98   See id., 709. A well-known instance of Mansfield's active participation in the Lords was his lengthy speech opposing the Rockingham administration's move to repeal the Stamp Act. 16 Parl. Hist. 172–77 (1766); J. Holliday, The Life of William Late Earl of Mansfield 242–51 (1797); 1 Oldham, 33 (collecting evidence of Mansfield's role in drafting the Marriage Bill) & 195; B. Donoughue, supra note 97, at 46–47, 87, & 120; 10 Holdsworth, 474; Langford, 709. In addition to taking positions favorable to the administration during debates, Mansfield also assisted in orchestrating the Crown's presentation. In December 1774, for example, Lord North sent the King "a plan of a speech which has been communicated to Lord Mansfield, & received his approbation, as it contains a detail of the plan for carrying on a War in America, together with an idea of a Commission much approv'd by Lord Mansfield." Lord North to King George III, reprinted 3 Correspondence of King George III 158 (J. Fortescue ed. 1927). Mansfield did disagree with the administration at times, as his opposition to repealing the Stamp Act shows. See Watson, 116–17; 1 Walpole, Final, 578; King George III to Lord North (Feb. 27, 1772), reprinted 2 Correspondence of King George III, supra, at 514; see 1 Oldham, 33. Mansfield's advice, however, was not always followed. For example, in 1770 when hostilities were threatened with Spain over the Falkland Islands, Mansfield advised against calling a joint session of Parliament. George hesitated at following this suggestion, fearing it would signal "that we are resolved at all events to accommodate the present dispute," and requested that Lord North discuss this factor with Mansfield. King George III to Lord North (Nov. 9, 1770), reprinted id., 166. The following day North reported that Mansfield had no objections to convening Parliament. See Lord North to King George III (Nov. 10, 1790), reprinted id., 167–68.

99   See 2 Oldham, 786-94, 814-28, & 833-43. On "calamitous decline," see 2 Oldham, 782.

100 King George III to Lord North (Mar. 17, 1771), reprinted id., 232; Lord North to King George III (June 17, 1770), reprinted id., 152; King George III to Lord North (Nov. 9, 1770), reprinted id., 166; D. Winstanley, Lord Chatham and the Whig Opposition 304 & 306 (1912). On Yorke, see Hoffman, 240–42; O'Gorman, 253–54; D. Winstanley, supra, at 296–315.

101 See Lord North to King George III (Sept. 17, 1776), reprinted 3 Correspondence of King George III, supra note 98, at 392–93; King George III to Lord North (Sept. 17, 1776), reprinted id., 393.

102 See 2 Christie, 27–54. For "political reality" quote, see Walcott, *Book Review,*

43 Am. J. Modern Hist. 322, 323 (1971). Junius quote is from Addressed to the Printer of the Public Advertiser (Letter No. 1, Jan. 21, 1769), reprinted Junius Letters, 32.

103 Tribunus, London Evening Post (Mar. 19, 1772), quoted in 1 Oldham, 33-34. On social tensions, see 2 Christie, 33-35 & 58; McCracken, 42; Rudé, 13-14. "Demise" quote is from J. Brewer, supra note 92, at 240-41 & 245. See Dickinson, 206. "The eighteenth and early nineteenth century was the high noon of mob disorder in England. Apart from the Jacobite attempts, rebellion had become a thing of the past, but with its disappearance riots increased Considerably." T. Hayter, The Army and the Crowd in Mid-Georgian England 1 (1978). Watson, 38-39 & 134. Ian Christie argues, however, that "there was a general awareness among the political class that occasional violent demonstrations should not be taken too seriously, that they usually arose over particular material grievances, and that they were not directed against the social system in general." 1 Christie, 35; see also id., 58. Christie has been criticized for his "rose-colored view of late eighteenth-century England," Kramnick, Book Review, 19 Eighteenth Century Studies 534, 535 (1986). Such events as the Wilkite riots may have concerned in part "material differences," but such issues as parliamentary representation were also at the forefront. For our purposes, however, the important point is that the ruling classes treated the Wilkite movement and other agitations seriously.

104 The original convictions arose out of Wilkes's publication of The North Briton No. 45, which could be construed as a personal attack on George III, and Essay on Woman, a bawdy and irreverent parody of Pope's Essay on Man. The two publications had been condemned by both houses of Parliament. See Rudé, 20-35. Wilkes, choosing to remain in Paris, failed to appear at his trial on these charges, and he was found guilty in a proceeding conducted by Mansfield; subsequently he was outlawed for failure to appear at sentencing. See 19 State Trials, 1075-77; 1 P. Fitzgerald, The Life and Times of John Wilkes, M.P. 258-61 (1888). The reports on the various proceedings involving Wilkes from 1763 to 1800 are reprinted in 19 State Trials, 1075-1138 & 1381-1418.

105 The deaths of Wilkes's supporters occurred when troops fired on crowds during the "Massacre of St. George's Fields," outside the prison where Wilkes was being held without bail pending trial (Mansfield had denied his bail). See Rudé, 47-56; J. Brewer, supra note 92, at 143-44. These events had followed a period of several months of sometimes violent agitation surrounding Wilkes's successful election to Parliament from Middlesex. See Rudé, 41-45; J. Brewer, supra, 129-30. Mansfield commented in his opinion for the case: "It is fit to take some notice of the various terrors hung out; the numerous crowds which have attended and now attend in and about the hall, . . . and the tumults which, in other places, have shamefully insulted all order and government." 19 State Trials, 1075-1079, 1082-83 n.° & 1111, quoted in J. Holliday, supra note 98, at 164. Mansfield's assertion that he was unfazed by the commotion appears infra text accompanying note 107. On criticisms of Mansfield's original rulings against

Wilkes, see 1 P. Fitzgerald, supra note 104, at 258; S. MacCoby, English Radicalism 1762-1785, at 94 (1955); P. Thomas, Lord North 26 (1976).

106 L. Kronenberger, The Extraordinary Mr. Wilkes 94 (1974); McCracken, 42; Rudé, 57. The technicality spotted by Mansfield was that the sheriff's writ recited that it was returnable "at my county court," whereas it should have specified the county (Middlesex) and stated that the court was "held for the County of Middlesex." 19 State Trials, 1114-16. Blackstone had warned, however, that "outlawry may be frequently reversed by writ of error . . . and if any single minute point be omitted or misconducted, the whole outlawry is illegal, and may be reversed." 4 Blackstone, 315. For the judges' opinion to the Lords, see 19 State Trials, 1127-1136.

107 Quoted in J. Holliday, supra note 98, at 149 & 165. Mansfield did have some rather severe critics in the press, but on the whole the newspaper accounts during the 1780s were rather favorable. See Oldham, 6-7. For Mansfield's denial of support for government, see 19 State Trials, 1112, quoted in J. Holliday, supra, 165; Junius's reply: To the Right Honourable Lord Mansfield (Letter XLI, Nov. 14, 1770), reprinted Junius Letters, 214.

108 See McCracken, 44-45; Rudé, 66-70; D. Winstanley, supra note 100, at 230-31, 244-47, & 255-71. The administration hoped that Wilkes's expulsion would bring an end to the rioting. Watson, 134-35. For Mansfield's statements, see 16 Parl. Hist. 959-62 (1770); J. Holliday, supra note 98, at 272-73.

109 See Brown, 276; Hoffman, 254-55; McCracken, 90-93; D. Winstanley, supra note 100, at 415-18. On the controversy over Mansfield's rulings on the role of the jury in seditious libel cases, see 2 Oldham, 775-800. There was contrary authority, in particular the *Seven Bishops' Case,* 12 State Trials, 183 (1688), but Mansfield chose to follow the traditional eighteenth-century authority, which since Chief Justice Holt's rulings on the subject had closely constrained juries in libel cases. Id., 777; Hamburger, *The Development of the Law of Seditious Libel and the Control of the Press,* 37 Stan. L. Rev. 661, 755-58 (1985). For quote on the crowd incident, see McCracken, 91; on the attempted investigation, see Brown, 293-94; Hoffman, 259-67; O'Gorman, 282-83; D. Winstanley, supra, 426-33. For Mansfield quote, see 4 Walpole, George III, 147; see 16 Parl. Hist. 1321-22 (1770). Camden had been Lord Chancellor until the previous January.

110 Edmund Burke to Marquess of Rockingham (Dec. 29, 1770), reprinted 2 Burke, 174. Walpole reported that Camden "declared he would meddle no further: he did not care to have all the twelve judges against him." 4 Walpole, George III, 149. See Hoffman, 262; London Chronicle (Jan. 17-19, 1771) ("skreen"), quoted in 2 Burke, 186 (editor's notes). The opposition was badly split over the proper approach to the issue of jury decision making in libel cases. Chatham, who was interested in embarrassing Mansfield, wished the legislation to declare in effect that the Chief Justice was in error by his rulings. The Rockingham-led opposition, however, thought that this was historically insupportable and that the bill should reform the existing law. Both Rockingham and Burke noted the futility of seeking declaratory legislation in the face of the nearly united opinions of the

common law judges supporting Mansfield. See Marquess of Rockingham to Edmund Burke (Dec. 15, 1770), reprinted id., 171; Burke, Speech in the House of Lords (Mar. 7, 1770), reprinted 2 Cavendish's Debates 352-77 (1770).

111 To the Right Honourable Lord Mansfield (Letter No. XLI, Nov. 14, 1770), reprinted Junius Letters, 207-9 & 211.

112 See C. Fifoot, Lord Mansfield 38 (1936); 12 Holdsworth, 471; 1 Oldham, 1-2, 18-20; 1 Walpole, George III, 207-23; Brown, 45; C. Fifoot, supra, at 33; E. Heward, supra note 95, at 150-60; Plucknett, 248-49. On Mansfield's decisions (some fourteen cases) concerning religious toleration, see 2 Oldham, 863-73; J. De Castro, supra note 51, at 36, 95-100; 2 Walpole, Final, 306; C. Hibbert, The Story of Lord George Gordon and the Riots of 1780, 112-18 (1959); J. Holliday, supra note 98, at 409-13; Rudé, 14. The bill in question, the Catholic Relief Act, 18 Geo. 3, c. 60, had passed the House of Lords without opposition in 1778. 19 Parl. Hist. 1143-46 (1778). Mansfield reportedly declined an armed guard to protect his house on the ground that he had nothing "to do with the Popery Bill."

113 16 Parl. Hist. 977 (1770), quoted in J. Holliday, supra note 98, at 242, 306; B. Donoughue, supra note 97, at 47. James Oldham interprets Mansfield's retreat from public statements about American affairs somewhat differently, but not inconsistently: "He was often featured in satirical prints as a co-conspirator with George III and the Ministers of State against the colonies. His early willingness to speak on the subject in the House of Lords receded as he became convinced that the less that was said, the better. This was because 'everything said in Parliament was immediately wafted to America, and converted to the purpose of counteracting the measures to which it related: Add to this, the frivolity of some parts of parliamentary Debate threw an air of consideration and levity upon the most serious subjects.'" 1 Oldham, 30, quoting Lloyd's Evening Post (Mar. 18-20, 1776) (statement of Mansfield).

114 See Edmund Burke to Charles O'Hara (Dec. 23, 1766), reprinted 1 Burke, 286 ("Lord Mansfield stood for the Constitution with his usual ability, and with an intrepidity that surprised friends and foes."); C. Fifoot, supra note 112, at 41. On Walpole's views, see 4 Walpole, George III, 34, 124-25, & 148. Walpole's charges against Mansfield were particularly vicious in the 1770s; 1 Walpole, Final, 216 ("Lord Mansfield . . . rarely abandoned mischief but from coward-ice."). Regarding the precarious tenure of the Chancellor, see Brown, 44 & 290; 12 Holdsworth, 472, 473 n.1; A. Mockler, Lions Under the Throne 161 (1983). Inexperience with Chancery matters could not have been the cause for Mans-field's disinclination because he had been a leading practitioner in that court. 12 Holdsworth, 472-73. For Newcastle quote, see Duke of Newcastle to Lord Mansfield (May 17, 1761), quoted in E. Heward, supra note 95, at 83. An example of Mansfield's declining to give an opinion to the House of Lords occurred in the debate on Chatham's corn embargo (described in text shortly hereafter). Although Mansfield delivered a speech on the limitations of prerog-ative powers, he declined to give a complete opinion on the ground that the

issue was before his court. See Lord George Sackville to John Irwin (Dec. 9, 1766), reprinted 1 Report on the Manuscripts, supra note 83, at 115.

115 Edmund Burke to the Marquess of Rockingham (Sept. 29, 1773), reprinted 2 Burke, 470; 1 Walpole, Final, 419; see 1 Oldham, 30; Brown, 290.

116 Id., 279; 18 Parl. Hist. 275 (1775).

117 Mansfield was Rockingham's uncle and former political mentor, and while their personal relations remained amicable, they had parted political company several years previously. See 3 Campbell, Justices, 370; Hoffman, 45. On the Chatham-Mansfield feud, see 3 Campbell, Justices, at 357; Brown, 26, 44, 247, & 293 (1967); Fifoot, supra note 112, at 38; Edmund Burke to the Marquess of Rockingham (Sept. 23, 1770), reprinted 2 Burke, 160 (referring to Chatham's "personal animosity" to Mansfield).

118 See O'Gorman, 196. For contemporary accounts of the corn embargo debate, see 16 Parl. Hist. 245-313 (1766); 2 Walpole, George III, 264; Lord George Sackville to John Irwin (Dec. 9, 1766), reprinted 1 Report on the Manuscripts, supra note 83, at 115; Edmund Burke to Charles O'Hara (Nov. 11, 1766), reprinted 1 Burke, 279. J. Adolphus, supra note 96, at 261-67. Walpole gave a cynical explanation for Mansfield's opposition: "Lord Mansfield, from aversion to Lord Chatham and his Chancellor Camden, was now the advocate of the Constitution. . . . Lord Camden answered with firmness, and with sharp irony, on the new Whiggism of the Chief Justice." 2 Walpole, supra, at 264. For examples of Mansfield's influence, see 3 Campbell, Justices, 370 (referring to advice to the Grafton administration); see, e.g., Charles Lloyd to Earl of Buckinghamshire (Sept. 10, 1767), reprinted 16 Report on the Manuscripts of the Marquess of Lothian 284-85 (1905) ("Lord Mansfield was in the Closet yesterday an hour and an half.").

119 Hoffman, 275, 260; see 1 Oldham, 33. Mansfield clearly was involved in both the drafting and the management of the bill in the House of Lords. "Political leprosy" quote is in Hoffman, 260.

120 See C. Fifoot, supra note 112, at 46-48; 1 Oldham, 47 & 51.

121 See Duman, 22 & 124; 1 Oldham, 28-29 & 124. Mansfield's personal wealth amounted to more than a half million pounds at his death—a fantastic sum for that period; he amassed this fortune largely from careful investments in mortgages and from the income of his office; see 1 Oldham, 28-29. Judicial pensions were not assured by law until 1799; see Duman, 124. Shelburne quote is in 18 Parl. Hist. 282 (1775); Chatham quote is in 4 Walpole, George III, 124.

122 See Brown, 232. It was noted in this period that places granted to holders for life tended to induce disloyalty, whereas those held only at the Crown's pleasure created influence over the person. See 1 Christie, 298 (citing statement of John Robinson, Secretary of the Treasury from 1770 to 1782 and the main organizer of Lord North's parliamentary supporters).

123 Pratt was Lord Chief Justice of the Court of Common Pleas. The quote is in the Diary of George Grenville (Dec. 17, 1763), reprinted 2 The Grenville Papers 239 (W. Smith ed. 1852). On Pratt's rulings, see Brown, 46 & 278-79; Rudé,

26-30. The report of Mansfield's remarks is somewhat vague, but it presumably relates to Pratt's actions of December 6, 1763, in which Wilkes recovered damages for his arrest under an improperly executed general warrant. See Wilkes v. Wood, 19 State Trials, 1154-76 (1763); see Brown, supra, at 278. Although Pratt avoided ruling on the overall legality of general warrants, only two years later Mansfield joined the other judges in erecting significant obstacles to the use of general warrants. See Leach v. Money, 19 State Trials, 1002-28 (1765); Brown, 279-81; Rudé, 30; see also Entick v. Carrington, 19 State Trials, 1030-76 (1765). Regarding Pratt's popularity, see C. Trench, Portrait of a Patriot 164 (1962). On the enhanced autonomy of judges, see Brown, 232; Mackintosh, 67.

124   On the Habeas Corpus Act, see 9 Holdsworth, 119-21; Speech of Lord Hardwicke (May 9, 1758), reprinted 3 Yorke, 12, quoted in 11 Holdsworth, 375 n.2 (1938); 3 Walpole, George III, 20. Walpole noted that one of the prior cases was that involving Admiral Byng. See id.

125   On occasion, Mansfield himself moved the Lords to require the judges' opinions and proposed the questions to be asked. See, e.g., 16 Parl. Hist. 316 (1767) (concerning the rights of religious dissenters). Mansfield also submitted to the House of Lords opinions from the other judges in pending cases. At a point when Mansfield was under attack for his views on the limited authority of juries in libel cases, he offered for support the written opinion of the judges of King's Bench in a case involving an alleged printer of the Junius letters. See 16 Parl. Hist. 1312-17 (1770); Fifoot, supra note 112, at 45; 4 Walpole, George III, 144. Lord Camden was furious at Mansfield's move, insisting that the opinion did not answer all the allegations brought against Mansfield, and he demanded that the judges answer "interrogatories" on the questions involved. Mansfield refused this request, which further aroused Camden, but the judges never were forced to answer. The judges' opinions are in 29 Journals of the House of Lords 337-38; 339-41; & 344-47, 353 (May 25, 26, & 30, 1758). Walpole reported that Mansfield spoke for more than two hours on June 2. Walpole, who generally criticized Mansfield sharply, wrote: "[p]erhaps it was the only speech, that, in my time at least, had real effect, that is, convinced many persons." 3 Walpole, George III, 121.

126   See 10 Holdsworth, 447-48; O'Gorman, 289-90. Horace Walpole provides a colorful, if slanted, view of George III's extraordinary efforts on behalf of the royal marriage legislation, which Walpole claimed was "undisguisedly disapproved by most of the Ministers, and even some of the King's own creatures." 1 Walpole, Final, 23; id., 23-24 & 27-71. According to Walpole, Mansfield advised the King "that his Ministers were divided (in truth they were in their hearts unanimous against the bill), and that he must oblige them to support it heartily, or change his Administration. The advice was taken and succeeded. The King grew dictatorial, and all his creatures kissed the earth." Id., 36. On Mansfield's involvement, see George III to Lord North (Feb. 21[?], 1772), reprinted 2 Correspondence of King George III, supra note 98, at 324; George III to Lord North (Feb. 21, 1772), reprinted id., 325; George III to Lord North (Feb. 27,

1772), reprinted id., 514; 1 Oldham, 33; 1 Walpole, Final, 23 ("bill drawn by Lord Mansfield"). On the Rockingham move, see Hoffman, 274; 1 Walpole, Final, 27–34. Walpole asserted, however, that "Lord Mansfield and the Ministers would not suffer" to allow Rockingham to ask the judges how far the King's prerogative extended beyond his immediate family, "because they were aware that the Judges could not answer it in a manner to justify what they were determined to enact." Id., 33. On the administration prevailing, see Hoffman, 275–76.

127   Stevens, 29; see also id., 28–34. In the year before this change, 1843, the judges were summoned to give guidelines on the insanity defense in criminal cases, which produced The M'Naghten Rules, 10 Cl. & Fin. 200 (1843). See Baker, 163 & n.32; 527 n.90, 598–99. On the 1873 law, see id., 163 ("treined judges"). On the eventual decline of advice to the Lords, see id., 163 n.32 & 527 n.90; Ellingwood, 23 & 28–30.

128   See 1 Christie, 18–19. "[I]n the later eighteenth century as so many times in earlier English history, those who defended the positions they sought by reference to ancient custom were in fact advancing new claims of a liberal and enlightened kind against old practices which no longer commanded general acquiescence." Id., 18. "[T]he fatal fear of eighteenth-century governments [was] offending a public known to be suspicious of all innovation." Watson, 73.

CHAPTER TWO: AMERICAN JUDGES PRIOR TO 1787

1   See Labaree, 134–35, 158, 167 & 403–8 (1930); Wood, 154–55 & 159–60; Friedman, 50–51. Among the positions most frequently granted the councillors were those of receivers general, naval officers, clerks of various sorts, and judges in the inferior courts. Labaree, 166.

2   See Friedman, 51 & 125–26 (2d ed. 1985); Labaree, 382–87 & 434–35; see, e.g., id., 162 (opinion on whether the governor could sit and vote with the council on legislative matters).

3   See Wood, 154.

4   See Wood, 156–61; Bailyn, 109–10; E. Douglas, Rebels and Democrats 26, 69–70, & 151–52 (1955); J. Greene, The Quest for Power: The Lower Houses of Assembly in the Southern Royal Colonies, 1689–1776, at 330–32, 343 (1963); Labaree, 388–401. The Declaration of Independence listed these as grievances: "He has obstructed the Administration of Justice, by refusing his Assent to Laws for establishing Judiciary powers. —He has made Judges dependent on his Will alone, for the tenure of their offices, and the amount and payment of their salaries."

5   Federalist No. 47, reprinted Federalist, 327; Federalist No. 48, reprinted id., 333 & 337.

6   See Wood, 154–56 & 160–61; F. Aumann, The Changing American Legal System 161–65 & 171–72 (1940); N.Y. Const. Art. 32 (1777), reprinted 5 The Federal and State Constitutions 2635 (F. Thorpe ed. 1909); N.Y. Const. Art. 5, § 1 (1821),

reprinted id., 2646; Federalist No. 71, reprinted Federalist, 483. Lawrence Fried-man discusses the New York example, as well as those of Connecticut and New Jersey, where the highest court was composed of variations of the governor and governor's council. Friedman, 139-40; Corwin, *The Progress of Constitutional Theory Between the Declaration of Independence and the Meeting of the Phila-delphia Convention,* 30 Am. Hist. Rev. 511, 514-15, & 519-20 (1925).

7 Adams, The Earl of Clarendon to William Pym, Boston Gazette, Jan. 27, 1766, reprinted 3 Adams Works, 480 & 481, quoted in Wood, 159; id., 456.

8 Mass. Const., Pt. 2, Ch. 3, Art. 2 (1780), reprinted 2 Federal and State Consti-tutions, supra note 6, at 1905; Opinions of the Justices to the Senate and House of Representatives, 12 Lathrop, 126 Mass. 547, 548 (1781); N.H. Const., Part 2 ("The Form of Government"). For a history of the provision for advisory opinions in the Massachusetts and New Hampshire constitutions, see Dubuque, *The Duty of Judges as Constitutional Advisers,* 24 Am. L. Rev. 369, 376 (1890); a digest of advisory opinions by Massachusetts and New Hampshire courts through the end of the nineteenth century is found in Dubuque, 378-80 n.1. No evidence of its use in New Hampshire prior to 1816 has been found. Ellingwood, 39. See Mass. Const., Pt. I, Art. 30 (1780), reprinted 3 Federal and State Constitutions, supra note 6, at 1893: "In the government of this commonwealth the legislature shall never exercise the executive and judicial powers, or either of them: the executive shall never exercise the legislative and judicial powers, or either of them: the judicial shall never exercise the legislative and executive powers, or either of them: to the end it may be a government of laws and not of men." See also N.H. Const., Pt. I, Art. 37 (1792) (three branches "ought to be kept as separate from and independent of each other, as the nature of a free government will admit").

9 See 2 W. Crosskey, Politics and the Constitution in the History of the United States 966 (1953); R.I. Acts and Resolves (1st Sess.) 3 (1786). Judge Howell's remarks were reported in a pamphlet printed in 1787, The Case, Trevett against Weeden, &c. (Providence, John Carter, 1787), reprinted 1 J. Thayer, Cases on Constitutional Law 73, 76 (1895), 2 Chandler's Crim. Tr. 327.

10 Coleman, Thomas McKean and the Origin of an Independent Judiciary, 34 Pa. Hist. 111, 113 & 125 (1967). McKean's acceptance of the Presidency of the Congress "caused a political explosion in Pennsylvania," and the Assembly passed a resolution declaring that a Supreme Court judge could not sit in Congress as a delegate for another state. Refusing to comply, McKean pointed to numerous instances in the revolutionary period in which judges of state Supreme Courts had been members of Congress. This included John Jay, who was Chief Justice of New York while he was President of Congress. Id., 127. Examples of the Pennsylvania court's advisory opinions include questions concerning the Penns' proprietary estates, whether a person condemned under a court martial should be retried in state court, and the matter of whether the state's admiralty court could issue general warrants to the French Vice Consul to search vessels for deserting French sailors. Id., 125 n.52. The Pennsylvania Supreme Court judges also performed an active role in law enforcement. "The Chief Justice [McKean]

received information concerning persons who had been apprehended locally, or who should be, and saw to it that the necessary writs were issued. The Attorney General and the Prothonotary traveled with the judges and served as prosecuting attorneys; on occasion the Attorney General even joined the judges in preparing (and signing) advisory opinions." Id., 126.

11 See id., 111-13 & 129.

12 1 The Law Practice of Alexander Hamilton 12 (J. Goebel ed. 1964); Morris, *Legalism Versus Revolutionary Doctrine in New England,* in Essays in the History of Early American Law (D. Flaherty ed. 1969); Friedman, 110-13; see Tachau, 78. For purposes of determining how Americans of this era would have viewed the practice of judges giving extrajudicial advice to the other branches, an important fact is that the reports and commentators available to them would have supported the assumption that advisory opinions were a customary part of the judicial role. Blackstone, of course, was their most likely source of information. Perhaps Coke's *Third Institutes* would have given them pause, but at the most it suggested that the practice should not be employed in criminal actions where the issue could return to the judges in a subsequent case. Moreover, Hargrave's notes to Coke's work, which were in the possession of at least some prominent American lawyers during the late eighteenth century (see H. Johnson, Imported Eighteenth-Century Law Treatises in American Libraries, 1700-1799, at 14 [1978]), acknowledged the lawfulness of these opinions. Justice Iredell, for example, not only consulted Hargrave but copied in his own hand the entire note on extrajudicial service. See Consultation with the Judges (undated notes written by James Iredell), cited 6 DHSC, appendix (forthcoming). Fortescue's reports, published in 1748 and available to American lawyers, listed a number of instances of advisory opinions; see chapter 1, note 39 and accompanying text. John Adams cited Fortescue in an important essay of 1773. See Adams, To the Printers, Boston Gazette, Feb. 1, 1773, reprinted in 3 The Works of John Adams 541-42 & 546 (C. Adams ed. 1851). In any event, many of the cases Fortescue cited would have been known owing to their notoriety. For example, the key documents in the *Case of Ship Money* could be read in an eight-volume 1721 collection published by John Rushworth. See Historical Collections, supra chapter 1, note 32. However, Eden's report of *Sackville's Case,* with its reservations about advisory opinions, did not appear until 1818; see supra, chapter 1, note 48.

CHAPTER THREE: THE FORMATION OF THE U.S. CONSTITUTION

1 John Jay, James Wilson, John Blair, James Iredell, & William Paterson to George Washington (Aug. 8, 1793), supra, intro., note 1.

2 John Jay to Thomas Jefferson (Aug. 18, 1786), reprinted 3 Jay Papers, 210; Federalist No. 47, reprinted Federalist, 331; Marcus & Van Tassel, 35; Wood, 150-59, 446-53, & 547-55; Federalist No. 48 (Madison), reprinted Federalist, 333; 2 Farrand, 35. Gouverneur Morris, who had "expressed great pleasure" two days earlier in hearing a suggestion that the President serve "during good behav-

ior," id., 33, commented: "One great object of the Executive is to controul the Legislature. The Legislature will continually seek to aggrandize & perpetuate themselves; and will seize those critical moments produced by war, invasion or convulsion for that purpose." Id., 52. On legislative domination of state governments in the postrevolutionary period, see R. Shalhope, The Roots of Democracy 88 (1990); Evans, *Executive Leadership in Virginia, 1776–1781*, in Sovereign States in an Age of Uncertainty 185–86 (R. Hoffman & P. Albert eds. 1981).

3 Federalist No. 48 (Madison), reprinted Federalist, 333; Federalist No. 47, id., 324 & 325 (emphasis added); Federalist No. 51, id., 347–48.

4 Federalist No. 51, id., 349; Federalist No. 10, id., 59. See J. Stoner, Common Law and Liberal Theory: Coke, Hobbes, and the Origins of American Constitutionalism 202–5 (1992).

5 See U.S. Const. Art. 1, § 1 ("All legislative Powers herein granted shall be vested in a Congress of the United States."); Art. 2, § 1 ("The executive Power shall be vested in a President of the United States of America."); Art. 3, § 1 ("The judicial Power of the United States, shall be vested in one supreme Court, and in such inferior Courts as the Congress may from time to time ordain and establish."); Federalist No. 9, reprinted Federalist, 51.

6 See 2 Jay, 1267–70; Holt, 1518; Federalist No. 80, reprinted Federalist, 535; 2 DHR, 569–70 (James Wilson, Pennsylvania ratifying convention, Dec. 11, 1787); 10 id., 1398 (Edmund Pendleton, Virginia ratifying convention, June 19, 1788) ("[T]he power of that Judiciary must be coextensive with the Legislative power, and reach to all parts of the society intended to be governed."); id., 1413 (James Madison, Virginia ratifying convention, June 20, 1788) ("[T]he Judicial power should correspond with the Legislative."); 4 Elliot's Debates, 156 (William R. Davie, North Carolina ratifying convention, July 29, 1788) ("[T]he judicial power should be coextensive with the legislative.").

7 2 Farrand, 289 (John Merecer); McCulloh v. Maryland, 17 U.S. (4 Wheat.) 316, 407 (1819). In the case of the judiciary, the Constitution was strikingly silent on the relation between the common law of England and the laws of the new United States. Article 3's provision for jurisdiction "arising under . . . the Laws of the United States" failed to specify what those laws were, although clearly the clause contemplated common law as well as statutes. See 2 Jay, 1255–56. A major controversy in the 1790s arose over whether the federal courts had power to define and enforce federal common law crimes. See Casto, 129–63; S. Presser, The Original Misunderstanding 67–98 (1991); 1 Jay, 103. By the end of the 1790s, Jeffersonian Republicans concluded that the maxim equating judicial and legislative jurisdiction had dangerous implications when juxtaposed with the "arising under" jurisdiction of Article 3. It meant that the judiciary's inherent powers would expand along with those of Congress, the scope of which Republicans thought the Federalists were aggressively promoting. More troubling to Republicans was their perception that the Federalists were claiming that national "laws" included the common law of England, thus implying that Congress had unlimited legislative powers. See 2 Jay, 1241–50.

8 Under the Judiciary Act of 1789, § 4, 1 Stat. 74-75 (1789), the Justices presided at circuit courts throughout the country. However, distances covered in the several circuits were significantly unequal, with the Southern Circuit being the worst. See 2 DHSC, 7. Justice Iredell complained severely about this inequity. See, e.g., James Iredell to John Jay, William Cushing, & James Wilson (Feb. 11, 1791), reprinted id., 132 ("[N]o judge can conscientiously undertake to ride the Southern Circuit constantly, and perform the other parts of his duty. Besides the danger his health must be exposed to, it is not conceivable that accidents will not often happen."); James Iredell to John Jay (Jan. 17, 1792), reprinted id., 238 ("I can no longer undertake voluntarily so very unequal a proportion of duty."). Jay—who had the far easier Eastern Circuit—acknowledged the inequity but replied that "[t]he Difficulties attending that Subject can in my opinion be removed by Congress only." John Jay to James Iredell (Mar. 3, 1792), reprinted id., 243. Congress did act in 1792 to provide that no Justice could be obliged without consent to repeat a circuit until all the rest of the Justices had taken the same assignment. See Circuit Court Act of 1792, 1 Stat. 253 (1792). This legislation was passed at the urging of Senator Samuel Johnston, who was Iredell's brother-in-law. See 2 DHSC, 236-37 (editors' note).

9 2 Farrand, 430. Because Madison's remark occurred during consideration of adding "cases arising under this Constitution," his concern for limiting the Court "to cases of a Judiciary nature" may relate only to constitutional questions, as opposed to federal law generally. It has been argued that there is no conclusive evidence that the Convention agreed with Madison's view: "An affirmative vote on any parliamentary proposal can never be evidence that the parliamentary body *agreed* with an objection to the proposal; the most that can be said is that it might not constitute evidence that the body *disagreed* with any particular objection." Lee, *Deconstitutionalizing Justiciability: The Example of Mootness,* 105 Harv. L. Rev. 605, 640 (1992). While this is true enough, it is not relevant to this incident, in which Madison purported to record the sense of the Convention—that "it [was] generally supposed" that Article 3 was "constructively limited to cases of a Judiciary Nature." Madison may not have accurately reflected the sentiments of the body, but that is a different objection.

10 See 2 Jay, 1254-62.

11 Judiciary Act of 1801, ch. 4, § 11, 2 Stat. 89, 92 (1801); Marbury v. Madison, 1 U.S. (1 Cranch) 137 (1803). There are numerous accounts of the repeal of the 1801 Judiciary Act and the accompanying constitutional questions. See, e.g., R. Ellis, The Jeffersonian Crisis 36-52 (1971); G. Haskins & H. Johnson, Foundations of Power: John Marshall, 1801-15, at 163-81 (1981). The Supreme Court upheld the repeal as constitutional in Stuart v. Laird, 1 U.S. (1 Cranch) 299, 308 (1803).

12 See U.S. Const., Art. 3, § 2. "Cases" encompass those actions in which jurisdiction is determined mainly by the subject matter at issue (arising under the laws of the United States, under the Constitution, or involving admiralty and maritime jurisdiction). The exception is that "cases" include suits "affecting Ambassadors, other

public Ministers and Consuls," in which jurisdiction is a function of party status. By contrast, "controversies" is used to designate the other heads of jurisdiction, all of which turn on the identity of the parties. The employment of different terms was deliberate. Early drafts of Article 3 used "cases" to cover all the proposed areas of jurisdiction. See 2 Farrand, 146-47 (first draft of the Committee of Detail). Without explanation, the Committee of Detail introduced the term "controversies," which remained intact in the final text. See id., 172-73 (Committee of Detail draft); Amar, *A Neo-Federalist View of Article III: Separating the Two Tiers of Federal Jurisdiction,* 65 Boston U. L. Rev. 205, 243-45 (1985). Further discussion of these two terms appears later in this chapter.

13 1 Farrand, 52-53 (May 31, 1787) (emphasis added). One of Samuel Johnson's definitions for "case" included "[c]ondition with regard to outward circumstances," "[s]tate of things," and "[r]epresentation of any fact or question." S. Johnson, A Dictionary of the English Language [unpaginated] (7th ed. 1785). Countless examples could be cited of similar usages: (1) "Mr. SHERMAN thought the cases in which the [Congressional] negative [on state laws] ought to be exercised, might be defined." 1 Farrand, 166 (June 8, 1787); (2) "On the question for extending the negative power to all *cases* as proposed [recording votes]." Id., 168. (June 8, 1787); (3) "Col. Mason observed that a vote had already passed . . . for vesting the executive powers in a single person. Among these powers was that of appointing to offices in certain *cases.*" Id., 101 (June 4, 1787); (4) "It had been observed that in all countries the Executive power is in a constant course of increase. This was certainly the *case* in G.B." Id., 100. (June 4, 1787) (Butler); (5) "Resolved that . . . the National Legislature ought to be impowered . . . to legislate in all *cases* to which the separate States are incompetent." Id., 21 (Randolph resolutions, May 29, 1787). Emphasis added in all examples above.

14 U.S. Const., Art. 1, § 8; see, e.g., Art. 1, § 7 ("But in all such *Cases* the Votes of both Houses shall be determined by Yeas and Nays, and the Names of the Persons voting for and against the Bill shall be entered on the Journal of each House respectively."); Art. 1, § 9 ("The Privilege of the Writ of Habeas Corpus shall not be suspended, unless when in *Cases* of Rebellion or Invasion the public Safety may require it."); Art. 2, § 1 ("In every *Case,* after the Choice of the President, the Person having the greatest Number of Votes of the Electors shall be the Vice President.); Art. 2, § 1 ("In *Case* of the Removal of the President from Office, or of his Death, Resignation, or Inability to discharge the Powers and Duties of the said Office, the Same shall devolve on the Vice president."). Emphasis added in all examples above.

15 For example, at the Convention, Samuel Johnson made this well-known remark in the course of the debate about the basis of representation in Congress: "The controversy must be endless whilst Gentlemen differ in the grounds of their arguments." 1 Farrand, 461 (June 29, 1787). Benjamin Franklin informed the delegates about Quaker customs: "It is an established rule with them, that they are not to go to law; but in their controversies they must apply to their monthly, quarterly and yearly meetings." Id., 84 (June 2, 1787). Many additional examples

could be provided. At times, "controversy" was used in the context of a court case to mean the underlying issues in dispute; see, e.g., id., 124 (June 5, 1787) ("Mr. WILSON opposed the motion on like grounds. he said the admiralty jurisdiction ought to be given wholly to the national Government, as it related to cases not within the jurisdiction of particular states, & to a scene in which *controversies* with foreigners would be most likely to happen."); Bill of Rights, Amend. 7 ("In Suits at common law, where the value in *controversy* shall exceed twenty dollars, the right of trial by jury shall be preserved."); Hylton v. United States, 3 U.S. 171, 171 (1796) ("But the parties, waving the right of trial by jury, mutually submitted the *controversy* to the court on a case, which stated 'the Defendant, on the 5th of June, 1794, and therefrom to the last day of September following, owned, possessed, and kept. . . . '"); Wilson v. Daniel, 3 U.S. 401, 406 (1798) (Chase, J.) ("It must be acknowledged, however, that in actions of tort, or trespass, from the nature of the suits, the damages laid in the declaration, afford the only practicable test of the value of the *controversy*."); Glass v. The Sloop Betsey, 3 U.S. 6, 10 (1794) ("The cases in [citations given] did not involve the question of prize; the sole *controversy* was, whether the taking of the vessel was piratical, or not."). See also S. Johnson, supra note 13 [unpaginated] ("controversy" defined inter alia: "[d]ispute; debate; agitation of contrary opinions: a dispute is commonly oral, and a *controversy* in writing. . . . A suit in law . . . a quarrel."). Emphasis added in all examples above.

16 Additional supporting evidence for this view may be found in the original Randolph resolutions, which described the national courts as "consist[ing] of one or more supreme tribunals, and of inferior tribunals to be chosen by the National Legislature." 1 Farrand, 21 (May 29, 1787). "Tribunal" readily connotes an institution that resolves disputes, whereas "court" more likely refers to a particular institution, one having more powers and duties than that of adjudication.

17 See, e.g., S. Johnson, supra note 13 [unpaginated] ("Case" defined inter alia: "The State of facts juridically considered: as, the lawyers cited many *cases* in their pleas.") ("Controversy" defined inter alia: "A suit in law."); Federalist No. 80, reprinted Federalist, 540–41 ("Case" used for certain suits designated in Article 3 as "controversies"); Virginia Resolutions Accompanying Ratification of the U.S. Constitution (June 27, 1788) ("11th. That in *controversies* respecting property, and in suits between man and man, the ancient trial by jury, is one of the greatest securities to the rights of the people, and ought to remain sacred and inviolable."); Dewhurst v. Coulthard, 3 U.S. 409, 410 (1799) ("The court, on the ensuing morning, returned the state of the case, declaring, that they could not take cognizance of any suit or *controversy*, which was not brought before them, by the regular process of the law."); Maxfield v. Levy, 16 F.Cas. 1195, 1196 (C.C.D.Pa. 1797) (Iredell, J.) ("[I]f it be not a *controversy* between citizens of different states, but between citizens of the same state, it not being one of those cases which entitle citizens of the same state to any exercise of jurisdiction by this court, it ought not to be determined here."); Pleasants v. Meng, 1 U.S. 380, 385 (Ct. Common Pleas, Phila., Penn. 1788) ("And the doctrine which applies in

the last case to support the commission there, applies to prove the invalidity of the one at present in *controversy*.") Emphasis added in all examples above. Justice Iredell argued that "cases" included both criminal and civil actions, whereas "controversies" was limited to civil causes; see Chisholm v. Georgia, 2 U.S. 419, 431-32 (1793) (dissenting), and this view has its followers; see, e.g., 1 Blackstone, pt. 1, 420-21 (S. Tucker ed. 1803) (editor's note); Fletcher, *Exchange on the Eleventh Amendment,* 57 U. Chi. L. Rev. 131, 133 (1990); Meltzer, *The History and Structure of Article III,* 138 U. Penn. L. Rev. 1569, 1575 (1990). Others have contended that the terms are interchangeable, see Amar, supra note 12, at 244 n.128, or the result of careless drafting, see Redish, *Text, Structure, and Common Sense in the Interpretation of Article III,* 138 U. Penn. L. Rev. 1633, 1640 n.28 (1990). Although this nice dispute is not relevant to this book — none of these commentators doubts that both usages are confined to justiciable lawsuits — the words do seem to mean the same. The examples at the beginning of this note are only a few of scores of contemporary uses of "controversy" in which the term is used in the same sense as "case" or "dispute." Iredell and Tucker offered weak explanations for their positions — Iredell said that criminal cases "respect the same governor only, are uniformly considered of a local nature, and to be decided by its particular law." Chisholm, 2 U.S., at 431-32. This ignores Hamilton's argument in Federalist No. 80, namely, that avoiding "an unjust sentence against a foreigner" was one of the objects of state-foreign citizen jurisdiction, even though "the subject of controversy was wholly relative to the lex loci."); Federalist No. 80, supra, 536. It is obvious that some of the "controversies" in Article 3 could be criminal. The drafters of the 1789 Judiciary Act took pains to qualify the Supreme Court's jurisdiction over certain "controversies" with the phrase "of a civil nature," see Judiciary Act of 1789, § 13, 1 Stat. 80 (1789), which hardly would have been necessary if the meaning were obvious at the time. Iredell rather lamely wrote that this addition "was perhaps a proper instance of caution in congress to guard against" a different reading. Chisholm, 2 U.S., at 432.

18 Justice Scalia has contended that Madison was addressing the problem of moot cases, see Honig v. Doe, 484 U.S. 305, 341 (1988) (Scalia, J. dissenting), but this is highly doubtful. See Lee, supra note 9, at 641 ("Madison might well have meant only that Article III should not be construed to authorize hypothetical opinions or any kind of judicial participation in pre-enactment review of legislation. This seems far more plausible than the possibility that Madison was alluding to justiciability, a concept whose earliest manifestations came in the mid-nineteenth century.").

19 2 Farrand, 34 (July 17, 1787). For example, in Chisholm v. Georgia, 2 U.S. 419, 452 (1793), Justice Blair wrote that "it follows that when a State, by adopting the Constitution, has agreed to be amenable to the judicial power of the United States, she has, in that respect, given up her right of sovereignty." Justice Wilson added: "What good purpose could this Constitutional provision secure, if a State might pass a law impairing the obligation of its own contracts; and be amenable,

for such a violation of right, to no controuling judiciary power?" Id., 465. Alexander Dallas argued in United States v. Peters, 3 U.S. 121, 125-26 (1795): "The three great objects of the judicial power are an authority—1st. to administer justice; 2d. to compel the unwilling, or negligent, magistrate, to perform his duty; and 3d. to restrain the ministers of justice within the regular boundaries of their respective jurisdictions."

20 Federalist No. 15, reprinted Federalist, 95. Any number of examples could be produced: Declaration and Resolves of the First Continental Congress (Oct. 14, 1774), reprinted 1 Journals of the Continental Congress 63-64 (P. Ford ed. 1904) ("Whereas, since the close of the last war, the British parliament, claiming a power of right to bind the people of America, by statute in all cases whatsoever."); Federalist No. 3, reprinted Federalist, 16 (John Jay) ("But the national Government, not being affected by those local circumstances, will neither be induced to commit the wrong themselves, nor want power or inclination to prevent or punish its commission by others."); A Declaration of the Causes and Necessity of Taking Up Arms (Continental Congress, July 6, 1775), reprinted 2 Journals of the Continental Congress, supra, 140: "If it was possible for men, who exercise their reason, to believe, that the Divine Author of our existence intended a part of the human race to hold an absolute property in, and an unbounded power over others, marked out by his infinite goodness and wisdom, as the objects of a legal domination never rightfully resistible, however severe and oppressive, the Inhabitants of these Colonies might at least require from the Parliament of Great Britain some evidence, that this dreadful authority over them, has been granted to that body." Federalist No. 15, reprinted Federalist, 95.

21 A fuller discussion of this episode appears in chapter 4; James Wilson, John Blair, & Richard Peters to George Washington (Apr. 18, 1792), reprinted Hayburn's Case, 2 U.S. 4089, 411-12 n.(a) (1792). The other justices (with the exception of Thomas Johnson, who was absent from his circuit that term due to illness) made similar statements. See John Jay, William Cushing, & James Duane to George Washington (Apr. 5, 1791), reprinted id., 410 n.(a); James Iredell & Samuel Sitgreaves to George Washington (June 8, 1792), reprinted id., 412-13 n.(a).

22 Wiscart v. D'Auchy, 3 U.S. 321, 327 (1796). See, e.g., Primer v. Supreme Court of Pennsylvania, 1 U.S. 452, 453 (Pa. Sup. Ct. 1789) ("Inconveniences of this kind have been perceived by the Legislature, or judicial power, of the most enlightened nations, and a remedy, in a greater or less degree, provided . . . and, in England, even before the statutes had given relief in the Courts of Common Law, the Courts of Equity endeavoured to provide for such cases."); 1 Farrand, 22 (May 29, 1787) (Virginia Resolutions) ("14. Resd. that the Legislative Executive & Judiciary powers within the several States ought to be bound by oath to support the articles of Union."); James Wilson, John Blair, & Richard Peters to George Washington (Apr. 18, 1792), supra note 21, at 411 ("[T]he people of the United States . . . have placed their *judicial* power not in Congress, but in '*courts.*'"); Ware v. Hylton, 3 U.S. 199, 261 (1796) (Iredell, Circuit Justice) ("But it is said that a declaration by Congress, that the treaty was broken by Great Britain, would be exercising a judicial power,

which by the Constitution in all cases of treaties is devolved on the Judges. Surely such a thing was never in the contemplation of the Constitution."). In reviewing English government, commentators typically would note that a portion of the judicial power was exercised by the legislative branch. See, e.g., Calder v. Bull, 3 U.S. 386, 389 (1798) (Chase, J.) ("The prohibition against their making any ex post facto laws was introduced for greater caution, and very probably arose from the knowledge, that the Parliament of Great Britain claimed and exercised a power to pass such laws, under the denomination of bills of attainder, or bills of pains and penalties; the first inflicting capital, and the other less, punishment. These acts were legislative judgments; and an exercise of judicial power."); Id., 398 (Iredell, J.) ("In England, we know, that one branch of the Parliament, the house of Lords, not only exercises a judicial power in cases of impeachment, and for the trial of its own members, but as the court of dernier resort, takes cognizance of many suits at law, and in equity."). James Wilson criticized the judicial function of the House of Lords, saying that "there is a very improper mixture of legislative and judicial authority vested and blended in the same assembly. This is entirely avoided in the constitution of the United States." 1 Works of James Wilson 323-24 (R. McCloskey ed. 1967); Johnson, supra note 13 [unpaginated] ("Judicial" defined: "1. Practised in the distribution of publick justice. . . . 2. Inflicted on as a penalty.").

23 1 Works of James Wilson, supra note 22, at 296. The Virginia Resolutions outlined a national judiciary "to consist of one or more supreme tribunals, and of inferior tribunals to be chosen by the National Legislature." 1 Farrand, 21. Similarly, the Paterson Plan proposed that a "federal Judiciary be established to consist of a supreme Tribunal." Id., 244. That the final version of Article 3 avoided the term "tribunal" perhaps suggests that the Framers might have intended the "judicial power" to extend beyond traditional lawsuits. However, the reverse seems more plausible: "one supreme Court" and "inferior Courts" were merely substitute expressions for "tribunals."

24 Montesquieu, The Spirit of the Laws, bk. 11, ch. 6, at 185 (G. & A. Ewing & G. Faulkner eds. 1751). "[T]here is no liberty, if the power of judgment be not separated from the legislative and executive powers. Were it joined with the legislative, the life and liberty of the subject would be exposed to arbitrary controul; for the judge would be then the legislator." Id. Federalist No. 47, reprinted Federalist, 324; see id., 325-26. The "power of judging" quotation is from Montesquieu, supra, 187. In the same essay, Madison quoted extensively from Montesquieu, including the excerpts in text here. Montesquieu understood "[t]he judiciary power" as residing in juries, "persons taken from the body of the people, at certain times of the year . . . in order to erect a tribunal that should last only as long as necessity requires." See Gwyn, 103 & 106; A. Cohler, Montesquieu's Comparative Politics and the Spirit of American Constitutionalism 107 (1988). The actual application of law to a case was a "mechanical" process, Vile, 89, whereby "the national judges are no more than the mouth that pronounces the words of the law, mere passive beings, incapable of moderating either its force or rigour." Montesquieu, supra, bk. 11, ch. 6, at 194.

25 John Jay to George Washington (Jan. 7, 1787), reprinted 3 Jay Papers, 227.

26 See, e.g., United States v. Curtiss-Wright Export Corp., 299 U.S. 304 (1936) (presidential authority over foreign affairs); United States v. Nixon, 418 U.S. 683, 705-6 n.16 (1973) ("[S]ilence of the Constitution" on executive privilege "is not dispositive," instead "that which was reasonably appropriate and relevant to the exercise of a granted power was to be considered as accompanying the grant."). The existence of administrative agencies may be the most glaring illustration. None of these modern developments leads necessarily to the conclusion that advisory opinions are constitutional; there may be other valid reasons of constitutional dimension to disapprove the practice.

27 U.S. Const. Art. 2, § 2; John Jay, James Wilson, John Blair, James Iredell, & William Paterson to George Washington (Aug. 8, 1793), supra, intro., note 1.

28 2 Farrand, 341 (Aug. 20, 1787).

29 On the Massachusetts provision, see chapter 2. On Pickney's press amendment, see 2 Farrand, 341 (Aug. 20, 1787). Pickney, along with Elbridge Gerry, moved on September 14 to insert this provision in the final text, but Roger Sherman objected that "[i]t is unnecessary—The power of Congress does not extend to the Press," and the proposal was defeated. Id., at 618. During ratification debates, the usual Federalist response to similar proposals would be: "The general government has not powers but what are expressly granted to it; it therefore has no power to take away the liberty of the press." 4 Elliot's Debates, 315 (Charles C. Pickney, South Carolina ratifying convention, Jan. 18, 1788); accord 2 DHR, 454-55 (James Wilson, Pennsylvania ratifying convention, Dec. 1, 1787); 10 id., at 1352 (Edmund Randolph, Virginia ratifying convention, June 17, 1788); 4 Elliot's Debates, 208 (Richard D. Spaight, North Carolina ratifying convention, June 17, 1788). Several other of Pickney's suggestions were not acted on, presumably because the Convention thought them to be details not needed in the Constitution, such as a provision for authorizing Congress to create the Great Seal and a requirement that commissions and writs "run in the name of the U.S." 2 Farrand, 342 (Aug. 20, 1787).

30 1 Farrand, 21 (May 29, 1787).

31 New York's constitution created a council composed of the governor, chancellor, and judges of the supreme court, who had the power to veto all legislation, subject to override by a two-thirds vote of the legislature. See 7 Sources and Documents of United States Constitutions 172 (W. Swindler ed. 1975); Morris, 12. Hamilton described the council in *Federalist No. 73*, noting that "[i]t has been freely employed upon a variety of occasions, and frequently with success. And its utility has become so apparent, that persons who in compiling the Constitution were violent opposers of it, have from experience become its declared admirers." Federalist No. 73, reprinted Federalist, 499. For Jay quotation, see John Jay to George Washington (Jan. 7, 1787), reprinted 3 Jay Papers, 226.

32 2 Farrand, 74 (July 21, 1787). For similar arguments at the Convention in favor of the council, see 1 id., 98 (James Wilson, June 4, 1787); 2 id., 73 (James Wilson, July 21, 1787); 1 id., 73-74 (Oliver Ellsworth, July 27, 1787); 2 id., 74 & 78

(George Mason, July 21, 1787); id., 75–76 (Gouverneur Morris, July 21, 1787); id., 79–80 (James Wilson, July 21, 1787).

33 See 1 id., 97–104 (June 4, 1787); id., 138–40 (June 6, 1787); 2 id., 73–80 (July 21, 1787); id., 298 (Aug. 15, 1787). The August 15 session considered a somewhat modified proposal for judicial participation in the veto. Madison "moved that all acts before they become laws should be submitted both to the Executive and Supreme Judiciary Departments, that if either of these should object 2/3 of each House, if both should object, 3/4 of each House, should be necessary to overrule the objections and give to the acts the force of law." Id., 298.

34 Id., 78 (July 21, 1787); see 1 id., 100–101 (Gunning Bedford, June 4, 1787) ("Mr. BEDFORD was opposed to every check on the Legislative, even the Council of Revision first proposed. He thought it would be sufficient to mark out in the Constitution the boundaries to the Legislative Authority, which would give all the requisite security to the rights of the other departments."); 2 id., 75 (Elbridge Gerry, July 21, 1787) ("He relied for his part on the Representatives of the people as the guardians of their Rights & interests.").

35 Id., 79 (Nathaniel Ghorum, July 21, 1787); see 1 id., 139 (Rufus King, June 6, 1787) ("If the Unity of the Executive was preferred for the sake of responsibility, the policy of it is as applicable to the revisionary as to the Executive power."); id., 140 (John Dickinson, June 6, 1787) ("Secrecy, vigor & despatch are not the principal properties reqd. in the Executive. Important as these are, that of responsibility is more so, which can only be preserved; by leaving it singly to discharge its functions.").

36 2 id., 75–77 (July 21, 1787); 1 id., 97–98 (June 4, 1787); id., 139 (June 6, 1787).

37 2 id., 76 (July 21, 1787); 1 id., 139 (June 6, 1787); see, e.g., 2 id., 73 (July 21, 1787) (Nathaniel Ghorum) ("He thought it would be best to let the Executive alone be responsible, and at most to authorize him to call on Judges for their opinions.").

38 Id., 80 (July 21, 1787); see also 1 id., 98 (Rufus King, June 4, 1787) ("[T]he Judges ought to be able to expound the law as it should come before them, free from the bias of having participated in its formation."); 2 id., 75 (Caleb Strong, July 21, 1787) ("[T]he power of making ought to be kept distinct from that of expounding, the laws. . . . The Judges in exercising the function of expositors might be influenced by the part they had taken, in framing the laws."). At the June 6 session, Madison addressed this argument, noting that it was one of the principal objections to the council. Acknowledging that the point "had some weight," he discounted the problem: "[I]t was much diminished by reflecting that a small proportion of the laws coming in question before a Judge wd. be such wherein he had been consulted; that a small part of this proportion wd. be so ambiguous as to leave room for his prepossessions; and that but a few cases wd. probably arise in the life of a Judge under such ambiguous passages." 1 id., 138–39 (June 6, 1787).

39 This could be the meaning of the remarks by Rufus King and Caleb Strong in the previous note.

40 2 Farrand, 298 (Aug. 15, 1787).

41 Id., 75 & 77 (July 21, 1787). See, e.g., 1 id., 110 (notes of William Pierce) (John Dickinson, June 4, 1787: "Mr. Dickinson could not agree with Gentlemen in blending the national Judicial with the Executive, because the one is the expounder, and the other the Executor of the Laws."); 2 id., 75 (July 21, 1787) (Elbridge Gerry: "It was combining & mixing together the Legislative & the other departments. It was establishing an improper coalition between the Executive & Judiciary departments.").

42 Id., 75-76 (July 21, 1787). "The truth was that the Judges in England had a great share in ye Legislation. They are consulted in difficult & doubtful cases. They may be & some of them are members of the Legislature. They are or may be members of the privy Council, and can there advise the Executive as they will do with us if the motion succeeds." Id.

43 Id., 300 (Aug. 15, 1787).

44 Id., 76 (July 21, 1787).

45 Corwin, *The Establishment of Judicial Review,* 9 Mich. L. Rev. 102, 118 (1910); 2 Farrand, 73 (James Wilson, July 21, 1787), 76 (July 21, 1787), 78 (George Mason, July 21, 1787), & 298-99 (John Mercer, John Dickinson, Aug. 15, 1787). Although a few states had taken tentative steps toward institutionalizing judicial review, many viewed the practice as "inconsistent with free popular government." Wood, 455. See W. Adams, The First American Constitutions 269-70 (1980): "The authors of the early [state] constitutions were fully aware that unconstitutional laws might well win the approval of the legislature. . . . But the two methods they devised for meeting this danger were not based on faith that the judiciary would have the ability, integrity, and authority to recognize such laws and annul them. The methods were based instead on belief in the value of a delaying veto . . . , and in the necessity for periodic review and revision of the constitution [e.g., New York's council of revision; Vermont's councils of censors]."

46 Labaree, 153; Wood, 138, 435; but see W. Adams, supra note 45, at 274-75: "But the executive councils never developed any political power of their own and remained little more than committees appointed by the legislature to watch over the activities of the executive branch. They were less powerful than the governors' councils of the colonial period, because most of the former councils' powers were transferred to the senates."

47 See, e.g., W. Humphrey, The Wise Men of Gotham, 1776 (engraving); The Plea of the Colonies (1776), quoted in G. Guttridge, English Whiggism and the American Revolution 104 (1963).

48 Sherman: 1 Farrand, 97 (June 4, 1787); Wilson: id.; Randolph: id., 90; Williamson: id., 71 (notes of Rufus King, June 1, 1787).

49 Franklin said, for example, that "[i]f the Executive was to have a Council, such a power [the veto] would be less objectionable." Id., 99 (June 4, 1787).

50 See id., 66 (June 1, 1787) (a council would "give weight & inspire confidence" in the executive); id., 70-71 (notes of Rufus King, June 1, 1787) ("[T]hey will be the organs of information of the persons proper for offices—their opinions may

be recorded—they may be called to acct. for yr. Opinions. & impeached—if so their Responsibility will be certain, and in Case of misconduct their punishment certain—"); id., 74 ("[A] Council ought to be the medium through which the feelings of the people ought to be communicated to the Executive.").

51 Ellsworth's idea clearly was preliminary, and by general consent it was laid over until Morris and Pickney could present their proposal, which appears to have replaced Ellsworth's. See id., 329 (Aug. 18, 1787). On the Morris-Pickney plan, see id., 342-44 (Aug. 20, 1787).

52 2 Farrand, 334-37 (Aug. 20, 1787) & 367 (Aug. 22, 1787). The Committee of Detail consisted of Rutledge, Randolph, Ghorum, Ellsworth, and Wilson.

53 See id., 473 (Aug. 31, 1787), at 495 (Sept. 4, 1787), at 537-39 (Sept. 7, 1787). Before voting on the committee's recommendation, George Mason made one last effort on September 7 to create a council of state. See id., 537 & 541-42. Mason's new council would have been appointed by either the legislature or the Senate, "to consist of six members, two of which from the Eastern, two from the middle, and two from the Southern States." Id., 542. Mason's hastily drawn scheme grew out of a concern that by "rejecting a Council to the President we were about to try an experiment on which the most despotic Governments had never ventured—The Grand Signor himself had his Divan." Id., 541. On the one hand, Mason particularly was worried about appointment of officers, which he thought was too great a power for the President to exercise alone. On the other hand, introducing the Senate as a check on appointments was ill-advised because it would require that body to be constantly in session, a prospect Mason viewed to be both dangerous and expensive. Id., 537-38. King objected, however, that "the people wold be alarmed at an unnecessary creation of New Corps which must increase the expence as well as influence of the Government." Id., 539. Although Franklin seconded a motion to commit the proposal to the committee for consideration, and drew favorable reactions from Madison, Dickinson, and Wilson, the Convention voted 8-3 against referral, effectively ending the last attempt to set up an executive council. Id., 542. The clause on September 7 included "ambassadors, and other public ministers (and Consuls)," "Judges of the Supreme Court," and "all other officers of U.S." Id., 542. On September 15, the Convention agreed to "vest the appointment of such inferior officers as they think proper, in the President alone, in the Courts of law, or in the heads of Departments." Id., 627.

54 Id., 542 (Sept. 7, 1787) & 329 (Aug. 18, 1787).

55 See id., 329 (Aug. 18, 1787) & 544-49 (Sept. 8, 1787). The connection with the Senate was made clear in Mason's unsuccessful proposal of September 7 for a legislatively appointed Privy Council, which Mason urged was preferable for considering appointments. In a more general way, this discussion was connected with the question of the Senate's role in the government, including whether it would be a body permanently in session to attend to great matters of state or simply another branch of the legislature. Viewing the Senate as an alternative to an executive council was natural, considering that colonial councils had a dual role as the upper body of the legislature and as advisers to the governor; in the new state constitu-

tions, the Senate often was the successor institution to the council. By the 1780s, however, there was a growing sense of the Senate as a branch of the legislature with the principal mission of checking the power of the people as represented in the House of Representatives. See R. Shalhope, supra note 2, at 89.

56 Pierce Butler "appealed to the example of G. B. where men got into Parlt. that they might get offices for themselves or their friends. This was the source of the corruption that ruined their Govt." 1 Farrand, 376 (June 22, 1787).

57 Wood, 158–59 & n.58 (listing constitutional provisions; 1 Farrand, 376 (June 22, 1787) (Mason); U.S. Const., Art. 1, § 6. The Articles of Confederation likewise provided in Article 5: "[N]or shall any person, being a delegate, be capable of holding any office under the united states, for which he, or another for his benefit receives any salary, fees or emolument of any kind." Article 2, § 1, of the Constitution responds to similar concerns: "[N]o Senator or Representative, or Person holding an Office of Trust or Profit under the United States, shall be appointed an Elector [for purposes of the presidential election]." Some voices to the contrary were heard at the Convention. James Wilson opined that "nothing seemed to be wanting to prostrate the Natl. Legislature, but to render its members ineligible to Natl offices, & by that means take away its power of attracting those talents which were necessary to give weight to the Governt. and to render it useful to the people. He was far from thinking the ambition which aspired to Offices of dignity and trust, an ignoble or culpable one." 2 Farrand, 288 (Aug. 14, 1787); see also 1 id., 381–82 (Alexander Hamilton, June 22, 1787); 2 id., 286–87 (Gouverneur Morris, Aug. 14, 1787); id., 491 (Nathaniel Ghorum, Sept. 3, 1787). However, both Wilson and Hamilton would have excluded legislators from plural office-holding but not from subsequent governmental service; see 1 id., 382 (Hamilton, June 22, 1787); id., 380 (Wilson, June 22, 1787) (Yates's notes).

58 The phrase "any office under the United States" would include judgeships, as the Convention apparently recognized. See, e.g., 2 Farrand, 491 (Charles Pickney, Sept. 3, 1787) ("Should [the disqualification] be agreed to, The great offices, even those of the Judiciary Depar[t]ment which are to continue for life, must be filled whilst those most capable of filling them will be under a disqualification [because they will be members of the first Congress]."); Marcus & Van Tassel, 36. The Paterson Plan, presented June 15, would have excluded the executive from "holding any other office or appointment during their time of service and for ____ years thereafter[,]" as well as prohibited judges from "receiving or holding any other office or appointment during their time of service, or for ____ thereafter." 1 Farrand, 244. Charles Pickney wanted the Constitution to include: "No person holding the office of President of the U.S., a Judge of their Supreme Court, Secretary for the department of Foreign Affairs, of Finance, of Marine, of War, or of ____, shall be capable of holding at the same time any other office of Trust or Emolument under the U.S. or an individual State." 2 id., 341–42 (Aug. 20, 1787). The debates on the disqualifying clause of Article 1, § 6, are collected in 2 1787: Drafting the U.S. Constitution 709–40 (W. Benton ed. 1986).

59 Although he sponsored the proposal for banning extrajudicial office-holding,

Pickney "strenuously opposed" the disqualification of congressional members from other offices, saying that "[h]e considered the eligibility of members of the Legislature to the honorable offices of Government, as resembling the policy of the Romans, in making the temple of virtue the road to the temple of fame." 2 Farrand, 490 (Sept. 3, 1787); see also id., 283-84 (similar remarks by Pickney on Aug. 14, 1787). The "skills of statesmanship" quote is from Wheeler, 127.

60 The Virginia Resolutions, the Paterson Plan, and the Pickney Plan provided for such protections. See 1 Farrand, 21-22 (Virginia Resolutions); id., 244 (Paterson Plan); 3 id., 600 (Pickney Plan). The delegates agreed on judicial tenure early in the proceedings and reaffirmed themselves throughout the summer. 1 id., 104-5 (June 4, 1787, approval of the Virginia Resolution on the judiciary); 2 id., 44-45 (July 18, 1787, approval in the Convention); id., 428 (approval of the Committee of Detail report, Aug. 27, 1787); id., 600 (Sept. 10-12, 1787, Committee of Style report). A minor dispute arose over whether Congress should be prohibited from increasing judicial salaries, and there was a brief debate over the terms of impeachment for judges. Id., 428-30 (Aug. 27, 1787); Bailyn, 74-75 & 105-8 ("controversial question throughout the century." Id., 105); Labaree, 388-401 ("widespread bitterness" regarding tenure of colonial judges; id., 400); Wood, 160-61, 407, 436 & 451-52 ("Judicial tenure had been one of the searing issues of the imperial debate." Id., 160). Madison wrote in *Federalist No. 39:* "According to the provisions of most of the [state] constitutions, . . . as well as according to the most respectable and received opinions on the subject, the members of the judiciary department are to retain their offices by the firm tenure of good behaviour." Reprinted Federalist, 252.

61 2 Farrand, 429 (Aug. 27, 1787) & 34 (July 17, 1787). Wilson was speaking in opposition to a motion to allow federal judges to be removed on a joint application by the two Houses of Congress to the executive.

62 The Essex Result (Report of the Delegates from Essex County, Mass., on the proposed Massachusetts Constitution, Apr. 29, 1778), reprinted The Revolution in America, 1754-1788, at 457 (J. Pole ed. 1970). *Trevett v. Weeden* is discussed in chapter 2. Hamilton linked security of tenure for judges to judicial review in *Federalist No. 78:* "If then the courts of justice are to be considered as the bulwarks of a limited constitution against legislative encroachments, this consideration will afford a strong argument for the permanent tenure of judicial offices, since nothing will contribute so much as this to that independent spirit in the judges, which must be essential to the faithful performance of so arduous a duty." Reprinted Federalist, 526-27.

63 Federalist No. 51, reprinted Federalist, 348; Federalist No. 78, id., 522 & 530. On the Act of Settlement, see chapter 1.

CHAPTER FOUR: THE WASHINGTON ADMINISTRATION

1 Comte de Moustier to Comte de Montmorin (June 5, 1789), quoted in 6 Freeman, 195.

2 Memorandum on a Discussion of the President's Retirement (May 5, 1792), reprinted in 14 Madison Papers 301 (Madison's account of a recent conversation with Washington).

3 George Washington to Catherine Macaulay Graham (Jan. 9, 1790), reprinted 30 Washington Writings, 496. Madison, Memorandum on a Discussion of the President's Retirement (May 5, 1792), supra note 2, at 301; see Flexner, 110–11 (dependence on the cabinet). Forrest McDonald wrote that "[m]ost of the problems with which he would have to deal as president were beyond his experience, and—harsh fact—many of them were beyond his ken as well. He determined that his only hope was to surround himself with able men, supervise them as closely as possible, and pray for the best." McDonald, Hamilton, 127.

4 Charles, 250; see Miller, 84–85.

5 See Combs, 20. For a balanced assessment of Jefferson's gubernatorial service, see Evans, *Executive Leadership in Virginia, 1776-1781,* in Sovereign States in an Age of Uncertainty 202-18 (R. Hoffman & P. Albert eds. 1981). Evans argues that Jefferson performed the best he could under difficult circumstances, and that overall "he did remarkably well" as governor. Id., 218.

6 The British parallel was quite striking, as the cabinet there also was composed mainly of the heads of departments, with the First Lord of the Treasury as the first among equals in the group. Hamilton modeled his office and financial program after the British system, and a strong case can be made that he sought a preeminence among cabinet officers similar to that enjoyed by the First Lord of the Treasury.

7 See Freeman, 200-202; 6 Washington Diaries, 68 n.; J. Alden, George Washington 238-39 (1984).

8 See Charles, 255. See, e.g., Jefferson, Anas, 121 (May 7, 1793: Washington opposed sending a letter to the belligerent powers on the effect of the Neutrality Proclamation but agreed because the vote was 3-1 in favor); Thomas Jefferson to James Madison (Aug. 11, 1793), reprinted in 26 Jefferson Papers, 649; 7 Jefferson Works, 474 (Washington favored calling Congress into session early but acquiesced to the majority view); Jefferson, Anas, 166-68 (Aug. 20, 1793: Washington disagreed with wording of a communication to the American minister in France but went along with the majority). On rare occasions, Washington would decide a question against the judgment of the majority of the cabinet. For example, on November 23, 1793, the cabinet discussed whether to send a message to Congress regarding Great Britain's failure to meet treaty obligations and its restraint on corn commerce; the issue was whether the communication should be secret or public. Jefferson recorded that although Hamilton, Randolph, and Knox favored total or partial secrecy, Washington spoke for public disclosure "with more vehemence than I have ever seen him show. . . . This was the first instance I had seen of his deciding on the opinion of one against that of three others, which proved his own to have been very strong." Id., 183.

9 See McDonald, Hamilton, 134: "When dealing with interdepartmental matters, or with Treasury matters in which he was not lawfully made responsible to

Congress, Hamilton was obliged to follow Washington's procedures—which, according to Jefferson, were so exacting that every letter sent or received by a department head was forwarded to the president before any action was taken." McDonald, Washington, 41.

10 On the origins and nature of the split between Hamilton and Jefferson, see J. Cooke, Alexander Hamilton 109–20 (1982); see also Miller, at 84–98; Stourz, 180–86; Charles.

11 Thomas Jefferson to William Short (July 28, 1791), reprinted 6 Jefferson Works, 290–91 & n.1 (the names of the men Jefferson mentioned appeared in code); Thomas Jefferson to William Short (Jan. 3, 1793), reprinted 25 Jefferson Papers, 15; 7 Jefferson Works, 204–5; Banning, *Republican Ideology and the Triumph of the Constitution, 1789 to 1793,* 31 Wm. & Mary Q. (3rd ser.) 167, 182–84 (1974).

12 See McDonald, Hamilton, 143–98; G. Wood, The Radicalism of the American Revolution 412 n.37 (1991); Banning, supra note 11, at 182–83; McCoy, *Republicanism and American Foreign Policy: James Madison and the Political Economy of Commercial Discrimination, 1789 to 1794,* 31 Wm. & Mary Q. (3rd ser.) 633, 637–42 (1974).

13 Alexander Hamilton to Thomas Jefferson (Jan. 13, 1791), reprinted 7 Hamilton Papers 426. Continuing, he said: "And I feel a particular reluctance to hazard any thing in the present state of our affairs which may lead to commercial warfare with any power; which as far as my knowledge of examples extends is commonly productive of mutual inconvenience and injury and of dispositions tending to a worse kind of warfare." Id.

14 See Buel, 32–34; Clauder, 16; DeConde, 74; Thomas, 20; McDonald, Washington, 120; McDonald, Hamilton, 269; Setser, 102–3; Charles, 227–28. Hamilton did not oppose protectionist policies in principle, as demonstrated by his support for such legislation in 1789; but he insisted that there be no discrimination among foreigners. See Combs, 24–25; Setser, 107. In the early 1790s, however, he clashed with Madison and Jefferson on the issue of adopting retaliatory trade laws against the British. Whereas Madison (with Jefferson's support) sponsored retaliatory tariff legislation in Congress, Hamilton successfully worked against passage, fearing that a trade war would be ignited with the British that could seriously damage his economic program. See Combs, 40–43.

15 Federalist No. 70, reprinted Federalist, 471 & 476. Hamilton's plan called for an executive elected by electors who themselves were chosen by electors selected by the voters; the executive would then hold office for life. See 4 Hamilton Papers, 208 & 244. Jefferson argued to Washington that Hamilton "had endeavored in the convention, to make an English constitution of it, and when failing in that, we saw all his measures tending to bring it to the same thing." Jefferson, Anas, 91.

16 Federalist No. 72, reprinted Federalist, 486–87.

17 N. Small, Some Presidential Interpretations of the Presidency 164 (1932); Pocock, 528; Banning, 176–78. On the issue of excessive influence of the British executive on Parliament, see chapter 1; Jefferson, Anas, 91 (Oct. 1, 1792);

Thomas Jefferson to Thomas Mann Randolph (Mar. 3, 1793), reprinted 25 Jefferson Papers, 313; 7 Jefferson Writings, 253. Jefferson was convinced that key members of Congress would personally benefit from such actions as funding of the debt, assumption of state debts, and creation of the national bank. In conversation with Washington, Jefferson said that his "wish was to see both Houses of Congr. cleansed of all persons interested in the bank or public stocks." Notes of a Conversation with George Washington (Feb. 7, 1793), reprinted 25 Jefferson Papers, 154; 7 Jefferson Writings, 104.

18 Alexander Hamilton to Edward Carrington (May 26, 1792), reprinted 11 Hamilton Papers, 429, 439 (emphasis in original); Alexander Hamilton to George Washington (Sept. 9, 1792), reprinted 12 Hamilton Papers, 349.

19 See Alexander Hamilton to George Washington (Sept. 9, 1792), reprinted 12 Hamilton Papers, 348; Thomas Jefferson to Thomas Mann Randolph (Mar. 3, 1793), reprinted 26 Jefferson Papers, 314; 7 Jefferson Writings, 253; McDonald, Washington, 94; McDonald, Hamilton, 261; Miller, 103; Stewart, 8–9 & 11; Jefferson, Mal-Administration of Treasury (Feb. 7, 1793), reprinted 7 Jefferson Works, 216.

20 George Washington to Marquis de Lafayette (June 3, 1790), reprinted 31 Washington Writings, 46. On Washington's attempts to reconcile Hamilton and Jefferson, see Miller, 95; see also Jefferson, Anas, 90 (Oct. 1, 1792) (recording a conversation with Washington, who thought Hamilton's presence in the cabinet served "to preserve the check of my opinion in the administration, in order to keep things in their proper channel, and prevent them from going too far"). McDonald, Hamilton, 296 ("For more than three years Washington had attempted to steer an intermediate course between the positions held by Jefferson and Hamilton, and the effort had rendered the administration virtually impotent.)"; Washington's doubt was recorded by Jefferson in his diary; see Jefferson, Anas, 90 (Oct. 1, 1792).

21 "And indeed every inch of ground must be fought in our councils to desperation. . . , for our votes are generally 2 1/2 against 1 1/2." Thomas Jefferson to James Monroe (May 5, 1793), reprinted 25 Jefferson Papers, 661; 7 Jefferson Writings, 309. This was addressed specifically to the course of American conduct regarding the French-British conflict of 1793. By the half-vote, Jefferson was alluding to Randolph, whom he thought was indecisive; the two other votes were Hamilton and Knox. See Thomas Jefferson to James Madison (May 12, 1793), reprinted 26 Jefferson Papers, 26; 7 Jefferson Writings, 324 ("Every thing, my dear Sir, now hangs on the opinion of a single person [Randolph], and that the most indecisive one I ever had to do business with. He always contrives to agree in principle with one, but in conclusion with the other.").

22 See DeConde, 39; McDonald, Hamilton, 264–65; Miller, 84–85. Forrest McDonald describes Hamilton as "hyperenergetic, impatient, and a compulsive meddler; and he often took the liberty, when policies in the province of the War or State departments were of interest to him, of attempting to initiate policy by preparing unsolicited position papers for the president's attention and

even by making private commitments that Washington was unaware of." Mc-Donald, Washington, 41.

23 See Lycan, 20–21; Miller, 115–16; Rufus King to Alexander Hamilton (Aug. 3, 1793), reprinted 15 Hamilton Papers, 173; John Jay to George Washington (Jan. 7, 1787), reprinted 3 Jay Papers, 226–27.

24 John Jay to George Washington (June 27, 1786), reprinted 3 Jay Papers, 204; John Jay to Robert Lowell, Feb. 29, 1796, reprinted 2 The Life of John Jay 265 (W. Jay ed. 1833); 4 Jay Papers, 204. See VanBurkleo, 239.

25 Speech at the New York Ratifying Convention (June 21, 1788), reprinted 5 Hamilton Papers, 43. "Hamilton put his trust in the privileged classes and considered their interests as inseparable from those of society as a whole." Charles, 245. See Stourz, 90–94.

26 3 J. Adams, A Defence of the Constitutions of Government of the United States of America 458 (Philadelphia 1787). For similar views by Hamilton, see Speech at the New York Ratifying Convention (June 21, 1788), reprinted 5 Hamilton Papers, 42.

27 Henry Marchant to Alexander Hamilton (Dec. 9, 1793), reprinted 15 Hamilton Papers, 447 (Marchant was making recommendations to Hamilton of individuals for appointment as federal district attorney in Rhode Island). On Federalists and the social elite, see Miller, 108–9.

28 McDonald, Washington, 95.

29 Thomas Jefferson to James Madison (Sept. 21, 1795), reprinted 8 Jefferson Writings, 192; James Madison to Thomas Jefferson (May 25, 1794), reprinted 6 Madison Writings, 217.

30 Jefferson, Anas, 145 (July 15, 1793). This was directly contrary to Hamilton and Knox's view that the cannons should be sent, as Knox said, "to every government to carry into effect orders of such importance." Id. Washington thought, however, that permanent defenses were the business of the states, although the federal government might issue "an occasional call on small parties of militia in the moments requiring it." Id. In the end, Washington acceded to the loan of cannons, but only because Knox already had ordered their loading on his own authority, and "taking them out of the boat again" would involve "disagreeableness." Id., 146. See also The Journal of the Proceedings of the President, 1793–1797, at 199 (D. Twohig ed. 1981). (Washington's diary entry on the incident, noting that he had "uniformly refused" such requests from state governors because "should [it] be granted to one, all would expect the same, & to gratify all would be attended with great inconveniences, even if it cou'd be done.").

31 Jefferson, Anas, 180–81 (Nov. 23, 1793). In the end, Washington decided to include the matter in his address, allowing that he would not recommend anything against the Constitution, but that "if it was *doubtful,* he was so impressed with the necessity of this measure, that he would refer it to Congress, and let them decide for themselves whether the constitution authorized it or not." Id., 181 (Nov. 28, 1793).

32 2 John Jay 12; Hamilton, Remarks on the Provisional Peace Treaty (Continental

Congress, Mar. 19, 1783), reprinted 3 Hamilton Papers, 295; VanBurkleo, 272. See H. Johnson, John Jay, 1745-1829, at 1 (1970); L. Wells, The Jay Family 21 (1938); Ernst, 68; Monaghan, 274-75.

33 John Jay to Benjamin Rush (Mar. 24, 1785), reprinted 2 The Life of John Jay, supra note 24, at 162. Jay expressed remorse that the New York Constitution — which he helped draft — contained no clause "against the continuation of domestic slavery." John Jay to Robert R. Livingston & Gouverneur Morris (Apr. 29, 1777), reprinted 1 John Jay 401; see E. Spaulding, New York in the Critical Period 1783-1789, at 89 (1932) (Jay unsuccessfully tried to include an antislavery provision in the New York Constitution). While negotiating the Treaty of Paris in 1783, Jay attempted to insert a clause banning the importation of slaves to America by British citizens. See infra note 50 and accompanying text. In 1785 he was a founder of the New York Society for the Manumission of Slaves, dedicated to raising funds to free slaves and lobbying for legislative reform. See Monaghan, 233-34; Monaghan, ed., *Anti-Slavery Papers of John Jay*, 17 J. Negro Hist. 481 (1932) (various documents relating to Jay's activities with the Society).

34 See Peter Van Gaasbeek to Aaron Burr (Mar. 28, 1792), reprinted 1 Political Correspondence and Public Papers of Aaron Burr 104 (M. Kline & J. Ryan eds. 1983) (Van Gaasbeek was a supporter of Jay in the 1792 New York gubernatorial race, but he was not optimistic about the probable outcome, because "[h]owever great the Abilities of Mr. Jay, his popularity was lost, or totally absorbed in the consequence of his exertions as is said in favoring of Manumitting the Slaves."); 2 John Jay, 13-14; John Jay to Peter Jay (May 23, 1780), reprinted 1 John Jay, 702 ("I bought a very fine negroe Boy of 15 years old at Martinico.") (Jay later manumitted this particular slave; 2 John Jay, 13).

35 John Jay & Rufus King, To the Advertiser, Daily Advertiser (New York), Nov. 26, 1793. On the context of this statement, see chapter 5, infra; John Jay to William Bingham (July 29, 1783), reprinted 2 John Jay, 571; John Jay to William Vaughan (May 26, 1796), reprinted 4 Jay Papers, 215-16; Charge to Grand Juries of the Eastern Circuit, Apr. 4 & 22, 1790; May 4 & 20, 1790, reprinted 3 Jay Papers, 387.

36 John Jay to George Washington (June 27, 1786), reprinted 3 Jay Papers, 204. See M. Lienesch, New Order of the Ages: Time, the Constitution, and the Making of Modern American Political Thought 51-52 (1988) (on Jay's denunciation of self-interest). Madison said much the same thing in *Federalist No. 10;* see Federalist, 59; John Jay to George Washington (June 27, 1786), supra, at 204-5.

37 See 1 Papers of Aaron Burr, supra note 34, at 105 n.1 (editors' note); A. Graydon, Memoirs of His Own Time 377 (J. Littell ed. 1846). Graydon was a Pennsylvania Federalist and leading advocate of the Constitution at the state's ratifying convention. His *Memoirs* are said to be "free from any deforming bias . . . [and] one of the best-known and most valuable historical sources for the period." 7 Dictionary of American Biography 525 (1931). Madison's statement was made in 1787, during the debates in Virginia over the ratification of the Constitution, quoted in R. Morris, Witnesses at the Creation 159 (1985). His acknowledgment was par-

ticularly notable in view of Southern furor over Jay's proposed treaty with Spain, which would have required Americans to forsake navigation on the Mississippi River for twenty-five years in exchange for trade concessions valuable to Northern merchants. See McCoy, *James Madison and Visions of American Nationality in the Confederation Period,* in Beyond Confederation: Origins of the American Constitution and National Identity 239-43 (R. Beeman, S. Botein, & E. Carter eds. 1987).

38 See Monaghan, 93–96; E. Spaulding, supra note 33, at 87 ("Jay was the dominant spirit in the committee appointed by the convention to draft a constitution, and the constitution seems to have been largely his."); D. Farber & S. Sherry, A History of the American Constitution 80 (1990). New York's governor served a three-year term (most other terms lasted only a year) and was not bound by a council as in a number of states. Although the governor had to consult a council of Senators for appointments and a council of revision for vetoes, the remainder of the executive power was exercised alone. Id. Moreover, the major justification for a council of revision was to allow the governor to join forces with the judiciary in order to strengthen the executive against the legislature. Quote from Jay: John Jay to Robert Lowell (Feb. 29, 1796), supra note 24.

39 Jay was a member of both the First and Second Continental Congresses, becoming President of Congress in 1778, a position that he held until elected minister plenipotentiary to Spain in 1779, where he served until 1781, when he was appointed as an American commissioner to negotiate with the British over what would become the Definitive Treaty of Peace (Treaty of Paris) in 1783. During his return voyage from these negotiations, Congress voted to make Jay Secretary of Foreign Affairs for the United States, a post he would hold until the formation of the new federal government. He became simultaneously Secretary of State (until Jefferson's appointment) and Chief Justice under Washington. After negotiating the Jay Treaty with the British in 1794, he returned to New York to find that he had been elected governor, a position Jay would hold until his retirement in 1801 at age 55. The chronology of Jay's life is conveniently presented in 1 DHSC, 3-7.

40 John Jay to Alexander Hamilton (Nov. 28, 1790), reprinted 7 Hamilton Papers, 167.

41 John Jay to James Duane (Sept. 16, 1795), reprinted 4 Jay Papers, 192-93; John Jay to George Washington (Feb. 25, 1795), reprinted 4 Jay Papers, 160-66; John Jay to George Washington (Dec. 14, 1795), reprinted 4 Jay Papers, 197. At about the same time that he was attacking "demagogues," Jay wrote with disdain about "the numerous herd of those who blindly follow their leaders, who judge without understanding, who believe without evidence, and who are to their demagogues what some other animals are to their riders." John Jay to James Duane (Sept. 16, 1795), reprinted 4 id., 193.

42 John Jay to Thomas Jefferson (Aug. 18, 1786), reprinted 3 Jay Papers, 210; Federalist No. 4, reprinted Federalist, 18-19; John Jay to William Livingston (July 19, 1783), reprinted 2 John Jay, 564; Federalist No. 64, reprinted Federalist,

434-35; John Jay to George Washington (Jan. 7, 1787), reprinted 3 Jay Papers, 226 ("In so large a body secrecy and despatch will be too uncommon.").

43 See F. Gilbert, To the Farewell Address: Ideas of Early American Foreign Policy 87 (1961); Federalist No. 4, reprinted Federalist, 20; John Jay to George Washington (Jan. 7, 1787), reprinted 3 Jay Papers, 226-27; John Jay to Thomas Jefferson (Aug. 18, 1786), reprinted 3 Jay Papers, 210; see also Charge to the Grand Jury of the Circuit Court for the District of New York (Apr. 12, 1790), reprinted 2 DHSC, 26 ("[W]ise and virtuous men . . . have at Length very unanimously agreed vizt That its Powers should be divided into three, distinct, independent Departments—The Executive legislative and judicial."); Federalist No. 64, reprinted Federalist, 436; Wood, 403-9.

44 See 2 John Jay, 14 ("Jay's letters . . . were heavily tinctured with Biblical allusions, as one would expect from a man of his deep religiosity."); Shalhope, *Republicanism and Early American Historiography,* 39 Wm. & Mary. Q. 334, 342 (1982) ("cosmopolitan elite"); see also Kelley, *Ideology and Political Culture from Jefferson to Nixon,* 82 Am. Hist. Rev. 531, 539 (1977). Writing in defense of the proposed federal Constitution, Jay admonished the public: "[g]entlemen out-of-doors [i.e., those not at the Philadelphia convention] should not be hasty in condemning a system which probably rests on more good reasons than they are aware of, especially when . . . recommended by so many men of distinguished worth and abilities." Jay, Address to the People of the State of New York (1788), reprinted 3 Jay Papers, 304.

45 Charge to the Grand Jury of the Circuit Court for the District of New York (Apr. 12, 1790), reprinted 2 DHSC, 26 & 30; see VanBurkleo, 250-51; Jay, Address to the People of the State of New York, reprinted in 3 Jay Papers, 299-301 & 313-15 (on the importance of the union to national commerce and navigation); John Jay to William Livingston (July 19, 1783), reprinted in 2 John Jay, 564; id., 15 (editors' note) ("One of the very first American continentalists, Jay had little patience with state and regional parochialism."). Prosperity, Jay maintained, "required maritime confrontations with ancient, well-defended monopolists; and successful interaction was doomed, he knew, without at least the appearance of internal harmony. Jay was obsessed with Congress's dubious respectability in Europe, and persuaded as well that circumstances could only deteriorate; for experienced mercantilists were not obliged to deal with upstart republicans inhabiting an unstable society." VanBurkleo, 255-56.

46 John Jay to Robert Goodloe Harper (Jan. 19, 1796), reprinted 4 Jay Papers, 200; Stewart, 18; E. Spaulding, supra note 33, at 243 (Jay's tardy support for the Revolution); R. Kelley, The Cultural Pattern in American Politics 114-15 (1979) (denunciation of Jay's treaty negotiations).

47 John Jay to Robert Goodloe Harper (Jan. 19, 1796), reprinted 4 Jay Papers, 199; Jay, Notes of a Conference Between His Excellency the Count de Florida Blanca and Mr. Jay at St. Ildefonso (Sept. 23, 1780), transmitted to Samuel Huntington (Nov. 6, 1780), reprinted 1 John Jay, 834.

48 John Jay to Sarah Livingston Jay (Nov. 14, 1783), reprinted 2 John Jay, 642;

Combs, 18-19 (contending that Jay's "anti-French tendencies" originated from his French Huguenot ancestry and had been exacerbated by his observation of French diplomacy while serving as an American minister negotiating peace at the end of the Revolution); John Jay to Robert Goodloe Harper (Jan. 19, 1796), reprinted 4 Jay Papers, 201.

49 Charge to the Grand Jury of the Circuit Court for the District of New York (Apr. 12, 1790), reprinted 2 DHSC, 26.

50 See, e.g., Monaghan, 200-203; 2 John Jay, 14, quoting Jay, Draft Treaty of Commerce with England (June 1, 1783) reprinted id., 540 ("During the course of the peace negotiations Jay, without being so instructed by Congress, ventured to propose a provision in the trade treaty that would have barred British subjects from importing slaves into America, and justified his proposal on the ground that it was the intention of the 'States intirely to prohibit the Importation thereof.'"); see also Perkins, *The Peace of Paris: Patterns and Legacies,* in Peace and the Peacemakers: The Treaty of 1783, at 203 (R. Hoffman & P. Albert eds. 1986) (at a critical point in negotiations for the Treaty of Paris, Jay "totally disregarded the instructions of 1781."); DeConde, *The French Alliance in Historical Speculation,* in Diplomacy and Revolution—The Franco-American Alliance of 1778, at 21 (R. Hoffman & P. Albert eds. 1981) (Jay and other "commissioners ignored their instructions and engaged in secret negotiations on their own with British representatives."); John Jay to Robert R. Livingston (July 19, 1783), reprinted 2 John Jay, 561: "But Congress positively instructed us to do nothing without the advice and Consent of the French Minister, and we have departed from that Line of Conduct. This is also true, but then I apprehend that Congress marked out that Line of Conduct for their own Sake, and not for the Sake of France. The object of that Instruction was the supposed Interest of America, and not of France. . . . Congress *only* therefore have a Right to complain of our Departure from the Line of that Instruction."

51 VanBurkleo, 264: "[E]nlightened statesmanship for Jay implied a certain freedom from structural constraints. The ends of government, after all, transcended one's momentary political assignment. The offices and institutional attachments of statesmen were vehicles toward those ends, not objects in themselves as legislators might have it." On Jay's pragmatism, see Casto, 173-83.

52 John Jay to Sarah Livingston Jay (Nov. 10, 1790), reprinted 3 Jay Papers, 404.

53 Charge to the Grand Jury of the Circuit Court for the District of New York (Apr. 12, 1790), reprinted 2 DHSC, 26-27.

54 VanBurkleo, 263-64: "Before 1789, Jay had argued repeatedly that this 'due Distribution' required cooperation between executives and jurists, whether through a council of revision, as in New York, or less formally through the 'interpretation and execution' of federal law. Consultation surely strengthened the authority of a few good men against throngs of legislators, and coordination in advance of public action prevented potentially damaging impressions of indecision or disagreement in high places. For these reasons, Jay freely provided informal advice to Federalists colleagues throughout his high court career."

55 Jay was nominated to be Chief Justice on September 24, 1789, and was confirmed two days later. He was already Secretary of Foreign Affairs, having continuously held that post since 1784. Jay agreed to remain as Secretary until March 22, 1790, when Jefferson assumed the office. See 1 DHSC, 6. On Jay's reputation for foreign policy expertise, see Morris, 32.

56 Donald Stewart summarizes the views of the opposition press: "Most reprehensible of all, his appointment while holding the office of Chief Justice . . . violated the principle of separation of powers. . . . Much was made of this last argument. If the President could use judges on foreign missions, he could sway the judiciary according to his will and make the courts subordinate to the Executive. Judges were not supposed to be assigned any duties other than judicial; in Jay's absence, how could impeachment proceedings against the President be completed, should the need arise? Might Jay himself be impeached for transgressions as an ambassador, and if the Supreme Court already complained of a crowded docket how was it possible to spare him?" Stewart, 189; see also Buel, 59–60; Link, 130–31; 1 Warren, 119–21; Randolph, 220. Randolph suggested that Jay resign before the appointment and become the resident ambassador in London. According to Randolph, Washington offered Jay this option, but he declined. Id.

57 See An Act establishing a Mint, and regulating the Coins of the United States, § 18, 1 Stat. 250 (1792); Wheeler, 140. The Sinking Fund was created by statute, An Act making Provision for the Reduction of the Public Debt, 1 Stat. 186 (1790), and the first meeting of the commissioners was on August 26, 1790; see 6 Hamilton Papers, 567. On the original justification for the fund as a debt reduction measure, see Hamilton, Report Relative to a Provision for the Support of Public Credit (Jan. 9, 1790), reprinted 6 Hamilton Papers, 106–8; regarding using the fund to intervene in the market, see McDonald, Hamilton, 171, 248–49. Another example in addition to the 1792 panic involved purchases of stock in the Bank of the United States shortly after its opening in 1791, which were designed to stabilize the market in bank stock. See Alexander, 243; McDonald, Hamilton, 223 ("Hamilton moved swiftly to counter the decline [in prices for bonds and scrip] with judicious purchases through the sinking fund, and in a week the market began to be stabilized.").

58 The coin inspectors consisted of the Secretary and Comptroller of the Treasury, the Secretary of State, the Attorney General, and the Chief Justice; see An Act establishing a Mint, and regulating the Coins of the United States, § 18, 1 Stat. 250 (1792). The Sinking Fund commissioners were the President of the Senate, the Chief Justice, the Secretary of State, the Secretary of the Treasury, and the Attorney General; see An Act making Provision for the Reduction of the Public Debt, § 2, 1 Stat. 186 (1790); Hamilton, Report on the Establishment of a Mint (Jan. 28, 1791), reprinted 7 Hamilton Papers, 606, cited in Wheeler, 141–42 n.87, Stewart, 41 & 100. In 1793, Rep. William Branch Giles, acting on the suggestion of Madison and Jefferson, launched a partisan attack on Hamilton's management of the Treasury; in particular, he raised questions concerning whether Hamilton had illegally disbursed proceeds from a loan. The Sinking Fund was involved in

this inquiry because Giles demanded, among other things, an accounting of all the fund's transactions. McDonald, Hamilton, 260.

59 See Marcus & Van Tassel, 44; Wheeler, 141.

60 See John Adams to John Jay (Mar. 21, 1792), reprinted 11 Hamilton Papers, 159; John Jay to Alexander Hamilton (Mar. 23, 1792), reprinted 11 Hamilton Papers, 173. On March 21, 1792, the Sinking Fund Committee voted to request that Jay come immediately to Philadelphia (he was on circuit duty in New York City) to discuss whether the statute setting up the committee constrained their purchases of securities in certain respects. John Adams to John Jay (Mar. 21, 1792), reprinted 11 Hamilton Papers, 159-60 (questions reprinted in id., 160 n.2). Jay responded by saying that he doubted the need for his personal appearance: "It appears from [Adams's] Letter to be a meer law Question. In that Case my opinion shall without Delay be formed and transmitted. . . . Why cannot I give my opinion on a Law Question in the city of New York as well as in the City of Pha?" John Jay to Alexander Hamilton (Mar. 23, 1792), reprinted id., 172-73. On March 26, the board resolved to send the questions to Jay. Id., 193 (the questions are reprinted in id., 160 n.2). Jay reported his answers on March 31, 1792, giving a legal interpretation of language in the act. Id., 214-16; Meeting of the Commissioners of the Sinking Fund (minutes of meeting, March 26, 1792), reprinted 11 Hamilton Papers, 193: "[I]t appearing to the Board, that the question turns upon the mere words of the law; that [Jay's] attendance . . . would interfere with his attendance as a judge, on the circuit courts. . . , *Resolved,* . . . That the said question be stated in writing, and forwarded to the Chief Justice, with a request that he transmit his opinion thereupon, as soon as convenient."

61 John Jay to John Adams (Mar. 23, 1792), reprinted 11 Hamilton Papers, 173. For their part, the commissioners resolved that their acceptance of the Chief Justice's absence was "dictated by special circumstances, [and] is not to be interpreted so as to form a precedent for obtaining the vote of an absent member on any other occasion." Meeting of the Commissioners of the Sinking Fund (minutes of meeting, Mar. 26, 1792), reprinted id., 193. Nevertheless, the attendance of Jay and his successor, Oliver Ellsworth, was probably not regular. See Wheeler, 143-44.

62 McDonald, Hamilton, 125; George Washington to John Jay (June 8, 1789), reprinted 30 Washington Writings, 344; 6 Freeman, 206 n.38. Washington had received a complaint from Maria Hammond, the wife of the captain; his vessel had been captured by the British, and he was now being held by the Portuguese. Jay was asked for his opinion on what procedures to follow. "Jay apparently advised Washington to make inquiries of . . . the governor of St. Jago," the island where Hammond was being held. 6 Washington Diaries, 38-40 (editors' note). On Washington's cabinet practices, see Boyd, 17 ("On important matters Washington was accustomed to ask the opinions of the Chief Justice and the Vice-President as well as the heads of departments."); Flexner, New, 213-14 (discussing Washington's main advisers and cabinet practices).

63 Lycan, 121-23; 6 Washington Diaries, 89. On the background of Beckwith's mission, see Boyd, 3-54.

64 Alexander Hamilton to John Jay (July 9, 1790), reprinted 6 Hamilton Papers, 488 (on Washington's initiating this request, see id., 488 n.1); 6 Washington Diaries, 94–95. Washington continued: "In a word, that the Secretary of the Treasury was to extract as much as he could from Major Beckwith & to report it to me, without committing, by any assurances whatever, the Government of the U States, leaving it entirely free to pursue, unreproached, such a line of conduct in the dispute as her interest (& honour) shall dictate." Id.; see Boyd, 48–49; Freeman, 269–70; Lycan, 11 n.22, 177–79. A long-standing debate has centered on Hamilton's conduct in his discussions with Beckwith. Julian Boyd argued that Hamilton only selectively revealed to Washington the content of his discussions with Beckwith, and misrepresented to the British via Beckwith the positions of the American administration. The alleged purpose of this was to further Hamilton's interest in the establishment of an alliance between the United States and Great Britain. See generally Boyd. Others have disputed this interpretation; see, e.g., Lycan, 122–23.

65 On Jay's limited legal experience, see Morris, 42–43. Edmund Randolph commented about Jay in 1792: "He has a nervous and imposing elocution; and striking lineaments of face, well adapted to his real character. He is clear too in the expression of his ideas, but that they do not abound on legal subjects has been proved to my conviction. In two judgments, which he gave last week, one of which was written, there was no method, no legal principle, no system of reasoning." Edmund Randolph to James Madison (Aug. 12, 1792), reprinted Randolph, 145. Jay's knowledge of the law of nations is demonstrated by several of his opinions to Washington, such as the one regarding the Nootka Sound incident, discussed later in this chapter. On the international political context, see Dickinson, *Changing Concepts and the Doctrine of Incorporation,* 26 Am. J. Int'l. L. 239, 241 (1932); Lint, *The American Revolution and the Law of Nations,* 1 Dipl. Hist. 20, 21 (1977). Many of the Framers wished to avoid military alliances and minimize the need for diplomacy and treaties. See F. Marks, Independence on Trial: Foreign Affairs and the Making of the Constitution 45–46, 155 (1973); W. Reveley, War Powers of the President and Congress 61 (1981); Farrand, 19, 24–25 (Edmund Randolph on the need for national authority to prevent violations of international law, which could result in war).

66 On the Nootka Sound controversy, see DeConde, 68–70; D. Pethick, The Nootka Connection (1980); Manning, *The Nootka Sound Controversy,* in Annual Report of the American Historical Association for the Year 1904, at 279–478 (1905); J. Wright, 50–65. Letters from George Washington to John Adams, Alexander Hamilton, John Jay, Thomas Jefferson, and Henry Knox (Aug. 27, 1790), reprinted 31 Washington Writings, 102–3 (draft of letter; signed copies are in Hamilton and Jefferson Papers, Library of Congress). The letter to Hamilton is reprinted in 6 Hamilton Papers, 572–73. Washington did not ask Randolph for an opinion, presumably because he would not arrive in New York until after Washington's departure. See George Washington to Edmund Randolph (Aug. 26, 1790), reprinted 31 Washington Writings, 101.

67 The opinions are collected in Boyd, 107–39; John Jay to George Washington (Aug. 28, 1790), reprinted Boyd, 115–16. Jay went on to predict that the Europeans would find it "more prudent for them at present to permit Britain to conquer and hold the Floridas, than engage in a War to prevent it," and thus "such Inquiries would be premature." He based this assessment on his view that "the State of their affairs strongly recommends Peace." Id.

68 Diary entries (Feb. 16, 1790; Feb. 17, 1790; Apr. 27, 1790) reprinted 6 Washington Diaries, 35, 68. 6 Freeman, 255–56. Ultimately, the Chief of the Creeks, Alexander McGillivray, was invited and came to New York, where a treaty was concluded. Id., 245–46 & 272–73.

69 George Washington to John Jay (Nov. 19, 1790), reprinted 31 Washington Writings, 155; John Jay to George Washington (Draft) (Nov. 13, 1790), reprinted 2 DHSC, 108; 3 Jay Papers, 405–8 (each is a partial, overlapping reprint); John Jay to George Washington (Draft) (Dec. 12, 1790), reprinted 2 DHSC, 117. This correspondence clearly indicates that Jay's letter of November 13 and Washington's of the 19th had crossed in the mail.

70 George Washington to John Jay (Sept. 4, 1791), reprinted 31 Washington Writings, 354. For example, Jay's response recommended that the surplus be used to pay additional installments of the French debt, and that Native Americans be treated "with benevolence." John Jay to George Washington (Sept. 23, 1791), reprinted 2 Life of Jay, 205–8.

71 George Washington to John Jay (Nov. 19, 1790), reprinted 31 Washington Writings, 155–56; John Jay to George Washington (Draft) (Dec. 12, 1790), reprinted 2 DHSC, 117; John Jay to Egbert Benson (Mar. 31, 1792), reprinted 3 Jay Papers, 418. In 1794, when Jay was in Great Britain to negotiate a treaty with the British, Washington wrote to him: "[A]nd for the honor, dignity and interest of this country; for your own reputation and glory; and for the peculiar pleasure and satisfaction I shd. derive from it, as well on private, as on public considerations, no man more ardently wishes you compleat success than I do." George Washington to John Jay (Nov. 1, 1794), reprinted 34 Washington Writings, 15–16. Jay responded: "Your very friendly letter of the 1st November last gratified me not a little." John Jay to George Washington (Feb. 25, 1795), reprinted 4 Jay Papers, 160.

72 Monaghan, 345.

73 See, e.g., 6 Freeman, 302: "Although John Jay still was called upon for counsel, it had to be remembered now that he might have to pass as Chief Justice on questions presented in their first form to the President. Jay must not be embarrassed or placed where he might be compelled to disqualify himself in hearing a case." Freeman cites no source for this statement.

74 After resigning as Chief Justice to become governor of New York, Jay continued to provide advice to Washington. In 1795, for example, Washington asked for "hints relative to those points which you conceive to be fit subjects for the further friendly negociations on the trade with G. Britain . . . which appears to have been in contemplation by the concluding part of the [Jay] treaty." George Washington to John Jay (Aug. 31, 1795), reprinted 34 Washington Writings, 293. Jay re-

sponded with three suggestions; see John Jay to George Washington (Sept. 3, 1795), reprinted 4 Jay Papers, 189. Similarly, Jay was sent a draft copy of Washington's Farewell Address, presumably for comments, and while Jay made several suggestions, these arrived too late for Washington to take them into account. See President's Journal, 343 n.1 (for entry of Sept. 19, 1796). Several times Washington asked Hamilton to consult Jay (when both were out of office) and provide Washington with advice. See, e.g., George Washington to Alexander Hamilton (June 26, 1796), reprinted 35 Washington Writings, 103 ("[A]s I have great confidence in the abilities, and purity of Mr. Jays views, as well as in his experience, I should wish his sentiments on the purport of this letter [questions included whether Washington could appoint an Envoy Extraordinary without Senate confirmation]; and other interesting matters as they occur, may accompany yours.") (Hamilton responded with Jay's views; see Alexander Hamilton to George Washington [July 5, 1796], reprinted 20 Hamilton Papers, 246–47); George Washington to Alexander Hamilton (Nov. 2, 1796), reprinted 35 Washington Writings, 254 ("As I have a very high opinion of Mr. Jay's judgment, candour, honor and discretion . . . it would be very pleasing to me if you would shew him this letter [regarding diplomatic matters] . . . and let me have, for consideration, your joint opinion on the several matters therein stated.") (Hamilton did so; see Alexander Hamilton to George Washington [Nov. 4, 1796], reprinted 20 Hamilton Papers, 372–73.). Jay also continued to pass on information and views to Washington without specific request; see, e.g., John Jay to George Washington (Dec. 14, 1795), reprinted 4 Jay Papers, 197 (saying that he had received "much intelligence from several quarters . . . that certain virulent publications have caused great and general indignation"). Washington responded in general agreement, adding: "The dregs, however, will always remain and the slightest motion will stir them up." George Washington to John Jay (Dec. 21, 1795), reprinted in 34 Washington Writings, 397.

75 Jay was on circuit assignment during the following periods: April 5–May 21 & October 4–December 7, 1790; February 21–23, April 5–June 22, & October 5–December 10, 1791; April 5–June 29, 1792; May 22–June 8, 1793; April 2–26, 1794. See 2 DHSC, 536–39 (listing of dates of circuit court sessions; does not include travel time before and after the circuit). He complained regularly about the time spent and the hardships of the journeys, as in this letter: "I am now [in a job] which takes me from my Family half the Year, and obliges me to pass too considerable a part of my Time on the Road, in Lodging Houses, & Inns." John Jay to Catharine Ridley (Feb. 1, 1791), reprinted 2 DHSC, 126.

76 See N. Emery, Alexander Hamilton 30 (1982); J. Cooke, Alexander Hamilton 11–12, 37 (1982); McDonald, Hamilton, 62, 114; Alexander, 161–62. Upon hearing of Hamilton's marriage to the daughter of a prominent New York family, Jay wrote from France to send congratulations: "You were always of the number of those whom I esteemed." Jay added that because of the marriage, Hamilton would of course be a New York resident, "of which I long wished you to be, and remain a citizen." John Jay to Alexander Hamilton (Sept. 28, 1783), reprinted 3

Jay Papers, 89. Jay had a fine portrait of Hamilton executed for himself by the painter John Trumbull in 1792. See Bland & Northcott, *The Life Portraits of Alexander Hamilton,* 12 Wm. & Mary Q. 187, 191 (1955).

77 "I beg leave to add that of the persons whom you would deem free from any constitutional objections—Mr. Jay is the only man in whose qualifications for success there would be thorough confidence and him whom alone it would be adviseable to send. I think the business would have the best chance possible in his hands." Alexander Hamilton to George Washington (Apr. 14, 1794), reprinted 16 Hamilton Papers, 278–79. Washington promptly offered Jay the position. See McDonald, Hamilton, 293–94.

78 See Alexander, 309. Jay also ran for the governorship in 1792, losing to the incumbent George Clinton in a contest that was tainted by charges of election misconduct against the Clinton camp. See Ernst, 174–80; R. Hendrickson, The Rise and Fall of Alexander Hamilton 341–42 (1981); Monaghan, 325–40. According to the editors of Hamilton's papers, "the traditional account of Jay's [1792] candidacy, repeated by most historians who have written on the subject, is that H[amilton] persuaded Jay to run and dictated his nomination to the New York Federalists." The editors, however, could find no letters by Hamilton to substantiate this claim. 11 Hamilton Papers, 38 n.2. Jay was selected to run for governor of New York at a meeting of Federalists in New York City on February 9, 1792. See id., 38 n.2. The election was held on April 13, 1792. For details of the election, see 11 Hamilton Papers, 378–79 n.4 (editors' note).

79 See John Jay to Alexander Hamilton (Apr. 19, 1798), reprinted 21 Hamilton Papers, 433; John Jay to Alexander Hamilton (Apr. 19, 1798), reprinted id., 434. Hamilton declined the Senate seat. See Alexander Hamilton to John Jay (Apr. 24, 1798), reprinted id., 447.

80 Alexander Hamilton to John Jay (Nov. 13, 1790), reprinted 7 Hamilton Papers, 149; John Jay to Alexander Hamilton (Nov. 28, 1790), reprinted 7 Hamilton Papers, 167. For example, Jay thought it would be helpful to station a revenue officer on the road to Canada and to allow the Collector of Boston a leave of absence in order to come to Philadelphia during the congressional session. Id. The latter recommendation was approved by Washington; see Alexander Hamilton to George Washington (Dec. 15, 1790), reprinted id., 342–43; Alexander Hamilton to Benjamin Lincoln (Dec. 17, 1790), reprinted id., 345.

81 See 12 Hamilton Papers, 305–10 nn.1–6 (editors' notes); Resolution of Sundry Inhabitants of the Western Counties of Pennsylvania, held at Pittsburgh, Aug. 21, 1792, reprinted 12 Hamilton Papers, 308 n.5 & 309 n.5. See generally L. Baldwin, Whiskey Rebels: The Story of a Frontier Uprising (1967); T. Slaughter, The Whiskey Rebellion: Frontier Epilogue to the American Revolution (1979); Tachau, *A New Look at the Whiskey Rebellion,* in The Whiskey Rebellion: Past and Present Perspectives 97 (S. Boyd ed. 1985).

82 Alexander Hamilton to John Jay (Sept. 3, 1792), reprinted 12 Hamilton Papers, 316–17 (Hamilton did not specify the offense, and he said that "[t]he point however is under submission to the Attorney General for his opinion." Id. at

316); Alexander Hamilton to George Washington (Sept. 1, 1792), reprinted 12 Hamilton Papers, 311–12. George Washington to Alexander Hamilton (Sept, 7, 1792), reprinted id., 331–33 (authorizing Hamilton to institute proceedings at the next circuit court should the Attorney General conclude that the offenses were indictable).

83 John Jay to Alexander Hamilton (Sept. 8, 1792), reprinted 2 DHSC, 294 (Jay wrote from New York to Hamilton in Philadelphia). "Probably Jay believed that a particular charge would be ignored, embarrassing the federal court, or tend further to inflame the passions of the westerners." Marcus & Van Tassel, 50. For Hamilton and King's suggestions about addressing Congress, see John Jay to Alexander Hamilton (Sept. 8, 1792), supra, 294. "[Congress's] address will manifest the Sense of the House, & both together operate more effectually than a Proclamation." Id. As to whether Washington should go in person to the scene, Jay replied that it would depend on the circumstances at the time; see id. "No sense of impropriety or violation of separation of powers informs Jay's reply to Hamilton." Marcus & Van Tassel, *supra,* 50.

84 On the conference of Hamilton, Knox, and Randolph, see 12 Hamilton Papers, 330 n.1 (as to the timing of these events in relation to Jay's letter, see Edmund Randolph to Alexander Hamilton [Sept. 8, 1792], reprinted 12 id., 336–40, which concluded that there was no basis at that time for prosecution of the protesters; Randolph agreed that a proclamation was necessary and within the President's powers); Alexander Hamilton to George Washington (Sept. 9, 1792), reprinted id., 344–46 (advising Washington, who was at Mt. Vernon, to issue a proclamation); George Washington to Alexander Hamilton (Sept. 17, 1792), reprinted id., 391–92 (indicating that the proclamation had been signed on September 15 and then sent to the Secretary of State for his countersignature); Proclamation of the President (Sept. 15, 1792), in the Philadelphia Daily Advertiser (Sept. 25, 1792), reprinted 12 Hamilton Papers, 330–31 n.1; Speech of George Washington, Nov. 6, 1792, reprinted 1 House Journal, 612. Regarding opposition to the whiskey excise taxes outside western Pennsylvania, see T. Slaughter, supra note 81, at 206–14 (rural East); Baumann, *Philadelphia's Manufacturers and the Excise Tax of 1794: The Forging of the Jeffersonian Coalition,* in The Whiskey Rebellion: Past and Present Perspectives, supra note 81, at 135.

85 The two letters have not been found, but they are referred to in Hamilton's letter to Jay of December 18, 1792. See Alexander Hamilton to John Jay (Dec. 18, 1792), reprinted 13 Hamilton Papers, 337–38 & nn.1 & 3 (includes editors' notes). Regarding public attacks on Hamilton, which centered on his economic plan, see Stewart, 34–47, 50–52, 55–56, & 59.

86 John Jay to Alexander Hamilton (Dec. 29, 1792), reprinted 13 Hamilton Papers, 384–85. Jay recommended that Hamilton keep memoirs: "[N]o other person will possess sufficient facts & Details to do full Justice to the Subject; and I think your Reputation points to the Expediency of memoirs." Id.

87 J. O'Connor, William Paterson: Lawyer and Statesman, 1745–1806, at 224 (1979); G. Wood, The Radicalism of the American Revolution 324 (1992); see C. Prince,

The Federalists and the Origins of the U.S. Civil Service 242-43 (1977); George Washington to John Jay (Oct. 5, 1789), reprinted 1 DHSC, 11; 30 Washington Writings, 429; George Washington to Edmund Randolph (Sept. 28, 1789), reprinted 30 Washington Writings, 418-19 ("[T]he due administration of justice is the firmest pillar of good Government, . . . essential to the happiness of our Country, and to the stability of its political system; hence the selection of the fittest characters to expound the laws, and dispense justice, has been an invariable object of my anxious concern."). Washington knew many of his judicial nominees from personal experience; see John Jay to Matthew Ridley (Oct. 8, 1789), reprinted 1 DHSC, 672 ("The Presidents personal Knowledge of distinguished Characters throughout the States, render[s] unnecessary for him to require or depend upon the Information or Recommendation of others."). This statement by Jay was not entirely accurate, for Washington frequently relied on the opinions of those he trusted—based on "the strictest inquiries," he said—in making judicial and other appointments. George Washington to Edward Rutledge (Nov. 23, 1789), reprinted id., 680.

88 C. Prince, supra note 87, at 241; 1 Holt, 1440-78; Ware v. Hylton, 3 U.S. 199, 220-45 (1796) (upholding a claim based on a pre-revolutionary debt owed to a British creditor); Chisholm v. Georgia, 2 U.S (2 Dall.) 435 (1793). "At stake [in *Chisholm*] was Georgia's ability to sidestep federal jurisdiction in disputes involving the Paris peace and hence to threaten an eventual rapprochement with Great Britain." VanBurkleo, at 267. On revenue prosecutions, see 2 Holt, 324-25 & n.95; Ifft, *Treason in the Early Republic: The Federal Courts, Popular Protest, and Federalism during the Whiskey Insurrection,* in The Whiskey Rebellion: Past and Present Perspectives, supra note 81, at 165. The carriage tax case is Hylton v. United States, 3 U.S. (3 Dall.) 171 (1796). The statute upheld was An Act Laying Duties Upon Carriages for the Conveyance of Persons, 1 Stat. 373 (1794).

89 "As far as the justices were concerned, the administration's neutrality policy was their judicial policy as well." 2 DHSC, 340; Buel, 235; Banning, 256-58; J. Miller, Crisis in Freedom: The Alien and Sedition Acts (1951); J. Smith, Freedom's Fetters: The Alien and Sedition Laws and American Civil Liberties (1956). The overall efficacy of these prosecutions is a separate matter, however, for in the end the public resentment they engendered "did the Federalists more harm than good." Buel, 236. All circuit courts that reviewed the Sedition Act upheld its constitutionality. In the process, they not only denied the right of juries to determine the question of constitutionality but also offended supporters of the Virginia Resolutions of 1798 by insisting that the federal judicial interpretation was binding on the states. Goebel, 645-51; Sedition Act, ch. 73, 1 Stat. 596 (1798).

90 Preyer, *United States v. Callender: Judge and Jury in a Republican Society,* in Origins of the Federal Judiciary: Essays on the Judiciary Act of 1789, at 178 (M. Marcus ed. 1992); Charge to the Grand Jury of the Circuit Court for the District of Virginia (Nov. 23, 1798) (Cushing, J.), reprinted Federal Gazette (Baltimore), Dec. 6, 1798, reprinted 3 DHSC, 306. "[O]ur judges are in the habit of printing their charges in the newspapers," Jefferson noted. Thomas Jefferson to Edmund

Randolph (May 8, 1793), reprinted 25 Jefferson Papers, 692; 2 DHSC, 373; see 2 DHSC, 5; Lerner, *The Supreme Court as Republican Schoolmaster,* Supreme Court Rev. 127 (1967).

91 See Marcus & Van Tassel, at 46. On Iredell's lobbying, see 2 Holt, 317–18 & 328–30; see, e.g., Samuel Johnston to James Iredell (Nov. 13, 1791), reprinted 2 DHSC, 231; Samuel Johnston to James Iredell (June 10, 1793), reprinted 3 Life and Correspondence of James Iredell 396 (G. McCree ed. 1857–58); Samuel Johnston to James Iredell (Feb. 27, 1796), reprinted 3 DHSC, 92; Samuel Johnston to James Iredell (July 5, 1797), reprinted 3 id., 212–13; James Iredell to Samuel Johnston (Feb. 28, 1799), reprinted 3 id., 324; Samuel Johnston to James Iredell (May 18, 1799), reprinted 3 id., 365–66.

92 See, e.g.. Henry Marchant to Alexander Hamilton (Dec. 9, 1793), supra note 27 and accompanying text. Another example involving Marchant occurred in August 1793, during the height of tensions over privateering activities by French and British ships off the American coast. Marchant wrote to Washington to inform him that the British ship *Catharine* had reportedly plundered an American vessel. Washington forwarded the letter to Jefferson at the State Department. See President's Journal, 220. On Marchant's correspondence with members of Congress, see Marcus & Van Tassel, 46.

93 See Goebel, 554–58; 1 Warren, 85–90; 2 Holt, 308–10. At the outset, two Justices rode each circuit, sitting at trials with a district judge. See Judiciary Act of 1789, § 4, 1 Stat. 74–75 (1789).

94 George Washington to the Chief Justice and Associate Justices of the Supreme Court (Apr. 3, 1790), reprinted 31 Washington Writings, 31–32 & 2 DHSC, 21.

95 See Letter (Draft) from the Justices of the Supreme Court to George Washington (c. Sept. 13, 1790), reprinted 2 DHSC, 89–91. Jay's arguments will be addressed in detail later in this chapter, as they may bear on the Chief Justice's attitude about advisory opinions. See also 2 DHSC, 92 n.1; 31 Washington Writings, 32 n.58 (no reply to Washington's letter was found in Washington Papers). In a draft of a letter to Washington dated November 13, 1790, Jay crossed out paragraphs that were to accompany a copy of the draft letter that Jay had circulated to the other Justices. In one of the excised sections, Jay noted that he had received no replies from the other Justices. He also struck a line saying that "The Report of the Atty Gen. (to whom I also sent a Copy of this proposed answer) will perhaps render the Delay less important." Letter (Draft) from John Jay to George Washington (Nov. 13, 1790), reprinted 2 DHSC, 108. Although these lines are struck, they suggest that Jay had decided to use Randolph's report to Congress on the judicial system as the vehicle for attacking circuit riding. The Randolph report is described later in this paragraph in text and note 96.

96 See H.R. Res., 1st Cong., 2d Sess. (Aug. 5, 1790), reprinted 3 Documentary History of the First Federal Congress of the United States of America 550 (L. De Pauw, C. Bickford, & L. Hauptman eds. 1977); Edmund Randolph to James Wilson (Aug. 5, 1790) (Society Collection, Historical Society of Pennsylvania), cited in 3 Holt, 345 n.11. On Randolph and Wilson serving together on the

Committee of Detail, see 2 Farrand, 106. Whether Wilson assisted Randolph is not known, but in later years Wilson provided advice to Randolph when the latter was Secretary of State. For the text of Randolph's report, see H.R. Rep., 1st Cong., 3d Sess. (Dec. 31, 1790), reprinted ASP-M, 21–36. For a thorough analysis of Randolph's report and Congress's reaction to it, see 3 Holt. No action was taken to abolish circuit riding until Congress passed the short-lived Judiciary Act of 1801, which halted the practice during the year it was in effect. See Goebel, 569.

97   John Jay, William Cushing, James Wilson, John Blair, James Iredell, & Thomas Johnson to George Washington (Aug. 9, 1792), reprinted 2 DHSC, 288; Washington presented the letter to Congress on November 7, 1792. See 1 Senate Journal, 455; 1 House Journal, 614. In their letter to Congress, the Justices noted that the original Judiciary Act of 1789 was understood as a "temporary expedient," rather than "a permanent System." Continuing, they said that the task of holding the numerous circuit sessions was "too burthensome," and had produced a "painful and improper situation." The Chief Justice, and the Associate Judges of the Supreme Court to Congress of the United States (Aug. 9, 1792), reprinted 2 DHSC, 289–90. See John Jay to William Cushing (Jan. 9, 1793), reprinted 2 DHSC, 343–44.

98   William Cushing to William Paterson (Mar. 5, 1793), reprinted 2 DHSC, 345; An Act in addition to the Act, entitled "An Act to establish the Judicial Courts of the United States," § 1, 1 Stat. 333–34 (providing that only a single Justice need attend a circuit court); John Jay, William Cushing, James Wilson, John Blair, & William Paterson to George Washington (Feb. 18, 1794), reprinted 2 DHSC, 442–43. Washington sent this letter to Congress on February 19, 1794; see 2 Senate Journal, 32; 2 House Journal, 66; Judiciary Act of 1801, ch. 4, 2 Stat. 89, repealed by Act of March 8, 1802, ch. 8, 2 Stat. 132. Turner [now Preyer], *Federalist Policy and the Judiciary Act of 1801*, 22 Wm. & Mary Q. 3 (1965).

99   James Iredell to George Washington (Feb. 23, 1792), reprinted 2 DHSC, 239–42, quoted in Marcus & Van Tassel, 45–46 & n.45; see, e.g., John Jay to Rufus King (Dec. 22, 1793), reprinted 2 DHSC, 434 ("Would it not also be adviseable to abolish the alternate sitting of the Circuit Court at York Town and Pha.? double places create double Trouble to all Parties."). Jay's suggestion was acted on two years later when Congress abolished the York sitting. See id., 435 n.1. In the same letter, Jay addressed the issue of marshalls who selected biased jurors, and he provided for an alternative location for Supreme Court hearings in the summer because of yellow fever outbreaks in Philadelphia. See John Jay to Rufus King (Dec. 22, 1793), reprinted 1 King, 509.

100 See Wheeler, 131–39 (discussing examples mentioned in this paragraph); An Act concerning Consuls and Vice-Consuls, § 1, 1 Stat. 254 (1792) (salvage); An Act to prescribe the mode of taking Evidence in cases of contested Elections for Members of the House of Representatives of the United States, and to compel the attendance of Witnesses, § 1, 1 Stat. 537 (1798) (contested elections). On remitting customs fines, see An Act to provide for mitigating or remitting the

forfeitures and penalties accruing under the revenue laws, in certain cases therein mentioned, § 1, 1 Stat. 122-23 (1790) (customs); see also An Act to provide for mitigating or remitting the Forefeitures, Penalties and Disabilities accruing in certain cases therein mentioned, §§ 1-2, 1 Stat. 506-7 (1797); An Act to repeal part of an act, intituled "An Act to provide for mitigating or remitting the forfeitures, penalties and disabilities, accruing in certain cases therein mentioned, and to continue in force the residue of the same," 2 Stat. 7 (1800) (extending the 1797 act indefinitely); An Act to provide for mitigating or remitting the forfeitures and penalties accruing under the revenue laws, in certain cases therein mentioned, § 1, 1 Stat. 122-23 (1790). On naturalization proceedings, see An Act to establish an uniform rule of Naturalization; and to repeal the act heretofore passed on that subject, §§ 1-2, 1 Stat. 414-15 (1795).

101 Militia Act of 1792, § 2, 1 Stat. 264 (1792); Conference Concerning the Insurrection in Western Pennsylvania (Aug. 2, 1794) (report of a meeting attended by Washington, Hamilton, Secretary of State Edmund Randolph, Knox, Attorney General William Bradford, and several Pennsylvania state officials, including the governor, attorney general, secretary, and Chief Justice of the state supreme court), reprinted 17 Hamilton Papers, 10; Alexander Hamilton to George Washington (Aug. 2, 1794), reprinted at id., 17; id., 12 (quoting Thomas McKean); Edmund Randolph to George Washington (Aug. 5, 1794), reprinted 17 Hamilton Papers, 11 n.9; 1 ASP-M, at 85; James Wilson to George Washington (Aug. 4, 1794), quoted in 2 DHSC, 438; Slaughter, supra note 81, at 192-221.

102 See 3 DHSC, 1-2 & n.6; Charge to the Grand Jury of the Circuit Court for the District of Pennsylvania (May 4, 1795) (Paterson, Circuit Justice), reprinted 3 DHSC, 41. Likewise, at the trial, Paterson charged the jury that "the object . . . to suppress the excise offices, and to prevent the execution of an act of congress, by force and intimidation . . . is high treason." United States v. Mitchell, 26 F.Cas. 1277, 1281 (C.C.D. Pa. 1795) (No. 15,788) (Paterson, Circuit Justice); see also United States v. Vigol, 28 F.Cas. 376, 376 (C.C.D.Pa. 1795) (No. 16,621) (Paterson, Circuit Justice). Tracking the language of the Militia Act of 1792, § 2, 1 Stat. 264 (1792), Wilson certified that there existed "Combinations too powerful to be suppressed by the ordinary Course of judicial Proceedings." James Wilson to George Washington (Aug. 4, 1794) (original in Library of Congress, Pennsylvania Whiskey Rebellion papers), quoted in 2 DHSC, 438.

103 The official title was: An Act to provide for the settlement of the Claims of Widows and Orphans barred by the limitations heretofore established, and to regulate the Claims to Invalid Pensions, 1 Stat. 243 (1792); §§ 2-4, 1 Stat. 244 (1792). For accounts of the proceedings in these cases, see D. Currie, The Constitution in the Supreme Court 6-14 (1985); 1 Warren, 70-82; Bloch & Marcus, *John Marshall's Selective Use of History in Marbury v. Madison*, 1986 Wisc. L. Rev. 301, 304-10; Farrand, *The First Hayburn Case, 1792*, 13 Am. Hist. Rev. 281 (1908).

104 James Iredell to Hannah Iredell (Oct. 4, 1792), reprinted 2 DHSC, 304.

105 Opinion of the Circuit Judges for the New York District (Apr. 5, 1792), reprinted

1 ASP-M, 50; see James Wilson, John Blair, and Richard Peters to George Washington (Apr. 18, 1792), reprinted id., 51; James Iredell and John Sitgreaves to George Washington (June 8, 1792), reprinted id., 52–53. The letters are reprinted as an attachment to Hayburn's Case, 2 U.S. (2 Dall.) 408, 410–12 n.(a) (1792).

106 John Jay, William Cushing, & James Duane to George Washington (Apr. 5, 1792), reprinted 1 ASP-M, at 50; James Iredell & John Sitgreaves to George Washington (June 8, 1792), reprinted id., 52–53; James Iredell to Hannah Iredell (Sept. 30, 1792), reprinted 2 DHSC, 301 ("I have reconciled myself to the propriety of doing the Invalid-business out of Court."); James Wilson, John Blair, & Richard Peters to George Washington (Apr. 18, 1792), supra note 105, at 51.

107 2 U.S. (2 Dall.) 408 (1792); Marcus & Teir, *Hayburn's Case: A Misinterpretation of Precedent,* 1988 Wisc. L. Rev. 527, 531 n.25, 539 n.83; An Act to regulate Claims to Invalid Pensions, ch. 17, 1 Stat. 324 (1793) (removing involvement of circuit courts in processing pension applications).

108 Marcus & Teir, supra note 107, at 534.

109 James Iredell & John Sitgreaves to George Washington (June 8, 1792), reprinted 1 ASP-M, 53.

110 For example, Iredell and Sitgreaves's letter comports well with Hargrave's account of advisory opinions; see chapter 1, text at note 20. At some point, Iredell copied Hargrave's published notes on this issue; see supra, chapter 2, note 12. Id.

111 See Morrison v. Olson, 487 U.S. 654, 677 (1988); Mistretta v. United States, 488 U.S. 361, 385 (1989); Buckley v. Valeo, 424 U.S. 1, 123 (1976); McGrath v. Kristensen, 340 U.S. 162, 167 n.6 (1950); Tutun v. United States, 270 U.S. 568, 576 (1926); Keller v. Potomac Electric Power Co., 261 U.S. 428, 444 (1923). The Court continues to cite *Hayburn's Case,* however, for the proposition that federal judges may be assigned extrajudicial duties, such as service on the United States Sentencing Commission. See Mistretta v. United States, supra, 402–4.

112 New Jersey Journal (Elizabethtown, N.J.), June 6, 1792, quoted in 1 Warren, 80 n.1; National Gazette (Philadelphia), Apr. 12, 1792, quoted in 1 Warren, 70 n.1.

113 See Fisher Ames to Thomas Dwight (Apr. 25, 1792), reprinted in 1 Works of Fisher Ames 117 (S. Ames ed. 1854).

114 See 2 DHSC, 236; General Advertiser (Philadelphia), Apr. 20, 1792, quoted in 1 Warren, 72–74.

115 2 DHSC, 235; An Act for altering the times of holding the Circuit Courts, in certain districts of the United States, and for other purposes, 1 Stat. § 3, 253 (1792). Prior to passage of the Act, circuit assignments were fixed to correspond to the individual Justices' place of residence at appointment. Thus, Iredell received the Southern Circuit, which by his estimate required riding nineteen hundred miles on the circuit; this was in addition to the distance from Philadelphia—where Iredell had moved after appointment—to the circuit and back again (eighteen hundred miles). James Iredell to John Jay, William Cushing, & James Wilson (Feb. 11, 1791), reprinted 2 DHSC, 132. According to Iredell, this was "at least 1000 miles more than the utmost of the others." James Iredell

to Thomas Johnson (March 15, 1792), reprinted 2 id., 246, also 2 id., 7 (editors' notes). The new Act was sponsored by Iredell's brother-in-law, Senator Samuel Johnston; see 2 DHSC, 236-37. On Iredell's correspondence with Johnston concerning circuit court reform, see supra note 91 and accompanying text.

116 Opinion of the Circuit Judges for the New York District (Apr. 5, 1792), reprinted 1 ASP-M, 50.

117 See John Jay, William Cushing, James Wilson, John Blair, James Iredell, & Thomas Johnson to George Washington (Aug. 9, 1792), reprinted 2 DHSC, 288-89; Opinion of the Circuit Judges for the New York District (Apr. 5, 1792), reprinted 1 ASP-M, 50, quoted in Marcus & Teir, 530-31. See James Iredell and John Sitgreaves to George Washington (June 8, 1792), reprinted id., 52 (Pension Act "founded on the purest principles of humanity and justice"), quoted in Marcus & Teir, 533.

118 See Warren, 76.

119 1 DHSC. The point about following British practice is made in 6 DHSC, appendix (forthcoming).

CHAPTER FIVE: DECLINING WASHINGTON'S REQUEST

1 George Washington to David Stuart Erskine, Earl of Buchan (Apr. 22, 1793), reprinted 32 Washington Writings, 428; Thomas, 14-18; Lint, 21. This attitude reflected "the principles on which the revolutionary leadership had conducted foreign policy during the Confederation period, when all believed the nation's interests would best be served by as great a separation as possible from European politics." Buel, 32; Combs, 15-23. Similarly, the Framers of the Constitution assumed that the United States would engage in a minimal amount of diplomacy and enter few treaties, with these being commercial in nature. F. Marks, supra, chapter 4, note 65, at 155; W. Reveley, War Powers of the President and Congress 61 (1981); J. Godechot, France and the Atlantic Revolution of the Eighteenth Century, 1770-1799, at 2 (H. Rowen trans. 1965); McDonald, Washington, 3.

2 Thomas Jefferson to James Monroe (June 4, 1793), reprinted 26 Jefferson Papers, 190; 7 Jefferson Works, 361; Clauder, 15-16 & 21-22; Jefferson, Report on the Privileges and Restrictions on the Commerce of the United States in Foreign Countries (Dec. 16, 1793), reprinted 8 Jefferson Works, 98-119; Lycan, 177; 2 W. Phillips & A. Reede, Neutrality: Its History, Economics and Law 31 (1936); Setser, 99-131; Flexner, 101, 131, & 143; McDonald, Washington, 135-36.

3 See DeConde, 82-85; Wright, 66-89.

4 W. N. Hargreaves-Mawdsley, Eighteenth-Century Spain, 1700-1788, at 139 (1979); 14 Hamilton Papers, 490-95 (editors' note); Thomas, 181-82; Letters from Thomas Jefferson to William Carmichael & William Short (Nov. 3, 1792; May 31, 1793), reprinted 24 Jefferson Papers, 566; 26 Jefferson Papers, 148-49; 7 Jefferson Works, 173 & 350 (saying that these events had been observed "for some months").

5 See 14 Hamilton Papers, 491 (editors' notes); Notes on Thomas Jefferson's Report of Instructions for the Commissioners to Spain, in 11 Hamilton Papers, 68-73 (editors' notes); Introductory Note, Opinion of the Depredations of the Creek Indians upon the State of Georgia, in 14 id., 492-93 (editors' notes).

6 Henry Knox to William Blount (Nov. 26, 1792), reprinted 4 Territorial Papers of the United States 221-22 (C. Carter ed. 1936); Henry Knox to William Blount (May 14, 1793), reprinted id., 257. Knox's letter was consistent with an opinion of the cabinet reached later in the month. See Opinion on the Depredations of the Creek Indians upon the State of Georgia, May 29, 1793, reprinted 14 Hamilton Papers, 494-95.

7 See Boyd, 3; Wright, 28, 46-48, & 50-85; Opinion of the Vice-President, Aug. 29, 1790, reprinted Boyd, 117. Jefferson expressed sentiments similar to Adams's; see Thomas Jefferson to James Monroe (July 11, 1790), reprinted 17 Jefferson Papers, 25; 6 Jefferson Works, 89-90.

8 Alexander Hamilton to George Washington (Sept. 15, 1790), reprinted 7 Hamilton Papers, 43; Opinion of the Secretary of War, Aug. 29, 1790, reprinted Boyd, 120; Wright, 66-67, 90-91; DeConde, 69; Lycan, 206. The Family Compacts consisted of a series of three treaties between the Bourbon monarchs of France and Spain (Treaty of the Escorial, 1733; Treaty of Fontainebleau, 1743; Third Family Compact, 1762). W. N. Hargreaves-Mawdsley, supra note 4, at 69-70, 80, 102-3.

9 See Treaty of Amity and Commerce, Feb. 6, 1778, reprinted 2 Treaties, 3; Treaty of Alliance, Feb. 6, 1778, art. 11, reprinted in id., 35, 39-40; Act Separate and Secret, Feb. 6, 1778, reprinted in id., 45. On the historical background of these treaties, see DeConde, *The French Alliance in Historical Speculation*, in Diplomacy and Revolution—The Franco-American Alliance of 1778, at 1-26 (R. Hoffman & P. Albert eds. 1981); L. Kaplan, Colonies into Nation: American Diplomacy, 1763-1801 (1972); R. Singh, French Diplomacy in the Caribbean and the American Revolution (1977); M. Smelser, The Winning of Independence 226-28 (1972); R. Van Alstyne, Empire and Independence: The International History of the American Revolution (1966).

10 Jefferson, Anas, 100-101 (Jefferson recorded this remark by Washington in his diary for December 27, 1792). Shortly thereafter, Jefferson wrote William Short, the resident American minister to the Hague, saying that Washington had told Jefferson that he "considered *France as the sheet anchor of this country and its friendship as a first object.*" Thomas Jefferson to William Short (Jan. 3, 1793), reprinted 25 Jefferson Papers, 15; 7 Jefferson Works, 204.

11 Buel, 39 (war declared Feb. 3, 1793); Thomas Jefferson to David Humphreys (Mar. 22, 1793), reprinted 25 Jefferson Papers, 426; 7 Jefferson Works, 266-67 (Humphreys was U.S. minister to Portugal); George Washington to Gouverneur Morris (Mar. 25, 1793), reprinted 32 Washington Writings, 402.

12 See Alexander Hamilton to George Washington (Apr. 8, 1793), reprinted 14 Hamilton Papers, 295-96; Thomas Jefferson to George Washington (Apr. 7, 1793), reprinted 25 Jefferson Papers, 518; 7 Jefferson Works, 275; George Wash-

ington to Alexander Hamilton (Apr. 12, 1793), reprinted 32 Washington Writings, 416.

13 Alexander Hamilton to John Jay (Apr. 9, 1793), reprinted 14 Hamilton Papers, 297–98.

14 Id., 297; Alexander Hamilton to John Jay (Apr. 9, 1793), reprinted 14 Hamilton Papers, 298–300. Prior to Washington's departure for Mt. Vernon, Jefferson had asked the President how Genêt should be treated if the French ambassador were to arrive before Washington's return to Philadelphia. Jefferson recorded Washington as responding that "he could see no ground of doubt but that he ought to be received." Jefferson, Anas, 116 (diary entry for Mar. 30, 1793, reporting events of Mar. 20, 1793). According to Jefferson, Hamilton expressed reservations to Washington at this time about receiving Genêt without qualification. Randolph concluded that he "should unquestionably be received; but he thought not with too much warmth or cordiality," a qualification that Jefferson viewed as "a small sacrifice to the opinion of Hamilton." Id.

15 John Jay to Alexander Hamilton (Apr. 11, 1793), reprinted 14 Hamilton Papers, 307–8, & 3 Jay Papers, 474. For the text of Jay's draft proclamation, see id., 474–77 & 14 Hamilton Papers, 308–10.

16 See George Washington to Alexander Hamilton, Thomas Jefferson, Henry Knox, and Edmund Randolph (Apr. 18, 1793), reprinted 32 Washington Writings, 420–21. Washington had arrived in Philadelphia on April 17. The questions are reprinted in id., 419–20. On Hamilton's authorship, see 14 Hamilton Papers, 327 n.2; 32 Washington Writings, 419 n.13; Thomas, 27–30; Jefferson, Anas, 118–19.

17 Pacificus No. II (July 3, 1793), reprinted 15 Hamilton Papers, 55–63, citing 2 J. Burlamaqui, Principles of Political Law: Being a Sequel to the Principles of Natural Law, at bk. 4, ch. 3, §§ 4–5 (T. Nugent trans. 1776); 1 Vattel, 138.

18 Question XIII, reprinted 32 Washington Writings, 420. On Jefferson's connection to this question, see Thomas, 29.

19 Cabinet Opinion on Washington's Question on Neutrality and the Alliance with France, Apr. 19, 1793, reprinted 25 Jefferson Papers, 570; 7 Jefferson Works, 281; see President's Journal, 114. Jefferson noted that issuance of the proclamation was "agreed by all." Cabinet Opinion, 25 Jefferson Papers, 570; 7 Jefferson Works, 281. On Hamilton and Knox's views, see 14 Hamilton Papers, 328. Jefferson recorded the scathing remark that "Knox subscribed at once to Hamilton's opinion that we ought to declare the treaty void, acknowledging, at the same time, like a fool as he is, that he knew nothing about it." Jefferson, Anas, 119; Jefferson took another dig at Knox: "I believe Knox's [written opinion] was never thought worth offering or asking for." Id.

20 Proclamation of Neutrality, Apr. 22, 1793, reprinted in 1 ASP-F, 140; 32 Washington Writings, 430–31.

21 Thomas Jefferson to James Madison (May 19, 1793), reprinted 26 Jefferson Papers, 61; 7 Jefferson Works, 336; see also Thomas Jefferson to James Madison (June 23, 1793), reprinted 26 Jefferson Papers, 346; 7 Jefferson Works, 408 ("[T]he drawing of the instrument was left to E.R."). On Randolph's authorship, see

Thomas, 43–45. Richard Morris contended that Jay "wrote an original draft of President Washington's Neutrality Proclamation." Morris, New England, 16 & 30.

22 Jay, Draft of Proclamation of Neutrality (Apr. 1, 1793), reprinted 3 Jay Papers, 474–77. Another contrasting feature of Jay's proposed proclamation was the use of several religious appeals, as in this example: "[W]e have abundant reason to give thanks unto Almighty God that the United States are not involved in that calamity [the war]. . . . [and Americans should] unite in rendering thanks to a beneficial Providence for the peace and prosperity we enjoy, and devoutly to entreat the continuance of these invaluable blessings." Id., 475–76.

23 Thomas Jefferson to James Madison (June 23, 1793), reprinted 26 Jefferson Papers, 346; 7 Jefferson Works, 407–8. Jefferson said that his objection "was so far respected as to avoid inserting the term *neutrality.*" 26 Jefferson Papers, 346; 7 Jefferson Works, 407.

24 See Elkins & McKitrick, 343; Stewart, 145–46; James Madison to Thomas Jefferson (June 19, 1793), reprinted 15 Madison Papers, 33; 6 Madison Writings, 127 n.1 (the *Gazette of the U.S.* was a pro-Federalist newspaper in Philadelphia published by John Fenno and supported by Hamilton). See also James Madison to Thomas Jefferson (May 8, 1793), reprinted 15 Madison Papers, 13; 6 Madison Writings, 128 ("The attempt to shuffle off the Treaty altogether by quibbling on Vattel is equally contemptible for the meanness & folly of it."); James Madison to Thomas Jefferson (May 27, 1793), reprinted 15 Madison Papers, 22; 6 Madison Writings, 130 ("I think it is certain that [Genêt] will be misled if he takes either the fashionable cant of the Cities or the cold caution of the Govt. for the sense of the public; and I am equally persuaded that nothing but the habit of implicit respect will save the Executive from blame if thro' the mask of Neutrality, a secret Anglomany should betray itself."); James Madison to Thomas Jefferson (June 13, 1793), reprinted 15 Madison Papers, 29; 6 Madison Writings, 130–31 ("I observe that the Newspapers continue to criticise the President's proclamation; and I find that some of the criticisms excite the attention of dispassionate & judicious individuals here. . . . I have been mortified that on these [criticisms] I could offer no bona fide explanations that ought to be satisfactory.").

25 Thomas Jefferson to James Madison (Apr. 28, 1793), reprinted 25 Jefferson Papers, 619; 7 Jefferson Works, 302; Combs, 107; Elkins & McKitrick, 336; Thomas, 35 & 48–49; Thomas Jefferson to Harry Innes (May 23, 1793), reprinted 26 Jefferson Papers, 100; 7 Jefferson Works, 343. See also Thomas Jefferson to George Washington (Apr. 7, 1793), reprinted 25 Jefferson Papers, 518; 7 Jefferson Works, 275 ("[It is] necessary in my opinion that we take every justifiable measure for preserving our neutrality."); Thomas Jefferson to Gouverneur Morris (Apr. 20, 1793), reprinted 25 Jefferson Papers, 576; 7 Jefferson Works, 282 (saying that Americans wished "to preserve a fair neutrality"); Thomas Jefferson to George Wythe (Apr. 27, 1793), reprinted 25 Jefferson Papers, 597; 7 Jefferson Works, 282 ("We shall be a little embarrassed [by French privateering in American waters] occasionally till we feel ourselves firmly seated in the saddle of neutrality."); Thomas Jefferson to James Monroe (May 5, 1793), reprinted 25 Jefferson Papers,

661; 7 Jefferson Works, 309 ("If we preserve even a sneaking neutrality, we shall be indebted for it to the President, and not to his counsellors.").

26 "I believe that through all America there has been but a single sentiment on the subject of peace and war, which was in favor of the former. The Executive here has cherished it with equal and unanimous desire. We have differed perhaps as to the tone of conduct exactly adapted to the securing it." Thomas Jefferson to James Monroe (June 28, 1793), reprinted 26 Jefferson Papers, 392-93; 7 Jefferson Works, 415; Thomas Jefferson to James Madison (May 13, 1793), reprinted 26 Jefferson Papers, 26; 7 Jefferson Works, 324 ("manly neutrality"); Combs, at 107-8: "Custom and international law at that time permitted a nation to do almost anything short of actual fighting and yet retain their designation as a neutral nation. Both Hamilton and Jefferson, while genuinely desiring that America remain neutral, favored making use of the latitude given to nations by custom and international law to stack America's neutrality in favor of either England or France, as their predilections dictated." See W. Hall, A Treatise on International Law 691-707 (P. Higgins 8th ed. 1924); L. Oppenheim, International Law—A Treatise 627 (H. Lauterpacht 7th ed. 1948).

27 W. Hall, supra note 26, at 691, 707; see H. Taylor, A Treatise on International Public Law 638-39 (1901) (The United States in 1793 "was suddenly called upon to restate with precision and force the very imperfect rules by which the law of nations then attempted to protect the sanctity of neutral territory."); Hyneman, *Neutrality During the European Wars of 1792-1815*, 24 Am. J. Int'l. L. 279, 308-9 & n. 124 (1930).

28 Alexander Hamilton to George Washington (May 2, 1793), reprinted in 14 Hamilton Papers, 368; see id., 371: "[T]he course of the Revolution [in France], has been attended with circumstances, which militate against a full conviction of its having been brought to its present *stage*, by such a *free, regular* and *deliberate* act of the nation, and with such a spirit of justice and humanity, as ought to silence all scruples about the validity of what has been done, and the morality of aiding it, even if consistent with policy." Id., 379-80, 382, 384, & 391 citing 1 Vattel, bk. 2, § 197, p. 188 (emphasis added by Hamilton). "But suppose the contest unsuccessfull on the part of the present Governing Powers of France. What would then be our situation with the future Government of that Country? Should we not be branded and destested by it, as the worst of Ingrates?" Id., 390.

29 Thomas Jefferson to James Madison (June 23, 1793), reprinted 26 Jefferson Papers, 346; 7 Jefferson Works, 408; Jefferson, Opinion on the Treaties with France (Apr. 28, 1793), reprinted 25 Jefferson Papers, 609; 7 Jefferson Works, 285-86. Although Jefferson's memorandum predated Hamilton's by several days, he had heard the latter's position articulated at the cabinet meeting on April 19. See id., 284.

30 See id., 292-96, citing 1 Vattel, at bk. 2, § 197, p. 188 (comparing Vattel to Grotius, Puffendorf, & Wolf) & id., bk. 2 § 158, p. 194. Jefferson interpreted Vattel's statement to mean that "the danger must be imminent, and the degree great," as opposed to the mere possibilities of danger suggested by Hamilton. Jefferson,

Opinion on the Treaties with France, 25 Jefferson Papers, 609; 7 Jefferson Works, 286 & 287-88. The language quoted is Jefferson's; in the section cited by Jefferson, Vattel wrote: "However, if this change [of government] renders the alliance useless, dangerous or disagreeable to him, he is at liberty to renounce it." 1 Vattel, bk. 2, § 197, p. 212). According to Jefferson, it was not "disagreeable" for the United States to follow the treaties. They were made, after all, when France was "under a despotic government," and now it is a "Republic extremely free." Jefferson, Opinion on the Treaties with France, 25 Jefferson Papers, 617; 7 Jefferson Works, 292 & 299-301. "But I deny that the reception of a Minister has any thing to do with the treaties. There is not a word, in either of them, about sending ministers. This has been done between us under the common usage of nations, and can have no effect either to continue or annul the treaties." 25 Jefferson Papers, 612; 7 Jefferson Works, 290.

31 See Thomas, 80-84. On Genêt's ambassadorship, see H. Ammon, The Genet Mission (1973); Letters from Thomas Jefferson to James Madison (Apr. 28, 1793 & May 9, 1793), reprinted 25 Jefferson Papers, 619; 26 Jefferson Papers, 61-62; 7 Jefferson Works, 301 & 337; Alexander Hamilton to unknown correspondent (May 18, 1793), reprinted 14 Hamilton Papers, 474; Jay, Draft of Proclamation of Neutrality (Apr. 1, 1793), reprinted 3 Jay Papers, 476-77.

32 Jefferson, Anas (diary entry for Mar. 24, 1793), 116. Several months later, Genêt bitterly recounted his reception in a letter to Jefferson (written after Genêt's recall had been requested by the United States), saying that he had been "extremely wounded" by Washington's reserved treatment, including the fact that the President had not "sa[id] a word . . . enouncing a single sentiment on our revolution; while all the towns, from Charleston to Philadelphia, had made the air resound with their most ardent wishes for the French republic." Letters from Edmond C. Genêt to Thomas Jefferson (Sept. 18, 1793, & May 23, 1793, reprinted 1 ASP-F, 143 & 173. On Genêt's reception, see 7 Carroll & Ashworth, 74-75; Thomas Jefferson to James Madison (May 19, 1793), reprinted 26 Jefferson Papers, 61-62; 7 Jefferson Works, 337; Thomas Jefferson to James Monroe (June 4, 1793), reprinted 26 Jefferson Papers, 189; 7 Jefferson Works, 361.

33 See Edmond C. Genêt to Thomas Jefferson (May 23, 1793), reprinted 1 American State Papers, Foreign Relations, 147; Thomas Jefferson to James Madison (May 19, 1793), reprinted 26 Jefferson Papers, 62; 7 Jefferson Works, 337. The French decree opening ports to American vessels on the same terms as French bottoms applied to France's colonies and certain other ports; it was motivated less by fraternity among Republicans than by France's urgent need for food and other provisions. Clauder, at 28-29. France soon imposed significant restrictions on American shipping, however; see infra, notes 104-5 and accompanying text.

34 See 14 Hamilton Papers, 451-54 (editors' note). Gouverneur Morris wrote to Jefferson from Paris in March, cautioning that Genêt would be carrying three hundred blank commissions for privateers, "which he is to distribute to such as will fit out cruizers in our ports, to prey on the British commerce." Gouverneur Morris to Thomas Jefferson (March 7, 1793), reprinted 2 The Life and Corre-

spondence of Gouverneur Morris 290, 291 (J. Sparks ed. 1832); see President's Journal, 128 (entry for May 4, noting that Genêt had blank commissions for privateers); Edmond C. Genêt to French Minister of Foreign Affairs (Oct. 7, 1793), reprinted *Correspondence of Genêt*, 2 Annual Report of the American Historical Association, 1903, at 246 (F. Turner ed. 1904).

35 See Thomas, 177–81. Jefferson noted in his diary that Genêt came to see him in a private capacity and informed him that he was organizing men in Kentucky under the command of "two generals in Kentucky" to "rendezvous" outside the United States for the purpose of taking New Orleans and then Louisiana. The plan was for Genêt to commission officers in Kentucky and Louisiana, with the ultimate aim of setting up "an independent State, connected in commerce with France and the United States." Jefferson reportedly responded that such "officers and soldiers . . . would assuredly be hung if they commenced hostilities against a nation at peace with the United States. That leaving out that article I did not care what insurrections should be excited in Louisiana." Jefferson, Anas, 130 (entry for July 5, 1793). Jefferson evidently did not report this conversation to Washington, and this lapse has been described as "intriguing" and "almost indefensible." 7 Carroll & Ashworth, 102 n.9.

36 These seizures and others are described in Thomas, 99–101. Washington had heard reports of privateering activity as early as April; see supra note 12 and accompanying text. See, e.g., Thomas Jefferson to James Madison (Apr. 28, 1793), reprinted 25 Jefferson Papers, 619; 7 Jefferson Works, 301–2 (reporting that a French frigate was bringing in as prizes ships that had left Philadelphia only two or three days before); Henry Lee to George Washington (Apr. 29, 1793), reprinted in 12 Writings of George Washington 287 n.1 (C. Ford ed. 1891) ("The minds of the people of my acquaintance are much agitated by reports of privateers being fitted out in some of our ports."); William Vans Murray to Alexander Hamilton (May 8, 1793), reprinted 14 Hamilton Papers, 425–27 (reporting from Maryland that a privateer commissioned in Charleston had brought a British ship into port as a prize; the prize master captain was quoted as saying that "a great number have fitted out [in Charleston] & will be.").

37 Thomas Jefferson to James Monroe (May 5, 1793), reprinted 25 Jefferson Papers, 661; 7 Jefferson Works, 309. See also Thomas Jefferson to Thomas Mann Randolph (May 6, 1793), reprinted 25 Jefferson Papers, 668–69; 7 Jefferson Works, 312 ("The *yeomanry* of the city (not the fashionable people nor paper men) shewed prodigious joy when, flocking to the wharves, they saw the British colours reversed and the French flying above them."); Thomas Jefferson to John Wayles Eppes (May 12, 1793), reprinted 26 Jefferson Papers, 7–8; 7 Jefferson Works, 341 ("Thousands & thousands . . . rent[ed] the air with peals of exultation."). Although much of the privateering was inspired by sympathy for the French cause, many privateers were motivated by simple profit. See Steven Higginson to Alexander Hamilton (July 26, 1793), reprinted 15 Hamilton Papers, 128; (Apr. 10, 1793), reprinted 14 id., 306.

38 George Hammond to Thomas Jefferson (May 2, 1793), quoted in 14 Hamilton

Papers, 452 (editors' note); see President's Journal, 125 (entry for May 2); Thomas Jefferson to George Hammond (May 3, 1793), reprinted 25 Jefferson Papers, 644; 7 Jefferson Works, 306 (noting the complaint and saying that the United States would "certainly not see with indifference it's territory or jurisdiction violated by either [belligerent], and will proceed immediately to enquire into the facts and . . . do what these shall shew ought to be done with exact impartiality"); see Thomas Jefferson to Jean Baptiste Ternant (May 3, 1793), reprinted 25 Jefferson Papers, 649; 7 Jefferson Works, 307 (enclosing a copy of the British protest and inviting a response from the French minister).

39 George Hammond to Thomas Jefferson (May 8, 1793) (copy in Library of Congress, Jefferson Papers), quoted in 14 Hamilton Papers, 452; see President's Journal, 131 & 132 n.3. The British also were concerned about French-owned cargoes allegedly being shipped fraudulently as American property on U.S. bottoms in order to be covered by a neutral's right to continue trading noncontraband goods with belligerents. See W. Phillips & A. Reede, supra note 2, at 43-44.

40 See, e.g., Thomas Jefferson to Brothers Coster & Company (May 21, 1793), reprinted 26 Jefferson Papers, 74; 7 Jefferson Works, 338-39. In this letter, Jefferson acknowledged the recipients' complaint of May 17 over seizure of their brig by a French privateer; he advised them to pursue private action for indemnification from the security posted by the privateers. Jefferson advised that only in the event there was no such security, or "that justice shall be refused you in resorting to it," would the United States "make it a subject of national complaint." 26 Jefferson Papers, 74; 7 Jefferson Works, 339.

41 See, e.g., William Ellery to Alexander Hamilton (Apr. 29, 1793), reprinted 14 Hamilton Papers, 355-56 (Ellery was Collector of Customs at Newport, R.I., and he asked for general directions on treating prizes brought by French privateers, including whether to collect duties on them); John Fitzgerald to Alexander Hamilton (May 17, 1793), reprinted id., 472 (Collector at Alexandria, requesting instructions respecting a recently captured British vessel); Otho H. Williams to Alexander Hamilton (May 28, 1793), reprinted id., 489-90 (Collector and Naval Officer at Baltimore, asking for instructions with regard to a recently captured prize by a French privateer).

42 Thomas Jefferson to Jean Baptiste Ternant (May 15, 1793), reprinted 26 Jefferson Papers, 42-44; 7 Jefferson Works, 329-30 & 332; Thomas Jefferson to George Hammond (May 15, 1793), reprinted 26 Jefferson Papers, 38; 7 Jefferson Works, 325-27. Jefferson added that the President's "expectation" was that the *Grange* and its cargo would be restored to its owners, and the crew released. For Randolph's report, see Edmund Randolph to Thomas Jefferson (May 14, 1793), reprinted ASP-F, 148-49.

43 Thomas Jefferson to Jean Baptiste Ternant (May 15, 1793), reprinted 26 Jefferson Papers, 43; 7 Jefferson Works, 331; see Thomas Jefferson to George Hammond (May 15, 1793), reprinted 26 Jefferson Papers, 38; 7 Jefferson Works, 327. In the letter to Hammond, Jefferson went on to inform him that "the proper law officer" had been instructed to institute proceedings against such offenders. 26 Jefferson

Papers, 39; 7 Jefferson Works, 327; see Thomas Jefferson to Jean Baptiste Ternant (May 15, 1793), reprinted id., 331.

44 Edmond C. Genêt to Thomas Jefferson (May 27, 1793), reprinted 1 ASP-F, 149-50.

45 Thomas Jefferson to Edmond C. Genêt (June 5, 1793), reprinted 25 Jefferson Papers, 195; 7 Jefferson Works, 362-63. Notwithstanding Jefferson's authorship of the letter, he disagreed with the decision to order the privateers to leave American ports. See Thomas Jefferson to James Madison (June 2, 1793), reprinted 26 Jefferson Papers, 167; 7 Jefferson Works, 357.

46 Henry Knox to Governors (May 23, 1793), reprinted 6 Calendar of Virginia State Papers and Other Manuscripts 377 (S. McRae ed. 1886), quoted in 15 Hamilton Papers, 77 n.6; see Henry Knox to Governors (May 24, 1793), reprinted id., 379; see also President's Journal, 147 (Washington approves the letters); Thomas Jefferson to Richard Harrison (June 12, 1793), reprinted 26 Jefferson Papers, 261; 7 Jefferson Works, 380-81; Thomas Jefferson to Edmond C. Genêt (June 17, 1793), reprinted 26 Jefferson Papers, 297; 7 Jefferson Works, 397; Alexander Hamilton to Collectors of Customs (May 30, 1793), reprinted 14 Hamilton Papers, 499. The advice to collectors was given after Hamilton, at Washington's suggestion, consulted Randolph for a legal opinion. Alexander Hamilton to Edmund Randolph (May 10, 1793), reprinted id., 431; President's Journal, 122-23 (entries for Apr. 29 & 30). On the treaty provision, see Treaty of Amity and Commerce, Feb. 6, 1778, Art. 19, supra note 9, at 16-17.

47 George Washington to Alexander Hamilton (May 7, 1793), reprinted 14 Hamilton Papers, 423. At Rawle's request, on May 29, 1793, Justice James Iredell ordered that a special session of the Circuit Court for the District of Pennsylvania be held on July 22, for the purpose of trying Henfield and others charged with neutrality offenses. 2 DHSC, 393-94 & n.2. The proceedings in the *Henfield* case are found in United States v. Henfield, 11 F. Cas. 1099, 1105-9 (C.C.D. Pa. 1793) (No. 6360); Engrossed Minutes (C.C.D. Pa., July 22-29, 1793) (U.S. Federal Archives and Record Center, Philadelphia). Secondary accounts are numerous; e.g., Casto, 130-36; DeConde, 214-16; Thomas, 170-74; Warren, 112-14; Hyneman, *The First American Neutrality,* 20 Ill. Stud. Soc. Sci. 130-31 (1934). On instructions to the New York district attorney, see Thomas Jefferson to Richard Harrison (June 12, 1793), reprinted 26 Jefferson Papers, 262; 7 Jefferson Works, 381.

48 See Christopher Gore to Tobias Lear (July 28, 1793) (Tobias Lear papers, Library of Congress) (the U.S. Attorney in Boston indicating that arrest warrants had been issued for two Americans serving on a privateer; Lear was Washington's personal secretary); Christopher Gore to Rufus King (Aug. 4, 1793), reprinted 1 King, 490-92 (saying that he had "now a prospect of attaining compleat evidence" against the French consul for fitting out privateers, and that he intended to prosecute the consul at the next session of the circuit court); William Loughton Smith to Alexander Hamilton (Aug. 22, 1793), reprinted 15 Hamilton Papers, 262 (reporting arrests of four men serving on the privateer *Roland* who were accused of capturing two vessels); The Boston Gazette and the Country Journal

(Aug. 26, 1793), quoted in id., 263 n.3 (reporting the arrest of the *Roland* crew); Cabinet Opinions on the *Roland* and Relations with Great Britain, France and the Creeks, Aug. 31, 1793 (written by Jefferson), reprinted id., 314; 26 Jefferson Papers, 795; 8 Jefferson Works, 8 (a discussion of a letter of August 24 from U.S. Attorney Gore, indicating that the French consul in Boston "rescued" the *Roland* "with an armed force from one of the ships of his nation"; the cabinet determined that if the report was true, the consul's exequatur should be revoked and Gore should "institute such prosecution as the laws will authorize" against the consul); Thomas Jefferson to Christopher Gore (Sept. 2, 1793), reprinted 8 Jefferson Works, 15 (referring to the consul's "daring violation of the laws," Jefferson reports Washington's desire to "institute such as prosecution against him, as the laws will," noting that "[y]ou know that by the law of nations, Consuls are not diplomatic characters, and have no immunities whatever against the laws of the land."); President's Journal (Sept. 2, 1793), 236 (approving the letter from Jefferson to Gore); id., 241 (Oct. 10, 1793) (recounting Washington's signing of the letter revoking the consul's exequatur "for his usurpation of powers injurious to the sovereignty of this Country, & persisting in the exercise of them."); id., 245 (Nov. 4, 1793) (noting a letter of Oct. 21 from Gore, reporting that the grand jury in Boston had declined to indict the French consul, but that it had returned true bills against four Americans and a Frenchman for privateering); Ghost of Puffendorf, To Citizen Genet, Connecticut Courant (Dec. 9, 1793) (noting that the grand jury had refused to indict the French consul in Boston by a margin of only one vote).

49 "[T]hey, who commit aid, or abet Hostilities against these [foreign] powers or either of them offend against the Laws of the united States, and ought to be punished." Grand Jury Charge of Jay, Circuit Justice (C.C.D. Va. 1793), reprinted 2 DHSC, 340 (editor's note), 383, 386–88 & United States v. Henfield, 11 F. Cas. 1099, 1102-4 (C.C.D. Pa. 1793) (No. 6360). This charge was reprinted on July 26, 1793, in *Dunlap's American Daily Advertiser* (Philadelphia), and in the *Diary or Louden's Register* (New York) at the same time. See 2 DHSC, 381 (editors' note). On other aspects of this charge, see infra note 89, and accompanying text.

50 Edmond C. Genêt to Thomas Jefferson (June 1, 1793), reprinted 1 ASP-F, 151; see 1 Jay, 1042–51. Congress subsequently enacted a statute on this subject; see An Act in addition to the act for the punishment of certain crimes against the United States, 1 Stat. 381–82 (1794), repealed by An Act in addition to the "Act for the punishment of certain crimes against the United States," and to repeal the acts mentioned therein, § 12, 3 Stat. 450 (1818).

51 Opinion of the Attorney General (May 30, 1793) (submitted to the Secretary of State), reprinted 1 ASP-F, 152. Similarly, Jefferson wrote James Monroe on July 14 that "I confess I think myself that the case is punishable, and that, if found otherwise, Congress ought to make it so." Thomas Jefferson to James Monroe (July 14, 1793), reprinted 26 Jefferson Papers, 502; 7 Jefferson Works, 448; Thomas Jefferson to Edmond C. Genêt (June 1, 1793), reprinted 26 Jefferson Papers, 160; 7 Jefferson Works, 352. Explaining his rationale, Jefferson

said: "Treaties are law. By the treaty with England we are in a state of peace with her. He who breaks that peace, if within our jurisdiction, breaks the laws, and is punisheable by them. And if he is punisheable he ought to be punished, because no citizen should be free to commit his country to war." 26 Jefferson Papers, 501-2; 7 Jefferson Works, 447. Jefferson also represented that his view "coincided with all our private opinions; & the lawyers of this state [Pennsylvania], New York and Maryland, who were applied to, were unanimously of the same opinion." 26 Jefferson Papers, 502; 7 Jefferson Works, 448. He acknowledged, however, that the U.S. Attorney in Philadelphia, William Rawle, "on a conference with the District judge, [Richard] Peters, supposes the law more doubtful. New acts therefore of the same kind are left unprosecuted till the question is determined by the proper court, which will be during the present week [when Henfield's trial commenced]." 26 Jefferson Papers, 502; 7 Jefferson Works, 448.

52 Edmond C. Genêt to Thomas Jefferson (May 27, 1793), reprinted 1 ASP-F, 150; see President's Journal, 139-40.

53 Jefferson, Opinion on the Restoration of Prizes (May 16, 1793), reprinted 26 Jefferson Papers, 50-51; 7 Jefferson Works, 333-35; Memorandum from Edmund Randolph to George Washington (May 17, 1793), quoted in Randolph, 149-51. Like Jefferson, Randolph determined that the question of the lawfulness of the capture must be judged "by the courts of the U.S. according to the rules of Admiralty." For the British to insist on "a certain rule and measure of procuring satisfaction for the insult by requiring the surrender of the vessel and restitution to the British subject, is to admit an unwarrantable intrusion into the[ ] internal police" of the United States." Id., 150.

54 Memorandum from Alexander Hamilton to George Washington (May 15, 1793), reprinted 14 Hamilton Papers, 455, citing 2 Vattel, § 15, pp. 7-8, id., 457-60. Secretary of War Knox also gave an opinion, similar to Hamilton's; see 14 Hamilton Papers, 454 (editors' note). A month after writing this analysis, Hamilton conceded that there was "much force" to an argument asserting that an admiralty court of a neutral nation would have jurisdiction in the case of a vessel captured within its territorial waters. Alexander Hamilton to Rufus King (June 15, 1793), reprinted 14 Hamilton Papers, 548 (the vessel referred to by Hamilton was the *William;* see infra note 63 and accompanying text).

55 Thomas Jefferson to George Hammond (June 5, 1793), reprinted 26 Jefferson Papers, 197-98; 7 Jefferson Works, 367-68; Thomas Jefferson to George Hammond (June 13, 1793), reprinted 26 Jefferson Papers, 271; 7 Jefferson Works, 382-84. This resolution related to a complaint on May 8 by Hammond regarding the capture of certain British ships, as well as actions by the French consul in Charleston condemning two British ships as prizes. See George Hammond to Thomas Jefferson (May 8) (copy in Library of Congress, Jefferson Papers), quoted in 14 Hamilton Papers, 452; see id. (editors' note). Referring to the seizure by the governor of New York of a formerly British prize ship that had been captured by the French and now was outfitted by them as a privateer,

Jefferson informed Genêt: "This transaction being reported to the President, orders were immediately sent to deliver over the vessel, and the persons concerned in the enterprise to the tribunals of the Country, that if the act was one of those forbidden by the law, it might be punished, if it was not forbidden, it might be so declared, and all persons apprised of what they might or might not do." Thomas Jefferson to Edmond C. Genêt (June 17, 1793), reprinted 26 Jefferson Papers, 298; 7 Jefferson Works, 397.

56 See Thomas Jefferson to Richard Harrison (June 12, 1793), reprinted 26 Jefferson Papers, 261-62; 7 Jefferson Works, 381; Cabinet Opinion (June 12, 1793), reprinted 14 Hamilton Papers, 534-35 (opinion of Jefferson, Knox, & Hamilton submitted to Washington); President's Journal (diary entry for June 12), 169 (Washington approves the opinion). The instruction to the U.S. Attorney concerned a vessel (the *Catherine*) that was the subject of a complaint from Hammond on June 11, 1793. Hammond was advised "to have the parties interested apprised without delay that they are to take measures as in ordinary civil cases for the support of their rights judicially." Thomas Jefferson to George Hammond (June 13, 1793), reprinted 26 Jefferson Papers, 270; 7 Jefferson Works, 382-83. In the same memorial, Hammond also asserted that the French consul in Charleston had condemned another British ship that had been captured within two miles of the town. See George Hammond to Thomas Jefferson (June 11, 1793); President's Journal (diary entry for June 12), 168. On actions by British shipowners, see Thomas, at 102.

57 Clinton remarked in his message to Washington "that to justify my employing the Militia in this Business, I conceive it necessary that they should be explicitly considered as called into actual Service under the Authority of the United States." George Clinton to George Washington (June 9, 1793) (original in National Archives, Washington, D.C., RG 59, Letters from Governors of States, at 114); Cabinet Opinion (June 12, 1793), reprinted 14 Hamilton Papers, 534-35 (opinion of Jefferson, Knox, & Hamilton submitted to Washington); President's Journal (diary entry for June 11, 1793), 167-68.

58 Thomas Jefferson to Richard Harison (June 12, 1793), reprinted 26 Jefferson Papers, 261; 7 Jefferson Works, 380-81; Cabinet Opinion (June 12, 1793), reprinted 14 Hamilton Papers, 534-35 (opinion of Jefferson, Knox, & Hamilton submitted to Washington); President's Journal (diary entry for June 12, 1793), 169 (Washington approves the opinion).

59 Treaty of Amity and Commerce, Feb. 6, 1778, Art. 19, supra note 9, at 16-17; Thomas Jefferson to George Hammond (June 13, 1793), reprinted 26 Jefferson Papers, 270-71; 7 Jefferson Works, 383; Thomas Jefferson to Edmond C. Genêt (June 17, 1793), reprinted 26 Jefferson Papers, 301; 7 Jefferson Works, 403. On May 17, 1793, Attorney General Randolph wrote an opinion for Washington on the subject of prizes, in which he noted that the treaty prohibited "officers of the U.S." from inquiring "upon a mere question of prize or no prize." The courts were authorized, he thought, to determine the validity of a privateer's commission. See Edmund Randolph to George Washington (May 17, 1793), reprinted Randolph,

150. The administration's resolution of June 12, 1793, which was communicated to the U.S. Attorney in New York, contemplated that if "no judiciary process will be adequate" to prevent the outfitting of vessels for privateering, that if the court refused jurisdiction, then the governor should detain the vessels by force until further advised by the "General government." Cabinet Meeting Minutes, June 12, 1793 (written by Jefferson), reprinted 14 Hamilton Papers, 535; Thomas Jefferson to Richard Harison (June 12, 1793), reprinted 26 Jefferson Papers, 261–62; 7 Jefferson Works, 381–82. The concern over whether the courts would take jurisdiction in these prize cases turned out to be well founded, as later in the year several district courts declined to hear them.

60 President's Journal, 178 (entry for June 15, 1793); see George Hammond to Thomas Jefferson (June 14, 1793) (original in National Archives, Washington, D.C., RG 59, Vol. 1, Notes from British Legation in the United States to the Department of State), quoted in 15 Hamilton Papers, 3–4 n.3; George Hammond to Thomas Jefferson (June 19, 1793) (original in National Archives, Washington, D.C., Vol. 1, Notes from British Legation in the United States to the Department of State), cited in President's Journal, 185 n.4; id., 184 (diary entry for June 20, 1793). Hammond also raised this question in his letter of June 14; President's Journal, 185 n.4; id., 183 (diary entry for June 19, 1793); Thomas Jefferson to George Hammond (June 19, 1793) (original in Library of Congress, Thomas Jefferson Papers), reprinted 26 Jefferson Papers, 321; President's Journal, 185 n.4; id., 186 (diary entry for June 22, 1793).

61 Thomas Jefferson to George Hammond (June 19, 1793), reprinted 26 Jefferson Papers, 322; 7 Jefferson Works, 405. "The interest we have in the Western posts, the blood and treasure which their detention costs us daily, cannot but produce a corresponding anxiety on our part." 26 Jefferson Papers, 322; 7 Jefferson Works, 405. For the original American inquiry, see Thomas Jefferson to George Hammond (May 29, 1792), reprinted 23 Jefferson Papers, 551; 7 Jefferson Works, 3. Hammond replied that the delay was probably a "consequence of the very interesting events, which, since the receipt of [the American complaint] have occurred in Europe," which Hammond speculated had distracted the British government from matters that may have been "regarded as somewhat less urgent." But Hammond "daily" expected instructions from his government, which would be communicated to the United States "speedily" upon "learn[ing] his majesty's pleasure on the subject of your representation." George Hammond to Thomas Jefferson (June 20, 1793) (original in National Archives, Washington, D.C., Vol. 1, Notes from British Legation in the United States to the Department of State), reprinted 2 Authentic Copies of the Correspondence of Thomas Jefferson, Esq., and George Hammond, Esq. 47–48 (1794).

62 Edmond C. Genêt to Thomas Jefferson (June 22, 1793), reprinted 1 ASP-F, 155–56. See also Edmond C. Genêt to Thomas Jefferson (June 14, 1793), reprinted id., 152 (requesting that the President "obtain immediately . . . restitution, with damages and interest, of the French prizes arrested and seized at Philadelphia, by an incompetent judge, under an order which I ought to believe

not genuine; and the like restitution, with damages and interest, of the vessels stopped and seized at New York").

63 National Gazette (June 22 & 28, 1793), quoted in 1 Warren, 107. See Findley v. The William, 9 F. Cas. 57, 59-61 (D. Pa. 1793) (No. 4,790). Peters expanded on these points in Moxon v. The Fanny, 17 F.Cas. 942 (D. Pa. 1793) (No. 9,873), which involved the same issue: "The party whose property is taken in a neutral country calls on the neutral sovereign to assert these rights, for the protection of those within the territory. If this cannot be done by negociation, it resorts to force, the only law among sovereigns where they differ upon public points. . . . I consider the judiciary as the expositors of the laws, and not partakers of the sovereignty for the objects of this suit. Their power is confined to matters of internal police; externally they have no power: they have none of the powers of peace or war. They have no right to command the forces of the country; and these are the means after negociation fails, by which sovereigns decide their disputes." 17 F. Cas. at 946-47. A similar ruling came in August from District Judge William Paca in the District Court for Maryland; see Glass v. The Sloop Betsey, 3 U.S. (3 Dall.) 6, 7 (1794), Goebel, 761-65; 1 Warren, 115.

64 Hammond pressed the necessity for protective measures; see George Hammond to Thomas Jefferson (June 21, 1793) (original in National Archives, Washington, D.C., RG 59, Vol. 1, Notes from British Legation in the United States to the Department of State); President's Journal, 187; Thomas Jefferson to Edmond C. Genêt (June 25, 1793), reprinted 26 Jefferson Papers, 358; 7 Jefferson Works, 411.

65 See Thomas Mifflin to George Washington (June 22, 1793) (original draft copy in Pennsylvania Historical and Museum Commission, Harrisburg), cited in President's Journal, 187. The *Little Sarah* had been captured in May by the French frigate *L'Embuscade,* shortly after leaving Philadelphia. For complete accounts of the episode, see DeConde, 217-22; Elkins & McKitrick, 350-52; Thomas, 137-43. On Washington's departure, see Carroll & Ashworth, 95-96.

66 See Jefferson, Anas, 131-42 (diary entries for July 8 & 10; reporting Dallas's recollection of his conversation with Genêt); T. Mifflin, Opening Address to the Pennsylvania Assembly (Aug. 29, 1793), reprinted 4 Pennsylvania Archives, 253-54 (4th ser., G. Reed ed. 1900) (recapitulating events relating to the *Petite Democrate*).

67 Jefferson, Anas, 137, 140. Jefferson wrote to Washington on July 9 that "it is inconsistent for a nation which has been patiently bearing for ten years the grossest insults and injuries from their late enemies, to rise at a feather against their friends and benefactors; and that too in a moment when circumstances have kindled the most ardent affections of the two people toward each other." Thomas Jefferson to George Washington (July 8, 1793) (enclosure to letter, titled Dissenting Opinion on the *Little Sarah*), reprinted 26 Jefferson Papers, 450-51; 7 Jefferson Works, 441; Jefferson, Anas, 139.

68 Id., 140; see Cabinet Opinion on the Case of the *Little Sarah* (July 8, 1793) (minutes of the meeting of Jefferson, Hamilton, & Knox), reprinted 15 Hamilton Papers, 70; 26 Jefferson Papers, 446; 7 Jefferson Works, 437 (a document in

Jefferson's handwriting, signed by all present). Genêt took the position that "the guns were all French property, and . . . he could name to me the French vessels from which he had taken every gun." Pressed for specifics, however, Genêt "was embarrassed and unwilling." Jefferson, Anas, 139–40.

69 See Cabinet Opinion on the Case of the *Little Sarah* (July 8, 1793) (minutes of the meeting of Jefferson, Hamilton, & Knox), reprinted 15 Hamilton Papers, 71; 26 Jefferson Papers, 446; 7 Jefferson Works, 437–38. Jefferson recorded that his cabinet counterparts wanted "to fire on the vessel and even sink her if she attempted to pass." Jefferson, Anas, 141–42; Reasons for the Opinion of the Secretary of the Treasury and the Secretary at War Respecting the Brigantine *Little Sarah* (July 8, 1793), reprinted 15 Hamilton Papers, 74–75.

70 Thomas Jefferson to George Washington (July 8, 1793) (enclosure to letter, titled Dissenting Opinion on the *Little Sarah*), reprinted 26 Jefferson Papers, 450; 7 Jefferson Works, 439–40.

71 Edmond C. Genêt to Thomas Jefferson (July 9, 1793), reprinted 1 ASP-F, 163; George Washington to Thomas Jefferson (July 11, 1793), reprinted 33 Washington Writings, 439–40.

72 See Jefferson, Anas, 142–43 (dated July 13, titled *A recapitulation of questions whereon we have given opinions*), 144 (diary entry describing the July 12 meeting: "Hamilton moves that the government of France be desired to recall Mr. Genet. Knox adds that he be in the meantime suspended from his functions. Thomas Jefferson proposes that his correspondence be communicated to his government, with friendly observations. President silent."); President's Journal, 212 n.1 (Jefferson's minutes of the August 2 cabinet meeting, which resolved to seek Genêt's recall); Thomas Jefferson to Gouverneur Morris (Aug. 16, 1793), reprinted 26 Jefferson Papers, 692; 7 Jefferson Works, 475–507 (detailing the case to the U.S. minister in France for Genêt's recall).

73 Cabinet Opinion on Vessels Arming and Arriving in United States Ports (July 12, 1793) (cabinet minutes taken by Jefferson), reprinted 15 Hamilton Papers, 87; 26 Jefferson Papers, 484; 7 Jefferson Works, 444–45; see Thomas Jefferson to Edmond C. Genêt and George Hammond (July 12, 1793), reprinted 26 Jefferson Papers, 487; 7 Jefferson Works, 445–46 ("You may be assured, Sir, that the delay will be as short as possible, and the object of it being to obtain the best advice possible on the sense of the laws and treaties respecting the several cases, I am persuaded you will think the delay well compensated."). This resolution also covered the British merchant ship *Jane,* which Genêt had complained was being augmented in force to cruise as a privateer. See Edmond C. Genêt to Thomas Jefferson (July 9, 1793), reprinted 1 ASP-F, 163; President's Journal (entry for July 30), 211 ("The Heads of Departments agreed that all new Carriages, port holes, Guns &c. which had been added to the Jane since she came into the Port was contrary to treaty & not to be suffered & that the Collector, Surveyor & Warden of the Port ought to make strict enquiry into the matter & report facts."). For further developments regarding the *Jane,* see infra note 103 and accompanying text.

74 See Jefferson, Anas, 153 (saying that Genêt had sent the vessel out "to obtain intelligence on the state of the coast"); Thomas Jefferson to Gouverneur Morris (Aug. 16, 1793), reprinted 26 Jefferson Papers, 697; 7 Jefferson Works, 500 (reporting Genêt's action).

75 See Thomas Jefferson to John Jay (July 12, 1793) (letterpress copy in Jefferson Papers, Library of Congress) (the letter notes at end: "The same to Judge Paterson."); Thomas Jefferson to James Iredell (July 12, 1793) (original in Ford Collection, New York Public Library). President's Journal, 196 (Washington approved letters to Jay and Paterson); George Washington to Thomas Jefferson (July 18, 1793), reprinted 37 Washington Writings, 575; see Wheeler, at 150.

76 Thomas Jefferson to the Justices of the Supreme Court (July 18, 1793), reprinted 26 Jefferson Papers, 520; 7 Jefferson Works, 451-52.

77 26 Jefferson Papers, 520; 7 Jefferson Works, 451-52.

78 President's Journal, 203 n.1; 6 DHSC, appendix (forthcoming). For the text of the questions, see 6 DHSC, appendix; 33 Washington Writings, 15-19. See 26 Jefferson Papers, 527 (draft of questions proposed by Hamilton, Jefferson, and Knox). On their delivery, see President's Journal, 204. Randolph did not participate in the meeting on July 18, as he had been on a tour of Virginia and Maryland, but he certainly had returned by July 19. See Carroll & Ashworth, 109 n.54.

79 Presumably the exclusions referred to items to be prohibited from each party's ships. Question 23 dealt with the right of each party to repair their vessels in each other's ports, that is, what types of repairs were allowable.

80 The administration already had taken a position on the subject of this question. Jefferson explained the matter in a letter to Genêt on July 24: "[B]y the general law of nations, the goods of a friend found in the vessel of an enemy are free, and the goods of an enemy found in the vessel of a friend are lawful prize. . . . It is true that sundry nations, desirous of avoiding the inconveniences of having their vessels stopped at sea, ransacked, carried into port and detained, under pretence of having enemy goods aboard, have, in many instances, introduced by their special treaties, another principle between them, that enemy bottoms shall make enemy goods, and friendly bottoms friendly goods. . . . but this is altogether the effect of particular treaty, controuling in special cases the general principle of the law of nations." Jefferson noted that "England has generally determined to adhere to the rigorous principle," whereas the United States had "adopted this modification in our treaties with France, the United Netherlands, and Prussia: and therefore as to them, our vessels cover the goods of their enemies, and we lose our goods when in the vessels of their enemies." Thomas Jefferson to Edmond C. Genêt (July 24, 1793), reprinted 26 Jefferson Papers, 557-58; 7 Jefferson Works, 457-58; see generally Jefferson, Opinion on Neutral Trade (Dec. 20, 1793), reprinted 8 id., 120-24. Instructions had been given to the American ambassador in Great Britain to seek the same agreement with them. See Thomas Jefferson to Thomas Pinckney (May 7, 1793), reprinted 25 Jefferson Papers, 674; 7 Jefferson Works, 313-14. Indeed, the American ambition was to gain acceptance of an even bolder principle, "declaring that nothing shall be contraband,"

a doctrine that had been incorporated in the U.S. treaty with Prussia. 25 Jefferson Papers, 675; 7 Jefferson Works, 315. There was, however, virtually no chance that the British would agree, for acceptance of the principle of "free ships make free goods" would provide France with a means to acquire much-needed foodstuffs. See 2 W. Phillips & A. Reede, supra note 2, at 32-33; Lord Grenville to George Hammond (Mar. 12, 1793), reprinted *Instructions to the British Ministers to the United States, 1791-1812,* in 3 Annual Report of the American Historical Association for the Year 1936, at 38 (B. Mayo ed. 1941) (instructing the ambassador to "very strongly inforce the principle . . . that Free Ships do not make Free Goods").

81 6 DHSC, appendix (forthcoming); John Jay, James Wilson, James Iredell, & William Paterson to George Washington (July 20, 1793), reprinted 3 Jay Papers, 487-88; George Washington to John Jay, James Wilson, James Iredell, & William Paterson (July 23, 1793), reprinted 33 Washington Writings, 28. The delay in responding may have been occasioned by Washington's referral of the Justices' letter to Jefferson on Saturday, July 20; Washington's response went out after a cabinet meeting on Tuesday, the 23rd. President's Journal, 205-6. At some point, Jay personally wrote out the entire list of questions, which indicates that he knew their contents. Unfortunately, the copy by Jay is undated. Jay's copy is now located at the Lilly Library, Indiana University.

82 William Bradford to Elias Boudinot (July 14, 1793) (John W. Wallace Collection, Vol. II, Hon. William Bradford, Attorney General, U.S.) (In January 1794, Bradford succeeded Edmund Randolph as Attorney General.). Bradford added in his letter that "[t]he abusive pieces against the President continue to be published, & [in] friday's Paper, he is charged with combining with Despots of Europe to crush the Liberties of France." Id.

83 Thomas Mifflin to Horatio Gates (July 17, 1793), reprinted 2 DHSC, 413.

84 General Advertiser (Philadelphia), July 17, 1793; reprinted Daily Advertiser (New York), July 19, 1793; Independent Gazette (Philadelphia), July 20, 1793; Boston Gazette (Boston), July 20, 1793; Virginia Gazette and Richmond and Manchester Advertiser (Richmond), July 25, 1793; National Gazette (Philadelphia), July 20, 1793; Baltimore Daily Repository (Baltimore), July 25, 1793; Stewart, 7-10.

85 Juba, Letter to the Editor, National Gazette, July 27, 1793 (dated July 25), reprinted Mercury (Boston), Aug. 6, 1793; Independent Chronicle (Boston), Aug. 8, 1793; Boston Gazette (Boston), Aug. 12, 1793.

86 United States v. Henfield, 11 F. Cas. 1099, 1105-09 (C.C.D. Pa. 1793) (No. 6360) (Grand Jury Charge of Wilson, Circuit Justice); see Engrossed Minutes (July 22, 1793), supra note 47. A more accurate copy of this charge, based on Wilson's manuscript, is found in 2 DHSC, 414-23, and will be used hereinafter as the primary citation.

87 Taking Wilson's conclusion about the treaty as true, it does not inevitably follow that a citizen is guilty of an offense for assisting one of the belligerents. After all, Wilson plainly stated that the treaty gave the United States the option of allowing France to use its ports for privateering purposes. Moreover, as Wilson pointed

out, under the law of nations a country was not expected to "superintend the whole behaviour of all the Citizens." 2 DHSC, 421; 11 F. Cas. at 1108. When all was said, Henfield was being prosecuted for violating the terms of the Neutrality Proclamation, which at the time was not a statutorily defined offense. On Wilson's answer as addressing some of Washington's questions, consider question 1, for example, which asked: "Do the treaties between the United States and France give to France or her citizens a *right*, when at war with a power with whom the United States are at peace, to fit out originally in and from the ports of the United States vessels armed for war, with or without commission?" 33 Washington Writings, 15. Indirectly, Wilson's response answered the next five questions and questions 11 and 13, which asked for details about the extent of France's right. Questions 6, 12, and 14 also were covered, as they inquired about the U.S. obligation to exclude the armed vessels of powers at war with France (Wilson said that the treaty imposed that obligation). Id., 15-17. By implication, he also denied that France had the authority to recruit Americans as soldiers and sailors, which was the subject of question 21. Id., 18.

88 Goebel, 626. That Wilson crafted the charge especially to deal with the neutrality crisis is evidenced by the contrast between this charge and his charge on June 7 to the grand jury for the Circuit Court for the District of Massachusetts, which was a lengthy and learned general dissertation on the nature of government and the citizenry's obligation to obey the social contract. See 2 DHSC, 396-404 & 414 (listing newspapers). The charge first appeared in three Philadelphia papers, *Dunlap's Daily Advertiser* (July 25), the *Federal Gazette* (July 25), and the *General Advertiser* (July 26).

89 Alexander Hamilton to John Jay (June 24, 1793), reprinted 15 Hamilton Papers, 20; 2 DHSC, 412; Grand Jury Charge of Jay, Circuit Justice (C.C.D. Va. 1793), reprinted 2 DHSC, 388, & United States v. Henfield, 11 F. Cas. 1099, 1104 (C.C.D. Pa. 1793) (No. 6360): "[A] State of Neutrality leaves us perfectly at Liberty to exercise every humane benevolent and friendly office towards the powers at War and their Subjects; and to continue our usual Commerce with them, excepting only those offices & that kind of Trade, which may be designed and calculated to give one party a military Preponderancy to the Detriment of others." Jay also charged that "aiding or abetting Hostilities" encompassed "carrying to [the belligerents] those articles which are deemed contraband, by the modern usage of Nations." Id., 383; 11 F. Cas. at 1102.

90 Engrossed Minutes (July 24, 1793), supra note 47 (true bill for misdemeanor). The report of this case erroneously indicates that the indictment was returned on July 27, which actually was the opening day of trial. Compare id. (July 27, 1793) with Henfield, 11 F. Cas. at 1109-15 (grand jury indictment); Engrossed Minutes (July 24, 1793), supra. A draft of the indictment appears in the handwriting of Randolph, with marginal corrections "apparently" by Hamilton, and a note to the effect that Lewis had suggested three of the counts. Henfield, 11 F. Cas. at 1115 n.3. A letter from Hamilton to Lewis comments on a citation that Hamilton thought would be useful for Rawle, and which Rawle in fact used at

the trial. See Alexander Hamilton to William Lewis (July 1793), reprinted 15 Hamilton Parpers, 156 (citing a treatise by Bynkershoek, which Rawle used in his argument; 11 F. Cas. at 1117 [the trial argument of William Rawle]). Another member of Henfield's crew, John Singletary, also was indicted on July 24. Thereafter, Singletary failed to appear for arraignment or trial; Engrossed Minutes (July 24, 1793), supra ("Deft. being called came note"); id. (July 29, 1793) (recognizance forfeited). On Henfield's defense, see Thomas, 171; see Malone, 120. At the time, Ingersoll was Attorney General of Pennsylvania.

91 Petit Jury Instruction, Henfield, 11 F. Cas. at 1119–20 (Wilson, Cir. Justice).

92 Id., 1120. Wilson relied on various treaty provisions between the United States and the European powers battling France—provisions that created a state of peace between these nations. Henfield's acts contravened these treaties, which "were in the most public, the most notorious existence, before the act for which the prisoner is indicted was committed." Id.

93 On the deliberations, see 11 F. Cas. at 1121–22; Engrossed Minutes (July 29, 1793), supra note 47.

94 From a Correspondent, National Gazette (Aug. 7, 1793). The same writer elaborated: "WHEN an Attorney General is brought forward, in an *extra-judicial* manner, to 'profane the sacred hall of justice,' with a *political declamation,* calculated to alarm the fears of a jury, and to substitute *political expediency* for *justice* and the *law of the land;* when the bench, instead of prohibiting such an unwarrantable proceeding, not only listen to the declaiming orator with pricked up ears, but afterwards address the jury in terms equally indecent and arbitrary, telling them, that if they do not pronounce a fellow citizen *guilty,* they are instrumental in plunging their country into all the horrors of war; in fine, when the most alarming measures are adopted, to stifle the calls of justice, and to intimidate an American jury into a verdict consonant with the wishes of a court-party, or British faction, it is high time for the virtuous citizens of America to be aroused to a sense of the dangers with which one of their dearest privileges, that of *impartial trial by jury,* is openly menaced."

95 See DeConde, 216; Stewart, 151–52, citing National Gazette (Philadelphia), Aug. 3, 28 & 31, 1793; 1 Warren, 114–15; General Advertiser (Philadelphia), Aug. 3, 1793; Star (Charleston, S.C.), July 12, 1793. Many contended that Henfield had violated no law because he became a citizen of France at the moment of his enlistment on the privateer. "Archy Simple," for example, asked: "Having voluntarily put himself out of the protection of the United States, how is he answerable to them? Having become a French citizen, by what law of the United States or of nation, can he be indicted and punished for doing his duty as a French citizen?" Archy Simple, Columbian Herald (Charleston, S.C.), Aug. 15, 1793. The same writer added that "[i]t is a policy peculiar to arbitrary princes and governments, to prohibit their subjects from migration."

96 See Lycan, 163–64; Thomas, 173–74; Hamilton, No Jacobin No. V, in Dunlap's American Daily Advertiser (Philadelphia) (Aug. 14, 1793), reprinted 15 Hamilton Papers, 246.

97 A South Carolinian, For the State Gazette, State Gazette (Charleston, S.C.), Sept. 5, 1793.

98 National Gazette (Philadelphia), Aug. 17, 1793; A South Carolinian, For the State Gazette, State Gazette (Charleston, S.C.), Sept. 5, 1793.

99 Quoted in Randolph, 183; Alexander Hamilton to George Washington (Aug. 5, 1793), reprinted 15 Hamilton Papers, 194.

100 See Hyneman, supra note 47, at 131, citing National Gazette, Aug. 3, 1793. On the French consul's prosecution, see supra note 48 and accompanying text; Thomas Jefferson to Gouverneur Morris (Aug. 16, 1793), reprinted 26 Jefferson Papers, 702; 7 Jefferson Works, 489-90; Lycan, 163. Henfield was later captured by the British. Henfield, 11 F. Cas. at 1122-23 n.7.

101 26 Jefferson Papers, 526, 579-81, 588, 603-5, & 607-10; President's Journal, 210 (July 29, 1793); Jefferson, Anas, 158-59.

102 George Washington to Alexander Hamilton, Thomas Jefferson, Henry Knox, and Edmund Randolph (Aug. 3, 1793), reprinted 33 Washington Writings, 35.

103 On the *Jane,* see supra note 73. The cabinet had discussed this problem on July 29 and 30 and had agreed at the second meeting not to permit an augmentation of the *Jane's* armaments. The port's Collector, Surveyor, and Warden were to "make strict enquiry into the matter & report facts." President's Journal, 211 (July 30). On August 1, these three reported that "they had examined the Ship *Jane* & found several augmentations to her force, & an increase of hands." Id., 212 (Aug. 1). The following day, August 2, the cabinet considered a letter from Ambassador Hammond to Henry Knox, which assured that the alterations to the *Jane* were proper and asked permission to complete the work. See id., 212 (Aug. 2).

104 The decree of May 9 was rescinded on May 23 following protests from the American representative in Paris, but on July 27 the French announced that they would seize ships carrying food supplies to enemy destinations. The 1778 Treaty of Amity and Commerce provided that such goods would be considered non-contraband. See generally Clauder, 28-30; DeConde, 400-401; 15 Hamilton Papers, 174 n.7 & 194-95 n.3 (editors' notes); 2 W. Phillips & A. Reede, supra note 2, at 34-37. The May 23 decree is reprinted in 1 ASP-F, 244; see McDonald, Hamilton, 280: "The American mercantile community was thrown into confusion, and insurance rates soared." Id.

105 Letters from Rufus King, Washington, and Hamilton in early August indicate that they were aware of the French decree of May 9 but not its recision on May 23. See Rufus King to Alexander Hamilton (Aug. 3, 1793), reprinted 15 Hamilton Papers, 173; George Washington to Thomas Jefferson (Aug. 4, 1793), reprinted 33 Washington Writings, 38; Alexander Hamilton to George Washington (Aug. 5, 1793), reprinted id., 194. Official notice of the recision was received from Paris on September 5. See President's Journal, 238 (dispatch from the American minister in France). Another related candidate for "fresh occurrences" is the possibility that Washington had received news that the British adopted an order of council on June 8, commanding that British warships seize certain grains on any ships bound for a French port; additionally, any ships attempting to enter

blockaded ports would be stopped and condemned. See Additional Instructions to the Commanders of His Majesty's Ships of War (Order in Council, June 8, 1793), reprinted 1 ASP-F, 240 & 264; see Clauder, 30-31. This order was transmitted to Ambassador Hammond by a letter dated July 5, 1793, which contained instructions for how to present the issue to the American government. See Lord Grenville to George Hammond (July 5, 1793), reprinted Instructions to the British Ministers to the United States, 1791-1812, in 3 Annual Report, supra note 80, at 40-42. The possibility of such an order had been considered earlier by the administration. Jefferson wrote on May 7 to Thomas Pinckney, U.S. ambassador to Great Britain, noting Pinckney's apprehensions about possible seizures of American grain vessels by belligerents, but saying: "Such a stoppage to an unblocked port would be so unequivocal an infringement of the neutral rights, that we cannot conceive it will be attempted." (May 7, 1793), reprinted 25 Jefferson Papers, 675; 7 Jefferson Works, 313-14. Arguing against this event as the "fresh occurrence" is the fact that the cabinet did not take up the issue formally until August 31, the day after Washington received an unauthenticated copy of the Order of Council from the U.S. consul in Liverpool. See Cabinet Meeting Minutes (Aug. 31, 1793), reprinted 15 Hamilton Papers, 315; 26 Jefferson Papers, 795; 8 Jefferson Works, 8-9 (written by Jefferson, signed by Hamilton, Knox, and Randolph); James Maury (from Liverpool) to Thomas Jefferson (July 4, 1793), summarized in 26 Jefferson Papers, 433, cited in President's Journal, 235 n.1; id., 234-35 (enclosing instructions to the British fleet). Pinckney was instructed to investigate the authenticity of the order, and if it was verified, to protest it as "manifestly contrary to the law of nations." Thomas Jefferson to Thomas Pinckney (Sept. 7, 1793), reprinted 8 Jefferson Works, 25; see Cabinet Meeting Minutes, supra (approving instructions).

106 Jefferson, Anas, 161. See DeConde, 270. Reports of the battle appeared in the Daily Advertiser (New York) on August 2, and it was mentioned in a letter from King to Hamilton on the next day. See Rufus King to Alexander Hamilton (Aug. 3, 1793), reprinted 15 Hamilton Papers, 172 & 174 n.3 (editors' note). The naval engagement was all the more interesting because it had occurred as a consequence of a public challenge by the British captain and resulted in widespread wagering on the outcome. Moreover, the *Boston* had been sent specifically to disrupt French attacks on the British merchant marine. See DeConde, 270-74; Carroll & Ashworth, 115-16 & n.107.

107 See McDonald, Hamilton, 279-80. See DeConde, 270-74; Carroll & Ashworth, 115-16 & n.107. On July 13, Jefferson gave Washington a letter from Lt. Gov. Wood of Virginia reporting the arrival of more than one hundred injured or ill refugees from the insurrection. See President's Journal, 196-97 & n.8, citing James Wood to Thomas Jefferson (July 8, 1793) (original in Jefferson Papers, Library of Congress); Thomas Jefferson to James Monroe (July 14, 1793), reprinted 26 Jefferson Papers, 503; 7 Jefferson Works, 449-50.

108 See Thomas Jefferson to George Washington (July 31, 1793), reprinted 26 Jefferson Papers, 593; 7 Jefferson Works, 462-63; Alexander Hamilton to

George Washington (June 21, 1793), reprinted 15 Hamilton Papers, 13 (indicating that he wanted to resign at the close of the next session of Congress); Jefferson, Anas, 161.

109 Washington listed the conflicts with Native Americans as one of several considerations for the cabinet to weigh in advising him on whether to convene Congress early. The other events he mentioned were the *Henfield* verdict and the decision to seek Genêt's recall. See George Washington to Alexander Hamilton, Thomas Jefferson, Henry Knox, and Edmund Randolph (Aug. 3, 1793), reprinted 33 Washington Writings, 36.

110 George Washington to Alexander Hamilton, Thomas Jefferson, Henry Knox, and Edmund Randolph (Aug. 3, 1793), reprinted 33 Washington Writings, 36. Not surprisingly, Hamilton advised against an early session, whereas Jefferson was favorably disposed. See Alexander Hamilton to George Washington (Aug. 5, 1793), reprinted 15 Hamilton Papers, 194–95; Thomas Jefferson to George Washington (Aug. 4, 1793), reprinted 26 Jefferson Papers, 619; 7 Jefferson Works, 465–66. Both Knox and Randolph counseled against calling a special session of Congress. See 15 Hamilton Papers, 196 n.4 (editors' note). Washington decided against convening the early session; Jefferson said that "tho' the P[resident] was in his own judgment for calling them, he acquiesced in the majority." Thomas Jefferson to James Madison (Aug. 11, 1793), reprinted 26 Jefferson Papers, 650; 7 Jefferson Works, 474; see Jefferson, Anas, 161 (entry for Aug. 6, noting the decision not to call Congress).

111 Thomas Jefferson to George Washington (July 31, 1793), reprinted 26 Jefferson Papers, 594; 7 Jefferson Works, 462–63; Thomas Jefferson to James Madison (Aug. 3, 1793), reprinted 26 Jefferson Papers, 607; 7 Jefferson Works, 465–66 (Jefferson enclosed a copy of the questions that had been posed to the Justices); President's Journal, 210 (July 29, 1793); id., 211 (July 30, 1793); id., 211–12 (Aug. 1, 1793); id., 212 (Aug. 2, 1793); id., 213 (Aug. 3, 1793); George Washington to Thomas Jefferson (Aug. 4, 1793), reprinted 33 Washington Writings, 37 (approving the rules and ordering publication "without delay"). The final version of the administration's "Rules on Neutrality" is reprinted in 26 Jefferson Papers, 608; 7 Jefferson Works, 460–61 n.1; 15 Hamilton Papers, 168–69 (draft of the rules). Further, the cabinet recommended that with respect to any prizes taken after June 5 by French privateers fitted out in American ports, France would be expected to pay restitution to the lawful owners. Failing that, the United States would indemnify the owners and obtain reimbursement from the French by deductions from the public debt to France. Cabinet Minutes (Aug. 3, 1793), reprinted 15 Hamilton Papers, 169–70 (written by Hamilton, also signed by Jefferson, Knox, and Randolph).

112 See Treasury Department Circular to the Collectors of Customs (Aug. 4, 1793), reprinted 15 Hamilton Papers, 178–81; Thomas Jefferson to Edmond Charles Genêt (Aug. 7, 1793), reprinted 26 Jefferson Papers, 633; 7 Jefferson Works, 468–70 (communicating resolves); George Hammond to Lord Grenville (Aug. 10, 1793), reprinted 15 Hamilton Papers, 163–64 (reporting the administration's

resolution, about which Hammond had been informed by a letter from Jefferson on Aug. 7); Cabinet Minutes (Aug. 5, 1793), reprinted 15 Hamilton Papers, 181–83 (written by Jefferson, also signed by Hamilton and Knox).

113 See John Jay, James Wilson, John Blair, James Iredell, & William Paterson to George Washington (Aug. 8, 1793), supra, intro., note 1. 1 DHSC, 217–19 (August term). Paterson took the seat of Thomas Johnson, who had resigned the previous January 16; John Jay to William Cushing (Aug. 6, 1793), reprinted 2 DHSC, 424 (giving the bad news that Cushing had been assigned the Southern Circuit in his absence). A surviving draft in Jay's handwriting of the letter to Washington indicates that he took care in considering its wording. Most of the changes in the draft are stylistic, as where he substituted "your usual Prudence, Decision and Firmness" instead of the less flattering "your Firmness and Decision." In one place, following the opening line, Jay struck a portion of a sentence that stated the question presented by Jefferson's original letter of July 18. Deleted were the following words: "Whether the Public may with propriety be availed of the advice of the Judges of the Supreme Court of the U.S." This would have repeated the question in the same words used by Jefferson. See supra, text accompanying note 76. Jay's editorial choice here may have been entirely stylistic, or he may have wished to avoid giving the President the impression that the Justices' advice could be solicited if the opinion were kept private. Another alteration was the deletion in the last line of the second paragraph of the words "the subordinate" prior to "executive Departments." John Jay to George Washington (draft, Aug. 8, 1793).

114 Jay & King, For the Diary, Daily Advertiser (New York), Aug. 14, 1793 (dated Aug. 2), reprinted 15 Hamilton Papers, 233.

115 Thomas Jefferson to James Monroe (June 28, 1793), reprinted 26 Jefferson Papers, 393; 7 Jefferson Works, 417. "I am doing every thing in my power to moderate the . . . dangerous opinion, which has been excited in him, that the people of the US. will disavow the acts of their government, and that he has an appeal from the Executive to Congress, and from both to the people." 26 Jefferson Papers, 393; 7 Jefferson Works, 417; Thomas Jefferson to James Monroe (July 14, 1793), reprinted 26 Jefferson Papers, 502; 7 Jefferson Works, 449.

116 Thomas Jefferson to James Madison (Aug. 3, 1793), reprinted 26 Jefferson Papers, 606; 7 Jefferson Works, 464. Jefferson added: "[Genêt] *will sink the republican* interest if they do not *abandon him.*" For accounts of the cabinet discussions over whether to publish Genêt's correspondence, see Elkins & McKitrick, 361–62; Thomas, 227–35; 15 Hamilton Papers, 233–39 (editors' note); Jefferson, Anas, 150 (entry for July 23, 1793, reporting Hamilton's statement at a cabinet meeting that day); id., 158 (entry for Aug. 2, 1793); Jefferson indicated that he would make the proposal to send the correspondence to Congress as a compromise. See Thomas Jefferson to James Madison (Aug. 11, 1793), reprinted 26 Jefferson Papers, 651–52; 7 Jefferson Writings, 464.

117 No Jacobin No. 1, in Dunlap's American Daily Advertiser (New York), July 31, 1793, reprinted 15 Hamilton Papers, 145; Elkins & McKitrick, 361–62; Stewart,

166: "As Jefferson had foreseen, administration supporters cleverly used Washington's popularity and Genêt's indiscretions to bolster the government's neutrality program and to lessen the popular sympathy for France. From all parts of the Union came resolutions pledging support to the President's proclamation and condemning Genêt's activities." On Morris's statement, see Jefferson, Anas, 150 n° (entry for Aug. 2, 1793, reporting Washington's recollection of his recent conversation with Morris, which "the President repeated twice" at the cabinet meeting, "with an air of importance").

118 Thomas Jefferson to James Madison (Aug. 25, 1793), reprinted 26 Jefferson Papers, 756; 8 Jefferson Writings, 7. Two weeks earlier, Jefferson wrote: "The towns are beginning generally to make known their disapprobation to any such opposition to their government by a foreigner, are declaring their firm adherence to their President, & the Proclamation is made the groundwork of these declarations." Thomas Jefferson to James Madison (Aug. 11, 1793), reprinted 26 Jefferson Papers, 651; 7 Jefferson Writings, 508. Madison responded that people in his area of Virginia who had been "attached to the French cause" were reacting with "suprize and disgust" at Genêt's conduct with respect to Washington; see James Madison to Thomas Jefferson (Sept. 2, 1793), reprinted 15 Madison Papers, 92; 6 Madison Writings, 191.

119 "While Hamilton was not a central figure in this dispute, he undoubtedly did his best—particularly in the controversy's earlier stages—to encourage Jay and King." 15 Hamilton Papers, 233 (editors' note); Hamilton & Knox, Letter to the Editor, The Daily Advertiser (New York), Dec. 3, 1793 (dated Nov. 29, 1793), reprinted 15 Hamilton Papers, 418-19. On Washington's knowledge of the contents of this statement, see Alexander Hamilton & Henry Knox to John Jay (Nov. 29, 1793), reprinted 15 Hamilton Papers, 419 (noting that an omission in the statement related to "a scruple about official propriety" that "concerned the President").

120 Genêt made an opening rebuttal to the rumor of his threatened appeal to the people in a public letter addressed to Washington, during the course of which he demanded that the President issue "an explicit declaration, that 'I have never intimated to you an intention of appealing to the people.'" Edmond C. Genêt to George Washington (Aug. 13, 1793), reprinted The Diary, or Louden's Register (New York), Aug. 21, 1793, reprinted National Gazette (Philadelphia), Aug. 28, 1793, quoted in 15 Hamilton Papers, 234 (editors' note). Jefferson replied on Washington's behalf with a letter that was later published in *The Diary*, saying that correspondence with the President should come through the Secretary of State. In any event, Jefferson explained, "[t]he President does not conceive it to be within the line of propriety or duty for him, to bear evidence against a declaration which, whether made to him or others, is perhaps immaterial. He therefore declines interfering in the case." Thomas Jefferson to Edmond C. Genêt (Aug. 16, 1793), reprinted 26 Jefferson Papers, 684; The Diary, or Louden's Register (New York), Aug. 21, 1793, National Gazette (Philadelphia), Aug. 28, 1793, quoted in 15 Hamilton Papers, 235. In November, Genêt wrote

to Jefferson that "my friends have called, in many papers, upon Mr. Jay and Mr. King, to produce the proofs of their assertion; . . . but the silence of these gentlemen was profound." Edmond C. Genêt to Thomas Jefferson (Nov. 14, 1793), reprinted The New-York Journal, & Patriotic Register, Nov. 27, 1793, quoted in 15 Hamilton Papers, 235-36.

121 Independent Chronicle (Boston), Sept. 5, 1793. Likewise, a Virginia critic pointed out that "[t]he certificate furnishes neither the time, place, nor circumstances, attending the expression. It is not stated, whether it was the result of some convivial humour? Whether the sudden ebullitions of the moment, preceded by some palliating circumstance, or whether it was urged in his official communications with the President." "A Uniform Federalist," The Virginia Gazette (Richmond), Sept. 9, 1793 (dated Aug. 24, 1793). On similar opposition challenges to Jay and King, see Stewart, 162-68.

122 Edmond C. Genêt to Edmund Randolph (Nov. 14, 1793), reprinted The New-York Journal, & Patriotic Register, Nov. 27, 1793, quoted in 15 Hamilton Papers, 235 (editors' note). Randolph replied that he would be willing to meet with Genêt to discuss the allegation. See Edmund Randolph to Edmond C. Genêt (Nov. 19, 1793), reprinted The New-York Journal, & Patriotic Register, Nov. 27, 1793, cited in 15 Hamilton Papers, 236; Jay & King, To the Public, The Daily Advertiser (New York), Dec. 2, 1793, quoted in 15 Hamilton Papers, 236 n.10 (editors' note). Jay and King noted that in Genêt's open letter to Washington he had denied only making the declaration *to the President;* they pointed out that this left "the question whether he had made it *at all,* entirely out of sight." Id.

123 Dunlap's American Daily Advertiser (Philadelphia), Dec. 6 & 9, 1793, quoted in 15 Hamilton Papers, 237-38 (editors' note). On December 19, 1793, Jay wrote to King that he regretted that Jefferson and Mifflin "still remain as it were in a back Ground" on the Genêt affair. "I am inclined to think that Letters, calculated for publication, from Col. Hamilton & Ge. Knox to Mr. Jefferson & Govr. Mifflin, calling on them to admit or deny the Facts in Question, wd. have been, and may yet be useful." John Jay to Rufus King (Dec. 19, 1793), reprinted 1 King, 469-70; John Jay to Alexander Hamilton (Nov. 26, 1793), reprinted 15 Hamilton Papers, 412-13; Rufus King to Alexander Hamilton (Nov. 26, 1793), reprinted id., 413-14. King pointed out the need for "immediate measures," as "[d]elay will give time for the formation of Parties."

124 See DeConde, 292-96; Ernst, 187-196; 15 Hamilton Papers, 239 (editors' note). King left an account of these events; see 1 King, 476-80; DeConde, 296; 15 Hamilton Papers, 239 (editors' note).

125 See DeConde, 286-87; Stewart, 160-68; Dunlap's Daily American Advertiser, Aug. 21, 1793, cited in Stewart, 162; National Gazette (Philadelphia), Sept. 28, 1793; Independent Chronicle (Oct. 7, 1793), quoted in Stewart, 164; "A Uniform Federalist," The Virginia Gazette (Richmond), Sept. 9, 1793 (dated Aug. 24, 1793). "Jay and King, who are known to have been amongst the foremost of [the "ministerial party"] have *heretofore affected* to despise the opinions of the people, have ridiculed their censorial influence, and have affected the almost necessary

infallibility of the constituted tribunals; at this particular juncture, and in this particular question, they are exhibited to the public, the avowed instigators of a popular clamour." Id.

CHAPTER SIX: EXPLAINING THE SUPREME COURT'S REFUSAL

1 Thomas Jefferson to James Madison (Aug. 11, 1793) (original in Madison Papers, Library of Congress), reprinted 26 Jefferson Papers, 653; 15 Madison Papers, 58. Jefferson continued: "I asked [Edmund Randolph] if we could not prepare a bill for Congress to appoint a board or some other body of advice for the Executive on such questions. He said he should propose to annex it to his office. In plain language this would be to make him the sole arbiter of the line of conduct for the US. towards foreign nations." Id.

2 See supra chapters 1-3. See 2 Holt, 332 n.127; Casto, 180-83.

3 John Jay, James Wilson, John Blair, James Iredell, & William Paterson to George Washington (Aug. 8, 1793), supra intro., note 1.

4 James Iredell & John Sitgreaves to George Washington (June 8, 1792), 1 ASP-M, 53.

5 See John Jay to New York Assembly (Feb. 23, 1801), reprinted 2 State of New York: Messages from the Governors 472-76 (C. Lincoln ed. 1909). The question involved an interpretation of § 23 of the New York constitution of 1777; Robert Roseboom, Ambrose Spencer, & De Witt Clinton to John Jay (March 17, 1801), reprinted id., 490-501.

6 John Jay to the Chancellor, Chief Justice, and Judges of the Supreme Court of New York (Mar. 18, 1801), reprinted id., 479-80.

7 John Lansing, Egbert Benson, James Kent, & Jacob Radcliff to John Jay (Mar. 26, 1801), reprinted id., 483. A fifth judge, Morgan Lewis, was unavailable to consult with the other judges, but he wrote through Chief Justice Lansing that "the Chancellor and Judges ought not to answer the question proposed; as it might possibly come before them in the shape of an impeachment." John Lansing to John Jay (Mar. 26, 1801), reprinted id., 481. Chancellor Livingston also wrote separately, without conferring with the others. Declining to answer as well, Livingston noted that the state constitution did not set up the "Judiciary [as] an advisory Council for the other branches of government," and therefore "it must have been intended that they should lend their support to, or discourage the usurpation of either, only in their judicial capacity." Like the judges, Livingston was concerned that an extrajudicial opinion "would have no more weight, or be more binding upon the party asking, or opposed to it, than that of any other gentlemen of equal standing in the profession of the law." This was of particular relevance to New York, where the highest court in the state was the Court of Errors, which consisted of the President of the Senate, the Senators, the Chancellor, and the judges of the Supreme Court. As Livingston explained, "[t]he members of the Senate make a large majority of the judges in the last resort," and if "the dignity of the Court and its constitutional competency is to determine

the doubt of the Executive," then Jay should direct his request to the Court of Errors. Livingston had an additional concern, namely, that if the judges were "bound to decide extrajudicially" at the behest of the governor, then "they are equally bound to give their opinions on the requisition of the Legislature. . . . [T]his would by degrees lead them into political controversies, incompatible with the duties of their office, and convert them into mantelets to receive the shot, while the leaders of parties fought securely under their protection." Robert R. Livingston to John Jay (Mar. 21, 1801), reprinted id., 481–82.

8 See Carroll & Ashworth, 348–56; Oliver Ellsworth to Jonathan Trumbull (Mar. 13, 1796) (original in Washington Papers, Library of Congress), quoted in id., 349. Washington refused the request from the House, citing "[a] just regard to the Constitution and to the duty of my Office," as well as his belief that compliance would "establish a dangerous precedent" by endangering the secrecy of treaty negotiations. George Washington to the House of Representatives (Mar. 30, 1796), reprinted 35 Washington Writings, 3 & 5. Peter Van Schaack remarked to Federalist Congressman Theodore Sedgwick that he "suppose[d] [the President] had consulted the heads of Departments or rather the Judges of the Supreme Court." Peter Van Schaack to Theodore Sedgwick (Apr. 4, 1796) (original in Theodore Sedgwick Papers, Massachusetts Historical Society). Van Schaack was a New York Federalist lawyer and friend of John Jay.

9 On "weighty points," see Timothy Pickering to Rufus King (July 27, 1796) (original in King Papers, Huntington Library). Pickering's actual words were "our first law-characters," but the context shows that he was referring to Supreme Court Justices. Shortly before this, Pickering asked Chief Justice Ellsworth for an opinion concerning French prize sales; see Timothy Pickering to Oliver Ellsworth (June 30, 1796) (original in Pickering Papers, Massachusetts Historical Society), quoted in Casto, 116; see Casto, *"I Have Sought the Felicity and Glory of Your Administration,"* J. Supreme Court Hist. 73 (1996). Ellsworth's response, if any, has not been found. James McHenry to Samuel Chase (Apr. 28, 1800) (original in American Philosophical Society Library, Philadelphia); Samuel Chase to James McHenry (undated, c. 1800) (original in American Philosophical Society Library, Philadelphia). Other judges of this period were reluctant to give extrajudicial advice, even in a "private" capacity. For example, Judge Edmund Pendleton of the Virginia Court of Appeals refused to give a legal opinion at the request of Governor James Monroe. Pendleton wrote that "it would be improper for me to commit myself in an Opinion, given by Anticipation, & without hearing an Argument, by which I might be afterwards embarrassed, & fear it would be difficult to separate the opinion of the citizen from that of the judge." Edmund Pendleton to James Monroe (Mar. 8, 1800) (original in Edmund Pendleton letters, Virginia State Library). Thanks to William Casto for this reference.

10 See Casto, 119; Wheeler, 220–23; John Rutledge, Jr., to Unknown Correspondent (Feb. 27, 1799) (original in John Rutledge Papers, University of North Carolina at Chapel Hill), quoted in Casto, 119 n.120. Marshall took the oath as Chief Justice on February 4, 1801, but remained as Secretary of State until March 3, 1801.

11 George Hammond to Lord Grenville (Mar. 7, 1793), quoted in Thomas, 87; Thomas Jefferson to Harry Innes (May 23, 1793), reprinted 26 Jefferson Papers, 100; 7 Jefferson Works, 343; Thomas Jefferson to William Carmichael & William Short (May 31, 1793), 26 Jefferson Papers, 149; 7 Jefferson Works, 351-52; Thomas Jefferson to William Short (July 28, 1791), reprinted 20 Jefferson Papers, 693 n.1; 6 Jefferson Works, 290-91 & n.1 (the names quoted in text were encoded in cipher by Jefferson): "It is prognosticated that our republic is to end with the President's life. But I believe they will find themselves all head and no body."

12 Thomas Jefferson to Jacques-Pierre Brissot de Warville (May 8, 1793), reprinted 25 Jefferson Papers, 679; 7 Jefferson Works, 322. Brissot was a leading Girondist whom Jefferson knew from his years in France; Jefferson had every reason to believe that Brissot still commanded influence in the National Convention. Brissot was a prime advocate of France's European war, and he had been responsible for Genêt's appointment as minister to the United States. See E. Ellery, Brissot de Warville: A Study in the History of the French Revolution 232-57 & 315 (1915); Malone, 82 & 91. A month before Jefferson wrote, however, Brissot had been denounced by Robespierre, and by the end of May, Brissot and the Girondists had fallen from power and were fleeing arrest; Bissot would be guillotined on October 31, 1793. See E. Ellery, supra, 351-86; M. Slavin, The Making of an Insurrection: Parisian Sections and the Gironde 14 (1986).

13 Thomas Jefferson to Jacques-Pierre Brissot de Warville (May 8, 1793), reprinted 25 Jefferson Papers, 679; 7 Jefferson Works, 322; Thomas Jefferson to James Madison (May 13, 1793), reprinted 26 Jefferson Papers, 25; 7 Jefferson Works, 324-25; Thomas Jefferson to James Monroe (May 5, 1793), reprinted 25 Jefferson Papers, 661; 7 Jefferson Works, 309.

14 Anonymous Letter, Independent Chronicle (Boston), Aug. 15, 1793. See A Uniform Federalist, The Virginia Gazette (Richmond), Sept. 9, 1793 (dated Aug. 24, 1793): "The opinions of parties respecting external politics, furnish an almost infallible index, to the internal objects of parties. It is singular, as it is true, that nearly the same division, is now found amongst official characters, respecting French and British politics, which has uniformly existed, respecting the construction of our own constitution and the internal administration of the general government. — Those, who have contended for confining the operations of government to the chartered authorities of the constitution, and denied the fanciful doctrine of implications unlimitedly, have uniformly sided with France. Those who have intrepidly overleaped the demarcations of the constitution, generated *power* from *convenience,* and despised the solemn obligations of LAWS, have almost unanimously sided with Britain; or to speak in a more courtly stile, the anti-ministerial party have sided with France, the ministerial with Britain. . . . [The "ministerial party"] know (whatever they may pretend) that all their artificial expedients, of *perpetual debts, perpetual taxes, of Banks, of Loans foreign and domestic,* &c. &c. &c. will prove but tender barriers, against enemies so formidable as the opinions and interest of the great majority of enlightened people."

15 Elkins & McKitrick, 288-89; Banning, 222; McDonald, Washington, 106-7. The

first quote is in Thomas Jefferson to William Short (Mar. 23, 1793), reprinted 25 Jefferson Papers, 436; 7 Jefferson Works, 269; the second quote is in Thomas Jefferson to Thomas Pinckney (Apr. 12, 1793), reprinted 25 Jefferson Papers, 536; 7 Jefferson Works, 277.

16 The first quote is from John Beckley, the clerk of the House of Representatives, quoted in Elkins & McKitrick, 288; Thomas Jefferson to Thomas Mann Randolph (Nov. 16, 1792), reprinted 24 Jefferson Papers, 623; 7 Jefferson Works, 179; Alexander Hamilton to George Washington (Aug. 5, 1793), reprinted 15 Hamilton Papers, 194. For Knox's concurrence (with which Randolph agreed), see id., 196 n.4 (editors' note); Jefferson, Opinion on Convening of Congress (Aug. 4, 1793), reprinted 26 Jefferson Papers, 615; 7 Jefferson Works, 465. In the end, Washington decided not to change the congressional schedule.

17 McDonald, Washington, 4; Miller, 99; Wood, 58-59; J. Trumbull, The Autobiography of Colonel John Trumbull: Patriot-Artist, 1756-1843, at 172 (T. Sizer ed. 1953).

18 This is Jefferson's account of a conversation with Washington. See Jefferson, Anas, 124; George Washington to Edmund Randolph (Aug. 26, 1792), reprinted 32 Washington Writings, 136. On the continuous danger of a breakup of the union throughout the 1790s, and on Washington's fear of a dissolution as a motive for his taking a second term, see Smelser, *The Federalist Period as an Age of Passion*, 10 Am. Q. 391, 393 (1958).

19 Id. On the "ferocity" of opposition to the Neutrality Proclamation, the escalating attacks on Washington himself, the criticism of Henfield's arrest, the handling of the *Little Sarah* incident, and the pro-British bias of the administration despite British depredations, see Stewart, 143-155. Regarding attacks on the administration for its interactions with Genêt, see id., 155-69. With respect to personal attacks on Washington and his resulting wounded feelings, see Slaughter, 156-57. During the first six months of Washington's second administration, "[e]xpressions against the government more and more were directed against the man at its head. As attacks focused on him, the invectives gained in unruly strength and in ugly spirit. The protests of an orderly and reasonable people fast were approaching the meaningless fury of a disorderly and unintelligible mob." Carroll & Ashworth, 119.

20 For an account of the various street disturbances in Philadelphia, see generally Carroll & Ashworth, 105-6 & 115-16 ("To any observer in Philadelphia, the heat of faction was high."); Flexner, 62-63 ("Washington was deeply worried, not only by the violence of the opposition gazettes, by reports of widespread discontents in Virginia, by the threats in New York of physical violence against Federalists, but by what he himself saw on the Philadelphia streets."); Lycan, 173-74. According to Donald Stewart, Democratic Societies "sprang up almost simultaneously with [Genêt's] arrival and . . . uniformly and enthusiastically supported him. They appeared suddenly, and Federalists who had been inclined to smile at popular manifestations of Francophile frenzy began to frown in worry or to protest harshly. Jacobin societies, not unlike these organizations, had come into being just prior to the uprising in France. . . . Clearly, they constituted a political

threat of no mean import, and they talked of coordinating their efforts through correspondence committees as had American revolutionaries two decades earlier. Jefferson watched their growth with a keen and benevolent interest; of such material would be compounded his opposition political party." Stewart, 169. See Buel, 48, 97–105 (on Federalist fears of Democratic Societies, and related concerns about popular disturbances); P. Foner, The Democratic-Republican Societies, 1790–1800, at 30–32 (1976); Link, 19 (explaining that the societies were only partly modeled after French Jacobin organizations and also had roots in English opposition associations and such American revolutionary groups as the Sons of Liberty). Both in America and Great Britain, there was a long history of political action through mob action. In America, "[e]xtralegal groups and conventions repeatedly sprang up to take public action into their own hands, to intimidate voters, to regulate prices, or to close the courts." Wood, A Note on Mobs in the American Revolution, 23 Wm. & Mary Q. (3rd ser.) 635, 640 (1966); see also Wood, 319–28; Maier, Popular Uprisings and Civil Authority in Eighteenth-Century America, 27 Wm. & Mary Q. 3 (3rd ser.) (1970). On mob activity in England, see chapter 1, supra, note 103.

21 Alexander Hamilton to Henry Lee (June 22, 1793), reprinted 15 Hamilton Papers, 14–15.

22 The seven Pacificus papers appeared in the Gazette of the United States (Philadelphia) on June 29, July 3, 6, 10, 13, 17 & 27, 1793, reprinted 15 Hamilton Papers, 33, 55, 65, 82, 90, 100, & 130. The nine No Jacobin letters were published by the American Daily Advertiser (Philadelphia) on July 31, Aug. 5, 8, 10, 14, 16, 23, 26, & 28, 1793, reprinted id., 145, 184, 203, 224, 243, 249, 268, 281, & 304. On Aug. 5, 1793, a single Philo Pacificus essay was printed in Dunlap's American Daily Advertiser (Philadelphia), reprinted id., 191. As to awareness of Hamilton's authorship, see Thomas Jefferson to James Madison (July 7, 1793), reprinted 26 Jefferson Papers, 444; 7 Jefferson Works, 436 (enclosing "Colo. H's 2d & 3d pacificus"); Thomas Jefferson to James Madison (Aug. 3, 1793), reprinted 26 Jefferson Papers, 606; 7 Jefferson Works, 464 ("the author is universally known"); Thomas Jefferson to James Madison (Aug. 11, 1793), reprinted 26 Jefferson Papers, 650; 7 Jefferson Works, 474 ("Pacificus has now changed his signature to 'No Jacobin.'"); Pacificus No. 1, Gazette of the United States (Philadelphia) (June 29, 1793), reprinted 15 Hamilton Papers, 43.

23 Pacificus No. 1, id., 37–38, 40, 42.

24 Id., 38 (emphasis added); Federalist No. 71, reprinted Federalist, 483.

25 Thomas Jefferson to James Madison (July 7, 1793), reprinted 26 Jefferson Papers, 444; 7 Jefferson Works, 436. The five essays appeared in the Gazette of the United States between August 24 and September 18, 1793; see Letters of Pacificus and Helvidius 53–102 (J. Gideon ed. 1845); 15 Madison Papers, 66, 80, 95, 106, & 113; 6 Madison Writings, 138, 160, 164, 174; Madison, Helvidius No. II–IV, in Letters of Pacificus and Helvidius, supra, 73, 78, 89.

26 Federalist No. 4, reprinted Federalist, at 20 (Jay).

27 John Jay to Robert Goodloe Harper (Jan. 19, 1796), reprinted 4 Jay Papers, 199;

Grand Jury Charge of Jay, Circuit Justice (C.C.D. Va. 1793), reprinted 2 DHSC, 389; United States v. Henfield, 11 F. Cas. 1099, 1104 (C.C.D. Pa. 1793) (No. 6360).

28 Buel, 47; Lycan, 154–55. Gouverneur Morris's diplomatic dispatches from France in the spring and summer are replete with news of military setbacks and civil strife. See Letters from Gouverneur Morris to Thomas Jefferson (Feb. 13, Mar. 7., 9, 25, Apr. 4, 9, May 20, June 25, 1793), reprinted 2 The Life and Correspondence of Gouverneur Morris 277, 290, 295, 299, 315, 317, 320, & 328 (J. Sparks ed. 1832). In the last letter of this series, Morris wrote: "No small part of France is in open war with the rest; and wherever the insurgents arrive, it appears that the whole country is friendly to them; so that, if one were to judge by what passes in that quarter, France would be very nearly unanimous in the re-establishment of royalty, should they come in force to Paris." Id., 331. A combination of crop failures and interdiction of food supplies by the British had raised the serious prospect of famine in France. See Thomas Jefferson to Thomas Mann Randolph, Jr. (May 7, 1793), reprinted 7 Jefferson Works, 312 ("I very much fear that France will experience a famine this summer.") Jefferson took these accounts in stride, and despite French losses he remained optimistic that "nothing can shake their republicanism." Thomas Jefferson to James Madison (June 29, 1793), reprinted 26 Jefferson Papers; Jefferson Works, 419; see Buel, 47. Jefferson also found comfort in the reports that Great Britain was in the midst of a serious financial crisis, which he thought might prompt the British to look favorably on France's reported overtures for peace. See Thomas Jefferson to James Madison (July 21, 1793), reprinted 26 Jefferson Papers, 545; 7 Jefferson Works, 455; Rufus King to Alexander Hamilton (June–July 1793), reprinted 15 Hamilton Papers, 44.

29 Thomas Jefferson to Justices of the Supreme Court (July 18, 1793), reprinted 26 Jefferson Papers, 520; 7 Jefferson Works, 451–52; Glass v. The Sloop Betsey, 3 U.S. 3 (3 Dall.) 6 (1794). By asserting admiralty jurisdiction over such cases, a federal district court could adjudicate a range of questions concerning the lawfulness of the capture and the validity of any cargo seizures. Such questions included what the effective offshore range of American territory was, what articles of commerce were considered contraband, and whether an armed vessel of a belligerent could follow an enemy merchant vessel immediately out of port for the purpose of taking it as a prize. See Casto, 40–41; 82–87.

30 John Jay, James Wilson, John Blair, James Iredell, & William Paterson to George Washington (Aug. 8, 1793), supra intro., note 1.

31 Jay, Address to the People of the State of New York, reprinted 3 Jay Papers, 305 (Jay was dismissing Antifederalist arguments that the proposed Constitution impliedly abrogated important individual rights).

32 John Jay to Rufus King (Dec. 22, 1793), reprinted 2 DHSC, 434; 1 King, 509. One proposed reform was to provide that marshalls be relieved of their authority to summon jurors "in every case in which the Court shall have Evidence to induce reasonable apprehensions of Partiality or Interest in the Marshall." This may have been prompted by the *Henfield* case, in which it was widely thought among

Federalists that the U.S. Marshall in Philadelphia had picked a jury with decid-edly Republican sympathies. Another of Jay's ideas was to establish an alternative location for the Supreme Court's August term, in view of the yellow fever epidemic that had plagued the city the previous summer.

33 2 DHSC, 434–35; 1 King, 509. A few days earlier in a letter to King, Jay had attacked circuit riding, pointing out that the rotation of Justices on the circuits had led to cases in which "one Set of Judges" was reversed in the next session of the circuit court by another panel of judges: "The natural Tendency of such Fluctuations is obvious; nor can they otherwise be avoided, than by confining the Judges to their proper place vizt the Sup. Court." Jay volunteered that he was willing to take a pay cut in exchange for the abolition of circuit assignments, "equal to the Expences of attending the Circuits." John Jay to Rufus King (Dec. 19, 1793), reprinted 2 DHSC, 434.

34 John Jay to George Washington (Sept. 23, 1791), reprinted 10 Washington Writings, 501 (J. Sparks ed. 1836). Jay advised: "All that ought to be done cannot be done at once." Id. Similarly, Randolph remarked to Washington that "judiciary topics should be rendered as mild as possible." Edmund Randolph to George Washington (Aug. 5, 1792), reprinted id., 513.

35 Thomas Johnson to George Washington (Jan. 16, 1793), reprinted 1 DHSC, 80 (saying that circuit riding was "excessively fatiguing," and that "I cannot resolve to spend six months in the Year of the few I may have left from my Family, on Roads at Taverns chiefly and often in Situations where the most moderate Desires are disappointed."); Egbert Benson to Rufus King (Dec. 18, 1793), reprinted 1 DHSC, 742 (reporting a conversation with Jay as to why the Chief Justice had agreed to compete in the New York gubernatorial election of 1792). Benson was a lawyer and Federalist congressman from New York.

36 Benjamin Bourne to William Channing (Feb. 21, 1792), reprinted 1 DHSC, 733 (saying that Jay had consented to placing his name in nomination only upon hearing that there was "no likelihood of an alteration in the present arrangement of the Federal Judiciary. [Jay] had got quite tired of the Circuits"); see 2 Holt, 327–28 & n.104; Egbert Benson to Rufus King (Dec. 18, 1793), reprinted 1 DHSC, 742.

37 Theodore Sedgwick to Peter Van Schaack (Dec. 18, 1793), reprinted 1 DHSC, 742; 4 Elliot's Debates, 164 (Samuel Spencer, North Carolina ratifying convention, July 29, 1788); see also Pennsylvania and the Federal Constitution, 1787–1788, at 779 app. (J. McMaster & F. Stone eds. 1888) (remarks of Robert Whitehill at the Pennsylvania Convention, as noted by James Wilson) ("The judicial department is blended with and will absorb the judicial Powers of the several States; and Nothing will be able to stop its Way."). Predicting an "extensive jurisdiction" for the federal courts, George Mason warned that it would include "all cases arising under the system, and the laws of Congress," which thus "may be said to be unlimited," 10 DHR, 1403 (Virginia Convention, June 19, 1788), because "[s]uch laws may be formed as will go to every object of private property." Id., 1402. Antifederalists typically associated the federal judiciary with "the direct

tendency of the proposed system . . . to consolidate the whole empire into one mass." Letters of Agrippa (V) (Dec. 11, 1787), reprinted 4 The Complete Anti-Federalist 77 (H. Storing ed. 1981). Others were convinced that "the powers of the judiciary may be extended to any degree short of almighty." 2 Elliot's Debates, 401 (Thomas Tredwell, New York Convention, July 2, 1788). Edmund Randolph, who reluctantly agreed to vote for the Constitution's ratification, believed it was defective "in limiting and defining the judicial power." Edmund Randolph to Virginia House of Delegates (Oct. 10, 1787), reprinted 3 Farrand, 127 app. A.

38 10 DHR, 1214 (Patrick Henry, Virginia ratifying convention, June 12, 1788); see id., 1447 (William Grayson, Virginia ratifying convention, June 21, 1788) (states would be unable to prevent suits by creditors in federal court); Essays of Brutus, reprinted 2 The Complete Anti-Federalist, supra note 37, at 429-31 (observing that "[e]very state in the union is largely indebted to individuals," Brutus predicted that the notes evidencing these debts would be transferred to out-of-state citizens, thereby creating diversity jurisdiction in the federal courts, and forcing states into court against their wills); Letters from a Federal Farmer, reprinted id., 245 (states will be "humble[d]" by being "oblige[d] to answer to an individual in a court of law"); see generally Fletcher, *A Historical Interpretation of the Eleventh Amendment: A Narrow Construction of an Affirmative Grant Rather Than a Prohibition Against Jurisdiction,* 35 Stan. L. Rev. 1033, 1047-48 (1983).

39 10 DHR, 1464 (Patrick Henry, Virginia ratifying convention, June 23, 1788); Hamilton, Federalist No. 81, reprinted in Federalist, 548 ("It is inherent in the nature of sovereignty, not to be amenable to the suit of an individual *without its consent.*"); 10 DHR, 1414 (James Madison, Virginia ratifying convention, June 20, 1788) ("It is not in the power of individuals to call any State into Court," but states could bring diversity actions as plaintiffs in federal court.); id., 1433 (John Marshall, Virginia ratifying convention, June 20, 1788) ("With respect to disputes between a State and the citizens of another State, I hope no Gentleman will think that a State will be called at the bar of the Federal Court. . . . It is not rational to suppose, that the sovereign power shall be dragged before a Court. . . . I see a difficulty in making a State defendant, which does not prevent its being plaintiff."); see generally Fletcher, supra note 38, at 1047-50. Edmund Randolph, however, acknowledged that states could be sued and defended this consequence in the Virginia ratification debates. See 9 DHR, 1084-85 (June 9, 1788); 10 id., 1453 (June 21, 1788); Fletcher, supra, 1050 & n. 70.

40 2 U.S. (2 Dall.) 419 (1793). Process also was ordered during the February term in similar suits against New York and Virginia, and on June 4, 1793, against Massachusetts. See Goebel, 734. As Charles Warren related it, *Chisholm* "fell upon the country with a profound shock." 1 Warren, 96; D. Farber & S. Sherry, supra, chapter 4, note 38, at 247 ("The negative reaction was immediate and almost universal."); Morris, 64 ("*Chisholm v. Georgia* burst like a bomb upon an unsuspecting nation and evoked an immediate response from states' rights supporters in all parts of the country."); 3 Annals of Congress 651 (Feb. 20, 1793). Action was postponed on the amendment until the next session; see id. 656 (Feb.

25, 1793); Independent Chronicle (Boston), July 25, 1793, quoted in 1 Warren, 99; see id., 96–100 (quoting various newspapers). Warren comments: "that this was no theoretical danger was shown by the immediate institution of such suits against the States in South Carolina, Georgia, Virginia and Massachusetts." Id., 99. See Stewart, 188–89; Independent Chronicle (Boston), July 18, 1793, quoted in J. Dressler, Shaping of the American Judiciary: Ideas and Institutions in the Early Republic 255 (Ph.D. dissertation, University of Washington, 1971); Independent Chronicle (Boston), Apr. 4, 1793, quoted in 1 Warren, 96.

41 See McDonald, Hamilton, 268 (estimating three million pounds sterling in total debts); Evans, *Planter Indebtedness and the Coming of the Revolution in Virginia*, 19 Wm. & Mary Q. (3rd ser.) 349, 511 (1962) (at the outset of the Revolution colonial merchants owed more than five million pounds); 1 Holt, 1430–35 (detailing sources of the five-million-pound debt); 3 Holt, 362-63 n.72, citing S. Bemis, Jay's Treaty: A Study in Commerce and Diplomacy 103 (1923) (listing the five-million-pound debt by state).

42 Art. 4, The Definitive Treaty of Peace, Sept. 3, 1783, reprinted 2 Treaties, 154; see generally McDonald, Hamilton, 268; Hobson, *The Recovery of British Debts in the Federal Circuit Court of Virginia, 1790 to 1797*, 92 Virginia Magazine 176 (1984); 1 Holt, 1438–58; F. Marks, supra, chapter 4, note 65, at 45 (creditor nations had a just cause for war under the law of nations if the debtor country did not provide a means for debt collection); 1 Holt, 1458 ("Debts, paper money, and violation of the Definitive Treaty of Peace by the nonpayment of British debts were among the forces impelling the Framers to travel to Philadelphia in 1787," and federal courts had been erected as a solution to these problems.).

43 Goebel, 545; D. Henderson, Courts for a New Nation 72–83 (1971); Tachau, 155–58; 2 Holt, 323-24; George Hammond to Thomas Jefferson (June 20, 1793) (original in National Archives, Washington, D.C., Vol. 1, Notes from British Legation in the United States to the Department of State), reprinted 2 Authentic Copies, supra chapter 5, note 61, at 48.

44 See Morris, New England, 16 & 29 (1968). On *Ware*, see 13 F. Cas. 1059, 1067-69 (C.C.D. Va. 1793) (No. 7,507) (Opinion of Jay, Circuit Justice); 3 U.S. (3 Dall.) 256 (opinion of Iredell, Circuit Justice) (the case is reported in *Federal Cases* under the erroneous case name of *Jones v. Walker*). Among the defenses overruled was the contention that the debt was voided by dissolution of the government that existed in Virginia at the time the bond was made. See 13 F. Cas. at 1061 (Jay: the defense was "unsupported by an principle recognized by the laws of nature or nations"); 3 U.S. (3 Dall.) at 257 (Iredell: the plea had been abandoned by the defense, but "undoubtedly, it is not tenable").

45 13 F. Cas. at 1063. See 13 F. Cas. at 1062 (Jay: even though a nation might voluntarily declare a treaty void owing to the other side's infractions, this decision was of a "political nature" unfit for the judiciary); 3 U.S. (3 Dall.) at 260 (Iredell: the defense presented "considerations of policy . . . entirely incompetent to the examination and decision of a court of justice").

46 3 U.S. (3 Dall.) at 277. "I should hope that the present plaintiff will still receive

his money, as his right to the money certainly has not been divested." Id., 279; 13 F. Cas. at 1069.

47 See Hobson, supra note 42, at 178, 182, & 192–95; "No issue in the politics and law of British debts was more bitterly disputed than the suspension of war interest." Id., 193. Juries, however, routinely disobeyed the instruction to add interest to the general verdict. Id., 194–95.

48 See Morris, 89; Stewart, 188–89; Edmund Randolph to George Washington (June 24, 1793), partially reprinted in Randolph, 153 (original in Washington Papers, Library of Congress). Henry had served as counsel for the debtors in *Ware* at the circuit court; see 1 Warren, 145; National Gazette, July 3, 1793, quoted in 1 Warren, 145 n.1.

49 See 2 Holt, 324–25.

50 Cf. Wheeler, 52 ("If the Court's advice were not followed the Court would appear weak, and if a case arose based on such an action there would be a tendency for the public to interpret a decision opposed to the President as vindictiveness and to regard a decision upholding him as obsequiousness.").

51 John Jay to Alexander Hamilton (Nov. 26, 1793), reprinted 15 Hamilton Papers, 412.

52 The timing of these events is detailed in chapter 5.

CONCLUSION

1 Allen v. Wright, 468 U.S. 737, 750 (1984), quoting Vander Jagt v. O'Neill, 699 F.2d 1166, 1178–79 (D.C. Cir. 1983) (Bork, J., concurring); Flast v. Cohen, 392 U.S. 83, 96 (1968), quoting C. Wright, Federal Courts 34 (1963); see Valley Forge Christian College v. Americans United for Separation of Church and State, Inc., 454 U.S. 464, 471–76 (1982); Warth v. Seldin, 422 U.S. 490, 498 (1975).

2 392 U.S. at 96, citing 3 Jay Papers, 486–489. The *Flast* opinion also cited Muskrat v. United States, 219 U.S. 346 (1910), which in turn had relied on the 1793 correspondence. See 219 U.S. at 354, 357.

3 392 U.S. at 96 n.14.

4 (1) Mootness: see Princeton University v. Schmid, 455 U.S. 100, 103 (1982); (2) Standing: see Sierra Club v. Morton, 405 U.S. 727, 732 n.3 (1971); (3) Ripeness: see United Public Workers v. Mitchell, 330 U.S. 75, 89 (1947); (4) Political questions: see United States v. Richardson, 418 U.S. 166, 170–71 (1974); (5) Independent state grounds: see Florida v. Meyers, 466 U.S. 380, 382 (1984); (6) Reaching constitutional questions only as a last resort: see Mills v. Rogers, 457 U.S. 291, 305 (1982); (7) Narrow basis for decision: see Watson v. Buck, 313 U.S. 387, 402 (1941); (8) Nonjudicial assignments: see Mistretta v. United States, 488 U.S. 361, 385 (1989). "Executive or administrative duties" quotation is from Morrison v. Olson, 487 U.S. 654, 677 (1988), quoting Buckley v. Valeo, 424 U.S. 1, 123 (1976), citing Hayburn's Case, 2 U.S. 409 (1792).

5 Allen v. Wright, 468 U.S. 737, 750 (1984), quoting Vander Jagt v. O'Neill, 699 F.2d 1166, 1178–79 (D.C. Cir. 1983) (Bork, J., concurring).

Index

Adams, John, 54, 85, 101, 116
Allen v. Wright, 172-73
Ames, Fisher, 109-10

Bacon, Francis, 15-16, 21, 198*n*25
Beckwith, George, 94-95, 249*n*64
Blackstone, Sir William, 10; on forms
of government, 22; influence of on
American legal practice, 56,
225*n*12; on judicial advising of the
House of Lords, 12, 13, 30, 150; on
judicial independence, 29-30; on
legislation, 23-24; on parliamentary
supremacy, 23
Blair, John, 63-64, 106, 107
Bradford, William, 137
Britain: debt collection by, 162-65;
Hamilton's support for, 81, 240*n*13,
240*n*14; in the Nootka Sound incident, 95-96, 115, 249*n*66, 250*n*67;
responds to French privateering,
124-25, 129-31, 266*n*39, 269*n*55;
United States foreign policy toward,
114-16. *See also* Neutrality crisis of
1793
British judges: administrative roles of,
11-12, 20; in criminal cases, 25,
211*n*62; independence of, 24-31; as
royal officials, 6, 10-11, 191*n*1,
191*n*2; suspensions of, 19, 204*n*40,
208*n*52; tenure of, 19-20, 21-22,
48, 205*n*44, 208*n*52, 208*n*53
—as advisors to the House of Lords, 4-
6, 12-14, 30, 46, 47-50, 194*n*12,
195*n*13, 196*n*17; continuation of
into nineteenth century, 7, 8, 31,
47, 50
—as advisors to the monarch, 4, 6,